PRAIRIE MAN

PRAIRIE MAN

*The Struggle between Sitting Bull and
Indian Agent James McLaughlin*

NORMAN E. MATTEONI

TWODOT®

GUILFORD, CONNECTICUT
HELENA, MONTANA

A · TWODOT® · BOOK

An imprint and registered trademark of Rowman & Littlefield

Distributed by NATIONAL BOOK NETWORK

Copyright © 2015 by Norman E. Matteoni

British Library Cataloguing-in-Publication Information available

Library of Congress Cataloging-in-Publication Data available

ISBN 978-1-4422-4475-7 (paperback)
ISBN 978-1-4422-4476-4 (e-book)

∞™ The paper used in this publication meets the minimum requirements of American National Standard for Information Sciences—Permanence of Paper for Printed Library Materials, ANSI/ NISO Z39.48-1992.

A warrior I have been
Now it is all over
A hard time I have.

—Sitting Bull's Surrender Song

Sitting Bull LIBRARY OF CONGRESS, LC-USZ62-111147

MAP OF THE GREAT SIOUX RESERVATION & KEY LOCATIONS WITHIN THE GENERAL AREA

(Adapted from the *Handbook of North American Indians,*
Vol. 13. Smithsonian Institution)

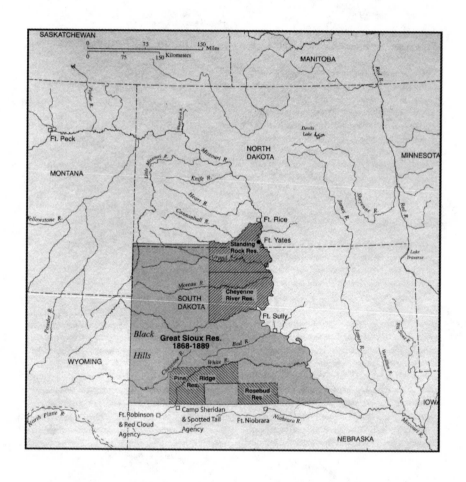

Contents

AUTHOR'S PREFACE: PERSPECTIVE

Frederick Jackson Turner, in his essay "The Significance of the Frontier in American History," declared the frontier closed as of 1890, based in part on the 1890 national census indicating the extent of the American population then living in the West.

That same year Sitting Bull was killed by his own people.

From the mid-1870s through the 1880s, Sitting Bull was the most-reported-about Indian in America. He was recognized as the leader of the Sioux in the battle with Custer in 1876. He was frequently photographed during his captivity after his surrender to the U.S. military in 1881. He even was featured in the Buffalo Bill show, the "Wild West," for one season. The fascination with his life continues. His role in the Sioux Wars of 1865–1877 has been chronicled in numerous books. During much of his life known to America, he was considered a "bad Indian," while at the same time many gave him celebrity recognition.

This book examines Sitting Bull's ongoing resistance and dissent to the American government's treatment of the Indian. It is a reader's journey of his escape to and exile in Canada, return to the United States and surrender, internment as a prisoner of war, and reservation life. The aspect of the man's life that attracts the most attention was his part in the Battle of the Little Big Horn. Sitting Bull is popularly credited with the killing of Custer; however, he was not a participant in the actual combat. His was the main voice that called together the many bands of Indians who gathered in the southeast Montana Territory in the spring of 1876; he preached the resistance of the Lakota to the U.S. government's campaign to force the roaming bands onto the reservation; and he and other leaders urged their people to respond to the attack that was certain to come.

The immediate national reaction to the defeat of the 7th Cavalry on June 25, 1876, was shock and outrage. It was the nation's first centennial. The American eagle was in full wingspread across the country—the Anglo-Americans inhabiting the United States in the late 1800s considered they were a superior and indomitable people. Seeking to explain how a reputed top military commander, known as a great Indian fighter with prior successful campaigns, and his entire outfit could have been annihilated, the press was susceptible to exaggerated accounts of hearsay from scouts, military personnel, and whoever offered an observation. There were no army survivors to the battle on the upper ridge (even the newspaper correspondent traveling with the 7th was killed); and the victors were not immediately available for interviews. Besides, they were branded as savages. The press labeled the battle a brutal massacre, idealizing the last stand of the dashing George Custer and his men and laying blame on Sitting Bull.

There were some who tried to explain the defeat with speculation that Sitting Bull was a product of West Point in the 1840s—a dark-skinned young man who carried the nickname "Bison." He was said to have graduated but was not commissioned. If not West Point, Sitting Bull must have attended another institution of higher learning. The theory was that he had to be schooled in military science. The truth was that Indian warriors were not organized by units nor commanded by any general; they fought more instinctively and under the leadership of several war chiefs at Little Big Horn, responding to an ill-conceived attack. Individuals followed these leaders out of respect and past experience.

The Battle of the Little Big Horn provides a vantage point for the later life of Sitting Bull. His reach went much further than the Sioux Wars. Thus, here the battle and events preceding and immediately following are recounted in early chapters for the purpose of understanding how they shaped what later occurred. At the same time, the book traces the path of James McLaughlin, a Canadian who came to Minnesota, married a woman of Sioux descent and would become the antagonist of Sitting Bull as his reservation agent. McLaughlin, well intended and convinced of the principles of the Bureau of Indian Affairs, embraced the role of shepherding the native toward Anglo-Americanization. That the two men would clash was predestined.

Sitting Bull was often referred to as a medicine man, not because he was a healer, but because he had wisdom—"his medicine was strong." He could see what others could not, and he had a deep spiritual side. He never gave up his role of chief and protector of his people, although many gave up on him. He sought to hold the diminishing native lands against the take of the white man.

He was a man whose soul was etched onto the prairie. The northern Plains, both harsh and bountiful, was Lakota land. The horse gave these people range. The buffalo was their sustenance—providing not only food but clothing and shelter from its skin and tools from its bones. While this book strives to be historically accurate, it is in part interpretive history, oftentimes based on varying accounts, some reconcilable and some contradictory. Admittedly, it seeks to fill in some blanks, but from the context of what was reported to have taken place. Recognize that interviews of Indians through a translator were often misunderstood or distorted; and some reporters found their own creation of history more interesting than the facts. Moreover, the Sioux story was told by oral history, which frequently was given years after the event. Fortunately, Sitting Bull's exile in Canada and reservation life is better documented.

The telling of the story presented here is heavily based on recalled or directly reported statements of the chief as well as conversations he had with others. Many quotations of conversation between Sitting Bull and Indian Agent James McLaughlin, during his years on the reservation, are from direct reports (primarily from the McLaughlin's journals and his book, *My Friend the Indian*, and Stanley Vestal's works, *Sitting Bull, Campion of the Sioux: A Biography*, and *New Sources of Indian History*). A few passages of dialogue are the interpretation of the author, drawn from what has been written of the two men's interactions and the events taking place about them. Always, the reader is directed to appropriate source notes.

What Sitting Bull and the Sioux faced in reservation life was summarized by Agent McLaughlin:

> *To the men of my time was appointed the task of taking the raw and bleeding material which made the hostile strength of the plains Indians, of bringing that material to the mills of the white man, and of transmuting it into a manufactured product that might be absorbed by the nation . . . .*[1]

Pretentious prose that simply meant "forced assimilation."

The lives of Sitting Bull and James McLaughlin were locked in a conflict of convictions for six and one half years. During those years, Sitting Bull did not seek to be a part of the white nation, although he was not opposed to learning from it. He refused to consider the Lakota were an inferior people; and the Indian agent continuously pushed the objective of making over the culture of the red man to that of the new American. McLaughlin, unable to convert Sitting Bull, came to the conclusion that he was an obstructionist to achieving that goal with other reservation Indians. The man had to be removed.

A different perspective was offered by Charles Eastman, a Santee Sioux with the native name of Ohiyesa, who crossed the assimilation line—attending Boston School of Medicine and coming back to Pine Ridge Reservation to serve as a doctor during the Ghost Dance craze in 1890: "I do not agree with Major McLaughlin in his estimate of Sitting Bull's character. He was no medicine man, but a statesman, one of the most farsighted we have had."

The advancement of American civilization across the Plains to the detriment of its native inhabitants was grounded on the belief of racial superiority and propelled by the country's insatiable appetite for land. The conquerors dictated how those who survived would be allowed to continue to live on America's land. The nation that proclaimed "all men are created equal" applied to its country's first peoples the philosophy of "kill the Indian to save the man."

Even Thomas Jefferson penned words for the Declaration of Independence characterizing these people as "merciless Indian savages." The commissioner of Indian Affairs in his annual report to the Department of the Interior wrote on October 30, 1876:

The management of Indian affairs is always attended with much of difficulty and embarrassment. In every other department of the public service, the officers of the Government conduct business mainly with civilized and intelligent men. The Indian Office, in representing the Government, has to deal mainly with an uncivilized and unintelligent people, whose ignorance, superstition, and suspicion materially increase the difficulty both of controlling and assisting them.

Mindful of the admonition of Victor Deloria, author of *Custer Died for Your Sins*, that today's American only presumes to know the Indian, I confess that I have no natural connection to the Lakota culture. Nor can I divorce my perspective from my heritage of a Californian of European descent.

I have chosen to tell a story out of the fabric of a period of American history, as I have found and analyzed it. In doing so, I give notice that most of the source material is written by non-Indians. Second, the recording of such history is not all fact; Western myth has touched parts of it. This author surely has fallen prey to passing on some of the myth. Hopefully that is at a minimum. If this effort produces criticism and/or comment, perhaps that exercise will provide a path toward better understanding.

In the larger view, this story is about the genocide of a native race. It was genocide by disease and alcohol, death, deception, and dispossession of land. Genocide made certain by military action, extermination of the buffalo, reservation confinement, disease and starvation, prohibition of use of native language, displacement of religious beliefs by Christianity, and treaty promises that were not kept. All of this was undertaken to destroy a people's culture. Sitting Bull witnessed it all. His life and murder underscore a terrible chapter of American history.

Because there was resistance, the culture endures while it adapts to changing times.

Timeline of Events

1851—First Fort Laramie Treaty

1862—Minnesota River Valley Uprising

1863—James McLaughlin comes to St. Paul, Minnesota, from Canada

1864—Sand Creek Massacre

1868—Red Cloud's war ends with the second Fort Laramie Treaty.
The Great Sioux Reservation is established, and unceded territory to the west is left to the roaming Indians who do not choose reservation life.
Sitting Bull refuses to sign Fort Laramie Treaty.
Custer comes to the Plains.

1873—Custer leads expedition into the Black Hills, sacred land of the Lakota Sioux and within the unceded territory, and discovers gold.

1875—Pressure builds in President Grant's administration to obtain the Black Hills from the Sioux.
Sioux living in unceded territory are given ultimatum to report to reservations.

1876—A three-prong military movement is set in motion to round up Indians in the unceded territory and relocate them in the Great Sioux Reservation.
On June 25, the Battle of the Little Big Horn takes place as Custer advances before supporting military units are in place. His strike against the camp of Lakota and Cheyenne is repulsed with devastating effect.
James McLaughlin becomes the agent at Devils Lake.
In the aftermath of the Little Big Horn debacle, the military intensifies its pursuit of the Lakota throughout the unceded territory.

1877—Sitting Bull takes his people to Canada.

1878—Sitting Bull confronts Terry Commission sent to Canada to seek his surrender.

1881—Sitting Bull agrees to return to the United States and surrenders at Fort Buford, Dakota Territory.
Sitting Bull is sent to Standing Rock Agency, where he first meets James McLaughlin, the new Indian agent.
Then the chief is made prisoner of war at Fort Randall.

1882—Edmunds Commission seeks to negotiate to reduce the Great Sioux Reservation. Outcries of fraud in securing approval from the Indians cause Congress to reject the negotiated agreement.

1883—Sitting Bull is released as a prisoner of war and returned to Standing Rock, now under the firm control of Agent McLaughlin.

1884—Sitting Bull moves from near agency headquarters to Grand River.

1885—Sitting Bull is permitted to go off reservation on a tour with Buffalo Bill.

1887—Congress passes the Severalty Act, designed to transfer commonality of tribal holdings within all reservations to individual ownership.

1888—First Sioux Act adopted to negotiate the reduction of the Great Sioux Reservation.

When negotiations are unsuccessful, Sioux delegations from the several agencies are invited to Washington, D.C.

1889—Second Sioux Act adopted and authorizes Crook Commission to negotiate the reduction of the Great Sioux Reservation.

Catherine Weldon comes to Standing Rock.

Crook secures the necessary consents at the several agencies to reduce the reservation.

Great Sioux Reservation is broken into reservations, corresponding to locations of agencies; 11 million acres are removed and made available to white settlers.

1890—Ghost Dance movement sweeps the Sioux reservations; it is viewed as a threat to reservation control of the Indians.

James McLaughlin plots the arrest of Sitting Bull.

Sitting Bull is killed by Indian Police.

PRINCIPALS TO THE STORY

Beyond the two central actors of this book—Sitting Bull (Tatanka Iyotanka or Tatanka Iyotake, which properly translates to "Buffalo Bull Who Sits Down") and James McLaughlin (the Indian agent at Standing Rock Reservation)—the following are the principal characters, by category, with a brief descriptive biography pertaining to the time of each person's involvement in the events reported:

INDIANS

American Horse—Oglala chief who served Red Cloud in the Powder River War and later was a progressive in reservation life who encouraged the signing of the Sioux Act of 1889 and was a frequent delegate to Washington

Andrew Fox—son-in-law of Sitting Bull who wrote chief's letter to McLaughlin

Big Foot—Miniconjou Chief (aka Spotted Elk); advocate of the Ghost Dance movement at Cheyenne River; leader of Indian band killed at Wounded Knee

Black Kettle—chief of Southern Cheyenne; killed at Washita River by Custer's regiment in 1868

Bull Head—lieutenant of the Indian Police at Standing Rock

Catch the Bear—ally and bodyguard of Sitting Bull

Chatka—lieutenant of Indian Police at Standing Rock

Chief Joseph—leader of the Nez Perce; surrendered to Colonel Miles

Crazy Horse—Oglala-Miniconjou war chief at Little Big Horn

Crazy Walking—captain of Indian Police at Standing Rock

Crow—ally of Sitting Bull who broke with him to return to United States from Canada

Crow Foot—son of Sitting Bull

Crow King—Hunkpapa war chief at Little Big Horn; broke with Sitting Bull in Canada

Dull Knife—chief of Cheyennes at Little Big Horn; attacked by troops of Colonel Mackenzie in the Big Horn Mountains and then sought out the protection of Crazy Horse's camp after the attack

Four Robes—one of Sitting Bull's wives; he also was married to Seen by the Nation at the same time

Gall—Hunkpapa war chief at Little Big Horn and later one of the leaders of progressive Indians at Standing Rock

Gray Eagle—brother-in-law of Sitting Bull; broke with chief in Canada; assisted Indian Police in the arrest attempt on Sitting Bull in 1890

Hawk Man—Police messenger who carried the letter authorizing arrest of Sitting Bull to Indian Police

Hawk Man 2—Police messenger who summoned military backup after the killing of Sitting Bull at Grand River

Her Holy Door—mother of Sitting Bull

Hump—Miniconjou Chief; advocate of the Ghost Dance movement at Cheyenne River

Iron Shield—Oglala chief (also known as American Horse) killed by General Crook's forces at Slim Buttes in September 1876

John Grass—reservation Indian and one of the leaders of the progressive faction at Standing Rock; considered an orator

Jumping Bull (aka Little Assiniboine)—adopted brother of Sitting Bull, named after his deceased father, who had originally taken this name when he had conferred his own name on his son, Sitting Bull

Kicking Bear—an Oglala who became a Miniconjou sub-chief from Cheyenne River; he introduced the Ghost Dance movement to the Sioux

Kills Enemy—represented himself as Sitting Bull in conference with Colonel Otis

Little Big Man—ally who assisted in arrest of Crazy Horse

Little Crow—Mdewakanton chief who lead the Minnesota River Valley Uprising in 1862

Little Knife—leader of scout party for Sitting Bull to Canada

Low Dog—ally of Sitting Bull who broke with him to return to United States from Canada

Many Horses—one of Sitting Bull's daughters

Nick Codotte—brother-in-law to John Grass; provided the barn for McLaughlin's clandestine meeting with Grass to secure the vote on the Sioux Act of 1889

One Bull—nephew and adopted son of Sitting Bull

One that Speaks Once—Sioux mother who addressed Terry Commission in Canada

Red Cloud—contemporary of Sitting Bull and chief of the Oglala Lakota; signed Fort Laramie Treaty of 1868

Red Tomahawk—Sergeant of the Indian Police at Standing Rock

Running Antelope—Hunkpapa chief; reservation diplomat

Scarlett Whirlwind—wife of One Bull and daughter-in-law to Sitting Bull

Shave Bear—leader of the ghost dancers at Grand River

Shave Head—Sergeant of the Indian Police at Standing Rock

Shell King—Standing Rock Indian with who Sitting Bull had differences

Short Bull—Oglala advocate of Ghost Dance at Pine Ridge

Spotted Tail—chief of the Brules; replaced Red Cloud as head agency chief in 1876

Two Moons—Cheyenne war chief at Little Big Horn

Walks Looking—daughter of Sitting Bull

White Bull—nephew and adopted son of Sitting Bull

Wovaka—Paiute mystic and prophet from Nevada who established the Ghost Dance movement and preached it to representatives of the Lakota and other tribes

Yellow Bird—medicine man with Big Foot's band at Wounded Knee

Young Man Afraid of His Horses—Oglala chief who replaced Red Cloud as one of the agency leaders at Pine Ridge Reservation

INDIAN AGENTS

Beckwith, Paul—Indian agent who succeeded Forbes at Devils Lake, and who was recalled and replaced by James McLaughlin

Forbes, William—Indian agent at Devils Lake who hired James McLaughlin in 1871

Love, Leonard—Indian agent at Cheyenne River Agency

McGillycuddy, Valentine—Indian Agent at Pine Ridge; at the time of the Ghost Dance movement, he was Assistant Adjutant General to Governor of South Dakota

Palmer, Perain—Indian agent at Cheyenne River Agency

Royer, Daniel F.—Indian agent at Pine Ridge, succeeding McGillycuddy

Williams, Henry—Indian agent to the Crow

MILITARY

Ahern, George P.—lieutenant assigned to Fort Randall who befriended Sitting Bull during his captivity

Andrews, George—colonel, commanding Fort Randall

Benteen, Frederick—captain under General Terry in the Yellowstone Campaign

Brooke, John—brigadier general, commanding the Department of the Platte

Brotherton, David H.—major assigned to Fort Buford who received the surrender of Sitting Bull

Chivington, John M.—colonel commanding the Colorado Volunteers

Clifford, Walter—captain at Fort Randall

Crook, George—general in the Yellowstone Campaign, leading one of the columns from Fort Fetterman, Wyoming Territory; lead commissioner in securing Indian approval of the 1889 Sioux Act

Custer, George A.—lieutenant colonel in the Sioux Wars and commander of the 7th Regiment of the 7th Cavalry at the Battle of the Little Big Horn

DeRockbraine, Andrew—soldier who assisted Sitting Bull in seeking release from Fort Randall

Drum, William—lieutenant colonel, commander at Fort Yates

Elliott, Joel—major under Custer at Washita River who was left in the field

Fechet, E. G.—captain under Colonel Drum stationed at Fort Yates who led the military backup for the arrest of Sitting Bull

Fetterman, William—lieutenant killed with his men in a trap set by Indians under direction of Crazy Horse

Forsyth, James W.—lieutenant colonel with the 7th Cavalry who directed the military search of Big Foot's surrendering band, resulting in the Wounded Knee Massacre

Gibbon, John—colonel in the Yellowstone Campaign, leading one of the columns from Fort Ellis, Montana Territory

Gilbert, Charles C.—colonel, commanding Fort Yates

Ilges, Guido—major who led the attack on Gall at Poplar Creek and pushed the surrendering Indians through the January snows to Fort Buford

Mackenzie, Ranald S.—lieutenant colonel who directed the charge of the Cheyenne camp in November 1876

Miles, Nelson A.—lieutenant colonel in the Sioux Wars who pursued Sitting Bull after the Battle of Little Big Horn; later general commanding the Division of the Missouri

Mills, Anson—captain who directed assault of Oglala camp of Iron Plume for General Crook in fall 1876

Otis, Elwell S.—lieutenant colonel who met with representatives of Sitting Bull on Cedar Creek prior to the meeting between Sitting Bull and Colonel Miles

Reno, Marcus—major under General Terry in the Yellowstone Campaign

Reynolds, Joseph J.—colonel who led the March 17, 1876, attack of Sioux and Cheyenne camps at Powder River

Ruger, Thomas—brigadier general, commanding the Department of the Dakota

Sheridan, Philip—general, commanding the Military Division of the Missouri

Sherman, William Tecumseh—general in chief of the army

Stanley, David—colonel and senior officer to Custer providing protection to railroad survey teams in 1873

Sumner, Edwin V.—lieutenant colonel charged with the duty of observing Big Foot in late 1890

Swain, P. T.—lieutenant colonel at Fort Randall who wrote up Sitting Bull's intended plan of action upon returning to Standing Rock

Terry, Alfred—general in the Yellowstone Campaign, leading one of the columns from Fort Lincoln, Dakota Territory

Whitside, Samuel—major with the 7th Cavalry who intercepted Big Foot and arranged for his surrender

NORTH-WEST MOUNTED POLICE OF CANADA

Crozier, Lief "Paddy"—post commander at Wood Mountain succeeding Walsh

Dewdney, Edgar—Canadian Indian Commissioner

Macleod, James—Canadian Military Commissioner

Mcdonnell, Alexander—inspector at Wood Mountain

Steele, Sam—superintendent at Fort Qu'Appelle

Walsh, James Morrow—inspector with the Mounted Police during time of Sitting Bull's stay in southern Saskatchewan Territory, Canada

OFFICIALS OF U.S. GOVERNMENT

Belknap, William—U.S. Secretary of War (1869–1876)

Belt, Robert V.—acting U.S. Commissioner of Indian Affairs (1890)

Dawes, Henry—U.S. senator from Massachusetts and author of the General Allotment Act of 1887

Edmunds, Newton—governor of Dakota Territory; treaty negotiator

Lincoln, Robert Todd—U.S. Secretary of War (1881–1885)

Logan, John—U.S. senator from Illinois serving on the Select Committee of the Senate under Senator Dawes, sent to investigate conditions of the Indian tribes in Montana and Dakota Territories in 1883

Manypenny, George W.—U.S. Commissioner of Indian Affairs (1853–1857); treaty negotiator

Morgan, Thomas J.—U.S. Commissioner of Indian Affairs (1889–1893)

Pratt, Richard Henry—founder of the Carlisle Indian School in Pennsylvania; led the commission seeking acceptance by the Indians of the Sioux Act of 1888

Vilas, William—U.S. Secretary of Interior (1888–1889)

Walker, Francis A.—U.S. Commissioner of Indian Affairs (1871–1872)

OTHERS

Allen, Alvaren—proprietor of St. Paul hotel who secured the services of Sitting Bull for a 1884 tour

Allison, Edwin "Fish"—interpreter and scout who attempted to arrange for the return of Sitting Bull from Canada

Bentley, Emma—woman at the Bismarck reception for Sitting Bull

Bland, Thomas A.—president of the National Indian Defense Association

Brughiere, Johnny—interpreter and scout

Burke, John—agent for Buffalo Bill

Carignan, John "Jack"—teacher at Grand River on Standing Rock Reservation

Cody, William "Buffalo Bill"—Indian scout, buffalo hunter, and showman

Collins, Mary—Congregationalist missionary at Standing Rock Reservation

De Smet, Pierre-Jean—Jesuit missionary who led peace commissioners to Sitting Bull's Northern Montana camp in 1868

Finerty, John—correspondent with *Chicago Times*

Hinman, Samuel—minister; part of the Edmund's Commission

Legare, Jean Louis—Canadian trader in Saskatchewan Territory who escorted Sitting Bull's band back to the United States for surrender

Marty, Martin—Catholic bishop of Dakota Territory

McLaughlin (Boisson), Marie Louise—wife of James McLaughlin

Oakley, Annie—sharpshooter and performer at Western shows

Primeau, Louis—Indian interpreter at Standing Rock Agency

Riggs, Thomas L.—Congregational minister at Oahe Station who assisted Sitting Bull at Fort Randall

Stephan, Joseph—Catholic priest and agent at Standing Rock prior to McLaughlin

Weldon, Catherine—member of the National Indian Defense Association and volunteer assistant to and confidant of Sitting Bull

Welsh, Herbert—a founder of the Indian Rights Association

Williamson, John—Congregational minister who assisted with letter to Secretary of War Lincoln asking for release of Sitting Bull

CHAPTER ONE

Fort Yates, North Dakota

December 1890

Dakota winters usually bite cold. And so it was in 1890 on the west side of the Missouri River the day they buried the body of a damned Indian who was killed by his own people. The site of interment was a corner of the post cemetery at Fort Yates, North Dakota.

There was no storm that day. No snow crusted ground. Just a December's chill to the bone.

A southeasterly wind cut across the river and pushed against a box coffin set beside a shoveled mound. No family or mourners gathered. Only three military officers and an Indian agent stood graveside. They came to witness the burial of a subversive Sioux chief. No one said a word on his behalf. Even if they were inclined to, the best they may have said of the man was that he was a misguided Indian. Sitting Bull had been an obstructionist to bringing civilization to the northern Plains for too long.

When it was done, the four men walked away from the soldiers' cemetery, each with the sense that the way of the Plains Indian had passed.

Numerous settlements and towns now spread over the land, and railroads reached into every region.[1] In less than a chronometer's turn of a century, the open prairie was gone.

Although questions were raised, the circumstances of Sitting Bull's death were quickly explained away. Thirty years later, dusty and suppressed memories would resurface. The Indian agent who had stood graveside at the burial was called back to Fort Yates. Both the occasion and weather were very different. An easy breeze riffled the Missouri's waters, keeping the temperature moderate for a midday reception. On a summery June 30, 1921, James McLaughlin was being honored for 50 years of exemplary service to the Indian Bureau.[2]

Fort Yates, originally established in 1863 as a post for the surveillance of the Teton Sioux, was now just headquarters for the Standing Rock Reservation.[3] McLaughlin had served there as Indian agent for 24 years, and Sitting Bull was in residence for six and a half of those years. James McLaughlin left in 1905 to become an agency inspector, declining the position of assistant commissioner of the Indian Bureau as a desk job too susceptible to the vagaries of politics. In time, he was appointed special inspector, overseeing all Indian agencies and reservations throughout the United States and reporting only to the Secretary of the Department of the Interior.[4]

The former agent greeted and embraced old Lakota and Yanktonia residents of Standing Rock. Officials from North and South Dakota and the bureau and former associates from his agency days were in attendance; others had sent congratulatory letters and telegrams.

He enjoyed the acquaintance of both politicians and Indians. He had survived petty attacks during his career. He had deflected charges of complicity in the events leading to the death of Sitting Bull. To local leaders and citizens he did what was necessary at a perilous time. The bureau fully accepted the immediate reports of its Indian agent and the military of the incident leading to Sitting Bull's killing. The reservation Indians stood silent. Sitting Bull's family and supporters scattered. Once ranks closed within the government, there was no one to effectively question the matter.

James McLaughlin had the reputation of a tireless worker for the betterment of the Indian, a diplomat, a humanitarian, and a gentleman. The good agent had faithfully served his country in pursuit of guiding his reservation charges toward assimilation in the American community.[5] He even wrote a book, *My Friend the Indian*, published in 1910—providing insights to understanding the Indian, management of reservations, as well as his characterization of Sitting Bull and the circumstances of the man's death. At age 79, he could be well satisfied with his career. He traveled extensively; he spent time at reservations and Indian schools listening to the complaints of the Indians and interceding on their behalf. At times he frankly told them that all that could be accomplished had been done within the system. His word was considered final, and he was trusted.

If there was one face of the bureau that the Indians of America knew, it was James McLaughlin. His recognition now surpassed that of Sitting Bull, who was remembered primarily in myth. To the American public, the chief had been branded as a renegade, the mastermind of the Custer Massacre, a coward, a prima donna, a malcontent old Indian chief, and a crazy man who was trying to raise Indian ghosts to rebel against the white man. He deserved no more than a common grave.

In 1921, there still resided at Standing Rock a few relations and old allies of Sitting Bull and more who had disagreed and broken with him. These people knew more than the myth. They had witnessed the dark side of the relationship between the chief and the agent. They had lived the events that set the two men at opposition. And they remembered the tense days preceding the chief's death.

In the late-afternoon shadows, away from the day's ceremony, old arguments flared anew: "Damn the man and the bureau for celebrating themselves here."

"You will not let go, forever blaming McLaughlin for Sitting Bull's death. Hell! Sitting Bull was out of touch and you know it. He always was living in old times. McLaughlin wanted to help, but . . ."

"But what? McLaughlin could never get beyond civilizing and Christian-making. You heard the same preaching today. Nothing's changed in thirty years."

"Sitting Bull was the one pulling us back to the past. He was the cause of our problems. He refused the hand of the agent. Instead of trying to work together, he always challenged the man."

"The old man even fought with his own people, because he could not give up being chief. His closest allies walked away."

"What do you mean? It was McLaughlin who turned the Indian Police on him. We would have done better listening to Sitting Bull."

"That is whiskey talk. The problem was that the son of a bitch thought that he could beat the reservation. No one can do that. You are just stirring up ghosts."

"We are the ghosts."[6]

For those with the longest memories, McLaughlin and Sitting Bull were preordained antagonists.

The conflict may well have been rooted in Sioux legend. A shape-shifter spirit, known as Iktomi, had warned the inhabitants of the Plains that a new kind of man was approaching from afar: "A strange sound is coming. A new voice. A new man. He is coming across the great waters to steal all the four directions from you. This man is clever, but he has no woksape [wisdom]. . . . He brings greed, and he weaves pretty lies wherever he goes."[7] This man was coming to take the land.

The new man would come fast and hard.

Sitting Bull DENVER PUBLIC LIBRARY, WESTERN HISTORY COLLECTION

CHAPTER TWO

The Northern Plains

The cross-purposes of the two men from Standing Rock came from each man's distinct vision of the northern Plains.

Sitting Bull was a native in an ancient country bound to a culture of extended family and sustained by the buffalo. James McLaughlin was the son of immigrants of Irish and Scottish descent.[1] One of the many new men, he came to a young country full of prospect. The problem was both the old and new countries occupied the same ground.

The prairie was ancestral land of the Plains Indians.

For nearly 500 million years, the middle of America had been accumulating horizontal strata.[2] Long before the Ice Age, the midcontinent was an inland sea. Then glaciers descended from the north to scour the seabed.[3] The earth form continued to evolve. Eons before the 1800s, the former sea had been transformed into an ocean of grass, rippling in waves blown by winds. Several years of dry periods were interspersed by above-average rainy seasons. These unpredictable cycles left the soft soils of the northwest (an area extending across the Missouri Plateau into the Alberta Plain) semiarid, held in place by blue gamma and buffalo grasses.[4]

Over the Upper Missouri Basin, the northern Plains stretch out west and north across the Dakotas and into eastern Wyoming and Montana toward the base of the Rockies. Here the climate has an inclination to run to extremes. Often within the same year or even same season, there are biting blizzards and twisting tornadoes. In the winter, temperatures plunge and drifting snows lay siege to frozen ground. From time to time, a chinook capriciously sends its warm air currents to drive the temperature from near zero into the forties; but freezing comes back hard. Even in summer there can be mad weather—thunderstorms delivering explosions of pounding rain and the harassment of outsized hailstones. Other times, heat can bake the ground, which when annually repeated over long summers produces years of drought.[5]

Always, there are constant currents to rub the land dry. Nature's forces arrive from every direction. They come from the opposites of the Arctic and Gulf. Westerlies charge out of the Pacific Ocean over the coastal ranges and Sierra, battering the Rockies, with each succeeding mountain range stripping the air of more moisture before racing over the flatlands.[6] High-pressure cells over the south hold back the moisture from storms out of the Gulf, and hot dry winds from the southwest raise summer temperatures.[7]

Nevertheless, the Teton Sioux thrived on these lands. Theirs was the strongest of bonds to the earth that provided for them. It was their country.

It was perfect grassland habitat for the buffalo. To Sioux, this animal appeared infinite in number.[8] The Pte were believed to regenerate by emerging from the womb of Mother Earth.[9] Massive at full size, the male American bison, or buffalo,[10] weighed from 1,600 to 2,000 pounds; the female grew to 900 to 1,000 pounds. Humped at the shoulders with a short, thick neck supporting a prominent elongated head covered in woolly fur, the animal appeared plodding. The buffalo roamed in herds and had endurance for the long run. Yet, when spooked, a buffalo could bolt to nearly 40 miles per hour. A galloping herd, combining mass and velocity, delivered hoof strikes that thundered upon the plain. Hunters drew their mounts alongside to deliver an arrow or bullet, and then swiftly veered away. Possessing a broad skull with short curved horns, the animal could easily gore and slam predators.

Like the buffalo, the Indians of the northern Plains lived in motion. Travel was in response to climatic forces, rhythms of the seasons, and, primarily, the migration of the buffalo. The Teton constructed their lives in concert with the weather's cycles. The prairie was land to follow the buffalo from spring to fall, and then to find hollows by tree-lined rivers and streams for protection against the assault of determined snowstorms, wrapped in buffalo robes and fed by stores of meat. For the Teton or Lakota, this landscape became one with their culture. The vastness of the land set no limits.

The first European report of the Sioux people was by French priests in the Great Lakes region during the mid-1860s.[11] The priests gave these people their common name, a contraction of what their Ojibwa (Chippewa) enemies called them—"Nadowesioux" or "Nadouesou,"[12] meaning "little snakes." (Others say that the name simply meant "speak foreign language.") They called themselves "allies" or "friends," according to dialect —"Dakota," "Nakota," and "Lakota."[13] The Lakota division was made up of seven subgroups or bands, known as "seven council fires," among which were the Oglala, Yanktonai, Miniconjou, and Hunkpapa.[14]

As they grew in numbers, many of the Lakota chose to move southwesterly toward and across the Missouri River; others did so unwillingly upon being dispossessed of their homeland by the more militant Ojibwa, who first acquired firearms from French traders. Migrating from woodlands of the north, the Lakota found a long plain of grasslands. They soon were known as Teton Sioux, from "Titonwan," said to mean "to live where they can see" or "dwellers on the prairie."[15] And everywhere on the prairie, there were multitudes of buffalo. The former agrarians and part-time hunters became dedicated hunters. The buffalo became all important, providing meat for food, hides for shelter and clothing, and bones for tools.[16]

The acquisition of the horse from the southwest produced a second shift in their way of life, vastly increasing the Teton's mobility and range.[17] They could move swiftly and far. Once mounted, they made themselves into skilled equestrians.[18] The horse did everything the rider asked of it. Horse and man completely trusted one another. The Teton prairie man emerged as a hunter-warrior. The migration of the buffalo no longer posed a hindrance, and the killing of the great animal became more efficient. Soon these Sioux dominated the northern Plains.[19] They made enemies of the Crow, Kiowa, Shoshone, and Assiniboine who shared in these lands.[20] They even took the Black Hills away from the Crow and wove it into their religious beliefs as a place of origin. Their territory covered hundreds of thousands of acres, extending from the Missouri River across what are now northern Nebraska and the two Dakotas into eastern Wyoming and Montana toward the Rockies and northward into Canada. The far horizon was a maybe boundary. The contours of streams, rivers, and hills were not firm demarcations. These topographical features offered areas to camp, graze horses, and hunt. Such was their life as the eighteenth century closed; the buffalo and the horse took care of their needs. There was no experience with the unrelenting drive westward of the new man.

The West attracted those seeking new opportunities, and the nation's leadership was intent on pulling the West under its control. In a remarkably short time, the Indian would no longer hold the middle ground between East and West.

This was land over which the Oregon Trail would give cross-country passage. This was land that would be scarred by miners and settlers. This was land that peace commissioners would appropriate and section off through ever-changing treaties with those in possession through gifts, threats, and promises of security in what was left over. This was land soon to be strewn with the bones of slaughtered buffalo. This was land that would be checkered with frontier garrisons of soldiers. And this was land that would be trampled and bloodied by recurring military campaigns to subjugate and annihilate the indigenous people of the Plains. Ultimately, this was land destined to be governed by the United States of America.

In 1803, a forward-thinking Thomas Jefferson, the third president of the United States, placed paper on the writing board of his wooden lap desk and penned instructions for a scientific study of the lands of the West: "to explore the Missouri river, & such principal stream of it, as, by its course & communication with the waters of the Pacific Ocean, may offer the most direct & practicable water communication across this continent, for the purposes of commerce."[21] Jefferson sought to define the extent of America. He asked for an assessment of whether the Missouri country could sustain a large population. He hoped that this "Great Interior Valley" would serve generations of yeomen. The president's ambition was an empire of democracy that in time would spread to the Pacific edge of the continent.

Appearing to fulfill the Iktomi prediction, the Corps of Discovery led by Captains Meriwether Lewis and William Clark embarked upon a reconnaissance mission at the bidding of the president. But these men were journeyers, charting what they observed. The Corps traversed the west river country of the Dakotas in both the fall of 1804 and the winter of 1805–1806. They treaded lightly, knowing they were traveling through lands where Indians lived.[22] Nonetheless, they carried the manifest of America's sovereignty. Their assignment was to map and chronicle the geography and flora and fauna of the countryside, determine an all-water passage to the Pacific, track the routes of the British from Canada who traded with Missouri Valley tribes, and learn as much as possible about the several Indian tribes encountered.[23]

Although the explorers hugged the river's course, they could not help being awestruck by the vastness of the country's center lands stretching away from view. The prairie presented a very different disposition from the lands to the east. Extending away from the river was a long lay of land devoid of trees, covered with grasses. Large humped-back cattle grazed on the American steppe. The discoverers concluded that the ground must be fertile, even though they were puzzled by a lack of trees. The vagaries of the temperamental Plains weather did not put them off.

As to the settlement potential of the area, Lewis and Clark were more concerned with the Teton Sioux, whom they had been warned against as "bad people." Upon first encountering these people in September 1804, they offered the usual gifts of tobacco, peace medals, and an American flag, adding for the head chief a red coat, cocked hat, and feather, to demonstrate good intentions. The president's directive to establish friendly relations was unrequited. There was no welcoming. The Teton menaced weapons and demanded tribute to pass through their territory. Captain William Clark, infuriated by the insults and extortion, wrote in his journal:

> *These are the vilest miscreants of the savage race, and must ever remain the pirates of the Missouri, until such measures are pursued, by our government, as will make them feel a dependence on its will for their supply of merchandise. Unless these people are reduced to order, by coercive measures, I am ready to pronounce that the citizens of the United States can never enjoy but partially the advantages which the Missouri presents.*[24]

Clark's observation placed an indelible mark against these people. His co-leader, Meriwether Lewis, advised President Jefferson that garrisons should be established in the north to interrupt the flow of merchandise through traders from Canada to make these Indians dependent on the United States.[25] Both captains understood there were national goals beyond scientific study and reconnaissance. The Teton Sioux also saw significance in the explorer's passage, marking it with a winter count pictograph in 1805, showing the flying of many flags.[26]

Later explorers who came to these lands ventured further away from the Missouri River's course and onto the prairie. Men such as Major Stephen Long correctly characterized these lands as semiarid; contemporary mapping labeled the outstretched plain the "Great American Desert." Major Long advised that the lands of the midcontinent were "uninhabitable by people depending on agriculture for their subsistence."[27]

Of course, the natives already knew this. Though they gathered roots and berries along rivers and streams, the Plains Indians were not agrarians. They were hunters. They hunted and harvested buffalo. Their very existence depended on the buffalo.[28] They warred against other tribes to protect their hunting grounds.

The predominate terrain of the Plains appears as a broad table of earth, caught in the rain shadow of the Rockies, from the eastern edge of those mountains to the 100th meridian (a north-south line running through the middle of the two Dakotas and Nebraska and south beyond the Texas panhandle). The skies often produce meager rainfall. Across this landscape are found sandstone, eroding sediments, and even sand hills. But it is not a wasteland.

Nor is it all flat; there are periodic interruptions of rivers and valleys. The ground gains gradual elevation in its long stretch from the Missouri River westward to the base of the Rocky Mountains. The rise is about 4,000 feet over 500 to 600 miles. It is a subtle climb. But not until leaving the North Platte Valley in western Nebraska is there a different character to the land—rock formations periodically jut skyward. Entering Wyoming and Montana, the land folds itself into foothills and scattered mountains—ranges such as Laramie, Bighorn, and Wind River all announce the coming of the Rockies.

Following the report to the president from the Lewis and Clark expedition, it was just a matter of time for America's westward expansion through the prairie. After all, the United States had bought the rights to the land from France in the Louisiana Purchase of 1803. The treaty between two sovereign nations did not seek approval of the native inhabitants; it was signed in Paris and ratified in Washington, D.C. The right of discovery by civilized people preempted any claim to the land by indigenous people who were classified as savages.[29] Thus the barbaric Indians only had a limited and extinguishable right of occupancy.

While there were earlier contacts by trappers and traders, the Corps of Discovery unlocked the gate to the West. Lines were drawn, and territorial administrations were given specific dominion over sections of the terrain over a succession of years. The establishment of the Louisiana Territory was immediate in 1804; in 1812, it was designated as the Territory of Missouri. The Territory of the Minnesota was established in 1849; Kansas, Nebraska, and Colorado quickly followed. The Dakota Territory was organized in 1861, made up of parts of the Minnesota and Nebraska Territories; it included what would become North and South Dakota and extensive parts of Wyoming and Montana.[30] Only the Civil War between the States slowed the American encroachments into these lands. When the war was over, the government commissioned surveyors on geologic and mapping expeditions to detail the lands beyond the 100th meridian. But it was left to the postwar restless and opportunists to make an impact on the ground.

The very earliest white intruders had been tolerated. These men made the effort to forge a cultural connection with the native population; basic survival demanded hunters, trappers, and traders adapt to the ways of prairie life. Equally important to their acceptance, traders brought the inhabitants highly prized metal goods—guns, knives, and kettles.

The new man had gained a foothold. He offered goods that increased the effectiveness of the hunter and strengthened the warrior. Of course, there was a price—the primary currency was fur pelts and buffalo hides. In retrospect, it was as if the Indians had partaken of a forbidden fruit.

Certainly, the Indians could understand people occasionally passing through. But they could not accept what became a constant flow of immigrants and settlements on the land. Even early entries produced adverse effects. To facilitate bargaining, traders introduced whiskey to the Indians.[31] Most devastating to families, the white man's diseases were easily communicated to the native population, who had no immunity to or medicines for typhoid, smallpox, cholera, and influenza. Such diseases had afflicted Indians since the white man's first arrival on the American continent;[32] more Indians were lost to these maladies than in battle.

As of 1840, the westward expansion of the United States was contained at the east bank of the Missouri River, flowing from the Rocky Mountains near Canada eastward and then south through the Dakotas and Nebraska, where it regained its easterly direction across Missouri to join the Mississippi at St. Louis. The lands on the left bank of the Missouri were known as Indian Territory. The first organized wagon train over the Oregon Trail was only a hundred travelers strong, departing in mid-May 1842.[33] During the 1840s to 1850s, this movement escalated to thousands heading west, by foot, by horse or mule, and by "wood that rolled."[34] (Ironically, the Plains Indians were categorized as nomadic, holding no legal title to these lands against the intrusion of discovers. But the nomads travelling the greatest distance were the white adventurers and settlers crossing the country.[35]) Curious observation by the Sioux and other tribes turned to harassment. Interference with wagon trains escalated. Horses and cattle were stolen. Tolls for crossing were demanded. Sometimes killings occurred along the trial. The hardship of passage was constant, but cross-country travelers experienced a measure of relief at the approach of geologic rock outcroppings and spires near the end of the prairie's long reach. Courthouse and Jail Rocks, Chimney Rock, Castle Rock, and Scotts Bluff stood as way posts, signaling a breaking away from the heart of Indian country.

In the late 1840s, sensational news shot cross-country from the far West. James Marshall discovered nuggets glinting in the gravels of the American River. "Gold in California!" was the siren's song. The ensuing rush for treasure exerted a pull westward stronger than any fear of danger in traversing the trackless ground beyond the Missouri River. Miners and settlers trampled the hunting lands of the central Plains, disrupting the migration of the buffalo and cutting scarce timber. So too began the littering of America's byways, as unwanted, useless, or just too-much-to-pack items were discarded along the trial. In retaliation, Indian stealth raids on livestock and outright assault were on the rise. In 1851, to assure safe passage for those heading West and others returning east through the Great Plains, the government sent out calls to various Plains Indian tribes to gather at Horse Creek, near Fort Laramie, Wyoming.[36] The purpose was not to buy land, but to secure a right of way through Indian Territory. The government was not ready to relocate these tribes as it had done with so many Indians in the east; here it sought a temporary fix. No reservation was proposed.

Representatives of the Sioux Nation, Cheyenne, Arapaho, Crow, Assiniboine, Gros-Ventre and Mandan (these were two distinct tribes bundled together in the treaty), and Arikara signed, agreeing to peaceful relations with the United States and to the right of the government to establish roads and military posts throughout Indian land. In return, the United States promised to protect the Indian nations against "all depredations by the people of the United States."[37] The lands of the seven Indian nations that signed, as well as the Blackfoot Nation, were defined with the intent of formalizing boundaries to preclude territorial disputes among the nations and to acknowledge the extent of the territory preserved.[38] (Of course, the delineation of formal boundaries was not a concept known to these tribes, who frequently crossed each other's territory.) The Indians were to be secure in these lands for "as long as the river flows and the eagle flies."[39] Additionally, for damages that "have or may occur" and other treaty stipulations, an annuity of $50,000 per annum was offered to be divided among the seven named Indian nations.[40] This was just over $7,000 per year over a period of 50 years to be paid to each of the seven groups signing.[41] Twenty-one chiefs or headmen put their marks to the document.[42] Where there were no chiefs, the government designated representatives to sign. Those signing were given gifts of military uniforms and swords for the occasion.[43] Most who gathered for council had no representative sign for them; paper chiefs meant nothing to the warrior societies within the tribes.[44] Pretend chiefs were an absurdity. Nonetheless, the United States imposed its "official" manner of business on the proceedings.

As occurred in all treaties with the Indians, more was spoken than put on paper, which itself had to be translated to those signing. The Indians understood the treaty to formalize reparations for destruction of the land from overland travel. One general called it a "molasses and cracker"[45] treaty—full of good-sounding words. But even some of the good words were later changed. The Senate in its ratification cut the time for payment of annuities to 10 years, allowing for a possible extension of five years at the discretion of the president.[46] To satisfy legal formality, the government sent out emissaries to secure sign-off from another set of designated chiefs for the amendment.

The territory of the "Sioux or Dahcotah Nation" was defined as running from the mouth of the White Earth River on the Missouri River southwesterly to the forks of the Platte River, then along the north fork of that river to a point known as Red Butte and along the Black Hills to the head waters of the Heart River to its mouth, coming back along the Missouri to the point of beginning.[47] This was a broad description covering the western regions of the Dakotas and Nebraska and extending into eastern Wyoming and Montana, which when read with later language in the treaty could only be a guideline. After dividing the lands among the signatory tribes, there was an acknowledgement that none abandoned any claim of right that they may have to other lands and they did not surrender the right to hunt, fish, and pass over any of the tracts. The Sioux had no intention of altering their movements over these lands or of making peace with their enemies.

While some of the Hunkpapa band of Sioux took presents and appeared to show interest, most voiced opposition. Rights to land could not be defined by words; Indians understood land only by what the earth provided them. Intertribal warfare was a way of life, and sometimes whites got in the way.[48] When roll was called, no Hunkpapa representative made his mark on the treaty paper. Besides, the tribe's primary range was several hundred miles to the north of the immigrants' crossing route. The paper document meant nothing to them. The Oregon Trial most affected the southern Sioux, the Oglala, whose home territory was along the Platte River and near the Black Hills.

Among the Lakota who observed the council sessions at Fort Laramie was a 20-year-old Hunkpapa.[49] Sitting behind his uncle, Four Horns, he watched and listened to leaders and elders within his band. From these men he learned that caution was the watchword when the white man extended the hand of friendship. More importantly, there was no reason to deal land to the white man. This lesson would last a lifetime.

Deliberative by nature, as a young boy this Indian was nicknamed "Slow."[50] But at age 14, he demonstrated no hesitation when a hunting party he was riding with encountered members of a hostile tribe. Confronted by greater numbers, the enemy scrambled to retreat. Pushing his horse forward, Slow cut to the lead of the chase. When the rearmost retreating warrior saw no escape, he wheeled his horse and dismounted while reaching for an arrow. Slow flashed forward and crashed a coup stick across the arm of his enemy as arrow was being pulled against bow string. The arrow went awry, and the charge of Slow's horse knocked the man to the ground.[51] When the enemy warrior tried to regain his feet, one of the young braves in the pursuit pack cut him down.

At the report of his son's exploit, the father bestowed on Slow his own name, "Tatanka Iyotake,"[52] ("Sitting Bull") and took for himself the name of Jumping Bull.[53] The maturing Sitting Bull advanced quickly within his band and soon achieved membership in the Hunkpapa warrior society. His mettle was widely recognized. He distinguished himself in encounters with tribal enemies and survived several wounds, all of which advanced his standing. By 1857, at age 26, he had risen to warrior chief.[54]

Round at the shoulders and broad across the chest, Sitting Bull was ruggedly built. A bit bowlegged, he stood not quite 5 feet 10 inches.[55] And he walked with a slight limp, the result of a bullet ripping through the sole of his left foot and exiting the heel in a fight with a Crow.[56] He had no swagger. His copper-colored visage carried a prominent nose and pronounced cheekbones; a well-cut jaw held a wide but fine-lined mouth that downturned slightly at the edges. His dark brown eyes were tightly contained under faintly arched brows within a broad face. Because his eyes occasionally tended to water, he had a soulful look that projected no fierceness. He typically parted his black hair down the middle and pulled it back across his ears, with braids wrapped in fur falling to the front of his shoulders. His manner of dress was most often simple[57] and at times a bit casual.[58] Although not striking in appearance, he was not lost in a crowd.

Lakota culture demanded daring and success in battle to achieve status. His war-making skill commanded high respect, but he was not all consumed by combat against other tribes. Equally important, Sitting Bull embodied the Lakota character trait of generosity to anyone in need. Even to an enemy he could show compassion. Once when his fellow warriors were about to execute a young Assiniboine after overcoming his band, he interceded and bade the boy forward. Not as a prisoner. Rather, because of what he saw as bravery, he adopted the youngster as his own brother over objection of his band. The young Indian was descriptively called Little Assiniboine. Later, after Sitting Bull's own father was killed in yet another fight with the Crow, Little Assiniboine was given the name Jumping Bull.[59] Compassion also could cut with a sharp edge. On another occasion, riding back to camp, Sitting Bull happened upon a group of shrieking women from his band about to set afire a harlot taken from another tribe. Seeing the captive, stripped naked, tied to a stake and kindling at her feet, he pulled his horse to a stop. He drew his bow and sent an arrow into her chest.[60] She was about to die; his way hastened the inevitable. The angry Hunkpapa shrews fumed among themselves; Sitting Bull's rejoinder was a long backward glance of disapproval as he reined his horse away.

Sitting Bull heard and saw what others could not. He was spiritual; he prayed often and sought visions for guidance.[61] His people followed because he possessed wisdom. It was frequently said that he had "good medicine,"[62] although he was not a healer or shaman. He was able to relate events to song, of which he was fond; he could comprehend the voice of animals. He particularly related to birds, with the magpie and meadowlark his favorites. He understood their language.[63] He listened; he observed.

He was his father's son, and his roots were those of his ancestors.

His first wife died during childbirth, leaving him a son who died four years later.[64] He remarried a woman called Snow on Her, who bore him two daughters. Shortly thereafter, he took a second wife, Red Woman. The arrangement was not a good domestic match. There was immediate dissension.[65] Snow on Her, always quarrelsome, constantly bickered with the younger woman and had to be dismissed from wedlock.[66] The daughters stayed with their father and the remaining wife. When Red Woman died within a year of giving birth to a son,[67] Sitting Bull turned to his mother, Her Holy Door, and other family members to rear the children. Even though he would have other wives, Her Holy Door was the woman of influence in his life. She was a slight but assertive woman, savvy in tribal matters. She was as persuasive as a counselor as she was protective as a mother. She often could see the knives of rivals being sharpened before he could. As long as she lived, her advice held weight in his decision making.

Pictograph of Sitting Bull by Four Horns
SMITHSONIAN

Along with possessing political power, he displayed a natural affability as well as a sense of humor.[68] He conversed as easily with women and children as with elders and warriors. He was not inclined to make a decision for the convenience of the moment. Many thought his adult name described intransience. There was no question that he could be unbending. And there were those who saw a forceful personality that they did not like. Lakota chiefs were not supreme leaders; they shared responsibilities.

They governed with advice from a council of elders and needed the allegiance of the warrior societies. Because Sitting Bull was not a hereditary chief, some questioned his standing. He was constantly confronted by factions within the bands.[69] It did not matter; Sitting Bull was convinced that he was chosen by the Great Spirit.[70] His will was iron forged. He spoke his thoughts in a firm resonant voice.[71] Chiefs were expected to be generous, selfless, forgiving, and all protective of their people.[72] He met all these prerequisites. Even though he was seldom vindictive, his detractors did not go away and in time became more numerous.

Following the 1851 treaty, the white migration across the country became constant.[73] Indian militants increased the harassment of immigrants, miners, and settlers. All of these deprivations drew the attention of the military. Protection was demanded by those who put themselves in the way of the Indian. The Lakota were quite proficient in skirmishes but did not have the numbers to defend the far edges of the prairie against the influx of westward migration. They had no standing army; and warriors bore the additional responsibilities in the field of family providers.

Under these circumstances, Sitting Bull's band considered it best to avoid the white man. The Hunkpapa continued to follow the buffalo and warriors clashed with tribal enemies in defending territory and stealing horses on raids. The cross-country travel route was left to the southern tribes to confront. The northern Plains remained Lakota land.[74]

Pressure to make it otherwise, however, was building. And the written word, first in the form of a book and second as legislation, heralded opportunity.

In 1860, a book by William Gilpin was published that changed America's perception of the Great American Desert. *The Central Gold Region, The Grain, Pastoral, and Gold Regions of North America* shouted "manifest destiny." Gilpin had attended West Point, was a member of John Fremont's 1842 expedition to find a suitable route over the continental divide, and was about to be appointed territorial governor of Colorado by President Lincoln. He was a futurist and booster; his book declared: "These PLAINS are not deserts, but the opposite and are the cardinal basis of the future empire of commerce and industry now creating itself upon the North American Continent."[75] The lands were for the taking and would become the "pasture-fields of the world."[76] (The book presaged the Dakota Boom during the late 1870s, a period of unusual rainfall, when nesters from the Midwest and Norwegians, Swedes, and Germans from Europe scrambled to claim farmland.[77]) No longer would the Plains be considered a "bleak monotony"[78] to be passed over.

Then with the Homestead Act of 1862, 160-acre quarter sections were made available without cost to those who would live on and improve the land. The gridding of the Plains was set in motion. Straight lines began to define territory. Title went to those who could measure and enclose the land.[79] Land was free for the taking to those hardy enough to seize the opportunity. Washington needed people to occupy the West and did not hesitate to provide encouragement.

Most Lakota, who never had known man-made borders, would not assent to having their lands mapped and redefined. Other tribes, however, succumbed to the government's reservation system, by now extending into Kansas and Nebraska, out of fear of the white man's power, hunger, and promises for their care. Even so, many of these men took leave during the spring and summer months to hunt off reservation. Even Sitting Bull was receptive to some of what the white man had to offer. During the early 1860s, he worked for a trader at Fort Berthold near where the Little Missouri meets the Missouri in the northern reaches of the Dakotas. He was a broker of buffalo robes. But when he was shorted on payment due him, he bargained no more.[80] Whatever he learned from this experience, trust of the white man was not one of them. It would not be the last time he was betrayed.

Meantime, a gold strike in Montana brought a run of prospectors to the northwest corner of the Plains.[81] Not only were adventurers crossing the hunting grounds of the Lakota, they were putting claims on the land. Roads and commerce quickly followed to support mining camps, as discoveries occurred in Bannack and Alder Gulch (later called Virginia City). Predictably, the intrusions produced friction between newcomers and natives; scattered skirmishes erupted around the camps and supply routes. Then in 1862, warriors raised the ante by boldly attacking a steamer carrying miners on the Missouri River.[82] With security demanded, Congress funded military escorts to protect the interlopers.[83]

While unrest in the northwest churned, a more immediate threat came out of the northeast. Following an unexpected Dakota uprising in Minnesota, shock waves were about to ripple into trans-Missouri territory. The Lakota would feel the hurt from a series of attacks by avenging infantrymen, recruited to fight for the Union army but directed against fleeing Minnesota Indians by aggressive commanders. What the Indians would encounter was not customary tribal warfare.

CHAPTER THREE

Minnesota River Valley Uprising

1862–1863

The Dakota Territory spread out from the western boundary of Minnesota. The primary demarcation is the Red River originating in Lake Traverse and flowing north to Canada along two-thirds of Minnesota's western edge. Just to the south of Traverse is Big Stone Lake, fed by the Little Minnesota River across from a divide altering the drainage pattern of the land from north to south; from this lake flows the Minnesota River southeasterly and then northeasterly to the Mississippi. The countryside on either side of the two rivers is similar. The woodlands and lakes of Minnesota gradually make their way toward the prairie; and the northeast Dakotas hold potholes, marshes, and lakes formed by glacial retreat. This is rich farming land, blessed with the greater rain that falls east of the 100th meridian than on the land on the far side of the Missouri.

The Red River boundary and two lakes were a definitive frontier line in the early 1860s. The Dakotas remained every bit Indian environment even though designated a Territory of the United States in 1861, while Minnesota progressed to statehood in 1858. The Anglo-American presence was well entrenched, particularly in and around St. Paul and east of the Mississippi River. This land was originally part of the Northwest Territory, running northward from the Ohio Valley up to the Great Lakes, incorporated by the United States in 1787. It was long-standing fur trading country; the French, the English, and the Americans all found opportunity to exploit an unlimited bounty. Yet there was a counterbalance at work because business depended on the native population as trading partners. The upper Mississippi River became a major transportation and commercial route. St. Paul, having an easily accessible landing at the Minnesota River's intersection with the Mississippi, grew from a few traders' stores and tents to a population nearing 10,000 by the time of statehood. Lake Superior dominated the northeast corner of the state, and thousands of smaller lakes dappled the land. The name "Minnesota" reflected a lake country, coming from the Dakota word for "sky-tinted water" or "cloudy-sky water." French-Canadian descendants were joined by Americans as merchants and traders in this new state; American farmers settled into fertile holdings scattered along the Minnesota River Valley to the southwest of St. Paul. The new commerce changed the way of dealing with the Indians. Former partners were now managed. The Indian clearly was the lesser.

The Dakota family of Sioux, known as the Santee, resided on the near side the Missouri, principally in woodlands of Minnesota. These people consisted of bands of Mdewakanton, Sisseton, Wahpeton, and Wahpekute.[1] They remained close to their original homeland and appeared to have adapted to the white civilization that had come to populate the area. But it was a coerced adaptation.

Dakota belligerence had been beaten down during the last half of the 1700s by confrontations with the Chippewa. Dwindling in numbers and pushed southward, the Santee had little strength to resist in the 1800s and accepted a treaty with the United States ceding most of their land for money and goods. They were granted a reservation along a portion of the Minnesota River and believed that the white man would look out for them. Many turned to farming and Christianity. Those who chose to work with the white man wore his manner of dress and cut their hair. Whatever benevolence the establishment chose to give went to these Indians. Others who stood their distance from the new ways dismissed their farmer brothers as "breeches men" and "cut hairs."[2] Short and long hair defined division. Relations between the two groups were strained. Adding to the dissention, mixed-bloods considered themselves superior to full bloods. The Santee found themselves pushed into serfdom.

Even for the so-called civilized Indians, amicable dealings with the whites were hard to maintain. Reservation boundaries were frequently ignored by farmers. Annuities provided by treaties were often late; traders commonly sold the natives goods at inflated rates. When annuity payments did arrive, reservation agents first took care of the traders' accounts. Such payment was always what was shown on the books; no dispute was mediated. Whatever was left over was for the Indians, and most of the time debt exceeded pay. Wages for work were below subsistence. Compounding this state of affairs, crop failures in 1860 and 1861 produced food scarcities.[3] The Santee were impoverished and malnourished; they were a misplaced people prodded from their cultural ties, while the white settlers and merchants prospered. There was no hiding the disparity. When the government was both late and short with annuity payments because of the priority of funding the Civil War effort, frustration ran to rancor.[4]

The Indians had been made dependent on the white man, and they suffered under failed promises. The Santee leaders' requests for assistance were ignored. Protests had no effect. Resentment that had simmered too long was about to boil over.

Come the summer of 1862, a riled group of destitute Santee men stormed an agency warehouse and helped themselves to more than one hundred sacks of flour.[5] Troops were called in, and the Indians dispersed without bloodshed. Still, the underlying causes of unrest remained. In early August, a community council was convened to attempt to assuage the Indians' grievances. But the whites looked for a measure of contrition. Little Crow, a prominent Mdewakanton chief and known as an accommodationist, advised: "When men are hungry, they help themselves."[6] "If they are hungry, let them eat grass," Andrew Myrick, a wealthy trader, bellowed back.[7] The insult would not wash away. It reflected a callousness that kept the Indians suppressed. The council was called to provide a salve not a solution; all that came of it was the release of some overdue food stuffs.

A few weeks later, on August 17, four young Indians returning from an unproductive hunt found a nest of eggs near a farm fence. When one of the boys reached down to steal the eggs, another scolded that he should not take what was not his.[8] They quarreled among themselves; there were taunts that the boy advocating leaving the eggs where they lay was afraid of the white man. Challenged to prove otherwise, he stomped on the eggs. The incident did not go unnoticed. A farmer named Robinson Jones saw the commotion from afar and ran over to accost the boys. He called them "dirty Injuns" and "dogs and thieves." They were not about to kowtow. Somehow a gun discharged, and the farmer fell to the ground.[9]

The carnage did not stop there. What took place next is not clear; the panicky young hunters themselves gave confused accounts. However, the reality was that the farmer and a postmaster, his wife, and two children in the Acton community were discovered murdered and four Indian boys walked away.[10]

Word of the killings raced through the Indian villages. That night a rally was called. It was certain that there would be reprisals as soon as the whites could respond; and the militant faction urged a preemptive strike: "Don't return to your homes to sit and wait for punishment." Little Crow sought to check the anger. He argued that there are too many white men: "If you strike at them they will all turn on you and devour you and your women and little children just as the locusts in their time fall on the trees and devour all the leaves in one day."[11] The assembled were already primed to strike back. They were fed up with white suppression. They would no longer bow to the establishment. Little Crow, having suffered criticism for appeasing the white man in past treaty negotiations, was derided. Reasoned discussion was not possible. The fractured light of bonfires and torchlights made the crowd appear more menacing. Confronted by mob hostility, Little Crow dropped any effort to calm the situation. In defending himself, he shouted out: "Little Crow is not a coward."[12]

Within minutes, he was at the lead of a rebellious band.

The next day, the Santee attacked farmers in the Minnesota River Valley.[13] By nightfall on August 18, over four hundred settlers were killed.[14] The ease in spilling blood only fueled the uprising. The rampage went on for weeks. It was a carnage run. Scattered farms were raided, settlers killed, women raped, bodies dismembered, livestock slaughtered, food stores looted, buildings burned. The body of trader Myrick was found shot with arrows and a scythe jammed into his rib cage.[15] Some said that his mouth was stuffed with grass.[16] If so, this was grass from land that no longer produced enough to feed the Santee. Outlying settlers were not able to defend themselves. They sent frantic runners to Fort Snelling, situated across the Minnesota River from St. Paul.

There was a call to arms. Not until late August could Minnesota militiamen effectively respond. Although the Santee did not have the means to sustain the fight, roiling anger and surprise propelled the early attacks.[17] Within a week, eight hundred white settlers were killed.[18] But when the United States Army joined with volunteer militia in September, the uprising was quick to finish. Both hostiles and bystanders were roughly rounded up. By December 1862, there were over a thousand Dakota men held captive. A military tribunal in summary proceedings found 303 of these Indians guilty of murder and rape and sentenced them to death.[19] President Abraham Lincoln intervened to personally review the evidence; he determined that only 39 deserved to be executed. And a reprieve was granted to one of the condemned at the last hour. This was an extraordinary intervention by Washington in response to a state populace gravely hurt, bitter, and angry. On December 26, 38 men were prodded from prison to a massive gallows at Mankato before a thousand or more Minnesotans who had gathered on a surprisingly mild morning to bear witness.[20] General Sibley stationed troops around the hanging platform to assure order. Those to be executed defiantly displayed feathers, painted their faces, and sang death songs. At ten o'clock in the morning, the signal was given to pull the floor door from the platform, and all swung at the end of ropes to the cheers of the crowd. They were buried in a single grave at the edge of town. Those not executed remained in prison, and the next spring they were transported downriver to be held in other stockades.[21] Indian families were expelled from the state, and reservation land was taken back by order of Congress. The Indians remaining in jail were sent to distant reservations in Dakota and Nebraska Territories. The only Santee who were not targeted for punishment were a small group of the Mdewakanton, Sisseton, and Wahpeton, who remained neutral during the conflict and in some cases assisted white settlers.[22]

Many Santee made their way into the Devils Lake area of northern Dakota Territory, hoping to avoid the hateful backlash for the death and destruction they visited on settlers of the Minnesota River Valley.[23] Rebellious bands that were able to escape the army went further west and eventually crossed the Missouri River to take up with the Teton Sioux.[24] Speculation was rampant that the escaped insurgents were reorganizing under Little Crow with other tribes to launch another attack; fear of terrorism ran through the border communities of the Dakotas.[25] Further to the west, the Teton Sioux alerted to what had happened offered protection to the fleeing Santee.

<hr />

The militia was not content just to see these Santee on the run. Generals Henry Sibley and Alfred Sully were ordered by Major General John Pope of the Department of the Northwest to give pursuit into Dakota Territory.[26] As a consequence, in 1863, the Lakota could no longer avoid confrontation with the white man. The Teton Sioux, having given refuge to their Santee brothers, became targets.[27] Troops came at them from the north and south. The initial thrust was from Sibley, followed by Sully.

Skirmishes and battles ignited the upper Dakota Territory. The first major encounter occurred east of the Missouri at Whitestone Hill. There followed Stoney Lake, Dead Buffalo Lake, and Big Mound.[28] Then the Missouri River was crossed in 1864, and the military attacked the Lakota in northwest Dakota at Killdeer Mountain and the Little Missouri Badlands.[29] Sitting Bull, now a warrior chief, was at the front in the later actions. But the army was the victor. In combat at the Badlands, a cavalry man's bullet struck the chief in the hip and exited the small of his back. Slumped over and clutching the mane of his horse, he rode out of range, where comrades pulled him to safety.[30] From these engagements Sitting Bull and fellow Lakota warrior leaders were given a harsh lesson about engaging in a pitched battle against American troops. Bows and arrows and old muskets were no match for the soldiers' rifles and cannon. The army was supplied by steamboat on the Yellowstone.[31] The force of the opposition was much more than they had ever experienced from tribal raiding parties. With no experience against a full military charge, to stand and fight proved disastrous. The Sioux could only run for distance from the field; the military considered it a rout. Yet, Bull was critical: "They stand still and run straight: it is easy to shoot them. They do not try to save themselves." He also felt that they had "no heart"; when a comrade fell, no one cried, no one cared.[32]

This was a shift in warfare that the Teton Sioux would valiantly strive to counter but ultimately they would be crushed by it.

Although Sully terminated his western Dakota campaign shortly after the invasion of the northern Badlands, the garrisons he established in the Upper Missouri stayed.[33] The lands of the Hunkpapa and other Lakota had become less remote. Nevertheless, Sitting Bull held to the belief that isolationism remained the best course for his people. Contact with the new man invariably led to trouble. The strategy would only provide a few years' respite. The traditional life on the Plains was fraying.

The execution of the Santee criminals was still the talk of the state, when an industrious 21-year-old Canadian disembarked from a train in St. Paul, Minnesota, on April 13, 1863.[34] St. Paul was the gateway to the old northwest[35] and a crossroads of commerce. It offered the promise of good employment.

James McLaughlin came to seek his place in the United States with the trade of blacksmith. He also was trained in the fundamentals of machinery.[36] At 5 feet 6 inches in height, McLaughlin did not have the hardy look of his occupation. In fact, with his fine facial features and manner of dress, he could be mistaken for an apprentice banker. His deep-set eyes, thick black hair, together with general good grooming, gave him a handsome appearance.[37] He was not a dandy but carried himself with confidence. Schooling through the eighth grade was enough for him to be a lettered man; this education would take him beyond manual labor. He was clear thinking, firm in his convictions, and resolute in pursuing his goals. He was not an ordinary scrubbed-face newcomer.

The energetic McLaughlin quickly obtained itinerant employment in nearby settlements.[38] He decided that a chin curtain of whiskers[39] provided a sturdier appearance to secure work in the countryside. Shortly after arriving, he was employed for a couple of months by the quartermaster at Fort Snelling.[40] This was a supply base for the military's Department of Dakota, which brought him into contact with soldiers and French-Canadian half-breed traders, known as "Red River Metis,"[41] all telling tales, real and embellished, about the recent Indian war and current conflicts in Dakota and Montana. These encounters produced impressions of the frontier that shaped his views.

Close by and east of the fort was the village of Mendota, where McLaughlin made the acquaintance of a merchant's daughter, Marie Louise Buisson. But she was more than a merchant's daughter; her maternal grandmother was an Mdewakanton.[42] Indians were more numerous than traders in Minnesota both at the time of her grandmother's and mother's marriages; it was not unusual for white men to take an Indian wife in this part of the country. James McLaughlin courted Marie Louise with good intent; at the same time he was aware of her family's standing in the community. They were married in 1864. The following year, he applied for United States citizenship.[43] Everything was falling into place in his new country.

Marie Louise was no ordinary woman of Indian blood; she had been schooled in the white world and reared in a mixed community. She was refined in her appearance and typically wore proper dresses. Yet her mother, Lucy Nancy "Mary" Graham, taught her Dakota traditions. As a child she was equally conversant in English and the Sioux language.[44] Her father, Joseph Buisson, was a French-Canadian Indian trader; just like McLaughlin, he came to the United States as a young man.[45] Buisson successfully conducted a trading post serving both settlers and Santee in Wabasha, Minnesota, some 60 miles southeast of St. Paul on the edge of the Mississippi River. The merchant did well by his children, and they did not suffer because they had Indian blood. At age 14, Marie Louise was sent to convent school in Prairie du Chien, Wisconsin.[46] But when her father died suddenly the next year, she returned home to her mother and Santee relatives.

Through his wife's family and his own itinerant work, McLaughlin came to know diverse Santee and mixed-bloods at St. Paul, Mendota, Wabasha, Faribault, and other communities throughout southeast Minnesota. He even acquired some knowledge of their language.[47] But he drew his conclusions about Indians primarily from his acquaintance of mixed-bloods. Based on what he learned of the Mdewakanton, it appeared that the native people remaining in Minnesota were well on the path to civilization, in contrast to the warring Indians whom McLaughlin heard about to the west in the northern Plains. The latter he called "trans-Missouri" Sioux.[48] While he came to know the native culture, he could never accept its preservation. As with most white men, he measured the Indian against Anglo-American culture.

Early on, he realized that his wife's family's Minnesotan merchant connections hastened his acceptance in his new country.[49] Equally important, Marie Louise's Sioux ancestry would prove instrumental in advancing her husband beyond the trade of blacksmith. In time, it would take him west of the Missouri River to Lakota country with a position of considerable influence.

James McLaughlin
STATE HISTORICAL SOCIETY OF NORTH DAKOTA

CHAPTER FOUR

Powder River War

1864–1870

The West was developing, and talk of it was everywhere rife; rail-roads building across the Plains, gold and silver to be dug in the hills of Montana, free land for the settlers, profitable hunting for fur and for buffalo robes, big money from the sale of firewood to the steam-boats. Naturally the most turbulent and adventurous were drawn to the West; and the United States Government was almost powerless to control them as the Indian chiefs were to manage their young men.
—GEORGE F. WILL, BISMARCK, NORTH DAKOTA[1]

Four years of North-South fratricide had physically and emotionally shattered the country. In the aftermath, the American people looked for a chance for renewal in lands not torn apart during the Civil War. Washington had already planted its flag on territories throughout the midcontinent; it added the Territories of Montana and Wyoming in 1864 and 1868. The government turned its attention to extending transportation routes and encouraging population growth into the West. Untapped resources lay on the other side of the Mississippi. The nation became outward bound. Promoters and immigrants surged westward, some stopping to establish settlements and towns within the Plains. Adventurers, miners, and then farmers all headed west—by trails, roads, and then rails.

The homelands of the Plains Indians bore the brunt of the onslaught, and the native inhabitants struck back. As the cross-country migration escalated and soldiers marched in, Sitting Bull's protectionist view stiff-ened and shaped his emergence as the ultimate resistance leader.

In the face of Indian raids on wagon trains, isolated settlers, and their livestock, particularly along the Platte River, citizens in Colorado, Kansas, and Nebraska stepped up demands for interdiction.[2] The army initiated a campaign in 1864 in the southern Plains to separate friendly Indians from hostile bands of Cheyenne, Kiowa, Arapaho, and Comanche. The goal was to move Indians onto the government-established reservations, even though those reservations were not able adequately to sustain the people already there. The rationale was that providing a fixed home and support was a fair trade-off for the country making room for westward expansion. The tactics were strong-arm terror, including burning villages, destroying food caches, and stealing and killing horses.[3]

Colonel John M. Chivington, a Colorado Methodist minister,[4] took those tactics to an extreme. Chivington had turned down a chaplain appointment to serve the Union forces in the Civil War to secure a fighting commission. In 1862, he played a key role at Apache Canyon in turning back a bizarre Confederate campaign out of El Paso, Texas. But when he did not advance in rank as he thought he should, he returned to Colorado. He urged early statehood and suppression of the country's Indian inhabitants. The territorial governor gave him charge of the volunteers for the 3rd Regiment of Cavalry. The "Fighting Parson" was a vengeful man running on manufactured hate, who whipped his militia into a frenzy to go after Indians, not fight rebels. The man was fired with ambition and conviction. He scorned those who urged treaty making. Still, he kept a firm hand on the Union flag, playing on the suspicion that agents of the Confederacy were inciting marauding Indians to kill white men on the central Plains.[5] In late November 1864, his Colorado Volunteers were on the march in southeastern Colorado looking for Indians. Learning that a Cheyenne band was camped on Sand Creek, the volunteers, most of whom had been drinking throughout the night, attacked the sleeping encampment at sunrise on November 29. Outside of the Cheyenne chief Black Kettle's tipi were staffed both American and white flags; many of the Cheyenne men were away on a hunt. Black Kettle believed his camp and Arapaho lodges that had joined up with his people were under the protection of nearby Fort Lyon. This was not a hostile camp. The signs of peaceful intentions mattered not. One hundred and five women and children and 28 men never saw another morning. The militiamen first ran off the Indians' horses to prevent escape. Then, cannon and rifle fire laid into the camp. Fleeing Indians were run down and shot, bladed, or beaten to death. A few managed to find hiding places in depressions dug along the creek bank;[6] but not for long. They were hunted down for killing. Yet, Black Kettle somehow managed to break away from the carnage. By noon, the assailants with knives in hand were mutilating the dead, removing sexual organs and taking scalps. When they returned to Denver, the militiamen reveled with their trophies of war before appreciative citizens.[7] Even heads were severed from bodies, put in buckets and sacks, and the skulls shipped to the Smithsonian for study.[8]

In the East, the killings and dismemberments of body parts were considered as monstrous barbarism. Unchecked madness. To those on the frontier, the Indians reaped what they sowed. It was well known that Indians had been guilty of raids and murdering settlers; who was to say these Indians were not guilty? The Western press presented Sand Creek as a preemptive strike to quell hostilities in Colorado.[9] Legislators in Washington reacted to a more urban constituency that took a different view. A congressional inquiry was initiated, and the Eastern press criticized both the Chivington raiders and Governor John Evans, to whom these men were ultimately responsible. Chivington maintained that his militia did battle to preserve the peace of the Territory as well as to thwart a rebel strategy. In the Senate Reports to the 38th Congress, the Joint Committee on the Conduct of the War entered its condemnation of the action: "[Chivington] deliberately planned and executed a foul and dastardly massacre which would have disgraced the veriest savage among those who were the victims of his cruelty."[10] "He surprised and murdered, in cold blood, the unsuspecting men, women, and children,"[11] who believed they were under the protection of the United States. Even the southern Plains Indian fighter Kit Carson was critical.[12] The colonel and his men felt the heat. They dodged reprisals by mustering out of the service before any disciplinary action was taken. Black Kettle was not as fortunate in avoiding repercussion from the calamity. Warriors pulled away from his leadership, casting him as a peace seeker who cost his people dearly.

James McLaughlin read the local newspaper reports about the military action in Colorado. In the company of his wife's relatives, he may have acknowledged that Chivington was a butcher, but he was willing to accept that the Indians at Sand Creek were different than those he knew in his new homeland. The Cheyenne were wild in untamed country. In that setting, bad things happen. Like most in the West, he did not take a close look. He was preoccupied with finding work in the settlements of southeast Minnesota, and he was convinced Indians needed to adapt to a changing world.

Word of the Sand Creek Massacre reached every corner of the untamed land. It galvanized resistance of the central Plains tribes, particularly the Cheyenne and Arapaho. When the news extended to the north, tribal leaders were outraged.

At the moment, however, there were few whites in the lands of the Lakota. Sibley and Sully believed that the army had demonstrated its supremacy in the 1863 and 1864 campaigns; the Indians had removed themselves to the hinterland. To the military, the Lakota had turned tail. The army's attention was directed elsewhere. However, remote had a way of changing within a short time. The discovery of precious metal brought miners on the run to Montana. Reacting to complaints that the routes to the gold fields were not direct, Congress authorized a survey from Sioux City, Iowa, for a road up the Niobrara River to pass through the western edge of the Black Hills and then extend to Virginia City. That path was ill-advised. The lands within the Black Hills were especially significant to the Lakota. They were both their spiritual home—a place of origin—and a game reserve. There was no way that the Lakota would accept a road through the Hills.

By 1863, John Bozeman, with the aid of John Jacobs—one a failed miner and the other a mountaineer—mapped an alternate trail from Fort Laramie, cutting diagonally northwestward through Wyoming and then west into Bannack, Montana.[13] The next year, Bozeman led a group of settlers up the trail. The army hurriedly came forward to convert a rough trail to a wagon road linked to the cross-country course of the Oregon Trial coming through Nebraska's Platte Valley. The journey north was thus shortened by hundreds of miles; the army engineers stayed well west of the Black Hills. The trouble was the route ran through the adjacent Powder River country, primary buffalo hunting range for the Lakota.[14] It crossed the headwaters of the Clearwater Creek, Powder River and Tongue River, and Little Big Horn River, all along the eastern edge of the Big Horn Mountains and then across their northern end, continuing to ford streams as it inclined westward—the Big Horn River, Clark's Fork, Stillwater River, Boulder River, reaching the Yellowstone, where it ran westerly for about 30 miles, moving from that river at its elbow flowing from the south, and over the East and West Gallatin Rivers, with a final southwest leg down into Virginia City. This constituted a permanent invasion of Indian land. As soon as the road opened, Sioux harassment rushed to close it. After the fact, the United States called for a peace conference to negotiate a right of passage. Preliminary talks arranged by the army during the spring of 1866 appeared favorable, and a conference was arranged for June at Fort Laramie, Wyoming.[15] The government sent E. B. Taylor to head the negotiations. But as insurance, General Sherman assigned a battalion under Colonel Henry Carrington to erect forts at key locations along the route.[16] Still, this would not be enough to secure the route; the regular army could only afford to deploy a limited number of men to the Western frontier, and most were untrained in basic military fundamentals.

Leaders such as Red Cloud, Spotted Tail, Red Leaf, and Man Afraid of His Horses came to the conference on June 13 and listened to Taylor promise to restrict travel to the narrow limits of the road and prohibit travelers from disturbing game along the route.[17] Later that same day, Colonel Carrington's men and wagons hauling construction materials for emplacements rolled into the fort. Taylor had mentioned nothing of this. Whether this was an inadvertent blunder or calculated intimidating conduct did not matter. The military's heavy hand was the ultimate in bad faith. Reaction was hot-tempered. Carrington's attempted explanation was shouted down. The great chief of the Oglala, Red Cloud, castigated the peace delegation for deception in a program of slicing away the Indians' land piece by piece. The soldiers had come to steal the road while Taylor talked peace. Any trace of goodwill evaporated. Red Cloud called for a united effort of tribes to drive the soldiers out.[18] Carrington

Red Cloud, Chief of the Oglala Sioux
LIBRARY OF CONGRESS

accelerated the installation of fortifications. The existing garrison of Fort Connor was reinforced and became Fort Reno as the first military post beyond Fort Laramie about 90 miles out; 60 miles further up the road Fort Kearny was established and 60 more miles beyond that was placed Fort Smith.[19] The northern tribes immediately challenged the escalating occupation. What came to be known as the Powder River War was ignited. Shoshone, Arapaho, and Lakota all took the offensive with frequent strike-and-run skirmishes along the route.[20] The Bozeman trail became a perilous corridor; the army could not provide enough men and supplies to the new forts.[21]

Sitting Bull, his bellicose view hardened by news of the Chivington bloodbath,[22] no longer tried to avoid the white man. The Hunkpapa marauded throughout the upper Missouri. The chief now surrounded himself with activists; the only white men he considered worth dealing with were traders.[23] In a communiqué from General Sully to the Department of the Northwest, dated August 8, 1865, "the man called Sitting Bull" was noted as making war against the government.[24]

Still, it was Red Cloud and the Oglala in the Powder River Country who dominated the clash against the United States soldiers. He forged an alliance of tribes to direct raids. He would not let the warriors withdraw to winter camps; it was year-round guerrilla warfare. And it was strategic. Both civilian and military wagon trains were shadowed and harassed. Stragglers were ambushed. Livestock was run off. Horses and mules were thieved. Food supplies were stolen. Miners killed. Isolated patrols and deserters were slain and scalped.

As always, there were those in the army who pressed to prove themselves as Indian fighters. Such men held an arrogant view of their own superiority. In December 1866, an ambitious, recently posted officer—William Fetterman—responded to Indian harassment of an army wood-gathering detail on a wagon road outside of Fort Kearny.[25] Engaging what appeared to be a small group of Indians, he ordered 30 cavalry and 50 infantry troops to make a hard charge.[26] The Indians feinted retreat, but sent a couple of warriors forward for a look-see. Those men then fell back over a hill. When the troops crested the ridge, there were Sioux, Cheyenne, and Arapaho warriors in wait.[27] Having taken the bait, the soldiers were confronted at the point and pressed on the flanks. Fetterman and all his men were killed and their bodies mutilated where they fell. The leader of the decoy was an Oglala-Miniconjou Lakota called Crazy Horse.[28]

The ambush was condemned as an Indian massacre. Reports of the dead, having been scalped, hacked to bits, and disemboweled, sent a message written bloody large that the Indians were carrying the attack against too few troops. The army pushed for retribution. General William Sherman, then the army's commander of the Division of the Missouri, went further, advocating "extermination—men, women and children."[29] Taking a different view, the Indian Bureau advocated new efforts at finding amity.[30] Sherman branded the opposition "Indian lovers"[31]—visceral frontier logic. The Indians could only see storm signals on the Plains pointing to belligerency; they did not pull back.[32]

Red Cloud's warriors maintained the upper hand against an army that was stretched thin.[33] Officers assigned to the West discovered the tactics of the Plains horsemen were far different than what had been encountered in Civil War campaigns.[34] The Indians did not mass troops, but would hit quick and run fast.[35] Sitting Bull, for his part, was constantly harassing the northern forts of Buford and Stevenson.[36] Few prairie men sought accommodation in the face of a military buildup. For the federal government, war was certain to be protracted and expensive.[37] This was not something that the country could afford after just coming out of a long and bloody War between the States. Compounding the matter was a pacifist mood in the Eastern power centers.[38] But it was clear that the Indians had to be moved aside as the nation continued its westward path. Indian land was always for the taking. Historically, whether displacement occurred by treaty or coerced relocation, territory had been appropriated along the Eastern Seaboard, then across the Appalachian Mountains, and into the Ohio Valley and to the Mississippi River. The Plains Indians were not about to let such a takeover happen on their ground.

A debate sparked between the military and Interior Department on how to secure control. The department's Indian Bureau, with support from humanitarian groups, argued that the army's intended response to the Fetterman disaster would lead to a terrible war. Practically, there were just too many bands in disparate locations for effective troop engagement. There emerged a policy of seeking peace by negotiation.[39] A new commission was dispatched by Congress in 1867, first to Medicine Lodge Creek, Kansas, to deal with the southern tribes and then Fort Laramie to negotiate with the northern tribes.[40] The delegation was headed by men intent on implementing the view of the Indian Bureau, but included military representatives appointed by the president—Generals Sherman, Harney, and Terry.[41] Sherman may have bristled under the Washington mandate of appeasement but followed orders.[42] He understood the reality of the time. Well aware that the army could not meet all the demands for protection on the frontier, the general wrote a letter published in the Cheyenne Star advising that the army must address priorities and scattered settlements needed to come together to provide their own protection. He explained that he ordered the military to remove those "who have not been drawn into war" to their proper reservations and to kill or destroy "all who have been involved in acts of hostility." Then he set out his limitations:

Nearly all the people of the Plains, even the governors of the states and territories, who ought to know better, seem to have an idea that I have a right to make war and peace at pleasure; a right to call out volunteers and pay them, and to do more in this connection than any monarch of a constitutional kingdom. I possess none of these powers. The Regular army is provided by Congress, and but a small portion

*of it is assigned to my command. With this small force I am required
to protect two railroads, the Missouri River, the various stage routes,
amounting in the aggregate to over eight thousand miles of traveled
roads, besides the incidental protection of tens of thousands of miles of
frontier settlements.*[43]

When the commissioners arrived at Laramie in September, only
a few Crow chiefs could be induced to meet with them.[44] Washington
had sent a delegation with a ready-made treaty, following the standard
formula of reserving a section of land exclusively for the Indians and
promising provisions to sustain the Indians within the reserved land. The
government offered iron pots, blankets, knives, and guns as a goodwill
gesture to Red Cloud, who was essential to putting together an armistice
package.[45] The Sioux leader held fast, sending word he would not come
to the fort to parley until the soldiers left the Powder River area.[46] With
no prospect of success, the commissioners went home.[47] Two successive
efforts had come up empty. A frustrated Sherman issued a warning: "The
railroads are coming and you cannot stop them any more than you can
stop the sun or the moon. You must decide; you must submit. This is not
a peace commission only; it is also a war commission."[48] Execution on his
threat would have to wait. In the spring of the next year, the commission
returned with authorization to abandon the three forts along the trail in
return for a signed peace treaty.[49] By then, Sherman, called to another
assignment, was replaced by an alternate—Colonel Christopher Augur.[50]
The Indians were given the promise of troop withdrawal. But the soldiers stayed put. Red Cloud was intractable—no removal, no treaty. The
government finally flinched, and troops pulled out at the end of the summer. The Oglala immediately torched the abandoned forts.[51] The purge
appeared to be complete. All the while the government treaty negotiators
knew there were substitute routes for the Bozeman Trail[52] as well as gross
inefficiencies in maintaining the contested forts.[53] The United States gave
up what it no longer needed.

The primary mandate was to clear Indians from the cross-country
travel routes to the West, particularly for the railroads.[54] The completion
of the Transcontinental Railroad was anticipated in 1869. A great track

of land and ongoing government provision for the Indians were promised. Negotiations went on for months. Finally, the treaty was consented to by those whom the officials recognized as the delegates and leaders of several bands. (Characteristically, where there were no chiefs, the commission simply designated whom they thought appropriate to have sufficient representatives attesting to the treaty.) As always, the words were written in English by government officials, and the Indians were told what the treaty provided by interpreters. Those signing made their marks on the document from April through November 1868. Red Cloud was one of the last to sign.[55] As he finished, he scooped dirt from the floor and made a gesture of washing his hands to indicate that bloodshed on the land was at an end.[56] He thought he had attained unconditional withdrawal of forts and troops. Later, Red Cloud would declare that he was never made aware of key provisions favorable to the United States.[57]

Sitting Bull, now a principal chief, was not near Fort Laramie during that summer. The Hunkpapa were encamped at the confluence of the Powder River with the Yellowstone. His band primarily hunted the northern region while the Oglala had the run further south along the North Platte River. Nonetheless, the government wanted the Hunkpapa, who had many run-ins with the military, to be part of the accord.[58] The Hunkpapa continued to hold their distance. Three commissioners were sent to Fort Rice in the heart of the Dakota Territory, together with the Jesuit priest Pierre-Jean De Smet. Father De Smet was a 67-year-old missionary who had long toiled among the northern Plains Indians and had gained their respect as a fearless but gentle man.[59] Moreover, his Catholicity did not get in the way of recognizing that Indians had their own form of spirituality. He usually referred to the creator as the "Great Spirit,"[60] giving recognition of a commonality of his God and that of the Indians. The good father had credibility. Without him, the three commissioners had not a chance. As always, he carried no weapons into Indian territory.[61] His black robe and crucifix were emblematic of peace. His courage was his passport.

De Smet was a short man, diminished from his former plumpness because of various afflictions in his later years.[62] It did not hurt his manner that his face retained something of a cherubic look and his effort was wholehearted. Yet his Belgium upbringing and Jesuitical commitment to spread the Gospel[63] produced his own view of manifest destiny.[64] And while he was a constant critic of the white man using the currency of whiskey to trade with Indians.[65] He allowed himself to be an emissary of the United States on the frontier. He may have been co-opted,[66] but he accepted no compensation.[67] For him, peace was paramount and his role was to protect the natives. He understood the danger to these people's way of life from the advancing encroachment of new men.[68]

Reliable sources reported that Sitting Bull's camp could be found over 200 miles west in Montana Territory. On the first of June 1868, Fr. De Smet and two interpreters—Charles and Matilda Galpin, set out under a banner bearing the image of the Blessed Virgin Mary.[69] Charles Galpin was an Indian trader with experience among the northern tribes, and his wife was Yanktonai Sioux.[70] They carried a message from Red Cloud urging friendship with the Great Father. The entourage was in the field several weeks and was escorted by a band of Indians. But in the shadows, Hunkpapa outriders maintained their own surveillance of the intruders. Upon arrival, the priest's appearance drew grunts from the camp. Undaunted, the priest-mediator offered liberal gifts of tobacco.[71] Sitting Bull may have questioned Red Cloud's assent to treaty, but he demonstrated no animosity toward the visitors. He offered words of welcome. He even took the delegation into his own lodge as a sign of protection.[72] In response, the black robe straightforwardly explained the purpose of his visit, asking that the Hunkpapa meet with representatives of the president who were waiting at Fort Rice: "Your Grandfather wishes you to live among your own people on your own lands. You will never starve. You will always have plenty of rations. You will not be captives, but at liberty."[73]

Sitting Bull's initial reply was that "the words sound good," but only if the whites would abide by the old treaty.[74] He wanted to know why the statements from past agreements were forgotten. Continuing to make his case, he said: "God gave us this land, and we are at home here. I will not have my people robbed. We can live if we can keep the Black Hills. We do not want from the hand of the Grandfather."[75]

That night, there was more solicitous conversation from the priest. The next morning, De Smet opened the council with a prayer. As "a token of my sincerity and good wishes for the welfare of the Sioux Nation," the banner of the Holy Virgin was presented to the gathering.[76] It was his shield of goodwill, and he gave it away. He said he was only an advisor and asked that Lakota "bury all your animosities against the whites, forget the past, and accept the offering of peace which is now just sent you."[77] Father De Smet preached the value of reconciling with one's enemies.[78] He asked nothing for himself. He made no threats.

Sitting Bull, sitting nearest to the priest, looked over to those attending the council to be sure that they heard the words of the black robe. He allowed other chiefs to speak before he did. Then he turned his attention to the priest, standing up and thanking him for coming to the Sioux camp. "I am a warrior chief, but I too want peace."[79] Remarkably, he offered to send representatives to meet with the commissioners. Stepping back, it appeared Sitting Bull had no more to say. He slowly stroked his fingers against the side of his face, only to let his hand fall away as he looked toward the priest. Almost nonchalantly, he said he had forgotten two things: "I wish all to know that I do not propose to sell any part of my country, nor will I have the whites cutting our trees along the rivers." The woodland groves "endure wintry storm and summer's heat."[80] Because they endure, they "flourish," not unlike his people. With this definitive explanation, Sitting Bull forever set his resolve on holding the Lakota's prairie land.

To even consider the treaty, the Hunkpapa chief told the priest that army forts must be removed from the upper Missouri and his people left undisturbed.[81] While similar, these conditions were beyond Red Cloud's demands that only related to the Bozeman Trail. Any accommodation with the United States required that his people be allowed to make their own way in their hunting lands. If the whites left him alone, he would leave them alone.

Two other chiefs with Sitting Bull—Gall (also called "Man that Goes in the Middle" for his willingness to go to the front in battle;[82] in time the appellation took on other meaning), who had expressed harsh words against the treaty, and Running Antelope,[83] who was more amenable— were solicited by De Smet. Sitting Bull instructed Gall to see what the commissioners had to say. But he cautioned: "Take no presents; we don't want them. Tell them to move the soldiers out and stop the steamboats; then we can have peace."[84] Upon leaving the northern camp, De Smet gave Sitting Bull a crucifix as a gesture of goodwill.[85] (This cross or a similar one was worn often by Sitting Bull and appears hanging from his neck in photographs, taken in the chief's later years of reservation life.) Both Gall and Running Antelope travelled with six others in the priest's company to Fort Rice. Gall initially held to his chief's directive, but when feasted and presented gifts, he succumbed.[86] Gall and the Lakota delegation signed the treaty on July 2. Gall trusted in the assurances of De Smet, yet did not understand the particulars of the treaty beyond the intent of a truce. The demands of the Hunkpapa were not met. Sitting Bull never signed.[87] Nevertheless, the Hunkpapa Lakota by the mark of these few representatives was considered to have signed onto the Fort Laramie Treaty.[88] The United States did not fully gauge the determination of Sitting Bull if it thought it could maneuver around him.

Congress ratified the treaty in February 1869. The first article of the document proclaimed that "[f]rom this day forward all war between the parties to this agreement shall forever cease."[89] The insincerity of the United States commitment was evidenced the next month by Congress recessing without voting on appropriations to fulfill Article 10's promise of food and clothing.[90]

Red Cloud emerged as a leader of what now became agency Indians, although his band continued to live in the outlands. There was no reason to change his way of living; he did not retreat to a reservation, but he did expect the annuities promised. He was satisfied that he had preserved the Powder River lands and Black Hills for his people. Sitting Bull stood alone as the primary chieftain of the nontreaty Sioux.[91] These Indians would be labeled as "hostiles" by the government. Sitting Bull did not forgive Red Cloud for touching pen to the treaty.[92] He told the Lakota who signed: "You are fools to make yourselves slaves to a piece of fat bacon, some hard tack, and a little sugar."[93] Two months after Gall and others made their marks at Fort Rice, Sitting Bull punctuated his desire to remove the white man from the northern Plains by leading a raid on the recently established Fort Buford, situated near the Canadian border in the northwestern corner of Dakota Territory.[94] Gall did not hesitate to join the warring party. Three soldiers were killed, and the Indians absconded with 250 head of cattle. Thirteen years later, Sitting Bull would come to know this garrison from the inside.

Now, Sitting Bull was branded as the main adversary at large in the northern Plains. Philippe De Trobriand, a French officer, assigned to the U.S. military in the Dakota Territory, wrote in his journal of 1868:

> *The principal chief is Sitting Bull, one of the most dangerous and most ill-disposed Indians in Dakota. A price has been successfully put upon his head by the authorities of Minnesota and of Montana. Now Dakota has become the theater for his depredations and assassinations. It is a fine play, the government leaving us in our posts without cavalry, without horses, and absolutely in no state to pursue and chastise him. He can thus wander freely and in all security over the prairies which he besmears with blood wherever it seems good to him.*[95]

The Treaty of 1868 provided an end to the war in the north and specified support, education, and the creation of the Great Sioux Reservation,[96] described in Article 2, covering the lower Dakota Territory west of the Missouri River.[97] (This was a huge territory of over 44,000 square miles.) That article further contained the "solemn" commitment of the United States that no persons other than authorized officers, agents, and employees of the government shall enter upon Indian reservations; and the Indians committed to relinquishing claims of possession to all other portions of the United States or its territories. This meant giving up rights to lands occupied east of the Missouri,[98] an area already speckled with the encroachment of white settlements.

An essential point of the treaty from the government's view was reinforcing a national reservation program designed to take the "wild" out of the Indian and accelerate the transition from red to white. To the white treaty makers the Indians should welcome this opportunity. (This type of thinking would remain the foundation of the Indian Bureau's management of the reservation system for decades.) At the same time, during the presidential campaign of 1868, candidate Ulysses S. Grant let America know that he would balance reform against military necessity. He declared that settlers in the West required protection "even if the extermination of every Indian tribe was necessary to secure such a result."[99] In Article 15, the Indians agreed to make the reservation their permanent home.[100] The intent here was to change the Indian way of life and culture. Hunters were to be farmers. Tipi dwellers were to live in houses. The Indian was to apply himself to education and Christianity. Those goals were thought to be generalizations to make the white man feel good. Many Lakota believed they had drawn limits to further white encroachments onto their prairie lands.[101] They had yet to comprehend the significance of the reservation system to the fulfillment of the United States' destiny.

The treaty formalized the elimination of the Bozeman Trail forts,[102] and the Indians withdrew opposition to the Transcontinental Railroad, which was completed the next year.[103] Moreover, the Indians pledged not to object to other railroads currently under construction and future railroads, wagon roads, and works of utility ordered or permitted by the government.[104] (So the Bozeman Trail was gone, but other roads were allowed to be constructed where the United States saw fit.) When such works were constructed through reservation land, damage would be assessed as established by three disinterested commissioners appointed by the president.[105] (An interesting exception to assuring the reservation lands to the Sioux forever.)

The original Sioux reservation extended north from the Dakota-Nebraska line to the 46th parallel, just north of what is now the common boundary of North and South Dakota, generally between the Cannonball and Grand Rivers; its eastern edge was the Missouri River, and it stretched west to the border with the Montana Territory, where the Black Hills are located.[106] The heart of the Black Hills, which spilled over into Wyoming, was not included, nor was the Powder River and Little Big Horn Valley in Montana. These areas were termed "unceded,"[107] meaning that were not granted to the United States. The Indians who chose not to live on the reservation were to be secure on the unceded lands—at least, for the time being. This gave the appearance of a key concession to those who chose to live outside the reservation. The treaty makers' long-range intent, however, was to force, cajole, or otherwise make those outside the reservation come in. General William Tecumseh Sherman was much more direct; he advised against the treaty's provisions, recognizing either the unceded land or hunting rights outside the reservation.[108] For him, it was the reservation or else; very quickly circumstances would present him the opportunity to prove his point.

To the south on the central Plains, pacification thought to be secured by the concurrent 1867 Medicine Lodge Treaty was unraveling. Bands of braves from the Cheyenne, Arapaho, and Kiowa refused to abide by the treaty directing them to move to a reservation in Western Indian Territory. Soon settlements and homesteads in central and western Kansas were terrorized by Indian raids. General Philip Sheridan, following his Civil War duty, had been assigned to the Military Division of the Missouri under General Sherman. Sheridan wanted immediate results on the central Plains[109] and did not see further negotiations as a means to that end. He knew that Indians made war during the summer when their movement was unrestricted, their horses were quick, and they could take food from the land, but not during the wintertime. In the cold and hard time, they hunkered down. A winter campaign was advocated; Sherman, the war general, approved. The military hawks would have their day.

These Indians were renegades in violation of treaty. What was needed was a proven field officer fired with ambition to quell the uprising.[110] The officer chosen was Lieutenant Colonel George Armstrong Custer, a young Civil War hero of the Union army, who had been sent West and was building his reputation as an Indian fighter. But first Custer had to be restored to duty. A court-martial proceeding the year before had resulted in his suspension for being absent without leave. General Sheridan, a supporter of Custer, cut through the bureaucratic process. And by late fall 1868, the lieutenant colonel had scouts following tracks through the snow southward into Oklahoma Indian Territory. This campaign got underway at the same time that the agreement ending hostilities in Powder River territory was being signed off at Fort Laramie.[111]

In the cold predawn of November 27, scouts found an Indian camp on the Washita River. Custer readied his troops and ordered the regimental song, "Garry Owen," played as the attack commenced at first light.[112] The troops swooped into a sleeping winter camp of Southern Cheyenne, who believed they were located on reservation land. Within a matter of minutes, 103 warriors (a number Custer later would say was greater) plus women and children, as well as Chief Black Kettle, who had survived the Chivington Raid four years earlier, were shot down. Custer also captured 53 women, children, and old people,[113] whom he counted as enemy combatants. He later observed, "[M]ost Indian women are as skilful in the handling and use of weapons as most warriors."[114] The camp was burned, and 875 horses were slaughtered; even Indian dogs were killed.[115] During the mop-up, the commander discovered that this was but one of a chain of camps in the area and more warriors were heading his way. Recognizing numbers now were moving against him, Custer withdrew and proclaimed victory.[116] In his haste, he failed to account for a detachment of 18 men under Major Joel Elliott that had gone downstream in pursuit of fleeing women and children.[117] Cut off from the main force, those soldiers were confronted and then trapped by Arapaho warriors. Two weeks later the naked and mutilated remains of Elliott and his men were found scattered across the frozen crust of the far side of a knoll.[118] The lieutenant colonel had been more interested in getting back to camp and taking captives, one of whom it was said he made his concubine.[119]

The tactic of a winter dawn attack was credited to Custer; it became the principal mode of operation against the Plains Indians in the years to come.[120] During Lieutenant Colonel Custer's return to Camp Supply, he was delivered a large envelope of letters, including a field order from General Sheridan congratulating him and his men for "gallant services" in the campaign against hostile Indians south of the Arkansas.[121] Many in the East saw it as another disgraceful raid.[122] It echoed the brutality of Colonel Chivington; again, the killing of women and children outnumbered the deaths of warriors.[123] Custer's response denounced the humanitarians as failing to understand the brutality of war on the Plains.[124]

Targeting family encampments was developing into the conventional practice of war on the Plains Indians. The intent was demoralization of the enemy. However, within a few months of the Washita attack, a gentler Custer turned to negotiation, using the Cheyenne women captives as go-betweens. During these amity talks, a Cheyenne chief warned Custer that if he ever made war on the Cheyenne again, he would die.[125]

Red Cloud, believing he had assured peace in the north, thought the Oglalas again held dominion over the Powder River country of Montana.[126] However, as soon as the treaty was approved, life on unbound plains again was compromised by outside forces. A fort named for Lieutenant Fetterman, just completed in the unceded area, remained.[127] It was on the south side of the Platte River about 60 miles northwest of Fort Laramie; the treaty did not speak to the removal of this fort. Roads and settlers entered. Trade was refused the Indians at Fort Laramie and rations and annuities were not delivered. All of this followed a nasty winter making game scarce.[128] Army and civilian representatives took to the field in the spring for discussions to encourage Red Cloud and others to take up the reservation life. The actual intent of the 1868 treaty was becoming evident—delineation of the unceded land was a stopgap that was to be eliminated as soon as possible. A recommendation, said to be consistent with the treaty, was put forward that an agency located along the Missouri River at Fort Randall would best serve the Oglalas.[129] It was not coincidental that it was well inside the Great Sioux Reservation. Red Cloud was adamant that he would never go to the Missouri.[130] The Oglala intended to hunt and camp as they always did, but wanted a convenient agency nearby for receipt of promised annuities and trade. The representatives offered Raw Hide Buttes, a long-standing crossroads for the Lakota, 40 miles north of Fort Laramie.[131] Red Cloud rejected this site out of hand, saying it would put white administrators too close to the sacred Black Hills.[132] He persisted that any agency should be at Laramie.

The government men would only bargain alleged treaty violations against concessions. At a stalemate, Red Cloud requested an audience in Washington.[133] The Interior Department, aware of members of his band and others still rebellious after the treaty, understood the importance of maintaining his presence as a moderate among the off-reservation Lakota.[134] The government granted the request and set the agenda. The Grant administration cast the 1870 visit as recognition of the great chief's role in negotiating a peace. Part of any Indian visit to the nation's capital was a display of power residing there. This visit included a tour of the National Armory and a display at the Navy Yard of an iron-clad ship and demonstration of a coastal defense cannon firing down the Potomac.[135]

Whatever impression may have been made, Red Cloud and his companions displayed little reaction. A White House dinner with President Grant was held. Then the commissioner of Indian Affairs counseled Red Cloud that it was far better to create a new agency for him and his people. For the government, agency and reservation went hand in hand; for Red Cloud, an agency was simply a point of service. He would not give his assent. But because the bureau needed him, Red Cloud would be sent home with some measure of relief in promise of more rations and modest ammunition for hunting. The location of an agency remained unresolved, and over the next couple of years various government emissaries would seek out Red Cloud to continue discussions.[136]

To further show goodwill, Red Cloud was allowed to travel from Washington to New York for a visit with various humanitarian groups friendly to the Indian. Invited to speak, he made an impression with his eloquence and was flattered by the attention. Red Cloud placed his trust in the overall negotiated peace, although he mistrusted the words given in 1868. The reality of Washington's power was sinking in. He had complained to the Secretary of the Interior at a conference following dinner with the president: "The white children have surrounded me, and left me with nothing but an island."[137]

As entreaties continued, the Indian Bureau appeared conciliatory, as long as Red Cloud was considering alternatives. He argued for an agency on the south side of the Platte near Fort Laramie.[138] The government countered with a site downriver. Negotiating with others in his absence, a temporary agency was set up in 1871 on the North Platt about 30 miles east of Fort Laramie.[139] To placate him, it was named "Red Cloud Agency." He said he did not want it. In 1872, he asked for another visit to Washington to talk directly to the Great Father. The president himself warned that northeast Nebraska was ripe for settlement.[140] Red Cloud well knew that Raw Hides Buttes was still in the government's plan; he now pushed for a location miles east of there, near the White River in Nebraska. The Interior Department had in mind a more distant location in Oklahoma at the Cherokee Reservation.[141] Finally, Red Cloud was able to secure the White River site as his best alternative, lying outside the reservation. As a warrior-turned-statesman, he was outplayed. He had argued and delayed for three years and at last was boxed in. Red Cloud could only hold a piece of Oglala land by taking what he could get in light of a harder assessment of the future. Instead of fewer restrictions, there would be more. When he returned, he told his people: "Make no trouble for our Great Father. His heart is good."[142] These words did not sit well with all; some of his warriors pulled away to join the Hunkpapa chief, whom they knew would not treat with Washington. In 1973, Red Cloud moved to White River and the government immediately established a cantonment nearby known as Camp Robinson ostensibly to protect the Oglala.[143] In time, the great chief would see his influence wane;[144] later even his agency would be taken from him.

During the immediate years following the 1868 treaty, fighting between the army and Indians subsided. As the wild land disappeared, an increasing number of Indians accepted the alternative life.[145] Not Sitting Bull, who derisively referred to agency ration centers as "gift houses."[146] The army pulled back, and the northern bands of Sioux turned their combative attention on their ancient enemies, the Crow.[147] The reduced hunting lands exacerbated old animosities, and intertribal fighting increased. This too became disruptive to the white man. Governor Benjamin Potts of Montana Territory beseeched the federal government to show a presence, citing fear of spillover raids on settlers.[148]

The Indians remaining in the unceded lands clearly saw the danger ahead. In 1869, Four Horns and other supporters made an unprecedented move of electing Sitting Bull supreme chief of the nontreaty bands in the north. He had a strong war record against both tribal enemies and the U.S. military; he was outspoken against reservation life; and he did not back down. Family and fractional interests were won over. The Blackfeet, Miniconjou, Sans Arc, Oglala, and Cheyenne joined the Hunkpapa in assent.[149] The various bands may have gone their separate ways for hunting, but Sitting Bull and his key associates could command their presence when necessary. His mother drew on this rise in tribal and intertribal importance together with greater family responsibilities to urge that he leave war making to others. Still, it was war or the threat of it, combined with broken promises that tightened the threads of his uncompromising stance. All nonreservation Sioux now looked to Sitting Bull; and even those on the reservation understood his imposing role. Not even Red Cloud at the height of his power on the central Plains had achieved such status. Although the population at reservation agencies rose, it was based on grudging resignation; dissatisfaction was everywhere. Over the next seven years Sitting Bull's word would become virtually absolute.

The career of James McLaughlin, the itinerant blacksmith in the Minnesota River Valley, also was advancing but on a dissimilar yet ultimately intersecting path.

For six years, McLaughlin worked various jobs to support his wife and growing family. He supplemented his metal working as a carpenter, traveling salesman, and clerk.[150] In 1871, Alexander Faribault, his wife's uncle, advised him that a new Sioux reservation was being established at Devils Lake just north of Fort Totten,[151] as part of a national pacification plan of the Grant administration. William Forbes, also Canadian born, had been appointed the Indian agent.[152] Forbes had long worked in the Minnesota Indian trade and was fluent in the Sioux language. He was looking for staff, and the Devils Lake Indians included the same band of Sioux as McLaughlin's wife's relatives in Minnesota.

Devils Lake was a small but unique agency. It was formed to provide some relief to the Indians gathered in the area. After the Minnesota uprising of 1862, many bands of Indians wandered the area east of the Missouri looking for food and shelter.[153] They often came to the fort with requests for handouts, which the military was forbidden to provide. While they were paid for work, it was subsistence wages.[154] They did not resist reservation life; they were too desperate.[155] The adjacent fort on the south shore of the lake was established in 1867 to guard transportation and mail routes through northern Dakota to Montana from Indian deprivations. It was 40 miles from Red River on the east (the upper Dakota Territory's common boundary with Minnesota) and 70 miles below the Canadian border.

The lake itself was known to the natives as "Spirit Water" or "Lake of the Spirit." The water was high in salinity, and frequent whirlpools abided there, thus giving evidence of a spirit living within. To the white man, because the water was brackish, the spirit the Indians thought to be living there had to be evil. The Indian words for the lake were corrupted in translation to Devils Lake.[156] As the largest natural body of water in upper Dakota, Devils Lake dominated the region.

On March 1, 1871, James McLaughlin sent a letter to Forbes:

> *I thought I would write to you to ascertain if you will have an opening in your employ for a man like me. I am a blacksmith by trade. Can do anything in that line. I have a fair knowledge of most kinds of business. If you should have anything in that line to let or need any person to assist in trading with or supplying the Indians & have not already any person, I would like to go with you.*[157]

He gave Faribault as a reference, and Forbes hired him.[158] James McLaughlin now had the sinecure of government employment; he believed he brought with him a unique understanding of the Indian. He certainly knew that natives were rapidly being displaced in their own country. He had witnessed assimilation to the white world by the mixed-bloods living in Minnesota. But more particularly, James McLaughlin believed that his wife's convent training had shaped and distinguished her from frontier Indians. As a church-going Catholic, he saw within his wife's Christianity an exemplar for the red man improving himself.[159] He now had a full mustache and imperial beard, evidencing a more authoritative appearance.[160]

Upon arrival at Devils Lake, William Forbes and his new employee received an indifferent welcome;[161] the Indians they came to serve had too long suffered hunger and outcast status. But Forbes, known as "the Major" because of his service as a Minnesota volunteer with the Union army during the Civil War,[162] showed a progressive approach toward his wards. He immediately purchased supplies and distributed them. He was able to secure the services of the Community of Grey Nuns from Montreal to run a school.[163] He saw to it that the Indians learned the elements of potato farming to provide for themselves. Major Forbes insisted on housing for his wards; they should live in log houses, not makeshift shelters. He put McLaughlin in charge of a detail to fell trees for building material; when the hand-sawing of the logs was too slow, the young assistant was allowed to order equipment for a sawmill. McLaughlin was up to the task; he built houses as well as basic furniture.[164] The Indians took well to the humanitarian treatment, and by 1875, Forbes reported that he had 102 good families in his charge.[165] His right-hand man was capable in both manual tasks and administrative duties. For the latter, McLaughlin whenever he could wore a suit, white shirt with a stiff color, and tie that he thought appropriate to his position.

Forbes was the good agent—a model of how to relate to reservation Indians. The lessons learned were lasting. When the Major's health failed, James McLaughlin became the general administrator of every labor carried on at the agency. He made sure Devils Lake worked smoothly and at the same time kept the surrounding community at ease.

CHAPTER FIVE

Papa Sapa

1871–1875

The Powder River War changed the United States' course of conduct toward the Lakota. With treaty in hand, the government backed away from military force and took a seemingly more liberal approach.

The establishment of the Great Sioux Reservation was paramount to the U.S. Indian program. The unceded lands were only an expedient, a temporary fix. It was now a matter of convincing the roamers to accept reservation life. One means to that end would be pernicious.

Upon becoming president in 1869, Ulysses Grant embarked upon a "peace policy" aimed at bringing all Indians onto reservations and civilizing them.[1] The country was in a long recovery from the economic impact of the military buildup for the Civil War; Quakers within Grant's cabinet provided the rationale to pacify the Indians without the risk of more armed conflict. A key feature of this policy was characterized as the "feeding system," the object of which "was to buy off the hostility of the Indians by maintaining them."[2] Indians who became dependent on the government were not going to cause much trouble. This, in turn, was contingent on the Indians recognizing the need for support from Washington. Thus, the scarcity of a food source on the Plains became part of the agenda of pacification.

The frontier generals, Sherman and Sheridan, understood the importance of the buffalo to the Plains Indians. Sherman knew the herds grazing between railroad lines of the Union Pacific through Nebraska and the Kansas Pacific and the under-construction Atchinson, Topeka & Santa Fe through Kansas had already been greatly diminished.[3] Sheridan observed that the extermination of the buffalo "is the only way to bring lasting peace and allow civilization to advance."[4] Treaty drafters had carefully crafted the words granting hunting rights in Article 11 of the Laramie accord—"so long as the buffalo may range thereon in such numbers as to justify the chase."[5] These words were not meant to say forever. The real peace policy was to create dependence; self-sufficiency was an illusion. The government knew that the principal food source of the Indian was in serious decline;[6] and the Plains Indians were fooling themselves that the Great Spirit would continue to send buffalo to them. The two generals promoted their Civil War stratagem of destroying the food supply of the opposing forces.[7]

This view had to contend with an emerging animal protection movement being advanced by women's groups in the East, combined with Eastern humanitarian organizations' compassion for the Indian. Faced with conflicting forces, the Secretary of the Interior endorsed the view of the generals. The logic was simple—if the Indians could not support themselves, they would be compelled to turn to the reservation. Once there, humanitarian efforts at civilizing them could be applied. The economic incentive of hunting for hides took hold from there. The army simply watched the onslaught.[8]

The years from 1871 to 1875 were a time of unrestrained killing by hide hunters and adventurers depleting the overall herd,[9] already affected by years of drought. The prairie was a virtual shooting gallery. Skinned buffalo corpses were left to rot in the sun. It was ecological devastation.

The Plains Indians themselves had been undercutting the sustainability of the buffalo for years by commercial hunts to secure robes for trade for goods and rifles from the 1830s into the 1860s.[10] Collateral damage was caused by livestock accompanying the pioneers across the country. Cattle cut a wide swath through the native grasses along the Platte River; cattle introduced into the river valleys throughout the plains competed for forage with indigenous game.[11] Sitting Bull sensed that when the last buffalo fell, it would be a "death wind"[12] for his people.

Following the completion of the Transcontinental Railroad tying the East to California, promoters and investors began planning another rail line westward from St. Paul to Seattle—the Northern Pacific Railroad. The country was on an accelerating roll west. After all, the Fort Laramie Treaty advised that there would be other railroads. Engineering survey teams began exploring the Valley of the Elk River (known to the military as the "Yellowstone"), where after being pushed out of the lower Plains most of the buffalo now grazed. Everyone knew that the Indians did not welcome railroad intrusion, and consequently there was expectation of sabotage and insurgency. The railroads brought more than construction crews and travelers to the Plains; hide hunters jumped aboard to gain quick access to the buffalo ranges.

Constrained by the small deployment of military personnel throughout the upper Missouri, a program recommended by the Commissioner of Indian Affairs, Francis Walker, referred to as "temporizing," was implemented.[13] Increased food provisions and clothing were made available to Indian friendlies. In the upper Montana Territory, near where the Milk River ran its course out of Canada and emptied into the Missouri River, Fort Peck was established as an agency trading post, with ample rations. Even arms were easy to secure.[14] Numerous bands soon encamped in the vicinity of the post. The 1805 advice of Captain Meriwether Lewis of dependence through trade had taken hold. There was even thought that Sitting Bull might succumb to opportunity to trade here. Instead he maintained his open hostility, deriding Red Cloud, who had been talked into reservation life but was in frequent quarrel with the Indian Bureau.[15] He drew increased attention from Lakota militants.

The view of the Indian Affairs Bureau was endorsed in eastern political circles. Reservations and rations replaced traditional roaming and hunting existence. Grant, upon his inauguration as president, however, cautioned that those not inclined to the peace policy "will find the new administration ready for a sharp and severe war."[16] Sherman and Sheridan were at the ready. The old way became more and more difficult to sustain. An ever-growing number of Indians walked or rode their ponies into the agencies.

Relative calm spread over most of the Plains; but in the north the military was called up to guard railroad engineering parties. By 1873, the Northern Pacific's rail line was in place from St. Paul to Bismarck, in the upper reaches of Dakota Territory. Railroads into the West were considered essential to converting the frontier. And the railroad companies for their part promoted the establishment of new towns, of which Bismarck was an example, and huckstered farmland to all the settlers who could be enticed to move nearby. All the while, more whites came into and through the prairie lands. During the 1870s, settlement within the Great Plains grabbed hold.[17] A period of favorable weather and cheap land was too much to resist. Farming flourished. What the settler saw as his American destiny, the Indian saw as a theft of the land.

Across the river from Bismarck and south of Mandan was located Fort Abraham Lincoln. Here the 7th Regiment of the Cavalry was posted in 1873; and its commander, George A. Custer, exploited the assignment to advance his renown as an Indian fighter.[18] It was not enough for him just to escort railroad men in the field. In the six years since Washita, he had been burnishing his reputation by writing of his exploits for the monthly journal *The Galaxy*; in 1874, his book, *My Life on the Plains*, was published.[19] The man understood the importance of the media and was quick to imbed correspondents into his expeditions. In return, the Eastern press eagerly gave him attention. Custer was in the field in the summer of 1873, although most of his time was spent hunting wild game. In fact, he was reprimanded by his senior officer, Colonel David Stanley, for wandering off escort patrol of railroad surveyors and setting his own course. But the young lieutenant colonel considered himself untethered. He was subordinate to a commander who took his sustenance from a whiskey bottle.[20] Custer, a teetotaler, did not respect Stanley, and Stanley loathed Custer for interpreting commands to match his purpose.

Sitting Bull and the young warrior chief, Crazy Horse, closely watched the movement of engineers and the troops that accompanied them. It was clear to the chief that the rails coming toward the Yellowstone were the herald of an invasion of Lakota land.[21]

But suddenly in 1873 this enterprise stalled. A financial crisis struck the nation, following a period of post–Civil War overexpansion.[22] Jay

Cooke and Company, an influential Philadelphia banking house, declared its financial failure on September 18, precipitating three years of economic crisis. The citizens were stunned. The banking firm, a key backer of the Northern Pacific Railway, was unable to market several million dollars' worth of bonds for the railway company. On September 19, the *New York Times* wrote of the fear that followed:

> *The news of the panic spread in every direction down-town, and hundreds of people who had been carrying stocks in expectation of a rise, hurried to the offices of their brokers and left orders that their holdings should be immediately sold out. In this way prices fell off so rapidly that even Vanderbilt could not have stemmed the tide.*
>
> *The Stock Exchange had been the arena of many desperate conflicts between bulls and bears, and it is hard to discriminate as to the violence of the respective melees, but it was said by old frequenters of Wall Street that no panic so frightful had ensued since the failure of the Ohio Trust Company in 1857 as that witnessed yesterday.*[23]

Banking houses collapsed, and stock prices sank. The Northern Pacific filed for bankruptcy. Railroad building came to a halt. The Yellowstone clashes ceased.[24] Breaking at the same time were scandals of political corruption involving numerous officials in the Capitol and state legislative houses.[25] The country suffered from post–Civil War overexpansion and unchecked speculation. The ongoing aftershocks brought on a deep economic depression.

However, conflict in the West would not go away. In the making was yet another white man's intrusion that would be of even greater consequence to the Sioux.

Custer was about to enter sacred Lakota ground.

Seduced by continuing rumors of gold, some prospectors could not resist venturing into the Black Hills.[26] The temptation grew when the editor of the *Sioux City Times* organized the Black Hills Mining and Exploring Association in February 1872 and began publishing articles about the likelihood of a mother lode. General Sheridan suggested the establishment of a military post in the Hills to better monitor the Lakota.

Custer's column advancing through Castle Creek Valley in Black Hills, 1874
NATIONAL ANTHROPOLOGICAL ARCHIVES, SMITHSONIAN INSTITUTION

Because these lands were relatively unfamiliar to the white man, the general ordered a reconnaissance mission to provide military mapping and information on minerals.[27]

The Black Hills (Papa Sapa) are a distinct landform rising above the surrounding prairie—eastern outliers of the Rockies. Most of the hills are in the Dakotas, but some cross over into Wyoming. They stretch east and west about 60 miles and are contained in an over-100-mile north-south axis, between the forks of the Belle Fourche and Cheyenne Rivers, both flowing toward the Missouri. The hills were formed by a geological uplift from the western Dakota Plains. Here the earth ascended to join with the sky.

The name for the hills came from the dark-green ponderosa pines and spruce, climbing the ridges of the hills, which from the distance appear black in contrast to the surrounding grassy plains. General George Crook, a civil war campaigner assigned to the frontier, understood the magnetism of the place:

> *The Black Hills was then a most interesting and beautiful country. It was like an oasis in the desert, for here was a broken piece of country covered with a beautiful growth of timber, filled with game of all kinds, surrounded as far as the eye could see with bare, uninteresting plains.*[28]

The Black Hills had long been considered spiritual by many tribes. Although the Sioux had occupied the northern Plains for perhaps just over one hundred years, they looked on the Hills as a place of origin.[29] It was the womb of the Earth Mother.[30] Buried within the hills is a small opening or spirit hole to what is known as the Wind Cave. Air passes through the opening, and Lakota belief holds that the first humans originated below and entered onto earth by this passage. The buffalo followed from the same passage as small insects and grew to full size as they breathed the air of earth.[31]

This place held sacred rock formations in Bear Butte (Mato Paha) and Bear Tower (Mato Tipila, but more commonly recognized by its American name of Devils Tower). Star maps tied constellations to sacred areas on the ground. Religious rituals and vision quests took place within these hills.[32] The land belonged to birds and animals. Wakan Tanka—the Great Spirit, lived there. The hills were also known as a "food pack," because they were rich in game and served as a reserve for the Lakota.[33]

Traveling through Spearfish Canyon, it is not hard to recognize that this was special earth for the Lakota. A cool, quick stream cuts along the canyon floor. This is flowing holy water. Walls of rugged cliffs stand on either side, with green pine seated on every bench and loft. Aspens are interspersed and autumn sun sets the foliage ablaze with golden hues, dancing to passing currents. The aspens reflect particles of light like stained-glass windows of a cathedral. And all of this is crowned with limestone spires, open to the sky.

The ever-opportunistic Custer was charged with leading an exploratory mission into the Hills. Over a thousand men were assembled at Fort Lincoln, and on July 2, 1874, the expedition began. His entourage included a geologist, a few miners, reporters, civilian employees, and soldiers. More than one hundred wagons and three hundred beeves followed.[34] It was a Lewis and Clark journey without the hardship; and few Indians were encountered. The natural beauty of the land enthused the scientists, who saw great potential in mineral and timber resources. Scientific exploration overtook military purpose.[35] When flakes of gold were found along French Creek, Custer issued accounts of gold discoveries "among the roots of the grass."[36] Newspapers ran with the story of new treasure to be found in the Black Hills.[37] Custer was a crier to a gold rush. The popular view supposed that Black Hills gold could pull the country out of its depression—"easy riches." Miners and settlers swarmed toward the Black Hills along the path Custer had taken,[38] soon to be known as the "Thieves Road"[39] by the Indians.

Recognizing the obligation to protect under the Laramie Treaty, President Grant felt compelled to contain the invasion of Indian land. Warnings of seizure of wagons and mining equipment and supplies, combined with the onslaught of winter, first appeared to do the job. This early effort, however, began to fade with the spring thaw. General Crook reported that he included an admonition with his warnings to leave the area that the miners agree among themselves "to respect each other's claims when it became lawful for them to go into this country."[40] Miners, who were told to leave, mostly circled back or simply ignored the troops with a wink. Faced with an impossible task, President Grant now asked for patience from the Sioux. Even though westerners argued that mineral resources preempted Indian occupancy, the order barring citizens from entry on Indian land remained in place. But the army understood it was to simply stand on the sidelines. It ceased any efforts at interdiction of miners. The treaty safeguarding the Great Sioux Reservation no longer fit the circumstance. Instead of ongoing protection promised by treaty, the United States looked to secure rights to the land from the Sioux.[41] (The talks may have been the same, but this was not to be treaty making. Congress had abolished the treaty system in 1871 in declaring that no

Indian tribe or nation shall be recognized as an independent power or nation. Washington now only would act through contract. Moreover, by legal interpretation a lease arrangement need not meet the three-fourths vote requirement of the 1868 treaty.[42]) At the end of summer 1875, a Senate commission came to the Red Cloud Agency at White River to lease the land or buy mineral rights.[43] They sought out the agency chiefs who proved themselves progressives after the Laramie Treaty in 1868. When word reached the chiefs of the northern hunting bands, they were furious and unyielding.[44]

The commission was headed by Senator William Allison of Iowa and included Major General Alfred Terry. They knew the Indians would never sell but thought they could talk them into leasing the land; besides, it would cost less and spread out the payments. While the distinction between lease and purchase was lost in translation, there was no misunderstanding of the intent to take away the Hills. Little Bear offered a reasoned response: "Our Great Father has a house full of money. Suppose a man walks right into that house and takes the money. Do you suppose that would suit everybody? The Black Hills are the house of gold for the Indians. We watch it to get rich. I want our Great Father to remember that and not to forget it."[45] Many, however, foresaw the loss of these lands as inevitable. Not Sitting Bull and Crazy Horse, who would not come to the gathering to negotiate but sent messengers urging the refusal of any offer.[46] The advice was pointed. Little Big Man, a firebrand who ran with Crazy Horse, warned those in council with the commissioners that he would shoot anyone who even spoke in favor of an agreement to sell.[47] Belligerent warriors mounted a mock charge on the commission in a show of intimidation.

Red Cloud, already compromised as an agency Indian, took a different tact, indicating a willingness to negotiate but recommending a high price. He wanted payment representing provision for his people for seven generations, asking for the best rations, wagons, and teams of horses and cattle, as well as farm animals: "I want some white men's houses at this agency to be built for the Indians. I have been into white people's houses and I have seen nice black bedsteads and chairs, and I want that kind of furniture given to my people."[48] Spotted Tail, the Brule chief known for his intelligence, stepped forward as the principal negotiator. He had prepared for this council by earlier having traveled with others from his agency to the Black Hills to assess the extent of mining activity and attempt to understand value of the land to the white man.[49] Since the government had a big safe, it should withdraw $70 million for payment. (It appeared that Lakota chiefs had learned something about the value of money; actually the number was suggested to them as sufficient to provide for care and feeding for generations to come.) The demand was far beyond consideration. When he asked for a written offer, the commissioners' response was $400,000 per annum in rent or $6 million as a buyout.[50] The Indian advocates who favored making an agreement were outnumbered. Negotiations were over. Frustrated commissioners advised Congress to unilaterally fix a price and present it as a fiat accompli.[51] Then, an upset Congress blustered, threatening to withhold rations at the reservations. There were those who argued that the Lakota had no need for the Black Hills; these Indians were nothing more than sometime visitors to the land they claimed to hold so dear.[52] And the mineral deposits meant nothing to them.

Sitting Bull and Crazy Horse were inflexible. Their patience had worn out. They were prepared to fight if the government sought to take the Papa Sapa. The Hunkpapa chief left no room for compromise: "I have no land to sell; I will not go to the reservation. We do not want the whites here."[53] These words were reported verbatim in the East; and outraged officials in Washington vilified Sitting Bull and other dissidents.[54] At the same time, Sitting Bull berated Sioux reservation Indians for a willingness to talk. Once on the reservation, talk was all they had. His former ally, Red Cloud, was on the road to a succession of failures. Sitting Bull's hard line convinced Washington of blatant hostility. More to the truth, it allowed Washington to convince the nation's citizenry of his hostility.

Miners now were citizens who required protection. Grant realized that the Hills had to be acquired, but certainly he was not giving in to a $70 million purchase price. The administration blamed the off-reservation Sioux for sabotaging negotiations and interfering with life at the agencies. Mining camps were increasingly subjected to raids. The military advised the president that it stood ready to enforce the miners' occupation. Reports were rampant that an outbreak of violence from "red devils" was threatened; and Grant, who had decided not to seek another term as president, was pressed to take action. It was not an act that either the miners or Indians expected. In late fall 1875, he quietly directed troop withdrawal, assuring even more adventurers rushing in.[55] The peace policy president now was willing to suffer an incident—a spark to action. The government's attitude decidedly had moved against the Indians. But it had to satisfy the Quakers within the administration and reformers that it had done all it could. It was the Sioux who could not accept changed circumstances. The repositioning of the Indians would take some political machination. A shift was taking place; the new man was determined to have the Hills.

—

In that same year, James McLaughlin's career reached a crossroads.

His boss and mentor, William Forbes, died in July 1875. McLaughlin believed he was the only choice for the agent position.[56] He knew everything about the job. He had put in his time and had the backing of the local community.

After personally accompanying the deceased agent's coffin to St. Paul for burial, McLaughlin took immediate steps to promote himself as the agent in waiting.[57] He first obtained an endorsement from Bishop Rupert Seidenbush, newly named the Vicariate of Northern Minnesota, which covered the Devils Lake area, to present his name as a candidate to the Bureau of Catholic Indian Missions in Washington.[58] The support of the Catholic Church was critical (at the time the Bureau of Catholic Indian Missions provided the vetting of candidates to reservation appointments). In a letter to the bishop, McLaughlin pressed his Catholic views, pledging to abolish polygamy and superstitions among the Indians. These practices, he wrote, were adverse to both "political" and "Christian civilization, this last being the only true, real & efficacious civilization."[59] The bishop was convinced. McLaughlin also gathered letters of recommendation from Alexander Faribault and other prominent persons in the area, including the commander of Fort Totten. His marriage to Marie Louise Buisson, with her Santee

Sioux lineage, was another strong qualification. She was well thought of by the reservation Indians; and McLaughlin himself had established a strong rapport with them over five years of service. He knew the people he would oversee.

However, another candidate's name advanced more quickly in Washington, bolstered by another set of endorsements; and Bishop Seidenbush's letter of recommendation was posted in the mail the day that the appointment of other man was confirmed by the Senate.[60] Paul Beckwith, a politician from South Bend, Indiana, whom McLaughlin called a "Catholic for the occasion,"[61] got the backing of the Indian Missions Bureau and the position. As soon as he arrived in September, he was at cross-purposes with McLaughlin. James McLaughlin got his first taste of the political spoils system at work. He quickly set out to reverse the appointment and received support from General Sibley, who had been instrumental in William Forbes's appointment to Devils Lake and served on the Board of Indian Commissioners.[62] When the new agent took temporary leave to arrange for his family to join him, McLaughlin made the initial move against the man. He sent a letter on October 12 to the Bishop Seidenbush and a missionary priest at Red River, complaining that Beckwith's wife was a Baptist, the agent discharged a good Catholic employee to make room for a Baptist brother-in-law, and he was on a path that would counter the good work of the priest and sisters ministering to the Indians at Devils Lake.[63]

Put off by the new agent's inexperience and insensitivity, the reservation wards disliked the man. McLaughlin used that animosity to his benefit. In November, he wrote to General Sibley in St. Paul:

> *The Indians have told me repeatedly that if their late Father [Agent Forbes] was living they would be better off this winter, as he could always get money for their use, that their present Agent is but a boy, and knows nothing about Indians, or how to get money for their use . . .* [64]

Knowing the northwest community's Catholic power base, he attacked the agent as a member of a Masonic lodge and having been married by a justice of the peace while professing himself as a strong member of the church.[65]

Agent Beckwith recognized that he was being undercut and would not have the allegiance of the Indians with James McLaughlin continuing as general manager. In February 1876, he sent a letter to the Commissioner of Indian Affairs advising that the position of assistant manager was no longer necessary.[66] Beckwith's goal was broader; until all long-standing employees under the prior agent were removed, he felt he would not have the confidence of the Indians.[67] He started at the top. He sought evidence to justify the discharge of McLaughlin. Hoping to find graft, he solicited information about the man's purchase of land next to the reservation, but he could not uncover anything incriminating.[68] Moreover, the commissioner did not respond to his suggested management reorganization. It did not matter; Paul Beckwith acted on his own authority. In early March, without providing a reason, he gave McLaughlin a notice of termination, but allowed him to stay the month if he agreed to resign.[69] That was not all; Beckwith removed Mrs. McLaughlin from her position of agency interpreter.[70] When McLaughlin refused to leave his job, he was ordered off the reservation grounds by April 5.[71] The reaction could not have been worse. The acrimony grew intense. Some Indians went off the reservation, declaring that they could not live under the new agent.[72] The chaplain at Devils Lake wrote to the Catholic Bureau in Washington, playing a fear card that the Santee Indians off reservation were highly agitated and may attack nearby settlements,[73] as had occurred in 1862. James McLaughlin moved his family to the home of a brother-in-law at the adjacent military base and headed for St. Paul.[74] He plotted the undoing of Beckwith and taking charge of the agency as his own.[75] Beckwith's support withered.

Pressure from Washington forced Beckwith to tender his resignation on April 29, but it was not to be effective until July 1. And McLaughlin still did not have the appointment. A disgruntled Beckwith did not give up. He worked through his contacts to undermine McLaughlin's bid and extend his own time at Devils Lake.[76]

McLaughlin countered. He pressed prominent men in Minnesota and Northern Dakota Territory for support, basing his case on evidence of the Devils Lake Indians' discontent with Beckwith. McLaughlin said he did not want this to appear as a personal vendetta; he postured that he sought the job for the good of the community and reservation. His campaign was unrelenting. And, indeed, it had become personal. His use of local influence outhustled Beckwith's political connections back East. In early June, the Senate confirmed James McLaughlin's appointment, and he got the job he desperately wanted.[77]

James McLaughlin discovered the power of well-directed correspondence. He also found that a properly placed rumor could stoke the fire. More to the point, he mastered how to effectively advance his position and counter an adversary. (Letter writing to influential persons and Indian Bureau administrators would consistently serve him during his professional life.)

McLaughlin was committed to the reservation program as the surest way to civilize the native. By temperament, experience, and Catholic righteousness, James McLaughlin intended to prove himself an able administrator and make Devils Lake an exemplary agency. But Paul Beckwith took a measure of revenge; he depleted provisions and returned unused funds to the bureau, then removed all the agency business records.[78] The new agent scrambled to pick up the pieces.

His ambition and hard work would carry him much further. He took on the mission of providing a transformation from the ancient ways. It was inevitable that civilization would overrun the Indian. One needed to look no further than the changes along the Eastern Seaboard a hundred years earlier. The problem was he could only see with Anglo-American eyes.

CHAPTER SIX

The 1876 Yellowstone Campaign

February 1876

Although the Papa Sapa was within the Great Sioux Reservation, the native right to the hills was on the verge of forfeiture. Political necessity had no patience for events to play out in taking the Black Hills.

The Lakota now were viewed as failing to keep the peace on their own lands; and the government was tired of waiting on the nontreaty Indians coming around. In this setting, the Grant administration devised its new strategy to undercut the standing of these Indians and maintain the more pliable Indians on the reservation. The roaming bands were judged disruptive to the reservation system. They were far too independent and able to provide for themselves, exactly the opposite of how reservation life was structured. Washington rhetoric cast the roamers as "hostiles."[1] They were "renegades," "raiders," and "ravagers."

A deadline for a peaceful resolution dictated by Washington was devised. If not met, military intervention would follow. The ploy was to appear reasonable. The voices of reformers and humanitarians had to be neutralized. The populace may not have wanted war, but the government knew it would accept a police action against rebellious Indians. A tripwire was placed to ensnare the nonreservation Lakota in a contrived provocation. The Secretary of War alerted the army to stand by to assist Indian Affairs.

In reality, by the early 1870s, the Sioux already had been compromised by the Laramie Treaty and other events. There was acceptance of reservation life by most, and the roaming bands occupied only the unceded territory, as was allowed to them, with some crossover from time to time. The Oregon Trail had been in place for years across the mid-section of the Plains and through the Rockies. The discovery of gold in California in January 1848 and the rush to riches put further strain on the midlands. California was quickly granted statehood in 1850; and 12 years thereafter, the building of the Transcontinental Railway was authorized to join East to West. Yet, safe journey cross-country to the Pacific was not enough. Civilization demanded that "savages" no longer be allowed to roam the Plains.

The off-reservation Indians were scattered throughout the unceded lands that had been set forth in Article 16 of the Laramie Treaty, north of the North Platte River and east of the Big Horn Mountains, where "no white person or persons shall be permitted to settle upon or occupy any portion of the same."[2] While Red Cloud's Oglala were promised in Article 11 continued hunting throughout lands north of the North Platte and along the Republican Branch of the Smokey Hill River as long as the buffalo grazed there,[3] that time had largely passed. The Lakota always considered the unceded lands as their own, and most of the Sioux leaders who roamed had refused to put their mark to the Laramie Treaty. What they failed to understand was the writer of the treaty also was its interpreter. The government alone determined their rights of occupancy.

In December 1875, President Grant issued an edict through the Office of Indian Affairs that all Sioux and Cheyenne had to be on a reservation by January 31, 1876.[4]

The pretext for Grant's ultimatum was centered on three factors—the Sioux's continued conflict with their old enemy, the Crow; the encouragement of agency Indians by free-roaming bands to take absences from the reservation; and Sioux harassment of whites moving into the lands in and around the Black Hills.[5] The real motive was the discovery of gold in the Black Hills. The wealth of the region should flow to the United States and not be left in possession of the Indians who had no need for the precious metal.[6] The government chose to secure the influx of prospectors and settlers into this preserve. No longer should the Sioux have range over those lands, as originally promised. The benevolent rationale was that only the sanctuary of the reservation could protect the Indians. And, of course, once put in place, the inhabitants needed to adapt to the civilization that was crowding them out of their lands.

The Indian agents had the responsibility of getting the word out to nonagency Indians that they must become reservation Indians or the army would force them in. Runners were sent out to find the outlying bands.[7] Not only was such notice unreliable, the timing was curious because any possible movement of the Indians would be hampered by the northern winter.[8] The Sioux did not roam during the cold months, but settled into camps and lived off stored provisions. Whether or not Sitting Bull received the directive,[9] he had no inclination to comply. The roaming bands did not come in out of the cold.

Failure to respond was answer enough. The Secretary of the Interior reported to Secretary of War William Belknap the day after the deadline that the Indians were still at large in the Powder River country. He formally turned over the hostiles' fate to the War Department.[10] On February 4, Secretary Belknap replied:

> *Sir: Acknowledging the receipt of your letter of the 1st instant stating that the time given Sitting Bull and his followers to repair to an agency having expired, and this chief still refuses to comply with the directions of the Commissioner, and turning over the case to the War Department, in accordance with recommendations of the Indian Bureau that hostilities be commenced against these Indians, I have the honor to inform you that the Adjutant-General has directed the General of the Army to take immediate measures to compel these Indians to remain upon their reservation, as requested by your department.*[11]

Grant had not expected the off-reservation Indians to come in. But he anticipated any resistance to be short-lived. The administration believed that full implementation of the reservation system was at hand.

"Locate Sitting Bull" was the cry. (Previously, General Sheridan thought the name was a general description of Sioux intransience or hostile Indians.[12] He was not certain that there was a Sitting Bull.) The man was identified as "the enemy Sioux general."[13] He was the face of the resistance. If he could be taken out, the rest of the Sioux would fall in line.

General Sherman directed a "double process of peace within the reservations and war without."[14]

A winter campaign was mobilized to catch the Indians snow-locked in a raw February. While the army was prepared to kill Indians, its overall aim was coerce submission by disrupting family shelters, destroying food supplies, and running off or stealing horses. Yet there was no thought of avoiding noncombatants.[15] After all, because it was the Lakota's choice to camp with their families, there were bound to be collateral casualties. Already strategically stationed, the army was deployed from three points—Colonel John Gibbon was to lead a column eastward out of Montana's Fort Ellis; General Alfred Terry's forces were to proceed westward from Fort Lincoln in Dakota Territory; and General Crook was to move out of Fort Laramie in the south. Wagons carried supplies for support. Relying on the advice of the Indian Bureau taken from reports of its reservation agents, the three commanders thought they were in search of about five hundred warriors scattered throughout the unceded territory.[16] The military should have known better than to rely on civilian agents. The prime areas targeted for search were the river courses of the Powder, Tongue, Rosebud, and Little Big Horn, flowing out of Wyoming and running northerly to the Yellowstone, between the Big Horn Mountains and the Black Hills. The Yellowstone River itself was a broad river that meandered northeasterly across Montana, after tumbling out of the Rockies in western Wyoming.

That February, a barrage of snowstorms battered the northern Plains, stalling any offensive.[17] Fierce gusts drove blizzards in the three commanders' paths; when the snowfall stopped, the winds were unabated. Large drifts built up. The Indians remained hunkered down in winter camp. Only General Crook's column was able to get underway during the winter but not until March 1. Crook commanded a force of eight hundred men, and they traveled with supply wagons and heavy artillery.[18] It was a slow haul.

John Gregory Bourke, aide-de-camp to General Crook, described the temperatures encountered on the trek north in terms of mercury congealing in the bulb and remaining solidified "during storms of Polar wind which howl across these plains."[19] He carefully catalogued the necessary apparel for the army to function in such weather:

> *For cavalry, great care is demanded to protect feet, knees, wrists and ears. Commencing with the feet, first a pair of close fitting lamb's-wool socks is put on, then one of same size as those worn by women, so as to come over the knees. Indian moccasins of buckskin reaching well up the leg are preferable to boots, being warmer and lighter. Cork soles should be used with them. Then comes the overboot, of buffalo-skin, hair side inward, reaching well up the thigh, and opening down the side and fastened by buckles or brass buttons like a pair of Mexican breeches. They should be soled, heeled and boxed with good leather, well tanned. Some prefer to wear leggings to buffalo skin, legs separate, strapped to pistol belt, and to use the clumsy buffalo overshoe of the Q.M. Department. This is a mode of attire more readily taken off during warm parts of the day, and for that reason, worthy of recommendation, but open to the objections that difficulty is generally experienced in getting the clumsy, awkward shoe into the stirrup. All people agree in denouncing as pernicious the practice of wearing tight foot-gear which by impeding the circulation assures the freezing of the lower extremities. For under clothing, first put on a good suit of lamb's wool or merino, then one of buckskin perforated to permit the escape of exhalations. Over this a heavy suit, the heavier the better. Finally a loose dark overshirt of thick texture or a heavy blanket blouse, made of a mission blanket, double-breasted; large buttons, well sewed on. If cold winds prevail, nothing will afford the body complete protection except a coat of beaver or buffalo skin, reaching to the knees or below and made loose at the elbows. For the head, a cap, loosely fitting over the cranium, of dark cloth, with leather visor to protect the eyes, and a border two inches to three in breath, of beaver fur to turn down, when required.*[20]

Bourke understood northern prairie winter.

When scouts discovered a Sioux and Cheyenne camp along the Powder River on March 17,[21] the general ordered Colonel Joseph Reynolds to attack. The colonel intended to make a run at first light, but snow flurries held back his troops. His men sat bundled up on their mounts, mittens protecting numbed fingers and woolen cloth strips fashioned into mufflers wrapped about faces from which exhale turned to vapor with the temperature subzero.[22] No matter, when there was a break in the weather, the men responded with a charge. But not with enough follow-through. Even though surprised, only a few Indians were killed; all the others were able to escape into hillside rock outcroppings west of their camp. From craggy redoubts they rained bullets upon the soldiers who were torching their village.[23] Supplies were lost. Horses were run off or taken, but most were later stolen back from unvigilant soldiers.[24] Escaping Oglala and Cheyenne found protection in the camp of Sitting Bull, miles down the Powder.[25] Crook fumed that Reynolds had bungled his mission.[26] He saw no choice but to head south to Fort Fetterman on the Platte River to regroup.[27] The retreat took his troops to within 50 miles from where the march began. The intended winter operation now was stalled on all fronts until later spring.

Up until this time, Sitting Bull was inclined to believe that his people were insulated in their traditional hunting grounds. He now realized there was no avoiding the white man's army. As the spring grasses were breaking winter's grip on the Plains, a dream came to Sitting Bull—a summer's whirlwind of dust charged from the east toward a white thunderhead in the northwest with currents pushing hard into the reaches of the large cloud. Sitting Bull saw soldiers on the march within the vortex of dust. He interpreted this as the U.S. Army riding toward where the Sioux were camped.[28] Outlying bands and hunters confirmed signs of soldiers to the east, west, and south. Whether the dream was real or manufactured, Sitting Bull used it to rouse the Lakota.

By the end of May, all three army columns were on the move. The overall force was nearly 2,500 strong with the support of Crow, Shoshone, and Ree (Arikaree or Arikara) Indian scouts.[29] The plan was to converge in the area around where the Big Horn River flows into the Yellowstone, the primary summer buffalo hunting grounds in the northern Plains. General Crook commanded the strongest outfit; after reorganizing at Fort Fetterman, his men now numbered 1,300, including 260 scouts.[30]

The leaders of the various bands received intelligence reports from hunting parties of military activity. For the roaming bands, it was unthinkable to submit to reservation life. They determined to fight any efforts to coerce them to do so. Council fires burned long into the nights.

Sitting Bull, as alpha chieftain of the nonreservation Sioux, sent out calls for a gathering of all hunting Indians.[31] The Lakota, Dakota, and Nakota, together with the Northern Cheyenne and Northern Arapaho, received word to join forces: "We are an island of Indians in a lake of whites. We must stand together, or they will run us out separately. These soldiers have come shooting; they want war. All right, we will give it to them."[32] By late spring, the assembly would build to somewhere around eight thousand Indians, including up to two thousand warriors, camped in the southeast Montana Territory.[33] Reservation Sioux heard the call, and several came on a run. Red Cloud heard the call as well, but having been treated to a full-dressed marine parade and shown the arsenal in Washington, he knew what lay ahead. He advised the Oglala to stay home. Typically a number of reservation Indians left in the warm months to hunt and visit relatives, drawn by the wild buffalo and a freedom to follow old traditions.[34] This season there was more purpose than taking temporary leave from the agencies.

The Lakota and Cheyenne were never better armed. For years, they had traded buffalo robes and ponies for arms with French-Canadian half-breeds (known as "Slotas" or "Metis").[35] They also bartered with reservation friendlies who acquired weapons directly from post traders. Their arsenal was gradually upgraded from single-loading guns to repeating rifles, placed in the hands of their best warriors.

As the summer solstice drew near in early June, Sitting Bull took a group of followers to a knoll in the Wolf Mountains to fast and pray for guidance. The chief stood for hours with arms outstretched, gazing skyward, over two days. On the third day, his nephew, Jumping Bull, took an awl to the chief's arms and from each cut away 50 strips of flesh in sacrifice.[36] Blood flowed down his arms as Sitting Bull slowly danced against the rays of the sun. He asked for wisdom from Wakan Tanka, the Lakota supreme being. Weakened from abstaining from food and water, he fell into an unconscious state. He lay prone for long minutes; his attendants watched over him and placed cool water over his forehead and wrists.[37] Upon awakening, the chief haltingly looked about to regain his bearings. As his head cleared, he spoke of a vision—he told the men on the mountain that he saw a hard storm carried by winds across the Plains, and it struck "blue coated, long knives" riding horses. Soldiers carrying lances together with their mounts were swept up, tumbling in the sky. Suddenly the wind stopped. Soldiers and horses plummeted back to earth, headfirst into an Indian camp.

He was preparing his people for what was to come. Sitting Bull proclaimed that the white men "have no ears."[38] The army ignored the Lakota demand not to occupy the lands of the Yellowstone, which had always been Indian country. He now foresaw that the attacking soldiers that appeared in his dream several weeks earlier were destined to die. In speaking of the vision, he admonished his people not to touch the bodies of the cavalry men that he foretold dying, less the Indians thereafter would covet the white man's belongings: "If you set your hearts upon the goods of the white man, it will prove a curse to this nation."[39]

In mid-June, the gathered camps were concentrated in the area of upper Rosebud Creek. While General Crook searched for signs of Indians on his second march northward, the Indians were equally intent on intercepting his troops. Sioux scouts had detected the military infiltration. On the night of June 16 under the sliver of a waning moon the fearless Crazy Horse guided his braves through the Wolf Mountains. At sunrise the next morning, he readied for battle. Crazy Horse hung a medicine stone behind his left ear and painted a lightning streak from forehead to cheek and blue spots (hail stones) on his bare chest. He placed hawk feathers, as his personal talisman for waging battle, into his hair; and then he sprinkled dust from a gopher barrow between the ears of his horse and over its hind quarters.[40]

Catching sight of some of the attack force, the army's advance Crow scouts opened fire. Alerted, Crook's forces scrambled to meet the aggressors. The soldiers and a pack train had been bivouacked along the Rosebud in the creek bottoms that were exposed and surrounded by ridges and bluffs to the north and south. The Indians held the high ground on the north. Although the Sioux, supported by Cheyenne, were about 900 warriors against the general's 1,300-man force with Crow, Shoshone, and Ree scouts, the military was not able to mass their troops, and the warriors continually cut the army picket lines.[41] Indians attacked from ravines and ridges and pulled back, attacked and pulled back. Both sides took causalities over six hours of fighting. With ammunition running low, Crazy Horse tactically disengaged.

George Crook could only be thankful that the warriors broke off the battle.[42] His report stated: "My troops beat these Indians on a field of their own choosing, and drove them in utter rout from it, as far as the proper care of my wounded and prudence would justify."[43] He backtracked miles to the south with knowledge that the hostile bands were larger and stronger than what intelligence from the agents described. In a June 19 report to Sheridan, he advised: "I expect to find those Indians in rough places all the time and so have ordered five companies of infantry, and shall not probably make any extended move-

General George Crook

ment until they arrive."[44] The conventional expectation of the Indians turning tail on the advance of the U.S. Army was in need of reassessment. And so was the number of warriors in the field. His battalion would not be a factor in the events of war about to unfold one week later.[45] More to the point, the *New York Herald* of June 24, based on the account of a correspondent, Reuben Davenport, traveling with Crook's expedition, opined: "The first regular battle between the United States forces and the hostile Sioux has resulted in what looks very like a defeat of the soldiers."[46] The journalist who sent in this story was ostracized by the command. But the plain fact was that General Crook did not get it done at Rosebud; during the remainder of his career he would be dogged by remarks that he lost this fight.[47]

Many Sioux believed that Sitting Bull's vision materialized at the Rosebud.[48] It was only an early glimpse of what was coming.

CHAPTER SEVEN

Soldiers Falling Upside Down

Spring 1876

By late June, there were thousands of Indians camped according to bands on west banks of the Little Big Horn River near the end of its waters run. From north to south, stretching more than three miles in length,[1] stood lodge circles of the Northern Cheyenne, Sans Arc, Miniconjou, Oglala, and the Blackfoot, Brule, and Two Kettle. The last three Lakota bands were congregated together just above the largest Lakota camp at the far end. The southernmost grouping of lodges was dominated by the Hunkpapa, joined by the Yanktonai and Santee.[2] One hundred or so yards from each camp circle, grazing on the sweet pasture further from the river, numerous horses of the several bands were held under watch of outriders. The Lakota and their Cheyenne allies had answered Sitting Bull's call to defend their homeland. The chief was at the height of his power. He had drawn together what was undoubtedly the largest assemblage of Indians on the northern Plains.[3]

The lowlands along the side of the Little Big Horn River were bracketed on the west by the Big Horn Mountains that run a crescent course of 120 miles south to north out of the Wyoming into Montana, and on the east by the lesser Rosebud and Wolf Mountains. The river originated in the Big Horn Mountains (known to the Sioux as the "Shining Mountains" because their peaks are covered with snow most of the year) and took its path northward to where it joined the Big Horn River, flowing northeasterly to the Yellowstone River and onto the Missouri. As it left the mountains, the Little Big Horn watercourse slowed through a series of switchbacks or loops, separating a flood plain on the west from hills on the opposite side. At the edge of the eastern banks there were steep bluffs, incised over years by the river's run, that climb into open hillside. The hillocks were creased with gullies and depressions; and, in places, the bluffs below were fragmented by washouts. The lower valley land carried the name "Greasy Grass" from the Crow, because the rich grass growing there provided good grazing for the buffalo and gave forage to their ponies.[4] Groves of trees hugged the stream banks and filled up the land within the loops.

The spring of 1876 had seen little rain, and by mid-June, the afternoon temperatures were near 100 degrees.[5] Grasses clutching the west-facing slopes above the river already were singed yellow-brown with random intrusions of short gray-green sagebrush.

In search of the roaming bands, General Terry, proceeding along the Yellowstone river route, directed Custer south along the Rosebud Creek.[6] Terry's and Gibbon's forces combined to continue west along the Yellowstone and then intended to go southward up the Big Horn River.[7] General Crook, who best knew the strength of the adversary, was not engaged.

George Armstrong Custer, now on his own, miles to the east of the Little Big Horn Valley, welcomed breaking away. He imagined his foe to be easy prey. It was just a matter of finding Indians; and that he was in a hurry to do. He declined wagon support and artillery; supplies were hauled by mules. His intent was to travel faster than Indians could decamp and move out. For three days, he pushed his troops on a hard ride.[8] When on June 24 Custer came upon the remains of an Indian camp near the Rosebud, to the east of the Wolf Mountains, he knew he was near.[9] Everywhere there were signs of recent large Indian movements.[10] His regiment quickened their step westerly along Ash Creek (later renamed Reno Creek) toward the Little Big Horn Valley 20 or so miles away, riding long into the night.

The next day's first flash of sun over the ridgeline splayed light along the edges of the river course below. Several camps on the Greasy Grass were starting to awake. Ten or so miles east, on a surveillance assignment, Crow scouts moved through shadowy draws toward a location known as "Crow's Nest." On Sunday morning, June 25, 1876, observing traces of smoke rising from camp fires, the scouts scanned the Little Big Horn with field glasses. A huge horse herd on the far side came into hazy view, and they knew that an imposing camp must be nearby.[11] The scouts warned the commander of the probable size of the camp.[12] (Because the actual encampment was screened by tall cottonwood groves near the river, the scouts could not see it.[13]) Custer decided to divide his exhausted regiment into three battalions to create a pincer movement that he thought would encircle whatever Indians were gathered in the location of where these signs pointed.[14] He would not wait on the scheduled arrival the next day of the Terry-Gibbon Column. Custer took the north side of Ash Creek and ordered Major Marcus Reno to move his men on the other side, each headed west.[15] Captain Frederick Benteen was sent further south with troopers and support wagons to determine whether there were Indians further upstream. Then he was to circle back to join Reno's battalion.[16] The Sabbath would be a killing day.

That morning, Sitting Bull evidenced no concern of any impending danger. He carried a buffalo tail stick, serving as a fly brush, to ward away the incessant summer flies swarming the Greasy Grass, as he strolled through the Hunkpapa encampment, talking to acquaintances.[17] There was no urgency in his movement. But he showed particular interest in warriors on his walkabout. He felt the time was closing on his vision, but to be calm was to be confident.

The fateful charge of Custer across the hillside above would make it a day like no other.

Near noon, a Lakota outrider saw dust rising in the hills to the east and rushed toward the southern camps to warn that soldiers were advancing.[18] Strangely, there was no great haste of reaction. Subsequent circumstances seem to indicate that the expected point of attack was the middle or northern reaches of the massive encampment; and the Indians were not at the ready in the south.[19] Some analysts say the Indians were reckless in not setting outer defenses.[20] Crook's withdrawal from Rosebud may have been taken as a sign that there were no soldiers in the immediate area. On the other hand, the Indians could well have anticipated the attack on June 26, when Gibbon was anticipated to join forces with Custer. Or perhaps, confident of Sitting Bull's vision, they did not expect a strong attack from the soldiers who were destined to fall upside down. Yet, there is no question that the Indians were able to scramble to readiness to meet Custer.

Reno moved his men across the Little Big Horn River about two or so miles above where the Indians were clustered.[21] Custer set his route along the ridges above the river. The sun was at mid arc in a cloudless sky.[22] Hidden by turns in the river and clusters of trees, Reno's column was not visible from the camps. Young boys, playing on the outskirts of camp, were the first to see soldiers coming. And the soldiers spotted them.[23] A rifle shot cut down one boy while the other ran to sound an alarm. As word reached the camps, warriors seized weapons and leaped to their ponies. Reno's job was to lead the shock troops while Custer first said he would follow with a second wave of troops. Instead he left Reno, whom he strongly disliked, at point and changed his own course to catch what he assumed would be scattering prey.

Advancing north along the Little Big Horn, Reno's forces caught sight of tops of tipis in the distance and spurred their horses; at about 70 yards they dismounted and began firing.[24] The camp of the Hunkpapa (the name means "those who camp at the end" or "end of the horn"[25]), which included Sitting Bull's lodges, was at the point of attack. Bullets ripped through the stretched buffalo skins of tipis.[26] Incoming fire killed two wives and a daughter of Gall.[27] Reaction was swift. Woman and children hurried to escape downstream to other encampments and westward into the hills.

Surprisingly to Reno, the Indian warriors did not attempt to take a defensive position to protect their camps; they raced directly toward the attackers.[28] (Again, the prevailing thinking was that the Plains Indians were only ambushers who would cut and run upon a show of force.[29] They were not army. They had no generals.[30] But for this fight, many seasoned warriors were within the gathering, and they were united in protection of their homeland.) Sitting Bull's nephews, One Bull and White Bull, were early to respond.[31] At the point of engagement, the military's line broke. Soldiers sought cover within trees along the river. Brush fire was added to arrows and bullets, driving the soldiers across the river against the high banks. Crazy Horse summoned several warriors to the attack and Gall led another charge.[32] True to the vision, soldiers began to fall. Facing heavy fire, Reno's battalion could only pull back.

Meanwhile, George Custer confidently continued to move his troops into position further north, without realizing Reno had called off his southerly prong of attack.[33] Custer's plan was to trap the fleeing Indians, flushed by Reno's troops. He intended a quick victory. Further south, Captain Benteen was bringing his soldiers to join with Reno's. Splitting the battalion proved to be a tactical mistake. Reno's men were dug in on a ridge under siege about four miles away from the Custer column.

Even as the command of Custer rode across rolling hills east of the river, the Indian combatants were readying their own assault. They could see dust clouds rising from the cavalry's horses canting over dry knolls and ridges. But Custer assumed that Reno continued to advance as he started northward.[34] When he crossed the upper reaches of a coulee called Medicine Tail at about 2:20 p.m., he saw tipis in the northern extreme of the encampment.[35] He also observed what appeared to be mostly women and children escaping from camp to the northwest. The brash commander believed he was about to close the trap.

There are differing accounts of Sitting Bull's movements at this time. One version later would be used to discredit him to his own people. Some claimed he fled with the women and children, while others said he shepherded these people to safety; and still others reported him remaining in camp encouraging the warriors forward.[36] He was not bloodied in the combat on the ridge. What is clear is that at 45 years of age, he was not an armed participant. His supremacy was beyond the particulars of battle. His reputation as a courageous warrior, wounded several times in skirmishes with both rival Indian tribes and the military, was well recognized.

The Lakota and Cheyenne were led by Crazy Horse, Gall, White Bull, Crow King, and Two Moons, all seasoned fighting men.[37] The braves who followed them were excellent horsemen.[38] They were not recent recruits as filled the army's ranks; they had ridden horses from early youth. Their horses were trained for hunting and battle.[39] A warrior's aim was not diminished while astride a galloping horse. In war, Indian horse and rider moved as one. (Even Custer earlier had written in praise of the Indian mounted warrior.) Colors of paints, bays, buckskins, roans, and sorrels seemed to swirl everywhere over the field. The Indians had some repeating rifles, but most still carried old muskets and muzzleloaders; and they did not have abundant ammunition.[40] The cavalry had breach-loading rifles, which sometimes jammed from soft copper shell casings.[41]

Advancing swiftly, warriors charged across the river and ascended the bluffs to the ridge. Custer knew from his own experience during the Civil War that a quick-hitting cavalry charge was highly effective. It had been his means to prior successes. Here he allowed the other side to seize the tactic; the Indians came at the soldiers on the hill like lightning strikes against the ground. Bold, sudden, and explosive. Gall and Two Moons streaked across the Medicine Tail's junction with the Little Big Horn River on the south.[42] Crazy Horse attacked from the north.[43]

In response, Custer made a doomed decision of dividing his troops on the ridge. He sent what was known as the "Gray Horse Group" under Captain Yates along Medicine Tail Coulee toward the river.[44] As soldiers attempted to cross the river, they were confronted and pushed back up the ridge.

Superior numbers and surprise tactics made it appear that Indians emerged from every draw on the east side of the river. (Reno would later write: "The very earth seemed to grow Indians."[45]) The hunter was now the prey. The Indians' rushes and battle cries and shrill whoops spooked the army horses, causing several to bolt. Others were shot out from under cavalrymen in the saddle. The 7th Cavalry became dismounted horsemen, disconnected from one another and disoriented, scrambling for cover in natural recesses of the open ridge.[46] Fallen horses and packs became breastworks.[47] Exhausted, frightened men, eyes wide, faces dank with sweat and dust, were scattered throughout the hill. There was no place to hide. With each assault, more bullets tore into horseflesh and human bodies. Then, archers sent arrows on parabolic trajectories that rained on the hunkered-down troops. Fire was put to grass in the ravines and swales so that winds carried smoke over the higher ground. Mounted and afoot, the Indians continued to press forward. War clubs were wielded in close. Dust, smoke, noise, and the sulfuric smell of burnt gunpowder covered the whole hillside. Everywhere there was chaos.[48] Then there was no sound at all.

When the firing stopped, the Indians went among the dead and dying. No one was allowed to live. Nor was there heed to Sitting Bull's warning a few weeks' earlier that the Lakota not touch the bodies of the dead cavalry men. Corpses were stripped of clothing and mutilated by women from the camp.[49] Some took revenge for past army atrocities against kin; others followed Sioux culture that a vanquished enemy should not be allowed to rise again in the afterlife. Booty of saddles, uniforms, carbines and revolvers, and rounds of ammunition were claimed.[50] Army horses were taken. Boys scrambled throughout the hills shooting arrows into the bodies of dead soldiers. The soldiers had recently been paid their military wages while on the march.[51] In stripping the bodies and ransacking the soldiers' packs, currency notes were loosened and dispersed by late-afternoon breezes to flutter over the knolls and catch in the grasses and sage. The soldiers no longer needed "pay money." Custer's body, while stripped, was not mutilated.[52] Yet, legend tells that a Cheyenne woman drove a sewing awl of bone into each of his ears, so that man who would not listen to the Cheyenne chief's warning after Washita would hear forever the death rattle of his command at Greasy Grass.[53] By the end of the afternoon, 210 members of the 7th Cavalry lay dead.

Custer and his troops all tumbled to earth from the ridgetop above Little Big Horn. The summer before, some of these same men were playing baseball at Fort Lincoln.

A glint in the grass next to a slain soldier caught the eye of a brave, who walked over and picked up a timepiece. Although the numbers on the dial meant nothing to him, he observed black arrows under a circular piece of glass pointing nearly straight up and down. This was white man's time of just after 6:00 p.m., but real time was in the afternoon. (The soldiers' chronometers were set to the time of nearest principal city and that appeared to be the East Coast, not Chicago.) He looked to the sky and saw that the sun was still high. When he heard the tick, tick of the watch, he drew it closer to his ear.[54] Fascinated, he kept it as a trophy of war. (To the Indian, time was not measured in such small increments. Rather, he related to day and night and the cycles of the earth.) The last clash on the ridge was quick to finish.[55] The overall battle of June 25 was fought in just over three hours.[56]

Captain Benteen reached Reno's embattled troops late that afternoon. As evening fell, the shooting stopped. But Reno's men remained dug in.[57]

The Indians took their dead and wounded from the field. There was an incongruous mix of reverberations in the village camps: wailing as the elderly, women, and children returned and woops from warriors celebrating victory and their individual deeds.[58] Some of the revelers were drunk from whiskey found in the canteens of the dead troopers.[59] Campfires crackled, and flames thrust jagged daggers at the darkness. The combatants were electric with exhilaration. They had defended their own ground and delivered a stunning defeat to the soldiers.

The next morning the Indians renewed the attack against Reno's men, some wearing army blue blouses and a few carrying the regimental guidons of the 7th Cavalry.[60] The Indians were now in command. The military adornments frightened the soldiers, who did not yet know what had happened to Custer and his men. Hours later, the attackers surprisingly left the field, setting ablaze grasses in the draws behind them.[61] Sitting Bull believed it was not necessary to complete the kill of all soldiers sent to Greasy Grass.[62] The warriors had delivered their message; 53 men under Major Reno were killed in action.[63] Now let the survivors recognize the resolute resistance of the Lakota and Cheyenne warriors. Through white eyes, this was a military mistake because there were sufficient forces to overwhelm Reno. That was not the Lakota way. Moreover, with troopers dug in and reinforced, the Indians pushing the attack were sure to take heavy causalities. The price to take out Reno's men would be too great.

Sitting Bull urged the camps struck.[64] He suspected other military forces were in the area and that retaliation would be coming. Singular engagement was the practice of the Plains Indians, not a war campaign. Moreover, the logistics of maintaining a large camp required movement; the necessity of new game areas for food and new grass for horses was constant.[65] Finally, he feared that his people having taken spoils from the dead "will covet the white man's goods," "be at his mercy," and "starve at his hands."[66] Withdrawal was the prudent course.

The Sioux placed their dead in funeral lodges; the Cheyenne took their dead into the western hillsides for burial.[67] Belongings and camp supplies that could not be easily carried were burned. The many bands trekked southwest toward the Big Horn Mountains.[68] Late afternoon on June 26 Major Reno's troops, clinging to defensive positions in the far eastern hills above the river, saw Indians moving up the first of a series of foothills,[69] single file and two abreast, afoot and on horseback, over several trails out of the hazy basin. Thousands of foot falls of animals and persons kicked up dirt; plumes of dust enveloped the procession. The victors were pulling out; Sitting Bull knew the likelihood that a bigger force was advancing. The Lakota had convincingly responded to the edict that they submit to the reservation. Now they wanted to be left to their own lands.

The Indians disappeared into the folds of the prairie. It was as if caravans of people were carried away on magic carpets driven by a slipstream from the battle ground. Actually, the converging army columns were both late and confused. While they hesitated in assessing the situation, the Indians covered great distances.

On June 27, the advance scouts of the contingents led by General Terry and Colonel Gibbon arrived. They discovered the bodies of Custer and his men. Two days of heat mottled dead flesh.[70] A terrible stench rose from the ridge, and flies swarmed everywhere.[71] A burial detail was ordered to cover the bodies with dirt where they laid.[72] Under the heat of a hanging sun, the men assigned this grisly task wore wet kerchiefs over nose and mouth and choked back nausea.

This was the event that defined Sitting Bull to the American people; there was no way he would outlive his reputation as a hostile. The Indians thought they were defending themselves. For the American public one word rang out: "massacre."

The Lakota would not see such a day again.

CHAPTER EIGHT

Reaction and Retaliation

July 1876

Field dispatches were taken by couriers to distant telegraph offices, most of which were closed for Independence Day celebrations. General Terry sent communiques by horseback riders west to Fort Ellis in Montana Territory and east to the Yellowstone and thereafter by steamboat to Fort Lincoln, to be telegraphed to Sheridan's Chicago headquarters and Washington, D.C.[1] Generals Sherman and Sheridan, who were in Philadelphia for the country's Centennial Exposition, received the wired messages with incredulity.[2] Sherman believed in the superiority of the U.S. military; and Sheridan had set the strategy for the Yellowstone Expedition. Neither expected the hostiles to be a force.

Over 600 miles removed from the Little Big Horn, James McLaughlin was making his way northwest to Fort Totten by wagon from Minnesota. He carried papers from the Commissioner of Indian Affairs, appointing him agent of the Devils Lake Reservation adjacent to the fort.

One would think this was an out-of-the-way corner of the Dakota Territory on the other side of the Missouri River, far removed from any consequence of the Indians victory at Little Big Horn. But Fort Totten had a cache of firearms and ammunition, and it was undermanned.[3] Confused rumblings from army couriers, scouts, and agency Indians were moving faster between frontier posts than authorized reports. The official word was not much more settled. The few troops present at Totten were apprehensive with talk of collateral repercussions directed toward the area. This was pure speculation arising out of fear that a major Indian

First Account of the Custer Massacre
STATE HISTORICAL SOCIETY OF NORTH DAKOTA

uprising was in the making. On the road, James McLaughlin had yet to hear of the battle.

It took over a week for the Little Big Horn story to reach the nation's newspapers. The first written account came out of Bozeman, Montana, where Fort Ellis was located, in an extra edition on July 3 at 7:00 p.m.;[4] the *Helena Herald* got its extra out on the afternoon of July 4,[5] and the *New York Herald* had the story on July 6.[6]

On July 5, a wire went to officials in Canada. The assistant military commander of the Canadian North-West Mounted Police sounded an alarm to his command in the southwest prairie of Saskatchewan Province, warning of the Sioux potentially escaping to Canada and using that as a base of aggression against the United States.[7]

News of the Indian's rout of the military rattled America's hundred-year celebration of nationhood. The Lakota and their allies had ignited a bombshell. The *Bismarck Tribune* issued its story on July 6, 1876, carrying the emotionally charged headline, "First Account of the Custer Massacre," and demanded retribution for a savage act.[8]

The newspaper detailed that "[t]he men in the companies fell, with their officers behind them in their proper positions. General Custer, who was shot through the head and body, seemed to have been among the last to fall."[9] This was the genesis of the last stand myth.[10] With soldiers confused and scrambling, Custer's heroic stand never may have occurred. Some analysts later concluded that he was killed early in the battle and his body was pulled up the hill by his soldiers.[11] For certain, there was panic on the ridge. Years later, Sioux warriors who survived the battle provided mixed testimony as to the events: some said the soldiers gave a good fight, while others said they were easy targets.[12] In desperate fear, there were even soldiers who turned pistols on themselves.

The immediate accounts of the battle claimed that an overwhelming number of Indian warriors was the predominate reason for the tragic defeat.[13] Some versions tempered this with the observation that Generals Sherman and Sheridan, who now knew the magnitude of what had occurred in southern Montana, considered Custer rash and foolhardy to have initiated the attack.[14]

The *New York Herald* blamed both the government that provided for reservation Indians, while hostile bands were killing soldiers, and the bureau that was considered too humane. Nevertheless, the Herald story of July 7 quoted an unnamed officer, as saying: "Custer's glorious death and the valor of his men will become a legend in our history. . . . We all think, much as we lament Custer . . . that he sacrificed the Seventh Cavalry to ambition and wounded vanity."[15]

The *Chicago Tribune* of July 7 was harsher:

> *It is time to quit this Sunday-school policy, and let Sheridan recruit regiments of Western pioneer hunters and scouts, and exterminate every Indian who will not remain upon the reservations. The best use to make of an Indian who will not stay on a reservation is to kill him. It is time that the dawdling, maudlin peace-policy was abandoned. The Indian can never be subdued by Quakers, and it is certain that he will never be subdued by such madcap charges as that made by Custer.*[16]

The next month, from a Sunday pulpit in Chicago, the Reverend D. J. Burrell was more reflective:

Who shall be held responsible for this event so dark and sorrowful? The history of our dealings with these Indian tribes from the very beginning is a record of fraud, and perjury, and uninterrupted injustice. We have made treaties, binding ourselves to the most solemn promises in the name of God, intending at that very time to hold these treaties light as air whenever our convenience should require them to be broken.[17]

This was a distinct minority view.

Across the southeastern corner of Montana, hot currents ran over the land, sending thermals against the Big Horn Mountains; thunderheads climbed into the high sky. Lightning flashed; rumblings in angry clouds detonated. Hard rains pummeled the ground.

For weather and other reasons, the army troopers in the field were slow to pursue.[18] Terry and Crook finally acknowledged that there were a greater number of warriors in the unceded territory than they had been lead to believe. They looked for direction from General Philip Sheridan. The delay certainly indicated they were waiting for reinforcements and supplies.[19] July saw no engagements by the military. The Indians looked for sources of food, camping in familiar territory on the Rosebud and Tongue.[20] The logistics of holding large groups together was too difficult. The bands began to go their separate ways. Crazy Horse led a contingent toward the Black Hills.[21] Reservation Indians went back to their agencies.[22] By July 7, General Sherman had proclaimed the army's response: "I will take the campaign fully in hand, and will push it to a successful termination sending every man that can be spared."[23] To seek and capture the hostiles, General Sheridan called for forces from every army post between Canada and Texas.[24]

The military had not been universally endorsed in the Indian Wars. Indeed, settlers and railroad companies demanded the army's defense, but people in the urban areas of the northeast felt that there were other ways to deal with the Indians. And Congress had to manage budget constraints in a country still struggling to recover from the physical and economic costs of the Civil War.[25] The reporting of the Custer Massacre changed these perspectives and galvanized support for the Army of the West.[26]

The brash Custer was now a martyr,[27] and the country rallied to send men and war materiel into Yellowstone country. The enemy was collectively symbolized in the person of one man. Sitting Bull was the anti-hero—the commander and mastermind of the savage slaughter at the Little Big Horn. His name was now known everywhere.

George Armstrong Custer

LIBRARY OF CONGRESS (LC-USZ62-62749)

The publication *Harper's Weekly*, on July 29, 1876, carried a political cartoon showing a congressman and wild-looking Indian with a bloody war club and rifle standing before the legislative chambers of the House. The two men are shaking hands after agreeing on retrenchment. The specter of Custer reaches over the handshake and points to a posting at the doorway, reading, "A WHOLESALE SLAUGHTER BY THE SIOUX OF OUR SOLDIERS" and advising that the Indians' intent is to further reduce the ranks of the military.[28] Clearly, the ghosted image called for retaliation.

Come August, there would be unrelenting pursuit by the army. One particular officer, Colonel Nelson Miles, intended a more calculated approach than had Custer. He would have much more success. Dispatched from Fort Leavenworth, Kansas, he lead his forces toward the Yellowstone.[29]

James McLaughlin arrived at Devil's Lake on July 2, just one week after the 7th Cavalry's defeat at Little Big Horn.[30]

Within days of his arrival, rumor raced ahead of fact. One had some of the Little Big Horn hostiles on a fast ride to Fort Totten to seek armaments, notwithstanding the long distance from the scene of the battle and lack of any knowledge by the Lakota that there was a cache of guns and ammunition to be found. Another tale claimed there were agency Indians, also miles removed in the middle of Dakota Territory at Standing Rock, emboldened by the success of the Lakota and Cheyenne in eastern Montana, off reservation and heading north.[31] Never mind that orders had immediately gone out for occupation of Standing Rock and other strategic agencies to prevent such an occurrence.[32] Adding to the local paranoia, there were locals telling Devils Lake Indians that they may be attacked as white sympathizers.

The post commander advised that the new agent should maintain close contact with the military. While James McLaughlin knew how to coexist with army officers, he had a strong sense of self-reliance. McLaughlin, while not a military man, fell heir to the title of his predecessor as "Major." The title suited him. While usually affable, he required recognition as the man in charge. He was a bureau man, and the bureau managed agencies.

Nor was he easily rattled.[33] Roaming Indians did not attack their reservation brothers. His long acquaintance with these Indians and his unruffled manner quieted their fears. In fact, no hostiles appeared at Devils Lake.

The real concern was directed elsewhere.

At the beginning, the massing of troops produced nothing but long marches and discontented soldiers. The Sioux set fires to timberland and prairies to disrupt or decoy the military's chase and deny grass feed to cavalry horses.[34] There were times when the sundown sky was awash in a blood-orange haze and a pervasive smell of smoke hung in the air. The hunted left their pursuers a scorched earth.

In mid-August, the columns of Terry and Crook ran into each other somewhere in the middle of nowhere in Montana.[35] Crook had seasoned soldiers and Terry recent recruits.[36] It did not matter; both were ineffective. The Indians could not be found.[37] Newspaper correspondents expressed doubts for the success of the campaign. The two generals parted shortly thereafter near the northerly terminus of the Powder River, and their marches were hammered by rain . . . rain . . . and more rain.[38] Terry went north along the Yellowstone and Crook headed east into Dakota Territory, then southward toward the Black Hills.[39]

The administration sent support and absolute direction to end the Indian problem now.[40] The commander of the army, William Sherman, pressed with new urgency his earlier position that all Indians belonged on a reservation. To implement that goal, General Sheridan instructed his field commanders to follow a twin strategy: one, pursue and find Indians in the field; two, occupy the agencies and confiscate horses and weapons to prevent aid from reservation Indians.[41] The overall order was "dismount and disarm" the Sioux.[42] There was no distinction to be made between hunters-providers and warriors; and reservation Indians were potential collaborators. Whatever remained of the horse culture of the Plains was swept from the lives of the so-called friendlies. The army occupied Standing Rock and Cheyenne Agencies and took control from the civilian agents in October.[43]

Any possible assistance from agency Indians to comrades in the field was cut off.[44] Some reservation Sioux were recruited as scouts against their own.[45] Others were enlisted to encourage any hostiles that could be found to surrender; even Red Cloud lent his assistance to this outreach.[46] If the various troop movements could not immediately locate the hostiles, they would disrupt hunting grounds, spooking and scattering game. Without food, the Indians in time would be flushed from hiding. In summer 1877, new forts were established in the unceded area, sustained by a constant flow of ordinance and supplies from steamships on the Missouri and Yellowstone.[47]

The Yellowstone country was dense with blue coats.

CHAPTER NINE

In Search of Indians

September 1876

Manpower and firepower belonged to the white man. No corner of the northern Plains would be overlooked. The new man was armed and angry and coming harder.

Summer receded into fall; Sitting Bull realized the Indians' success at Little Big Horn did not dissuade the army aggression. With the risk that the army would not go away, he considered two options in council with other chiefs. He could go south into Mexico or north into Canada.[1] Both countries provided borders that the Lakota believed were hard lines that the U.S. military would not cross. The land across the border in central Canada was familiar to the Sioux. They had hunted there. Their ancestors had fought for the British in the War of 1812. They had longtime contacts with traders in the area. Moreover, the prairie land extended north and there were buffalo feeding grounds above the border. Finally, the Canadian government was not at war with Indians. Although Mexico also proffered another political power outside the United States of America's control, it was not well-known territory.

Many of the Lakota elders counseled going north; the chief's mother, Her Holy Door, also urged her son to take this path.[2] Some of those who had dispersed from the great gathering had already made their way to Canada. But Crazy Horse refused to go north.[3] Sitting Bull for once was not decisive. He vacillated, holding to the hope that the roaming bands could exhaust the military. He did not intend to be run out of Lakota land. Of course, he did not a have the benefit of reading what communiqués from Washington's generals and the press had to say. Reluctance to leave home ground was soon confronted by hard reality.

Well into late August, persistent rain drummed the earth in the path of soldiers crossing the headwaters of the Heart, Cannonball, and Grand in western Dakota Territory.[4] Crook ordered his troops to leave their tents behind, each man permitted to carry only a poncho and blanket.[5] The intent was to move more quickly. The opposite occurred. They continued to march. The weather remained wet. Downpours mired down the men and their horses. Mud was everywhere.[6] Tired and overburdened horses sunk into ground that had turned to gumbo; when the animals could not be removed, they were shot.[7] Soldiers were forever scrapping muck from their boots. Clothing was saturated. Sleeping, cold and damp, sitting or curled up, was sporadic. Esprit de corps matched the dismal weather.

John Finerty of the Chicago Times, who was traveling with the Crook forces, did not think much of the military's effort; he sent a letter report, dated August 28, published in his newspaper nearly a month later on September 22:

> *Incertitude is the order of the day at present. Many camp followers, including some of the correspondents, are leaving the expedition; I have not yet made up my mind what is best for me to do. I hate to leave at this stage of the futile campaign, and yet by remaining I shall see very little else than mud, misery, and rough country. One good battle and a decent wind-up to this wretched business would just suit me now. But I fear very much that the last shot of this section of the campaign has been fired.[8]*

The newsman thought the Lakota had the upper hand. Nonetheless, General Crook was not about to call a halt.

The scattering of those who came together on the Little Big Horn may have made the individual groups difficult to find,[9] but it also weakened their ability to counter when they were eventually located by the army.[10] Finerty attributed the getaway to the cleverness of Sitting Bull: "Like a greedy gambler, he won a large stake and then, when the chances were almost equalized, he draws out and leaves us in the lurch."[11] From

Sitting Bull's standpoint logistics and the general independency of bands prevented again drawing together the Lakota and Cheyenne for a major battle.

After days of slogging south with food rations exhausted and subsistence dependent on horse and mule meat,[12] Crook's troops cried for relief. They questioned the ongoing campaign. "What is the old man thinking? There are no Indians in this muddy hell." "This is a goddamned horsemeat march."[13] Finally, an Indian village above the Black Hills in an area called Slim Buttes was stumbled upon. It was an Oglala camp under Chief Iron Shield (sometimes known as American Horse).[14] In a cold rain on September 9, Captain Anson Mills directed an assault.[15] Although most escaped, Iron Shield was mortally wounded, his gut ripped open by buckshot. He emerged from a cave where he had taken refuge to surrender, holding his intestines. His wife wrapped him in her shawl, and he sat down to let his life go.[16] The hungry soldiers looted the abandoned camp in search of dried meat and other provisions, then burned the lodges (Mills thereafter would be called "Burns Lodges"[17] by the Sioux). Ironically, the stores of dried meat found in camp were the product of butchered Indian ponies;[18] the Indians on the run were also short on fresh provisions. Over three hundred horses were taken by the army to replenish mounts that either had worn out or died during the unforgiving drive.[19]

Couriers ran from the attack to nearby camps of Crazy Horse[20] and others. The camps mounted up in response to their comrades. Warned of retaliation from these allies, the military reformed ranks and laid down rifle fire against advancing warriors. The Sioux quit the fight.[21] Thereafter, General Crook dispatched a released captive to find Sitting Bull with a message; the communication plainly declared that the army would not go away until the last hostile was killed or taken prisoner. "Surrender was a better alternative to exposing woman and children to accidents."[22] (A pointed choice of words for an army leader who always asserted U.S. troops did not attack woman and children.) When Sitting Bull and his warriors later came upon the burnt remains of the village, he reflected: "What have we done that the white people want us to stop? We have been running up and down this country, but they follow us from one place to another."[23] Sitting Bull could not avoid the chase.

The general declared a victory; the army finally had struck back. Barely. Some of the groups of Indians attacked had been on their way to surrender at the nearest agency; and the troops were driven by the need to find a new a source of provisions. It was an untidy and limited first success.[24] But it provided a strong lift to the military morale. If Crook's troops were experiencing difficulties in tracking, the Indians had their own problems: they were without a source of supplies, had families to feed, and were on the run.

With the hostiles in retreat and the military occupying the agencies, the government got on with unfinished business—taking dominion of the Black Hills. While the army's Yellowstone campaign chased Indians, Congress initiated its own action. It had tired of the expense of care and feeding of reservation loafers. The 1868 treaty intended Indians to become self-supporting farmers. They had not done so and were not likely to. If Congress was to continue to make appropriations it was entitled to something tangible in return. In late summer, another commission from Washington brought pressure on agency Indians to consent to the transfer of the Black Hills. The commission was headed by George W. Manypenny, a seasoned negotiator of Indian Treaties and former Commissioner of Indian Affairs.[25] The directive was to acquire all rights to the Black Hills as well as to the Powder River country. The United States already had de facto control of the North Platte. As usual, the commission came with the agreement of the treaty already written. It also carried the same dispatch as the Allison Commission of 1875: terms were to be dictated not negotiated. The reservation Indians were advised that to be protected from being overrun by miners and settlers, the hills must be in the hands of United States.[26] The government would not devote resources to safeguard the Sioux in the land that was guaranteed to them. This time, to make certain there was no misunderstanding, an ultimatum was given—"sign or starve."[27] Under the terms of the 1868 Treaty, it was contended that time had expired on the government's honorable promise to make provision for these people, although they had not achieved the self-sufficiency anticipated under agency management. The bureau, by mistake or compassion, continued to send support. Now, Congress pointedly voted to cut off appropriations for rations to the agency Sioux.[28] The tribute of land was demanded for full stomachs. The immediacy of martial presence added exigency. Put more plainly, it was government extortion.

Red Cloud and other reservation Indians succumbed within hardly more than a month of discussion and signed away the lands. The commission deemed it unnecessary to meet the requirement of the Laramie Treaty of 1868 that there be consent to any cession of the Great Sioux Reservation by at least three-fourths of all adult male Indians occupying or interested in the land. Congress ratified the contract of amendment with less than 10 percent of the adult Sioux male population touching pen to paper. Of course, the hostiles were excluded from this agreement; and many of those on the reservation who did sign on were bought with bribes and whiskey. By the end of October, Manypenny and his fellow commissioners had what they came for. In February 1877, Congress ratified the revision of the treaty. There no longer could be any question that what Red Cloud had won in Powder River War was lost in provisions written into the treaty concluding that war.

The new western boundary of the Great Sioux Reservation was moved eastward about 60 miles to the 103rd meridian of longitude. From where the meridian touched the northern border of Nebraska, it traced due north until it met the Cheyenne River, where it followed the course of the river around the Black Hills. The northerly boundary was extended somewhat to the Cannonball River, which came by its name from sandy concretions found there and described by Captain William Clark as large cannon balls. The Sioux were given 900,000 acres to the north and lost 7.3 million acres to the west.[29] Thus, the Lakota were stripped of their sacred landscape; they signed under coercion what they would not agree to sell for money.[30]

As soon as the signatures were secured, the army seized the horses belong to the Red Cloud and Red Leaf bands.[31] They were treated no better than what took place at Standing Rock and Cheyenne Agencies, the home of hostile sympathizers. Red Cloud stiffened at the occupation of his agency; he and some followers pulled out. In October, he was arrested and made to walk back 40 miles to Camp Robinson, Nebraska.[32] Then, he was deposed as head agency chief and replaced by Spotted Tail of the Brules.[33] These were betrayals that would long simmer. But when word reached Sitting Bull of what had happened, he castigated his former allies, Red Cloud and Spotted Tail, as "rascals" who had sold out their people.[34]

To Sitting Bull, the reservation Indians had traded away their tribal inheritance. It was the inevitable result of submission to reservation life. His warriors continued their defiance, harassing smaller troop movements and supply lines with sudden strikes and just as quick disappearances. These raids produced only a few ponies and provisions to sustain his people in flight. Young militants demanded more formidable retaliation. Again, Cheyenne and Sioux at the agencies were recruited to join the military effort against their own people.[35] The government took all available means to bring in the roaming bands.

Sitting Bull returned to the Rosebud and the Tongue, west of the Powder.[36] He desired to stay in the northern Plains, but to do so meant repeated relocations. On one move in mid-September, his forward riders crested a knoll on their way toward a water impoundment. At the foot of the incline below laid carcasses of 12 buffalo cows and calves, ravaged by wolves and carrion scavengers. Three more decomposing bodies of buffalo were in the mud of a wallow. There were spent cartridge casings in the grass on the knoll. Soldiers had passed through, shooting and leaving the carcasses maybe four to five days earlier. Constant hounding was as important to the army as combat.

But the Lakota knew too how to harass. In mid-October, an army supply train was sighted going north along the Tongue River toward a new cantonment established by Colonel Nelson Miles. (By the end of summer, low waters on the upper Yellowstone prevented steamboat passage to serve military outposts.[37]) That night, when the men manning the supply wagons camped, raiders swooped near to set fires and shout yelps, stampeding 47 mules from the army's corral.[38] The following day, the Sioux intercepted the wagons, shooting some mules in their traces. Guerrilla tactics designed to discourage the army but not kill men. The damaged wagon train doubled back to where it had come. The civilian teamsters refused a second trip and were replaced by military personnel with an escort of two hundred soldiers, headed by Lieutenant Colonel E. S. Otis.[39] The train drew another attack, but this time the Sioux were held at bay by troopers firing long-distance rifles. White Bull, a nephew of the chief, was hit in the left arm in an attempted charge.[40] Next morning, one of Sitting Bull's men staked a message from the chief a mile or so ahead of the path of the ongoing train.

> *I want to know what you are doing on this road. You scare all the buffalo away. I want to hunt in this place. I want you to turn back from here. If you don't I will fight you again. I want you to leave what you have got here and turn back from here.*[41]

Stealing a line he had heard from American negotiators, Sitting Bull signed the note with the closing: "I am your friend." A postscript asked for rations and powder.[42] Was this man deranged? Otis was quick to reply, sending a scout to tell any Lakota in the way that the supply train would proceed and, if the Indians wanted to fight, he would accommodate them.[43] (Otis's commanding officer, Colonel Miles, when he later heard of the communication staked to the ground, thought the words "your friend" most curious in the context of what the colonel viewed as war. Was the note authentic or an attempt at black humor by some army scout?[44])

That same day, two Indians from Standing Rock visited Sitting Bull's camp under a white flag, carrying an Indian Bureau request to quit running.[45] Other advisors pressed Sitting Bull to parley with Otis. At least it would give him the opportunity to assess the strength of his pursuers. He consented to the reservation emissaries riding back to the soldiers to offer a meeting on the open prairie. Otis agreed to talk, but only in his camp.[46] For this conference the chief hedged, sending others on his behalf with Kills Enemy passing himself off as Sitting Bull.[47] The Indian delegation claimed they were tired of war and asked the army to show goodwill by providing food and ammunition. Otis at first refused, saying he was not there to make peace. The Lakota harangued that he and his men did not belong in this territory. Otis eventually dropped packets of bacon and hard bread on the ground alongside his supply train and moved on.[48] The gift of food ended the confrontation. But Colonel Miles, awaiting the delayed supply train, put his regiment in the field. A few days later, Sioux scouts caught sight of infantry troops under Miles, coming toward Cedar

General Nelson A. Miles

Creek, on the divide between the Yellowstone and Missouri Rivers.[49] White dustings were on the mountain peaks, and a chill clutched the river's course. (The Indians called Miles "Bear Coat" because he wrapped his uniform with a great fur coat for the winter campaign.[50]) A flag of truce again was shown by two lead Indians and a parley arranged.[51] Knowing his distance from reinforcements, Miles agreed to talk. He would take firsthand measure of Sitting Bull and how many warriors were with him. While the chief did not want a fight here, he was not about to accept the army on Indian land.

The two men met on open ground, each with a main attendant and five supporters.[52] No one was to be armed, but Miles later admitted that he and his people carried revolvers under their coats.[53] Further back clustered the troops and warriors for each side. The council would extend over two days; but Miles had one goal—Sitting Bull must surrender. With Sitting Bull was a half-breed named Johnny Brughiere, whom the chief had befriended when the man came into camp unannounced. Others had misgivings about including Brughiere; the man was on the run from a murder charge arising out of a drunken brawl at an Indian Agency.[54] Nonetheless, he was knowledgeable in English and Lakota, previously having served as an interpreter at Standing Rock Agency for the Hunkpapa.[55] Miles immediately sought the upper hand, telling Sitting Bull that sources informed him not only where the Indians were, but where they were going. The chief was not impressed. He calmly demanded the soldiers leave this land. But behind the facade Sitting Bull was irate, suspecting treachery by agency Indians who traded information to Miles for favors.

Sitting Bull met the accusation of his warriors thieving mules from freighters with the rejoinder that soldiers had stolen ponies from his people.[56] The colonel accused Sitting Bull of always being against the white man. Sitting Bull replied: "No. I never thought that I was against the white man, but I admit I am not for him."

"You are against white people, ready to fight white people, and you like to fight all the time."

"I never had any such idea."[57]

The men sparred—Miles intent on making Sitting Bull the aggressor and the chief maintaining that his people were only defending what was theirs. At times, the adversaries appeared to find a measure of self-satisfaction in the verbal exchange. The real purpose was to assess an adversary, and each held his own in the exchange.

"Then why is that everybody keeps saying you are so strong against the whites?"

"They are all wrong. I have always been glad to see white men. I like to be friendly. I don't want to fight, if I don't have to."

"All the same, that is what I've heard. They say you are well known to be hostile to the white man."

"That's all wrong. All I am looking out for is to see how and where I can find more meat for my people, more game animals for my people, and to find what God has given me to eat."

"Nevertheless, that is what they are saying about you all the time."[58]

Sitting Bull countered that "[e]very time the army came into Indian country, it was only to fight, and that is why you are now here."[59]

Miles tried another approach. In more compromising tone, he promised a reservation anywhere south of the Missouri, something he had no authority to deliver. The new course of conversation lessened some of the tension. Pushing the proposal of living at an agency, Colonel Miles went so far to tell Sitting Bull could have an agency of his own.[60] Sitting Bull was not swayed. When asked why he would not accept reservation life, the response was hard line:

Because I am a red man and not an agency beggar. The blue coats drove us west of the Missouri, they robbed us of the Black Hills, they have forced us to take this land from the Crows, but we wish to live at peace. You have no right to come here. You must withdraw all your troops and take all settlers with you. . . . I have not declared war against Washington, but I will fight when you push me to the wall. I do not like strife. It is not pleasant to be always fleeing before your guns. This western world is wide; it is lonely of human life. Why do you not leave it to us? All my days I have lived far from your people. All that I got from you I have paid for. My band owes you nothing.[61]

He was bargaining on reputation. He wanted the Yellowstone country free of soldiers and the settlers who were certain to come after them. The Indians should be free to follow the buffalo and continue to trade.[62] He still did not seem to comprehend the end game of the pursuit.

At a stalemate, Sitting Bull advised that he would continue his hunt. He pushed the matter further, saying he wanted to live in the Black Hills. Then he added a strange twist, suggesting Bear Coat join him on the hunt,[63] as though a Lakota hunting experience would make for better relations. Having offered what he felt was a gesture of friendship, the chief pressed his assumed advantage with a request for food and ammunition from the military that was pursuing him. Miles was amused and put off at the same time. As the day closed, both sides agreed to meet the next day. But suspicions of each other remained. When some soldiers were spotted nearby the next morning, the Lakota women began to strike camp.[64]

On the second day, representatives of the Miniconjou and Sans Arc, who had been debating ongoing resistance in their own council, joined Sitting Bull in the meeting. Sensing backsliding within the ranks, the chief felt undercut and lost sharpness in the ensuing discussions.[65] He sometimes fumbled for words and other times just sat back letting others carry the discussion. But when his nephew, who had been watching the rear guard, came up and whispered that Miles's soldiers were readying for an engagement, Sitting Bull scolded the commander. "All that you have said is lies."[66] Standing on Lakota principle, he declared: "The Great Spirit made me an Indian, and not an agency Indian. I have no intention of living on a reservation."[67] Both men stiffened; any détente dissolved. Sitting Bull called the parley to an end and got up and signaled his people to walk back to camp. Bear Coat struck out to join his waiting troops.

But not before Miles issued a warning to the backsides of Indians that "[u]nless you accept the terms of our Government and laws, as all other Indians had done, you will be pursued until driven out of the country or until you succeed in driving the troops out. Return to camp, but in fifteen minutes, if you do not accept the terms offered, my troops will open fire."[68] It is not clear whether the Indians heard the ultimatum or understood its immediacy. (Fifteen minutes was not a concept known to them.[69]) However, the Indian women who had started to pull down tipis at the end of the prior day had the camp ready to move out.

Neither side was ready for all-out confrontation.

Yet, Miles was determined to show the army's might. Upon the expiration of the allotted time, he ordered his men to advance on the Sioux camp a few miles distant.[70] With the first shots fired, White Bull immediately sought to meet the attack; Sitting Bull held him back.[71] An exchange of gunshots at long range allowed the families to withdraw. A grass fire was started between the retreating camp and the oncoming soldiers;[72] then the warriors gathered behind the withdrawal of their families to provide cover. The army's foot soldiers could do nothing more than keep the Indians moving, and the chase extended over 40 miles.[73] There would be no long-term winter camp.

The colonel wrote in his recollections published in 1896 an assessment of his adversary from this discussion at Cedar Creek:

On first meeting Sitting Bull I naturally studied his appearance and character. He was a strong, hardy, sturdy looking man of about five feet eleven inches in height [more probably he was shy of 5 feet 10 inches], well built, with strongly-marked features, high cheek bones, prominent nose, straight, thin lips, and strong under jaw, indicating determination and force. He had a wide, large, well-developed head and low forehead. He was a man of few words and cautious in his

*expressions, evidently thinking twice before speaking. He was very
deliberate in his movements and somewhat reserved in his manner. At
first he was courteous, but evidently void of any genuine respect for the
white race. Although the feeling was disguised, his manner indicated
his animosity toward those whom he had to meet. During the conversation his manner was civil and to some extent one of calm repose.
He might have been mistaken for a mild, plain-spoken, inoffensive
man until I developed the other side of his nature. In the course of the
conversation he asked me what I came into that country for with that
large body of soldiers. I informed him that I came out after him and
his people.*[74]

More contemporaneously, in a letter to his wife after the encounter, Miles
wrote that Sitting Bull was a man of great influence and a thinking person. "I think he feels that his strength is somewhat exhausted and he
appeared much depressed, suffering from nervous excitement and loss of
power."[75] Now it was Miles who did not fully comprehend the will of his
opponent.

Sitting Bull directed his followers south below the Yellowstone,
between the Little Big Horn and the Powder, in search of buffalo; then
he turned north.[76] His band entered the land of the Crow and found a
freshly killed buffalo. Examining it, they discovered its meat had been
injected with poison. (It was a practice of what were termed "wolfers"—
hide hunters—to slay a buffalo and lace it with strychnine, which in turn
would be ingested by wolves that came to prey.[77] Then the wolfers would
come back to harvest pelts from the dead wolves.) The poisoned buffalo
carcass served as a harbinger of the difficulty of finding game.

The Miniconjou and Sans Arc now openly spoke their disagreement
with Sitting Bull's intransigence and considered surrender as the only
course. He admonished them:

*Are we coyotes? Shall we slink into a hole and whine? You have eaten
too much white man's bread. It has taken the heart out of you. Do you
wish to be the sport of our enemies? Then go back to the agencies and
grow fat on the scrap they will throw you.*[78]

They could not be dissuaded. Some broke away and sought further dialogue with Miles.[79] In quick time, nearly all gave into the colonel and were sent to the Cheyenne River Agency.[80] White Bull, a Miniconjou, also had dissented from his uncle but initially held back from capitulating. Then, fearing relatives placed on a steamer were in danger if other nearby Miniconjou did not surrender, White Bull brought his family band to the Cheyenne Agency.[81]

Continual running exacted its toll. Unity was unravelling. Miles had succeeded in drawing numbers from Sitting Bull's followers. For the moment, he would accept defections. The military had one purpose and the means to succeed.[82] The Sioux warriors were not alone in the field; the bands consisted of families with children and the elderly. They had to live off the land. Without supply lines, their resources dwindled each day. The army received continual supplies along the Missouri and Yellowstone Rivers by steamboat, offloaded to pack trains for transport to forts and outposts.

With the Lakota forced further north, Sitting Bull was talked into sending an exploratory party to Canada as a potential sanctuary. Sometime in November, about a dozen Lakota traveled to Wood Mountain, where they came upon a trading store. The proprietor was a rugged and imperturbable trader of Canadian-French descent named Jean Louis Legare. He caught sight of the Indians approaching but remained inside the store. The leader, Little Knife, rode up on his horse and peered through a window of the building, watching the goings on within. In a short while he entered the store, leaving the door open but saying nothing, and sat on the floor. Then others entered one after another. Legare appeared to look on this as an ordinary occurrence, only arching an eyebrow in the visitors' direction. Perhaps two hours later, the visitors finally bestirred themselves to greet storekeeper and his assistant.[83] One said that they came because they cannot sleep in peace in their homeland.[84] Jean Louis had been hired by a half-breed—Antoine Quellette, to establish a trading business in southern Saskatchewan. Working with mixed-bloods of Canadian Indian and French parentage allowed him an understanding of these Lakota travelers. Rather than confrontation, he offered provisions.[85]

Shortly thereafter, Little Knife's contingent was met by a patrol directed by Inspector James Walsh of the North-West Mounted Police.[86]

Walsh well knew of the Custer Massacre and the press accounts attributing it to Sitting Bull. In fact, by the winter of 1876, newspaper reporters had written much about the Lakota Chief, with scant hard facts. His ability to elude the military's search added to the public's interest in the fugitive Indian chief. He was taking on the mantle of legend. The inspector commanded an outpost in the Cypress Hills area, about 180 miles west of Wood Mountain, in southern Saskatchewan Territory. Walsh immediately admonished the Sioux party that Canada was not a staging ground for raids to the south. He knew of Colonel Miles's posturing to cross the border to hunt down any raiders; he also understood that his northern government would not accept a foreign power on its soil.[87] If the Sioux wanted sanctuary, there were rules to obey. A few determined to stay: and a report was sent to Sitting Bull that the road was open to Canada. Others would follow later. Sitting Bull remained cautious, thinking that white people were all alike. Yet he did not hold back those who wanted to go.

On the south side of the international border, in late November, one of Crook's commanders—Lieutenant Colonel Ranald Mackenzie—led a charge on the Cheyenne camp of Dull Knife and Little Wolf on the Powder River at Red Fork.[88] The Indians scattered upon the attack; but 40 warriors were killed. Lodges were burned, food supplies destroyed, ammunition lost, and seven hundred horses taken. The Cheyenne would not recover from these losses. In weather ranging to 30 below zero, they tramped forward in search of Crazy Horse's camp. It was clear that parley was no longer the priority of the military.

The travails of Sitting Bull's band continued. Colonel Miles was intent on intercepting Sitting Bull. He kept his troops in the field in the below-freezing winter.[89] Johnny Brughiere, whom Sitting Bull had taken in months earlier, turned coat by selling his services to Miles. In exchange for the colonel's promise to assist him in beating his pending murder charge, he agreed in December to help get Sitting Bull to surrender.[90] Brughiere told Lieutenant Frank Baldwin, one of the colonel's officers, where he could find Sitting Bull's camp in the Missouri bottoms near the entry of the Milk River to the bigger river in upper northeast Montana. It was just days before that he had been in Sitting Bull's camp. Baldwin almost succeeded in locating Sitting Bull on the morning of December 7, but passed by the camp without seeing it, as snows blustered into white-out conditions.[91] Later in the day, the storm subsided and the overlooked camp broke. The Lakota band crossed the frozen river, taking up hiding just above the river. Toward evening an advance military party crossed the iced-over waters; the Indians fired on the troops, pushing them back. Long-range rifle shots were exchanged until renewed snows lashed at both sides. At the onset of darkness, Baldwin put his command on a forced march back to Fort Peck. Sitting Bull went north. Trading first with the Slotas to secure more ammunition and then traversing southeast, he sought to join his band with that of Crazy Horse. By this time, Baldwin had regrouped at Fort Peck and was again out on the trail. On December 16, Sitting Bull's camp was found.[92] When the Sioux rose up to confront the advancing soldiers, Baldwin fired a howitzer he had hauled on the march.[93] The Lakota had no effective response. The Indians immediately withdrew from the fight, gathering their families in retreat. Sitting Bull managed to get his people out of the way and saved the horse herd but lost vital lodges, dried meat, and robes.[94] Bear Coat's forces kept coming.[95]

That winter held no forgiveness. The Lakota only wanted to tie down their tipis along wooded streams as they always had in winter, slanted away from the winds with backsides shouldered to slip the brunt of the season's storms. Instead, there was constant movement. They could not set up camps. There was no mending of clothing and tipis. Food stocks were low. The buffalo were hard to find. There was no respite. Sitting Bull traveled toward the Big Horns looking for Crazy Horse.

Crazy Horse had his own run-in with Miles in January. Dull Knife's Northern Cheyenne had joined Crazy Horse in early December. Winter had come early, and game was scarce. Stores of meat were exhausted, and the Indians were living off of horse flesh of dying ponies.[96] Consideration of surrender was pressed upon Crazy Horse by his cohorts. They convinced him to send a delegation to discuss peace. As these men approached the cantonment at the Tongue River, Crow scouts disregarded the flag of truce and killed five of them.[97] Crazy Horse was outraged, and any talk of peace was now out of the question. Instead, there was a retaliatory strike on government mail carriers. A few days later, the Oglalas stole 250 head of cattle before departing from the area.

In late December, Miles led a column southwest in subzero temperatures with frequent river crossings in search of Crazy Horse. He was so intent on taking out Crazy Horse that he pressed his command through the bitter cold.[98] Iced-over rivers did not always hold; and men, horses and wagons dropped into the freezing waters. Miles ordered fires built wherever a river was to be crossed to provide heat to any man who fell into the water.[99] Crazy Horse, for his part, invited the search by having decoy parties engage in small skirmishes to be sure the army pressed forward. On January 8, 1877, Crazy Horse was ready to spring his attack. Miles's troops had been discovered in bivouac on a flat portion of ground where Battle Butte Creek flowed into the Tongue in the Wolf Mountains. However, army scouts gave warning of the approaching Indians, and soldiers rushed to set up a defensive perimeter as warriors dismounted and established their own firing lines.[100] The battle was fought on the ground and continued over several hours.[101] Not making the mistake of Custer, Miles had brought heavy guns.[102] He ordered his field artillery up just prior to yet another Montana blizzard blowing onto the battlefield. Enveloped by swirling snow, the Indians retreated as shells exploded in their midst.[103] Although the battle did not result in heavy losses, it underscored the army's ability to carry the fight wherever it chose during the winter months.[104]

The roaming bands continued to lose numbers. Black Moon took his people north in December;[105] and Four Horns would add more than 50 lodges by the following March.[106] Others left to sneak into agencies, hoping to be absorbed as reservation Indians, to wangle food and shelter. Some just gave up straightaway.

Crazy Horse, as elusive as ever, brought his people to the Little Powder, but he too felt the double bind of hounding pressure of the military and the difficulty of feeding his followers. Sitting Bull and Crazy Horse met for the last time on January 15 where the Tongue River dropped out the mountains at Prairie Dog Creek near the southern edge of Montana.[107] Within a week, the bands separated.[108] Sitting Bull was inclined to go to Canada and let Crazy Horse hold the northern hunting grounds. The split would weaken both as Crazy House and his followers stood alone in the homeland.[109]

By May 1877, the militant Crazy Horse could run no more; he delivered eight hundred of his people to Camp Robinson.[110] Red Cloud, either still willing to trust the government or, more likely, to assure the safety of an old ally, acted as a go-between to facilitate the submission. He rode into the fort alongside the warrior chief and presented Crazy Horse to General Crook.[111] Crazy Horse now was under government eyes, but he still walked his own path.

Upset about the army's recruitment of former Sioux warriors to fight the Nez Perce in the north, Crazy Horse openly talked of leaving the agency.[112] He chaffed under reservation rule; he gave contradictory signals of pulling out and enduring the new way. Crook promised a northern reservation, but Washington had no intention of creating a home for Crazy Horse in his old haunts.[113] Frequently sullen, Crazy Horse rode alone into the hills and would be gone for days. Former supporters withdrew; even an old friend—Little Big Man—distanced himself.[114] Spies reported his behavior as a malcontent, and his own people were sent to bring him to Camp Robinson for a parley. When he saw that he was being escorted to a guard house, he pulled away. Little Big Man, grabbed him by the arms (Little Big Man later explained that he was trying to quell a dangerous situation). Crazy Horse drew a knife and slashed the arm of Little Big Man in an attempt to break his grip. Other reservation hands reached out and held him fast while a soldier ran a rifle bayonet through his back. The blade tore into vital organs; his body collapsed.[115] Someone wrapped him in a blanket. Crazy Horse was taken to the post surgeon's office and laid on the floor. Post Surgeon Valentine McGillycuddy eased the pain with shots of morphine.[116] On September 5, the Lakota lost their strongest war chief.[117]

When Sitting Bull heard this, he was stunned. He grieved that his closest comrade in arms had been forced onto the reservation only to be killed at the hands of former allies. The reservation was no place for an Indian.

CHAPTER TEN

Northern Sanctuary

1877

Desperate to avoid capture, Sitting Bull finally determined to go north.[1] He led an inconsequential raid on a camp of white men along the Milk River, driving off their horses.[2] Then he left the Sioux homeland, crossing into the Dominion of Canada during the first week of May 1877.[3] There was no thought of possible return.

The open grasslands above the cairn stacks marking the border were rimmed on the northwest by Cypress Hills arcing eastward and Wood Mountain 100 miles to the east. Rivers and streams from this plain flow south to the United States. The feel of the terrain was familiar to the Sioux. The Lakota had escaped enemies before. They believed they were beyond the reach of the U.S. Army. This was the Queen of England's country. And they expected buffalo on the Canadian prairie to sustain them.

It was not a stealth relocation. Canadian newspapers played up the story of Sitting Bull guiding an army of warriors into Canada.[4] Predictably settlements on the Saskatchewan Plains felt threatened.[5] A dangerous situation was in the making; and the Mounted Police were tasked to maintain the peace. Moreover, there was political sensitivity in Canada's ministry about how to deal with American Indians on Canadian soil.

One hundred thirty-five lodges set up near Pinto Horse Butte[6] in the western Wood Mountain area, about 30 miles above the line separating the British Dominion from the territory of the United States. For the Sioux this border was known as the Medicine Line,[7] with the faith that it would hold back the blue coats. Canada was sanctuary. At the moment,

Commander Sherman was satisfied to have the hostiles run out of the country, and orders went out to Miles not to cross the border. With Sitting Bull in Canada and Crazy Horse having surrendered to reservation life, General Phil Sheridan sent a report to the Secretary of War in July 1877 that the Sioux war problem was solved.[8]

Facing the prospect of relocation from the Red Cloud Agency to a reservation on the Missouri in the fall, some of Crazy Horse's former band deserted and came north.[9] It was estimated that there were five thousand American Indians who found asylum in Grandmother Queen Victoria's land.[10] Lakota tipi abodes were tied down on the southern plains of Canada. Although their movements were limited, they still held onto traditional life, while the two governments postured and talked. The best alternative for the United States was to have Canada make the Lakota its own by providing a reservation; the second was to send the refugees back.[11] The Canadian government would not do the first; and return was up for discussion. Yet, Sitting Bull was determined to reestablish the Lakota people in the North Country.[12]

The general populace of the Territory worried that Sitting Bull would stir up Canada's own native peoples; while the Canadian tribes were alarmed about the impact of the newcomers on their lives.[13] Sitting Bull, for his part, extended himself to the northern tribes, assuring their chiefs that the Lakota wanted only refuge and there would be no problem from his people.[14] The home tribes remained wary; it was not the reputation of the Sioux to move into new terrain seeking peace. The chief well understood that his band had to get along in order to stay.

The border may have been a hard line to the military but not to others. Several U.S. newspaper correspondents were able to reach Sitting Bull for interviews.[15] As a renegade in exile, the chief drew increased interest from the press. Other emissaries were dispatched to his camp in attempts to negotiate his return. He was in contact with more white men than at any time before. He carefully took their measure. All the while, he knew he was the Indian of interest to both Canada and the United States; and he thought he could play Canada against the United States.

Almost immediately, the federal government had the need for its own eyes and ears on the scene. A Catholic priest, Martin Marty, and two other Americans, a scout for Colonel Miles and a translator,[16] were the first to seek out Sitting Bull in late May.[17] The presence of the Miles scout did not invite dialogue. After an initial refusal to meet with the visitors, the chief consented out of courtesy to the host government. The Mounties exacted a promise that Sitting Bull would not harm the American emissaries.[18] The chief rightly assumed the purpose of the meeting was to talk him into going back to the United States. He would have none of it and preempted the discussion, invoking his usual grievances against the Americans. He told Father Marty that he listened to his to his own god, Wakan Tanka, who had directed him north.[19] Sitting Bull made it clear:

> *What should I return for? To have my horses and arms taken away? What have the Americans to give me? They have no land. Once I was rich, plenty of money, but the Americans stole it all in the Black Hills. I have come to remain with the Grandmother's children.*[20]

The first official overture from the United States had failed.

At the same time, Canada struggled to establish its political position. It could not tolerate an incident on its soil. Commissioner James Macleod of the Mounted Police made recommendations on May 30, 1877, for dealing with the Sioux refugees in a formal letter to the Canadian prime minister:

> *I would respectfully suggest that communications be opened with the United States Government to ascertain upon what terms they would receive them back, and I fancy they would be only too glad to have them return, as their presence—so near the boundary—cannot but be a source of continual anxiety and trouble, and it would be impossible for the police to keep them in check over such an extended frontier; that the Indians be then told of the terms of the United States Government; that they cannot be recognized as British Indians; that no reserves will be set apart for them, and no provisions made for their maintenance by our Government; that by remaining on our side they will forfeit any claim they have on the United States, and that after a few years their only source of support—the buffalo—will have failed and they will find themselves in a much worse position than they are at present.*[21]

While Canada took issue with the United States on other matters affecting international relations,[22] the government in Ottawa was committed to find a way to peacefully return Sitting Bull to the United States.[23] Canada may have questioned how the United States handled its Indians, but it could not afford the burden of maintaining the Sioux. It was buying time for a diplomatic solution that produced some concessions to Canada. Nor did it want to use military action that could spark its own Indian war.

Ahead were four years in exile, and each succeeding year found the Lakota more distressed.

Although the Queen's government allowed the Sioux to hunt and trade for provisions, it firmly refused to establish a reservation or authorize a government ration program.[24] For the first year, there seemed to be plenty of buffalo across the Saskatchewan grasslands between Cypress Hills and Wood Mountain. But the new arrivals were competing for the same food sources as Canadian tribes. In fact, the northern government would soon give approval for its own tribes' free movement across the international boundary in search of buffalo.[25] If the Lakota could come north, the Cree could go south. The buffalo were overhunted.

Despite the government's constrained approach, Sitting Bull made two strong friends in Canada: one a military man and the other a frontier trader. Each understood the plight of the Lakota and was supportive. The official stance of no rations was often ignored by the Mounties under James Walsh, who witnessed firsthand the harsh effects of food shortages on these people.[26] Additionally, Jean Louis Legare, the storekeeper and Metis dealer, extended provisions when the Sioux had nothing to trade.[27]

Inspector Walsh (who preferred the title "Major") had been sent to the Cypress Hills in 1875 to establish a military post that he was permitted to name for himself.[28] Fort Walsh was located on the south slope of the western hills above the prairie, both to provide a vantage point and to facilitate receipt of most of its supplies from the United States. Walsh was tough, decisive, and practical.[29] He also showed a flare in his manner of dress, often in buckskins and a slouched hat instead of the military dress of the Red Coats, and he sported a well-trimmed imperial beard. Walsh first encountered Sitting Bull within a few days of his arrival at Pinto Horse Butte. This day he was in his issued scarlet coat with gold braids

James Morrow Walsh

and accompanied by several redcoated Mounties. Walsh confidently dismounted, strode forward, and extended a welcome. After an exchange of greetings, the major took up the task of laying out the rules of Canadian accommodation: "You must obey the White Mother's laws if you want to stay in her country."[30] Canada was never to be used as a base of operations against the United States. Sitting Bull professed that his "heart was good."[31] He explained: "The White Forehead Chief walks to my lodge alone and unarmed. He gives me the hand of peace. This is a good thing. A new hope enters my heart. I am in another land, among wasichus different from any I have known."[32] He promised no wrong would be done unless there was an attack by American soldiers.

Hearing this pledge, Walsh warranted that his government would not allow the United States to make a preemptive strike to take the Sioux back. These words affirmed the decision of crossing the Medicine Line. There would be occasions when Walsh had to assert strong authority over the Indians, but they appreciated his courage and directness. He did not tell lies. In time, he became a champion of the Sioux people residing in Canada.[33]

The U.S. Army remained in striking distance playing a waiting game. Colonel Miles operated primarily out of Fort Keough on the south side of the Yellowstone near the Tongue River. His patrols evidenced a continued threat of pursuing the Sioux into Canada.[34] However, holding back other American Indians from crossing into Canada took priority. The Nez Perce, who refused an order to reservation confinement in a takeover of their homeland, were on flight from eastern Oregon and the Idaho Territory. These Indians under White Bird, Looking Glass, and Chief Joseph were pushing east across the Bitterroot Mountains into Montana and then across the Rockies. General Oliver Howard from the West and Colonels John Gibbon out of Montana and Samuel Sturgis out of Wyoming were in pursuit. The Nez Perce could not shake the military. Major battles were fought at White Bird Canyon, Clear Water, Big Hole, Camus Meadows, and Canyon Creek. These and other skirmishes killed warriors, women, and children and exhausted resources.[35] In the fall, Bear Coat joined his forces to the army's running 1,500-mile campaign. The Indians now were on a northward track to Canada to join the Lakota. The U.S. Army was not going to let that happen. The indefatigable Miles led a march out of the Tongue River cantonment on the Yellowstone across the Big Horn Mountains to intercept the Nez Perce.[36]

Ironically, after running the Lakota out of the United States, pressure began to build to bring them back.[37] While Canada worked through diplomatic channels, fearful settlers along the northern Montana border wanted Sitting Bull under U.S. control.[38] The United States was confronted with conflicting issues of the Canadian political asylum, pressure to extradite the renegades and not wanting to provide concessions to those it drove north.[39]

Even when peaceable, Sitting Bull was viewed as the treacherous mastermind, ready to spring another surprise attack.[40] He was never able to shed the role the American people assigned to him at the Battle of Little Big Horn. Yet, he and his people were now refugees in Canada.[41] Sitting Bull could only hang on. The Canadian government strove to persuade, not to provoke. At the invitation of the prime minister,[42] a commission headed by General Alfred Terry, the Sioux's old adversary, came to Fort Walsh in October 1877 to discuss bringing the Lakota back to the United States. The arrival was within days of the Nez Perce being trapped by Colonel Miles in the Bear's Paw Mountains just below the international border.[43]

The Nez Perce War came to an end just 40 miles below the Medicine Line. Though Chief Joseph surrendered, some of his people escaped the last battle and made their way to Canada. Those escaping included wounded women, children, and warriors. True to Lakota culture, Sitting Bull's camp provided food and care to the new refugees. Former adversaries were accepted as victims of the same common enemy. Concern heightened that the army may take the escape as reason anew to invade Canada to reach both the Nez Perce and Sioux.[44]

The Wood Mountain Indian village was in a dark mood. Sitting Bull refused to attend the conference.[45] He saw no friendship in the hard fist of the military. General Terry had pursued the Lakota on the Plains; Miles's troops remained on watch at the border and now had chased down the fleeing Nez Perce. The chief's disposition grew more irritable with the recent death of his young son to a white man's illness.[46]

He was riled by the visit. Why meet with the U.S. representatives? "They are all liars."[47] He told Walsh that it was stupid for the Americans to send Terry as head of a peace commission; he "was the one sent to kill us at Greasy Grass."[48] Sitting Bull would never bend to the commission's entreaties. The major spent three days urging the chief at least to come to hear what would be said. Sitting Bull eventually succumbed to the request in order not to embarrass Canada. But he exacted a condition that the Mounties stand watch during the Lakota attendance at the Fort Walsh Mess Hall for the conference.[49] When the commissioners entered, Sitting Bull made a show of shaking hands with officials of the Mounted Police and demanded that all spectators be removed.[50] He consented to a stenographer and some newspaper correspondents remaining. There even was discussion about the seating arrangements. Sitting Bull and his people sat on the floor on buffalo robes, and he told the commissioners to do the same. When one of the commissioners pointed out that it was their habit to sit on chairs, the table separating the two sides was removed.[51]

General Terry opened the meeting with expressions of the desire of peace and said there would be a full pardon to those who surrendered. He appeared conciliatory and humble:

The President has instruction us to say to you that he desires to make a lasting peace with you and your people. He desires that all hostilities shall cease and that all shall live together in harmony. He wishes this not only for the sake of the whites, but for your sakes too. He has instructed us to say that if you return to your country and refrain from further hostilities, a full pardon will be granted you and your people for all acts committed in the past, and that no matter what those acts have been, no attempt will be made to punish you or any of your people. What is past shall be forgotten, and you will be received on as friendly terms as other Indians have been received.

We will explain to you what the President means when he says you will be treated the same as other Indians who have surrendered. Of all the bands that were hostile to the United States, yours are the only ones not surrendered. All other bands have come into their agencies. Of these bands, not a single one has been punished. Every man, woman, and child has been received as a friend and all have received food and clothing. Every one of you will be treated in the same manner. It's true that these Indians have been required to give up their horses and arms, but part of these have been sold, and whatever money was received for them will be expended for their owners' benefit.[52]

Terry continued, outlining a key term of surrender:

Of one thing, however, it's our duty to inform you: that you cannot return to your country or your people with arms and ammunition in your possession, and should you attempt to do so, you will be treated as enemies of the United States. We ask you to consider carefully what we have told you, and take your time and weigh your answer.[53]

This was the militant stand Sitting Bull anticipated, hiding behind sweet opening words. His response was scathing:

I did not give you my country, but you followed me from place to place, and I had to come here. I was born and raised here with the Red River Mixed Bloods [exaggerated rhetoric], and I intend to stay with them. I was raised hand in hand with these people, and that is why I shake their hands. That is the way I was taught. That is the way I intend to go on doing. See how I live with these people.

Look at me. I have ears, I have eyes to see with. If you think me a fool, you are a bigger fool than I am. This house is a medicine house. You come here to tell us lies, but we do not to listen to them. I don't wish such language used to me, or any such lies told to me in my Grand-mother's house. Don't say two more words. Go back home where you came from. This country is my country now, and I intend to stay here and raise people up to fill it.[54]

Others followed the chief's oration with similar scorn. Sitting Bull even arranged for a woman to speak to the commissioners. He intended this appearance as an insult to the commissioners, playing off the chauvinism that men only were appropriate participants in such discussions. The woman's name evidenced her ability—The One that Speaks Once. She addressed the commission as a mother who desired to bring up her children in her own country, but was denied such a home. Her voice was so hushed that the interpreter had to ask her to speak up. Then he translated for Terry: "She says, General, that you won't give her time to breed."[55] The woman closed her remarks by saying that she chose peace and would stay with the redcoats.

Sitting Bull had a larger audience in mind. He wanted the attending officers of the Canadian government to hear of the abuses his people suffered at the hands of the United States. He aimed to convince the northern government of the injustice of the United States. When General Terry spoke again, he asked what he should tell the president, who had sent the peace overture. "Are we to understand from what you have said that you refuse those offers?"[56]

Sitting Bull was abrupt: "I could tell you more, but this is all I have to say. If we told you more—why, you would pay no attention to it. I have no more to say."[57]

Crow, another chief, rose to underscore his leader's stand. He, too, embraced Walsh and Commissioner Macleod before speaking:

This country is not yours. . . . The redcoats hide nothing from us. We will live with them. You want to hear more from us? For sixty-four years you shook hands with our people, but you always betrayed us and brought us new hardships. You can go back where you came from and stay there. We will stay here.[58]

The newspaper representatives from several cities in the United States, attending the meeting, saw a different Sitting Bull than what was his reputation—he was not just tough, he was articulate.[59] He brilliantly presented his case. The Chicago correspondent who had ridden with the Crook command after Little Big Horn, John Finerty, described him:

He had a strong personal magnetism. His judgment was said to be superior to his courage, and his cunning superior to both. He had not, like Crazy Horse, the reputation for being recklessly brave, but neither was he reputed a dastard. Sitting Bull was simply prudent and would not throw away his life so long as he had any chance of doing injury to the Americans.[60]

The newspapermen's attentiveness served as acknowledgement that Sitting Bull remained the spokesman of the Lakota.

In interviews arranged by Walsh, the news reporters naturally asked about the events of June 25. To such inquiries, Sitting Bull revealed little.[61] He was quick to point out that Custer came to destroy his people; he did not seek out Custer. To him, that was long ago. And he was clear about the Canadian retreat: "You call us 'savages.' What are the white men? The buffalo come north. We have come north to find them, and to go away from a place where people tell lies."[62]

The Canadian officials knew they had work to do. James Macleod, in a behind-the-scenes discussion with the Hunkpapa chief, made it clear that the Sioux were not British Indians; this was not their country.

Your only hope of livelihood is the buffalo, but in another two to three years there will very few of them left. Hunters in your country are killing them off so quickly that there won't be enough of them left to

migrate north of the border. When that happens, you can't expect any-
thing from the White Mother except protection as long as you behave
yourselves. She will have enough of her own Indians to look after. Your
decision to reject the offer of a pardon by your White Father will affect
not only your own lives, but those of your children. It is well to think
about this before it is too late. I urge you to carry my words to your
people and to think about them fully.[63]

Sitting Bull stayed on point by recounting many wrongs inflicted upon his people:

We did not give them our land any more than you would have done
had it belonged to you. . . . We want to live in this country and be
strong and happy. . . . You will see more of our tribe crossing the line.
The Great Spirit gives us plenty of buffalo. . . . I could never live there
again. . . . We did not wish to fight; they started it. . . . If they liked me,
as they say, why did they drive me away?

We are friends with you and the other officers; it was on that account
that we came to meet the Americans today.[64]

Appreciative that Sitting Bull at least had consented to meet with the commission, Macleod ordered ammunition and provisions to be given to the Sioux delegation.[65]

Below the border, fear of what Sitting Bull might do persisted. Northern Montana Territory was rife with rumor that Sitting Bull was making alliances with the Canadian tribes to invade the United States.[66] The government at Ottawa wanted firsthand reports of what was taking place with the American Indians in Saskatchewan Territory, and Walsh was called to the capital. To get there he traveled through the northern United States. On stopovers he was sought out by the press; he had come to be known as "Sitting Bull's Boss,"[67] and he did not shy from the recognition. But he consistently offered testimony that Sitting Bull, whom he usually referred to as Bull,[68] was not hostile. He discounted newspaper stories of Sitting Bull seeking a coalition of tribes to oppose the whites as based on rumors started by army scouts. These were yarns for the gullible or pure mischief. He advised that the larger problem for the future "will be dissatisfaction with life on the reservations, with Indian agents holding out on food they're supposed to be giving the Indians."[69] Reports of Walsh's candor were not well received in Ottawa.

As to the rumors that the chief would surrender to agency life, Bull himself was emphatic:

> *I have forbidden my people to use my name to the Americans. I have always said to my people in council: 'If any of you want to go back, tell me.' None has done so yet. I am looking to the north for my life and I hope the White Mother will never ask me to look to the country I left although it is mine, and not even the dust of it did I sell, but the Americans can have it.*[70]

The ensuing winters grew harsher; and buffalo were more difficult to find. The Blackfoot, Piegans, Bloods, and Crees complained of the Sioux presence within their hunting grounds. The Medicine Line was not a barrier to the migrating buffalo, and there were frequent hunting excursions across the border by both Canadian tribes and Sioux young men in search of game.[71] The hunts were commonly tolerated by the Mounted Police, but raids on American settlements were unacceptable. Bear Coat, for his part, only sent patrols as far as the area between the Milk and Missouri Rivers, but his was a continuing presence near the border. Although the colonel's orders were not to create an incident with the Queen's government, his men were suspected of setting fire to the prairie grasses on the south side of the international line to disrupt the migration of buffalo to the north.[72] Others said the Canadian Blackfoot Indians started fires on the north side of the boundary as a means of forcing the Sioux to leave.[73] But this was unlikely because the Blackfoot would be hurting themselves. In June 1879, newspaper correspondent Stanley Huntley somehow was able to arrange an interview with Sitting Bull, who was then camped in Montana. The reporter quoted the chief to his readers: "We want meat. Our women and children are hungry. There is nothing for us but wild game. . . . The buffalo have left us. We have followed them."[74]

After a spell of poor hunts, the Sioux were reduced to begging for food from the Mounties. There were more stealth hunts and some raids on homesteads across the border for livestock, requiring Walsh's men into extended service to attempt to police the situation. The Canadian government authorized establishing a new post at Wood Mountain with Walsh in command to better prevent these border runs. Sitting Bull viewed Major Walsh's new proximity at the edge of the Hunkpapa camp as an opportunity. In the chill of an autumn night, Sitting Bull accosted Walsh at his office. With him were Four Horns and Black Moon, old allies, and a few young braves. Walsh, whose handling of the Sioux was under question by his own government, was testy. The chief demanded provisions. The major was annoyed:

> *What gives you the right to barge into my office and make demands? You, Sitting Bull, you have been nothing but a bloody nuisance, you and your young men with their horse stealing. You've given me and my men no end of god-damned trouble. Have you forgotten that you are American Indians? You haven't any right to be in Canada. The only reason that you're in this country is because American soldiers chased you out of your own country. Now you come here and break our laws, even though you promised not to. You seem to think all white men are afraid of you. Well, they're not. Get your provisions at the trading store and get the hell out of here, before I throw the whole damned lot of you in the guard room.*[75]

Bull reacted. He mimicked Walsh: "Who do you think you are talking to?" Then, he answered his own question: "You are talking to the leader of the mighty Sioux nation."[76]
Walsh lashed back:

> *I know damned well who I'm talking to. What I said still goes. Now get the hell out of here, and if there's any more horse stealing by any of your people, I'll clap irons on you too and toss you in the guard room, you god-damned red son of a bitch.*[77]

Sitting Bull snapped: "No man can speak to me like that."

Walsh did not back down: "Are you threatening me? Are you threatening the Mounted Police? Damn it all! Behave yourself or I'll throw you out of here."[78]

The two were toe-to-toe, shout-to-shout. Sitting Bull reflexively squeezed his right hand and reached to his waist for a revolver tucked into his belt. Walsh saw the move (certainly Sitting Bull did not want to execute on his indignation) and grabbed the chief's wrist. Again, the chief was told to leave and this time shoved out the door. There were hard stares between the two men now standing outside the office and the braves bunched behind their chief. When Sitting Bull again reached for his revolver, Black Moon and Four Horns, having also exited the office, took hold of him. They pushed him hard against an outer wall, telling him not to challenge his friend. Sitting Bull released his grip on the revolver, but held his ground for a short while, then muttered about sparing Walsh's life, mounted his horse, and rode off. Walsh sent a call to the barracks, and men tumbled out; if there was another encounter, he wanted armed attendants. Within minutes, Sitting Bull and several young bucks galloped back fast, hooping and brandishing rifles. Walsh told his men to draw their weapons and yelled out "Far enough!" Sitting Bull at the lead refused to rein in his horse until within steps of the major's boots. Walsh did not flinch: "You've caused enough trouble for one day. Go back to your camp."[79] In this standoff, there were more than enough Sioux to take out the redcoats. Nonetheless, Sitting Bull, now suppressing his temper, turned away, uttering something about another day. His braves followed after him, with guttural sounds and bad eyes toward the Mounties. It was a flare of bad temper from a man who usually picked when to let his ire show. Under stress, he was lashing out even at friends.

Just a week later, Walsh was back to his role of guardian. Bull himself was on a hunt to the south, when confronted by Crows accompanied by a young U.S. military officer. The Crows opened fire, and the blue coat—Lt. William Clark—dashed off to warn his superiors. The ever-ready Miles sent reinforcements. A Crow scout had recognized Sitting Bull in the distance; sensing an opportunity, the scout bolted forward on horseback firing his rifle. The shot fell short, kicking up a trace of dirt. Watching as the Crow continued to advance, Sitting Bull steadied his horse, wiped his hand across his eyes, then raised a rifle to his shoulder, aligning the front post on the barrel to a sharp bead in the V of the rear sight. He slowly squeezed the trigger. There was a crack as the primer sparked powder. The shot hit the Crow in the head; his body toppled from the horse.[80] Sitting Bull rode away without a backward glance.

The army's forces responded to Clark's alarm; Miles ordered up artillery fire.[81] Before the big guns could be set for action, a fast-approaching storm let loose a hard rain. Sitting Bull and his braves vanished with a wet wind at their backs across the Milk River toward Canada. Bear Coat trailed as far as the border.[82] Walsh quickly was apprised of the confrontation. He first met with Sitting Bull and accepted the chief's explanation that the Crows had attacked a hunting party. The major then traveled to Bear Coat's camp and spent the night, assuring Miles that this had not been a raid. He contended that Sitting Bull had no hostile intent and the Mounted Police could handle the situation.[83] Miles acquiesced.

Walsh, acting the go-between, returned to Sitting Bull's camp with a message from Bear Coat—"If the Sioux want to come across the line, they'll have to surrender themselves, give up their horses and guns, and agree to go a reservation. None of them will be harmed, and they'll be given enough food. I'd like you to pass that on to Sitting Bull."[84] Miles sent his own emissary, the embedded journalist, John Finerty, ostensibly to give the journalist an opportunity for a story but more importantly to take stock. Finerty spent three days in the Lakota Camp. Walsh explained Finerty was neither a soldier nor government agent. Sitting Bull, although having seen the man at the time of the Terry visit, refused to talk to him, but let others inquire how long the army intended to patrol the Milk River. Before Finerty could answer, the major sharply said that as long as the Lakota did not go down there, it was none of their business.[85]

Colonel Miles continued his waiting game.

CHAPTER ELEVEN

The Making of an Outlier

1880 –1881

The Saskatchewan prairie had become a landmass with too many Indians and not enough game. During 1880–1881, food shortages and general impoverishment afflicted both the Sioux and Canadian tribes. There was fear of famine.

More disturbing to the citizenry, increased speculation had Sitting Bull expanding his reach beyond Canadian tribes to the Gros Ventre and Blackfeet, even the Metis, to make war.[1] There always were more assumptions about the man's intentions than actual knowledge. In reality, food shortages and demise of the buffalo were splintering the uneasy relations among the tribes of Canada and United States. The Sioux for their part sent more hunting parties south of the international line in search of game, and the hunters sometimes returned with stolen horses and cattle.[2] Young men rode out with or without Sitting Bull's assent. Either way, the Mounties had to respond. Political reaction took over.

The Saskatchewan citizenry's fear reached Ottawa. The government grappled with the awkwardness of continued presence of the Sioux on its soil. The ministry of Canada needed to rid itself of the uninvited guests. It was annoyed at Walsh's advocacy on behalf of Sitting Bull in pursuing a reservation for the Lakota in Canadian territory. The major had become too sympathetic to his Lakota charges. Walsh wrote in his 1880 official report: "The conduct of these starving and destitute people, their patient endurance, their sympathy, the extent to which they assisted each other, and their strict observance of all order would reflect credit upon the most civilized community."[3] When times were difficult, the Mounties had dispensed food to the Sioux. Such disregard of policy no longer would be tolerated. Ottawa wondered who was in charge of whom at Wood Mountain. The election of a new prime minister hastened a change of policy.[4]

In July 1880, Bull heard that Walsh was reassigned to Fort Qu'Appelle about 200 miles northeast of Wood Mountain.[5] Worried about the consequences, he scrambled to catch up with Walsh and pleaded for help. The major was blunt: "It will be a wasted labor on my part to try to do any such thing, and a waste of time on your part to await a result."[6] Sitting Bull gave his first indication of a possible return to America:

> *If the White Mother is determined to drive me from her country into the arms of those waiting for me like hungry wolves, will you talk to the White Father and ask him whether I will be treated like a man and not like a dog if I go back? Will I get the same treatment others of the Lakota have received? Or will I be grabbed and hung up on a tree?*[7]

Major Walsh agreed to try to talk to the Great White Father, "if the White Mother's government will allow me to."[8] Walsh explained that his position was tenuous.

The new post commander—Lief "Paddy" Crozier—was directed to implement his government's tougher stance.[9] He was experienced in dealing with Indians, but displayed none of the compassion of Walsh. Yet he realized he could never get away with telling Sitting Bull he was a "god-damned red son of a bitch." Crozier's approach was to refuse to acknowledge Sitting Bull as a leader and to undercut him with his people. His specific assignment was to find a way to force Sitting Bull out of Canada.[10] The instructions from Ottawa were absolute—do not furnish provisions to the American Indians. This strategy broke Sioux solidarity; defections followed. Actually, the new commander was working on an already reduced number of Indian refugees; as many as 3,700 had departed the Grandmother's country because of distressed living conditions before he took command.[11] On the other hand, the harsh enforcement of his orders spurred increased horse stealing, not for mounts but for food. The Canadian plains were greatly overhunted. Lakota women were butchering dying ponies and making stew. Malnourished children were constantly ill.

When Superintendent Crozier failed to convince the chief, lesser head men were approached. Sitting Bull stalled while waiting on what he thought would be Walsh's return; others gave in. One of those to leave was Gray Eagle, Sitting Bull's brother-in-law. (This was not a loss because there were strained relations between the two over discipline imposed by Sitting Bull.[12] Sitting Bull had been informed by the Mounties that his brother-in-law was part of a horse-stealing ring; to make amends, the chief ordered his brother-in-law to return the horses and then had Gray Eagle tied to a tree without food or water for a day.[13])

Meanwhile, Major Walsh again tried to intercede in a letter to his government:

> *I believe, and Sitting Bull's Indian friends believe, that if the U.S. Government would give Bull a reservation at the head of the Tongue River, he would accept it. It is a small concession for the U.S. to make in order to end this vexed question, and the people would find that by settling this man on a reservation, the Indian problem on the frontier can be more easily resolved, and with more satisfaction than the other way.*[14]

By this time, Walsh's critics were many; they said his closeness to the chief only aggravated the situation.[15] The independence and take-charge attitude that served him so well on a frontier post were turned against him. His actions now were viewed as bordering on insubordination. There was talk of cashiering him from the Mounted Police.[16] Walsh lost all effectiveness. Others now were working toward Sitting Bull's return to the States. The two governments offered to pay anyone who would assist in the removal of the Sioux. Various persons sought to claim the monetary compensation, as well as the notoriety, for bringing Sitting Bull back. The emphasis turned to convincing his key supporters that sustaining their position in the north was untenable. Moreover, Canada would exact promise from the United States of no reprisals.

The approach of Edwin "Fish" Allison was both distinct and calculated. A longtime scout and interpreter along the upper Missouri, he earned the nickname "Fish" because he had a slippery tongue when it came to the truth.[17] Allison caught up with Gall, who was on a hunting trip in northern Montana, while the scout was on a cattle drive through the same area. Gall frequently absented himself from Wood Mountain; to the close observer there seemed to be some growing distance between Gall and Bull.[18] Fish Allison sensed an opening. He invited Gall and his riders to a steak dinner (Gall never could resist the offer of a hearty meal) and then introduced the idea of arranging a meeting with Sitting Bull. Gall agreed to set it up. Allison had secured the approval of Major David Brotherton from Fort Buford, situated just over the border, to facilitate surrender. Fish was in Sitting Bull's camp sometime in November. He told Sitting Bull he was authorized to promise the chief that he would not be singled out for punishment because of the Custer Massacre. A full pardon was ready to be given. The scout also brought presents and food (not unlike the customary indications of friendship the Americans showed the Indians in making treaties).[19] Fish argued that life on a U.S. reservation would mean the Lakota would no longer go hungry. This was the significant bargaining chip. The buffalo were gone, and Sitting Bull had to know that Canada put its own tribes first. He and his people had been reduced to beggars in a foreign land. Further, Allison gave assurances that those who had already left were safe and Sitting Bull's band would join relatives on the reservation. The Indians were protected by the agencies; the one understandable condition was that horses and weapons had to be relinquished. Anticipating objection, he said that this would not be permanent. To a hunter-warrior, the reassurance based on future restoration did not cut the bitter taste of the medicine offered.

The commissioner of the North-West Mounted Police followed up with Sitting Bull; others came to urge return before the hard winter hit. Sitting Bull insisted that he would wait for Walsh before deciding. More stalling. More intransience. Fish Allison gave up on Sitting Bull and directed his appeal to the more malleable Gall, promising that he would be head chief if he returned to the States.[20] Knowing how much the situation had deteriorated in Canada, Gall was willing to accept a lead role in getting out. But he still would not act unilaterally.

Sitting Bull was challenged by his war lieutenant and key adviser. Gall thought Sitting Bull foolishly stubborn not to acknowledge that staying in Canada was no longer viable. The argument hastened a distance between the two, and Gall was emboldened. By December, Gall broke with Sitting Bull and led four hundred of his people back to the United States.[21] Running with him was Crow. Sitting Bull had the harshest of words for his longtime ally.[22] Gall was called a "weak heart." Although he had earlier said those who want to leave were free to do so, the chief was stung by the departure of Gall. He needed strong men about him; Gall had been an enforcer, quelling dissent from others. The cohesiveness of the bands was tearing fast; the naysayers came to the front.

Sitting Bull realized his word was no longer absolute. Low Dog was in conversation with Crozier, telling him that there were other camps that wanted to leave, but because of Sitting Bull's stance they needed encouragement.[23] The superintendent made a point of visiting those camps. Within a week, Low Dog left and took several able men with him.[24] Now Sitting Bull was overseeing mostly old men and women and children.[25] These people stayed with him because they were family or long-standing friends. His constant brooding tested their loyalty. He was becoming a chief without Indians. Those who left believed he was at the lead of a lost cause. Recognizing an escalating exodus, Sitting Bull confronted the futility of his position. He told Superintendent Crozier: "If I could get a good letter from the soldier-chief at Fort Buford that he will treat us well, I might go. I will see about it."[26] Straightaway, word went across the border to Fort Buford, and the post commander dispatched a letter providing assurances through the Mounted Police to Sitting Bull.[27]

Gall, still having a warrior's brashness, did not rush his return. He had announced that he would surrender at Poplar Agency, but instead he made camp on a flood plain of the Missouri just below the agency. There followed talks with the military that his band would submit at Fort Buford when the weather was more favorable to travel. To do so immediately, meant an already suffering people would be made to travel at least four days in freezing temperatures. Crow echoed that they intended

Chief Gall
STATE HISTORICAL SOCIETY OF NORTH DAKOTA

to wait until spring. With some bravado he said they wanted to hunt for skins to clothe their people along the way. "We will go to Buford someday. It is cold and stormy, so we cannot travel. We want to wait for Sitting Bull."[28] Apparently, the break from the chief was not complete.

Major Guido Ilges was now in command at nearby Fort Keough, Nelson Miles having been elevated to brigadier general. Ilges was an impatient man; no Indian would dictate to him the time of surrender. Nor could he accept any remaining control by Sitting Bull. These Indians remained enemies of the United States. Troops crossed the frozen river and formed two columns to converge on the encampment. With the intent of coercing the Indians from camp, artillery was set up and shots were fired. When eight Indians were wounded, Gall hurried forward showing a white flag.[29] Ilges's men moved in and burned the tipis and then force marched the Sioux in the bitter cold to Fort Buford.[30] All arrived on January 10, adding to the growing population of returnees at the fort.

Sitting Bull continued to hold out. During this time, Sitting Bull and a party of Lakota struck out on a hunting trip in the border lands along the Milk River. With him was one of the chiefs from Little Big Horn, Crow King. The ever-maneuvering Allison intercepted them and convinced Crow King and two others to accompany him to Fort Buford to check the state of affairs for themselves. Crow King came back satisfied with what he saw.[31]

General Terry commended Ilges for taking decisive action at Poplar. Then, learning of Sitting Bull's whereabouts, he cancelled Fish Allison's assignment and ordered Ilges to capture Sitting Bull while he was over the international line. Capture on American soil would make the matter so much simpler. But Sitting Bull was a step ahead. Immediately upon hearing of the attack on the surrendering Sioux, the chief called for his hunting party to return to Canada.[32] Crow King thought this unwise and the two argued with each other. Crow King broke with Sitting Bull. He took with him 350 more Sioux who arrived at Buford on February 5.[33] By this time there would be nearly one thousand prisoners there. Major Ilges lost his chance to snare Sitting Bull.

But on February 7, Ilges learned that Jumping Bull (also known as Little Assiniboine[34]), the adopted brother of Sitting Bull, was camped with his band west of Poplar at Wolf Point, along the Missouri River. Here was another hostile across the international line. He ordered the Indian's arrest and placed him in a guard house, shackled in irons. When Sitting Bull heard what had happened to his brother, he only foresaw harsher prospects for himself.[35] The chief anguished over the treatment that befell his brother, Gall, and the others.

Back in Canada, a suitor sought the chief's daughter, Many Horses. Sitting Bull would have none of it; he refused to consent to the marriage. He told his daughter to remain in his lodge while he searched for a way to stay on Canadian soil. He was in denial that these were his final days in the north. For weeks he held to his own thoughts, preferring to be alone. Then he embarked on a pointless mission. Thinking Walsh was at distant Fort Qu'Appelle (actually the major had spent only five days there before the Canadian government put him on leave), he set out to meet him. Upon arrival, he found Inspector Sam in command. The chief nonetheless pressed his appeal for a reservation for his people. That was an impossible request to grant. Canadian Indian Commissioner Edgar Dewdney showed up a few days later to flatly state that the White Grandmother wanted the Lakota band back in its own country. Even the lieutenant governor came to Qu'Appelle to reinforce his government's position. He reminded Sitting Bull of the chief's recorded words refusing to cede away the Black Hills, which he labeled a mistake of intractability. He told

Sitting Bull that the Sioux had a reservation of their own on the other side of the Medicine Line. Finally, he offered that if Sitting Bull would surrender to the U.S. military, the Canadian government would provide rations for his people's journey south.[36]

In Ottawa, Major Walsh was ordered to remain in place by Sir John A. Macdonald, the prime minister; Walsh could not go to Washington to intercede on behalf of Sitting Bull. The official position was that a mounted policeman did not have the standing to meet with the president of the United States.[37] Sitting Bull's presence had become an international issue that required higher authorities working to solution. James Walsh remained on forced leave and would not see Sitting Bull again.

On his return to Wood Mountain, he found his people on subsistence food supplies. A chastened Sitting Bull could only grovel for provisions. Inspector MacDonnell, now in command, told him: "You have been given good advice to go back where you came from, where you can get all the food you need." Sitting Bull despaired: "I am thrown away."[38] Observing multiple defections over the last several months, the Canadian government was certain that the prospect of starvation would force the remaining Lakota back to the U.S.. Ottawa's inhospitality became as pointed as a policeman's pistol against one's back.

Losses kept coming. In the chief's absence, his daughter had eloped and returned to the United States. Sitting Bull for the first time was cut off from most of his people, with only a dwindling band of about 180—all tattered, ill, and underfed. There was no hope of obtaining a reservation in Canada. His iron will barely holding, Sitting Bull stood alone against two governments. Asylum was collapsing.

Although reined in by his own government, Major Walsh, while on leave, contacted a general he knew who was now with the Indian Bureau in Chicago, asking him to intervene on behalf of Sitting Bull. The general gave his word that he would speak to responsible parties in Washington to secure a safety.[39] Walsh managed through unofficial channels to send a message to Sitting Bull that the U.S. government would treat him fairly.[40]

Even his strongest Canadian friend saw that surrender was the only course available.

Stepping into the breach was Sitting Bull's other Canadian friend—Jean Louis Legare. The trader bluntly advised there was no way to stay. Bull heard that money had been offered to Legare.[41] But there was nowhere else to turn.[42] By mid-1881, the loss of allies, lack of provisions and poor living conditions could not be swept aside with hope of a better day. The Lakota spirit was crushed; a shaky state of affairs had changed to doom. Sleep at night was restless, and waking in morning brought no respite. Those who remained were an apathetic band, unable to do for themselves. They had no items to trade. The pocket watches and other mementos taken from the dead of the 7th Cavalry had been bartered away long ago. They were threadbare blanket Indians. The old people either shuffled about or sat and stared. Sitting Bull had to realize that there was no way for his people to reclaim their lives in the Grandmother's country. The remaining Lakota were prisoners of their own circumstance. The *Bismarck Tribune* carried an article on May 6, 1881:

> *First, he is starving; second, the continual desertion of the several . . . bands from his camp have left him so weak that he is afraid to leave Wood Mountain to hunt, there being so many enemies on the watch for him. Third, Low Dog, one of his chiefs, left Wood Mountain a short time ago with 20 lodges or 30 families, and came over to Poplar River to surrender.*[43]

At last, Sitting Bull was ready to surrender. He forced himself to ask Crozier for formal assurance from Post Commander Brotherton that those at Fort Buford were well cared for. Crozier quickly obliged. He asked his second in command to escort four Sioux south for a look for themselves. When they returned, one of the Sioux claimed conditions were not good. Paddy Crozier was furious at what he considered an outright lie. Sitting Bull erroneously had been informed that his own daughter was in irons at Fort Buford.[44] He knew how Ilges moved against Gall and his adopted brother while they sought respite in winter camps near Poplar Creek.[45] To Sitting Bull, the two governments spoke in falsehoods. Once again he changed his mind. When some of his band returned to camp with stolen horses, he deluded himself that the new mounts would help find game.

He refused to leave. In the meantime, Legare escorted others back.[46] The refugees processed at Fort Buford were transported south to Fort Yates (a former cantonment in mid-Dakota Territory, renamed in 1878 for Captain George Yates, who led the ill-fated Gray Horse Group at Little Big Horn). They were placed at the Standing Rock Agency, located beside the fort within the Great Sioux Reservation. Legare continued to provide food to those who remained in the north. And he brought word that the Americans had treated fairly the earlier surrendering Lakota. The Canadian government offered no sustenance to hold these people together. Sitting Bull was certain that there was a price on his head, but the impoverished condition of his remaining followers removed choice. He could not ignore his people's vulnerability to all manner of illness and the specter of ongoing food shortages. No one would intercede. The remaining Lakota in exile were a shattered people. Although he distrusted the assurances given, a beaten Sitting Bull admitted defeat. "My people are cold and hungry. My women are sick, my children freezing. I will do what the Great Father wishes. I will give my guns and ponies into his hands."[47] Legare pulled up trading wagons to transport Sitting Bull's remaining band;[48] both the Canadian and U.S. governments promised to reimburse the trader.

The news reports ran the story that Sitting Bull finally was on his way to surrender to the U.S. military. Arrangements were made to receive him at Fort Buford, about 60 miles from the Canadian border, where the Yellowstone flowed into the Missouri. The overall trip, however, was nearly 200 miles. The journey started on July 12. As they rolled through the Canadian prairie lands, they saw the scattered bones of slaughtered buffalo. The image seared as a reminder of what they had lost. Each mile traveled further wore down the returnees; they were coming back to their homeland without the ability to truly go home. The journey stutter-stepped. Even facing the inevitable, Sitting Bull sought stoppages with requests to make council with his people, breaks for smokes, late-morning starts and tea drinking.[49] The procrastinations exhausted Legare's provisions for the trip. The trader sent ahead a request for assistance and wagons with supplies came to meet him.[50] Within a few miles of crossing the international border on July 17, an advance party from the fort led by Captain Walter Clifford intercepted Legare's train of carts south. At first seeing the blue coats approaching, the Indians pulled up and some shouted warnings to those behind, but Clifford had with him just a couple of soldiers, Louis Legare reassured that the soldiers had come to help and Sitting Bull favorably recognized the lead officer from an earlier contact.[51] With Sitting Bull almost within reach of the United States, the commander at Fort Buford simply was not about to let the chief change his mind.

As the blue coats came up, a crow flapped its wings and lifted from the branch of a nearby tree, cutting a long arc and disappearing into a hole in the sky.

Sitting Bull had followed the prairie north to sustain the Lakota way of life. He always recognized the Canadian experience would bring about changes; he wanted to believe the trade-off was worth it. In the end, he found there was no protective barrier at the international border. The Grandmother's country would not provide for his people, and they could no longer make their own way. All that he achieved was a sharper awareness of the guile in politics. The Sioux had wandered the plains of Saskatchewan for four years and gained no relief to their plight.

By July 19, the warm weather of summer withdrew. An overcast sky produced a persistent drizzle, pushed by a stony wind from the northwest.[52] Shortly after noon, the Lakota crossed through the gates of Fort Buford.[53] These refugees from Canada were a ragtag bunch. Sitting Bull and a few others rode in on gaunt ponies—ribs outlined against their hides and heads downcast; the rest were hauled aboard the traders' carts with wheels screeching from the lack of grease. The few possessions that did not fit in the wagons were dragged by travois. Dogs brought up the rear. Captain Clifford observed that "nothing but nakedness and starvation have driven this man to submission."[54] Sitting Bull asked that his people be allowed to rest. They turned over their horses and weapons, with the exception of the Winchester rifle that Sitting Bull said he would give up at the formal proceedings. Then they were taken outside of the fort to a meadow to camp overnight. The party consisted of only 44 men.[55] While Sitting Bull had been considered as a threat, the reality was that he had long since lost his ability to make war. He advised his young son:

"If you live, you will never be a man in this world, because you can never have a gun or pony."[56] At best, the chief would become an agency Indian, which he had resisted since at least 1868. The man who was the face of the Lakota was now a shadow of his former self. Fort Buford, the scene of so many of his raids, now was the place where he would say "no more." After weathering so many storms, exhaustion took hold.

Canada played the role of intermediary, convincing the exiles of their untenable position and the need to return. The promise of money was the guarantee of delivery. Sitting Bull recognized the machinations of both governments but accepted his deliverance at the hand of a friend. Legare was paid $2,000 by the Canadian government but denied reimbursement of expenses of $13,412 by the U.S. government.[57]

During the years of Sitting Bull's declining station in Canada, James McLaughlin's standing with the Indian Department was on the rise. He proved himself a skillful manager at Devils Lake, advancing the bureau's policies while maintaining the respect of his wards. McLaughlin forbade old traditions,[58] putting an end to the sun dance.[59] But the agency Indians did not rebel. The mission school system was strengthened under his administration.[60] Although underpaid, he did not succumb to diverting funds and falsifying accounts, as was the case with so many Indian agents.[61] McLaughlin understood the negative reputation of Indian agents and commented in a letter to the Bureau of Catholic Indian Missions that there is a duty to "try to prove by our acts that there are some honest agents."[62] The influential Catholic Bureau considered James McLaughlin the ideal agent. He got along with missionaries, traders, and soldiers. When salaries were cut for all agents by Washington, he was given aid through the Catholic mission fund and officers at Fort Totten.[63] But James McLaughlin did not like being beholden to others; to maintain a sense of self-esteem, he sold property he had earlier purchased in Minnesota for the support his family.[64]

In central Dakota Territory, the Standing Rock Agency was beset with problems.[65] There had been a growing population of former exiles who had followed Sitting Bull to Canada and then deserted him. Thus, it was home to many of the Lakota who had participated in the Battle of Little Big Horn;[66] this created friction between both officers and enlisted men posted at Fort Yates and the reservation wards. Although the agent, Father Joseph Stephan, was a hard-working man, he constantly quarreled with military personnel. McLaughlin drew consideration as a replacement.[67] He had acquired strong experience and was well regarded within the bureau. In April 1880, McLaughlin was invited to Standing Rock to assess the situation. Because he had demonstrated the ability to work with the soldiers at Fort Totten, Generals Sherman and Terry endorsed him for the job.[68] But it took over a year for the Bureau of Indian Affairs to work out the resignation of the existing agent and the appointment of McLaughlin. McLaughlin hurriedly accepted and took steps to move his family in the summer of 1881.[69]

Father Stephan had the last word. In his letter of resignation, he stated the whites, not the Indians, were the "trouble-some element" at Standing Rock.[70] Major McLaughlin was confident that he could meet the challenge.

James McLaughlin and Sitting Bull were each moving toward the same destination but from very different circumstances. One invited; the other coerced. One confident; the other unable to fathom what lay ahead.

CHAPTER TWELVE

Surrender at Buford

Summer 1881

The overcast of the preceding day persisted, but this day's clouds brought a harder rain. The long trip, the weather, and the unknown all spoke bleakness for the Lakota. The official surrender was scheduled one hour before midday on July 20, 1881.[1]

Sitting Bull understood his deliverance to the army was a celebrated moment. For the United States it formalized the end of the Sioux Wars. Various representatives of the military and press attended. Inspector MacDonnell was dispatched from Canada by Crozier to assist in any arrangements, and Major Ilges and Fish Allison were present. (Allison later wrote a book, *The Surrender of Sitting Bull: Being a Full and Complete History of the Negotiations Conducted by Scout Allison*, supporting and embellishing his role in bringing about the surrender.[2]) Already, the St. Paul and Minneapolis Pioneer Press had its headline written: "BAGGED BY BROTHERTON."[3]

The chief chose to submit in his own fashion. He entered the parlor of the commander's quarters with several of the men who had long followed him together with his young son—Crow Foot.[4] In his hand was his Winchester rifle that he laid at his feet as he was motioned to take a chair next to Major Brotherton. He was not dressed as a chief, but in plain clothes with no adornments. A simple bandana wrapped his head, pulled low and partially covering his eyes, one of which was infected. His shirt was dirty calico, the arms of which appeared to have painted stripes; he wore old leggings, and a frayed blanket was drawn low across his back.[5] The man was as worn as his clothes. But there was purpose to his appearance.

The terms of the surrender were read by Major David Brotherton; Sitting Bull was to be sent to Standing Rock Agency to join his daughter and other Lakota. For surrendering arms and ponies, he would be pardoned. When asked for a reply, he uttered no words.[6] The monophonic strikes of a pendulum wall clock punctuated his silence. Some of the gathering shuffled with impatience. Sitting Bull did not look about. The bandana drew his eyes downward. His façade impassive, his captors awaited his response. Certainly the lull heightened his presence. He knew the speaker's art of the pregnant pause. An attaché whispered something to the major; Brotherton looked at the clock and responded "What does a few minutes matter at this point."[7] Then Brotherton renewed the question of whether Sitting Bull intended to speak. The chief gestured to his son to come to his side; and he gave the boy the rifle from the floor, motioning him toward the major. As his son handed the rifle to Brotherton, the chief declared: "I want it known that I am the last of my people to lay down my gun."[8]

Sitting Bull said that he came back so that his son could be taken care of: "I wish him to learn the habits of the whites and to be educated as their sons are educated."[9] This sounded a conciliatory tone.

As Brotherton and the assembled officials eased in their chairs, Sitting Bull spoke for himself, saying he intended to continue his existing ways. He would travel to and from Canada whenever he chose, and he would hunt wherever.

> *This is my country, and I don't wish to be compelled to give it up. My heart was very sad at having to leave the Grandmother's country. She has been a friend to me, but I want my children to grow up in our native country, and I also wish to feel that I can visit two of my friends on the other side of the line—Walsh and Captain MacDonald, whenever I wish, and would like to trade with Louis Legare, as he has always been a friend to me.*[10]

His demeanor shifted from submissive. Even though weary, he refused to cower. He was still a chief. He asked for his own reservation on the Little

Missouri, as once promised by Colonel Miles, and he requested that his daughter be brought from Standing Rock to visit him at Fort Buford. He declared he did not want to leave Buford until all his people came from Canada.[11]

Sitting Bull underscored his position: "This land I have under my feet is mine again. I never sold it. I never gave it to anybody. If I left the Black Hills five years ago, it was because I wished to raise my family quietly."[12] This was not unconditional surrender. This was not recognition of the military in charge. But the military was in charge. None of his demands would be met. To the assembled dignitaries, Sitting Bull did not understand that his role of chief entitled him to no concessions. Rather, for the United States, because of who he was—a fugitive insurgent, he was in no position to dictate terms. He undid any act of contrition with what could only be taken as arrogance.

Already higher authorities were discussing the fate of Sitting Bull. Some advised against sending him to Standing Rock because he was a destabilizing force. His defiance at Buford gave further reason not to allow him to join his people. Although not accused of breaking any treaties (he had signed none), nor other criminal acts (he had not even killed any whites at Little Big Horn in defense of his people), the dialogue back in Washington focused on declaring him a prisoner of war and placing him in a detention camp. But for the moment America would show its humanitarian side and let him rejoin family and old friends. The steamboat General Sherman, which ran the upper Missouri, was called upon to transport him and his band downriver to the Standing Rock Agency, or more particularly to the adjacent Fort Yates. He remained under the control of the military. He departed on the morning of July 29.[13]

What was to become an inconsistent manner of treating Sitting Bull began here. The City of Bismarck located downriver sent a request that the prisoner be allowed shore leave for a visit. The nation's reaction to the Battle of the Little Big Horn and newspaper interviews during his years in Canada made him a Western celebrity. Perhaps for no other reason than to show off the prisoner, the military consented. He was allowed to disembark on the following Sunday, July 31, under guard at Mandan, a town across the river from Bismarck.

The municipality of Bismarck was founded in 1872, in response to the coming of the Northern Pacific Railway—the same railroad whose extension into the unceded lands originally brought Custer to Fort Lincoln and was resisted by Sitting Bull. Originally called Edwinton the town had changed its name within a year to Bismarck in recognition of the chancellor of Germany to appeal to German immigrants in the area. Now the town elders saw an opportunity to be on the national stage. They even enlarged the visit to include a reception.

The local community recognized its chance to witness history. The attention lifted his spirits. But there was a difference in perspective. He understood his importance as the Lakota chief who came home; the whites recognized him as the notorious slayer of Custer who eluded the army for four years after the battle at Little Big Horn. So the inquisitive came to see the infamous Indian outlaw. They were voyeurs to a turn of history.

Sitting Bull chose not the trappings of a great chief for the visit.[14] Rather his appearance was marked by reddish streaks painted on his face and a pair of smoke-colored spectacles that had been given to him to protect his eyes.[15] For the townspeople, these were distinct accents to his careworn appearance. Some of the observing press believed he had purposefully chosen the manner of dress to underscore the distress of his people.[16] All could see that there was no fat in these people. There were no insolent stares, no look of the warrior. One of the crowd remarked that the great warrior chief appeared much subdued from his fierce reputation.

A delegation met the chief at the landing and arranged transportation into town. Present were the editor of the *Bismarck Tribune*, the post trader at Standing Rock, officers from Fort Lincoln, several local society women, and Fish Allison, who had finagled an ongoing job of interpreter. Sitting Bull appeared obliging. But when offered a ride in a locomotive on a spur line from the levee, he refused.[17] The Northern Pacific's extension into Lakota territory still rankled. Instead he accepted a carriage ride. If the citizens of Bismarck wanted to see him, he wanted to see what they were all about. He knew he was in the white man's world. Sitting Bull and his retinue were feted with a luncheon at the Merchant Hotel. Although never before in a city, they handled themselves well. Sitting Bull was served his first taste of ice cream, commenting that he did not understand how something so cold could be made in the heat of the summer.[18] Always an engaging storyteller and schooled from his earlier interviews, he played to a receptive audience, but he kept his remarks focused on family. He provided autographs, having been taught to write his name while in Canada. He posed for a photograph by Orlando Goff, and received a fee.[19] He had not been as cooperative aboard the steamer; when a pencil sketch had been drawn of him, the chief grabbed and shredded it.[20]

The so-called hostile Indian, always comfortable in the presence of women, showed particular interest in the ladies. Sitting Bull questioned an attending officer how the white man kept their woman looking so well. The women at the reception did not display the rough edges of pioneer stock. The officer replied that the white men did not work their women hard. When approached by a young woman, Miss Emma Bentley, who gave him a pear, he tasted it. Finding it pleasing, he reciprocated by taking a ring from his hand and tendering it to her.[21] His comfort increased upon being introduced to Miss Lulu Picotte Harmon, the daughter of Matilda Gilpin who had accompanied Father De Smet on his peace mission in 1868.[22] Just as her mother, Miss Harmon was fluent in Lakota and more trusted than Edward Allison as a translator. At the end of the meal, he presented his pipe to Captain Batchelor and his glasses to Mr. Vermilye, private secretary to the manager of the Northern Pacific Railroad.[23] (It was Lakota custom to reciprocate upon being shown hospitality.) He signed the hotel register and returned with his family to the river to camp overnight. He performed as a seasoned diplomat, without the artfulness of a politician. He was a gentleman.

On August 5, the *Bismarck Tribune* was caught between reporting on his conduct at the reception and questioning "Can this be the instigator of the Custer Massacre?"[24] There was no middle ground, however, for Elizabeth "Libby" Custer, who waged an ongoing public relations campaign in the East against the Sioux on behalf of her martyred husband.[25] She would not let the people in Washington forget.

Sitting Bull had charmed his way through the layover. In taking the next leg of his journey, his life was about to change dramatically.

On Monday he arrived at Fort Yates. A large throng gathered on the riverbank as the steamer readied to dock. Gall was there; and Sitting Bull could see the makings of a grand reception. The chief in exile had returned. A band played, some of the Lakota began singing, and soldiers stood between the crowd and the steamboat landing.[26]

Sitting Bull at Bismarck
LIBRARY OF CONGRESS

Even though it was a momentous occasion, his resumption of leadership was not certain. The crowd was respectful, but most were relatives and old allies—recent arrivals. Others came out of curiosity to see how he would handle the reservation life he so long avoided. Sitting Bull looked for the welcoming embrace of his people.

Tears traced down the cheeks of Sitting Bull. An agency chief, Running Antelope, an old ally who earlier had withdrawn from Sitting Bull in Canada, was chosen as the person to greet him, and he was allowed to board the boat. The Hunkpapa chief had hoped it would be Gall who first would receive him, even though he, too, had deserted him. Gall was like a brother as well as a longtime supporter and confidant. Sitting Bull wanted reconciliation. Gall neither sought this nor offered it. The Man who goes in the Middle stood on the bank, arms folded across his chest. Running Antelope hastened to embrace the chief, who seemed put off.[27] Sensing what he believed to be sadness, Running Antelope was consoling:

"Brother, don't weep; everything will come out all right."[28] The words rang hollow; Running Antelope was considered a sellout by Sitting Bull.[29] (Years later, that impression was given literal currency; Running Antelope's likeness was imprinted on the United States' Five Dollar Silver Certificate issued in 1899.) Sitting Bull could only question to himself: "Who put this man in charge?"[30]

The surrendering Hunkpapa came ashore but were not allowed to register at the adjacent Standing Rock Agency. They were held above the bank of the river near the fort's landing under military supervision. Members of his family and others were allowed to visit, at least fulfilling the promise made at his time of capitulation at Fort Buford that they were safe at the agency. He was relieved to find his daughter well and not bound in chains. But placing him apart from those at the reservation was designed to undercut Sitting Bull reclaiming his chiefdom. It did not quite work; old friends and several head men who had earlier submitted to reservation life came by to visit. One night Sitting Bull managed to slip away from his river camp to make council with other chiefs at their camp.[31] He was thoroughly briefed on the workings of the agency as well as the status of other recent arrivals. From what he could see of the new environment, there were no lean and hard-bodied braves.

There was no overly harsh treatment, and the food was adequate. The returnees' stomachs again felt full at mealtime. But the encampment near the banks of the Missouri under watch had its effect. He confided to Brotherton, who had come to Fort Yates:

> *What law have I broken? Is it wrong for me to love my own? Is it wicked for me to do so, because my skin is red, because I am Sioux, because I was born where my fathers lived, because I would die for my people and my country? What treaties have the whites made that the red men have broken? Not one! What treaties have the white men made with the red men that they have kept? Not one!*[32]

The interlude proved nothing more than time for the Washington bureaucracy to finalize his status as a prisoner. He was not to be allowed to reemerge as principal chief. The army recognized that the longer he was in residence near the agency, the more other former hostiles sought his counsel. Even Gall came around to see him. Clearly, he could not stay with his people. It was far better that more pliable Lakota men advance as leaders at the agency. This man required special handling. Some recommended he be placed beyond the Great Sioux Reservation. A month passed without decision. Then, Secretary of War Robert T. Lincoln issued the order that Sitting Bull be sent to Fort Randall, miles downriver, alongside the Nebraska border, but still within the reservation.[33] It was a form of solitary confinement in an out-of-the-way garrison, with the added burden of accompaniment by the beleaguered last of his Canadian followers. The General Sherman was again called on to provide transportation. In a coincidence of time and location, James McLaughlin was a passenger on board the ship steaming down the Missouri. McLaughlin was on his way to Standing Rock.

A low-ranking officer informed Sitting Bull of the order that came from Washington. Furious, the chief demanded a meeting with the post commander—Colonel Charles C. Gilbert. He threatened rebellion and swore that he would not go.[34] He railed because he had no other way to resist. He decried another breach of an American pledge. He blustered to show that he still was at the front for his followers. Edward Allison provided translation. Exact or exaggerated, Allison's interpretation did not change the result. Sitting Bull simply had confirmed his irascibility.

On the day before Sitting Bull was to be sent south—September 8—James McLaughlin arrived at Fort Yates with his wife and family.[35] From the deck of the Sherman, he could see bayoneted infantrymen watching over a clustered group of Indians on the upper bank to the right of the dock. He knew Sitting Bull had to be among them. As McLaughlin walked off board, Sitting Bull took notice of the man dressed in a dark-gray suit and bowler hat. A professional appearance had become his constant look. Here was the new Indian agent assigned to the home of the trans-Missouri Sioux appearing eager to get to work. Before the Indians could be herded aboard, Sitting Bull made a surprisingly desperate move. As McLaughlin was being received by the fort commander, word arrived that Sitting Bull wanted an audience with the agent.[36]

Sitting Bull stood waiting on the boat's deck. He had thought out his argument, premising it on the Indian Bureau not the military being in charge of agencies.[37] McLaughlin knew that the chief and his band had to be coerced from camp to board the Sherman for its ongoing passage down the Missouri River. As a government man, he well recognized the import of the Secretary of War's directive. His call on the chief was part protocol and part personal assessment. The new agent evidenced no hesitation and actually welcomed the opportunity. It underscored his importance.

In addressing the new agent, Sitting Bull changed his manner from ill-tempered to cooperative, saying he needed to make friends because he wanted to stay with his family at Standing Rock. Having gotten McLaughlin's attention, the chief could not hold back a run of what he knew as abuses of the reservation system.[38] He offered to work with the agent to correct the abuses. He assumed too much. McLaughlin, tilting his bowler hat back on his head,[39] cut him off and said at this point the military was in charge.

"But, you, Mr. Agent, are said to be a friend to the Indian."

"Give me some time; and I will see what I can do. But I offer you this advice—take the time to prove your cooperativeness."[40] The new agent of Standing Rock was not about to preempt the army.

If Sitting Bull thought something positive would come of this conversation, he did not understand the ways of this agent. James McLaughlin was not going to be his advocate. Upon rejoining the post commander, McLaughlin said: "That Indian is mendacious. He has an evil face and shifty eyes."[41] Agent McLaughlin looked at his pocket watch for a moment and then back to the stern wheel steamer pushing into the main current of the Missouri. "There is no way that I want that Indian here."[42] McLaughlin knew that Standing Rock had a large population of late hostiles; he did not need Sitting Bull in this mix while he established himself. Nor was the chief's standing high among all of the reservation Indians. Some had been at the agency for a long time, and others, recently returned from Canada, were bitter over having been led on a doomed odyssey. Time was needed for all agency Indians to simmer down. Whether he was playing to the post command or actually believed what he voiced, James McLaughlin's initial negative characterization of

Sitting Bull would not wash away. His relationship with the Sioux chief would be far different than that of Walsh.

Yet, McLaughlin did have an excellent reputation as an agent.[43] McLaughlin cared about these people, and he was conscientious. But his views were a product of both his religion—Catholic—and his belief in the principles of the Indian Rights Association.[44] That organization was made up of liberal-minded people in the northeast who viewed themselves as supportive of the Indian. The underlying tenet of the organization held that the only salvation for the Native American was assimilation into civilized America.[45] Herbert Welsh, a founder of the Indian Rights Association and executive secretary, wrote in 1882:

When this work shall be completed the Indian will cease to exist as a man, apart from other men, a stumbling block in the pathway of civilization; his empty pride of separate nationality will have been destroyed, and in its place the greater blessings which he or his friends could desire will be his, an honorable absorption into the common life of the people of the United States.[46]

The government promised a stimulus package of employment and housing. To reach that end required the Indian to adopt a work ethic in farming, attend school, and embrace Christianity. The Office of Indian Affairs in Washington had been espousing this approach for some time, but it now had outside reformers to give it new urgency.[47] America could dispossess the Indian of his land, but conquest had a price—the native should be educated to civilization.[48] An enlightened nation professed a conscience. Religion was viewed as a necessary ingredient to converting the savage. Padres had accompanied the early Spanish soldier-explorers to convert the pagans in the new world; now the ministers and Indian agents followed the U.S. military on the Western frontier. Although the Sioux were a deeply spiritual people, native rites and rituals were considered heathenism. No one asserted the First Amendment's directive of separation of church and state against churches spreading Christian doctrine within the reservation.

Ancestral knowledge and influence were to be forgotten; culture and tradition were forbidden to speak to future generations.

James McLaughlin well understood his assignment to make the Indian an American. He had risen to a professional position by hard work and faith in his religion. The red man must take the same road. Agent McLaughlin was a perfect fit for the bureau.[49] He unfailingly advanced its objectives and policies.[50] All the while, he considered himself a friend to the Indian. But he was not reluctant to play factions against one another to suit his overall purpose.[51] McLaughlin would run the Standing Rock Agency from 1881 to 1895.

Standing Rock was a successor agency to what was established as the Grand River Agency in 1869, and it extended above the 46th parallel to the Cannonball River, about 30 miles south of Bismarck in the North Dakota area. (The name of the agency came from a rock formation that Lakota legend interpreted to be either a pouting solitary woman or woman sitting with a child on her back turned to stone.[52]) Its headquarters was another 30 miles downriver, adjacent to Fort Yates standing on its southern edge to provide military reinforcement. The agency's jurisdiction ran to the south into what is now South Dakota and shared a boundary with the Cheyenne River Agency. Other than bottom lands along the Missouri and its tributaries, the agency's land was not readily adaptable to farming.[53] The greater reservation land ranged from the rutted ravines and pinnacles of the Badlands in the south to rolling hills and shallow valleys, with some scattered woodlands and lakes. The thinking was that hard work would make it farmable. The agency was headquartered along the Missouri by specific plan; the Indians were placed away from the heart of the grasslands so that they might forget their hunting days.

Early the next morning, Sitting Bull and the Hunkpapas who had stood by him began their river passage to Fort Randall.

McLaughlin did not see Sitting Bull again for 21 months. Not until he heard insiders' talk that the authorities in Washington were seriously discussing the transfer of the man from the War Department to Indian Affairs would McLaughlin step forward. And that was to advise the commissioner how the Sitting Bull should be managed.[54] McLaughlin always claimed he greatly assisted in the man's eventual release.[55] To the contrary, there were those who said he had lent his affirmation to the decision to make the chief a prisoner of war.[56] What was clear is that James McLaughlin used the chief's absence to promote others to solidify his hold over the agency.

The chief who epitomized Lakota resistance was consigned to a far corner of the prairie.

CHAPTER THIRTEEN

POW at Fort Randall

1881–1883

Fort Randall was in the lower reaches of the Dakota Territory, just below an east-west elbow in the Missouri River before it rolled into Nebraska.[1]

This was the area Lewis and Clark traveled in 1804 before encountering the Teton Sioux further upriver. Here they recorded sightings of jackrabbits, antelope, mule deer, magpies, coyotes, and, of course, the "buffalow." A group surveying biotics was fascinated by a small scamp of an animal on the plain. On a chilly September morning, the men spotted a burrowing rodent that barked, sat up to look about, and then scurried into a dirt hole—it was their first view of a prairie dog. When they saw more of these animals, they poured water down burrow holes to flush out at least one critter for capture as a specimen. The grand cross-country journey had just begun; and despite a week's worth of storms, all was well.

For Sitting Bull, sent in the opposite direction on the Missouri in 1881, the steamboat journey took eight days over 300 river miles from Fort Yates.[2] The prisoner-passengers were disillusioned. They had not been pardoned. They were not reunited with their own people. The pledges at Fort Buford were ignored. Sitting Bull stood at the steamer's rail watching the passing riverside and listening to waters slapping the boat's bow. He felt each mile of the increasing distance from Standing Rock. Solitude was preferred to time with his traveling companions. The past pulled away, and the future was not recognized. He cursed the mendacity of the U.S. officials.

In its early years, Fort Randall was important as part of a line of
fortifications on the upper Missouri and a central supply depot. The fort
stood to protect settlers on their trek along the Platt River westward;
then it became a point of deployment of troops to fight the Sioux during
the 1860s and 1870s.[3] Now it was a garrison with its most exciting days
in the past; the soldiers' tasks were routine—maintenance of the fort,
patrol of nearby wagon roads, and processing of supplies to the upper
Missouri. Particularly during the winter, one could feel the slowness of
the long months with frequent winds pushing against the fort's buildings and traces snow drifting between the uplands and the breaks along
the river.

On September 17, the Sherman drew beside the Randall landing.
Sitting Bull and his followers were allowed to make camp about a mile
west of the fort, but were kept under surveillance. They erected their own
tipi shelters, and the army issued food rations. Treatment by fort personnel proved surprisingly fair. The man in charge when the Hunkpapa
arrived was Colonel George Andrews, who quietly held the opinion that
there was no need to treat Sitting Bull as a prisoner of war. The Andrews
watch of the Indians was gentler than what was experienced at Yates.
Another positive occurred; he finally rid himself of Fish Allison. The
interpreter had accompanied the prisoners from Buford to Yates and then
to Randall. He operated as though his service was indispensable to the
army, and the Lakota were in no position to complain. Allison, hardly an
honorable man, claimed a young Indian woman from camp and later took
the wife of a headman as his own. The second affront was too much; the
Lakota protested. Colonel Andrews found this conduct reprehensible and
ordered Allison off the post, sending him back to Fort Buford.[4]

Sitting Bull, nonetheless, felt the binds of compassionate confinement. There was nothing to constructively occupy the daylight hours; the
only required activity was responding to the officer of the day taking roll.[5]
So, there were long hours of conversation, smoking, and gambling among
the men. The time spent was for the most part just time spent. The chief
counted days of clouds marching on the backs of other clouds. He felt
every moment of the hot currents over the land during the long days and
short nights. He felt chilling blasts blowing over the cold earth during

the short days and long nights. He felt the sky's showers and downpours, warm and cold according to the year's cycle. Unable to roam, the rhythms of the prairie no longer worked for the man confined to camp. His mind played out thoughts, but to what purpose. He fell into periods of despondency. He did not attempt to hide his pain. He told the fort commander: "It is not easy for me to sit down as a prisoner and dream out the future. It is all dark to me."[6]

Fortunately, there were some distractions to break the monotony. Visitors frequented the fort, usually via steamboats. Most often these guests requested the colonel to arrange a meeting with Sitting Bull. The colonel permitted correspondents and even Sioux chiefs from the several agencies to call on the chief.[7] He complained to one correspondent:

> *The life of the white men is slavery. They are prisoners in towns or farms. The life my people want is a life of freedom. I have seen nothing that a white man has, houses or railways or clothing or food, that is as good as the right to move in the open country and live in our own fashion.*[8]

For the interview, he exacted two dollars and some tobacco.[9] But he impressed the scribe as a great man—priest, doctor, politician, and warrior.[10]

When the German artist Rudolf Cronau came to do a painting, the chief appeared in his finest.[11] Cronau was able to arrange an exhibit at the fort that included paintings of notables such as Gall and other former comrades of the chief.[12] Sitting Bull sat several times for photographs by visiting men carrying camera and equipment.

Many photographs during this time showed him sitting with family before a tipi, often with his mother, two wives, and children gathered around him. It was the first time that the outside world considered him as a family man; and it was obvious that he was close to his family and cared about his children. But no camera box captured even a hint of contentment. One photograph showed him with chin in hand, blanket pulled around and looking forlorn, with four young children (three were his and one was a white child), all to his right bundled against the winter's cold, and one of his wives, Four Robes, carrying the youngest child over her shoulder, all to his right, and Sally Battles, niece of the post commander, to his left. Captain Charles Bentzoni with a military cape over his shoulders astride a white horse was in the background.[13] It was an incongruous juxtaposition: Sally Battles was in a long maroon outfit showing two rows of long pleats flaring below a dark waistcoat, a ruffle at the throat, wearing gloves and short brimmed rounded crown hat—a sort of English woman's riding cap; and the white child was in a three-quarters length woolen, double-breasted overcoat, long stockings, with a knit hat pulled down low. Miss Battles was seated on a stool, a head above the rest of the group, and the Indian family was all wrapped in blankets, sitting on the ground. The officer's presence within the photograph was hardly accidental. It emphasized Sitting Bull's captive status.

Missionaries and others came to interview Sitting Bull; in those encounters the chief was cautious about what he said.[14] Incoming mail and requests for autographs multiplied.[15] Sitting Bull turned the attention to his advantage, demonstrating he was not a rogue but rather a significant personage and foremost a Lakota chief. He became a model prisoner—accommodating and well behaved. He said the right things. No more outbursts; no challenging of his overseers. Still the great chief's people at Standing Rock were beyond his reach. There is no doubt that he wanted out of the restraint of Fort Randall.

One of the officers stationed at Randall had secured pictographs depicting exploits of Sitting Bull's and his adopted brother's lives. The officer sought authentication from Sitting Bull.[16] These were copies made by his uncle, Four Horns, originally as a gift to his adopted brother, Jumping Bull, that somehow had fallen into other hands. During his time as a prisoner, he recreated most of these pictographs on ledger paper (omitting the ones showing him attacking soldiers) and gave them to persons who befriended him at the fort. His symbolic signature was a sitting buffalo with a line attached to the mouth of the Indian figure; but on some he used a cursive signature.[17] He was at his obliging best.

He asked his new friend Cronau to carry a message for him back to Washington:

When you go to the Great Father, I beg you speak in my interest, for I am of the opinion that up to now no one has brought my wishes before the Great Father. Tell him, that he may allow me to visit to speak with him personally, tell him that I should like to live like a white man and own a farm that could feed me, for I do not want to live on the rations given to us daily. I like to help myself. I should like to live on the Cannon Ball or Grand River. There is good land, water and wood. There also is the place where I was born.[18]

He was obviously promising to conform—a serious compromise of principles—but it was to no avail. Then President Chester Arthur was not interested in even hearing such a request. Sitting Bull had letters written to Agent McLaughlin at Standing Rock asking for assistance; McLaughlin did nothing, but later reported he "gave good advice."[19] Persisting, with the help of one of the post officers, the chief wrote in August, 1882 to the Commissioner of Indian Affairs:

I never signed a treaty or benefited from a treaty. Therefore, I could not have violated a treaty. I voluntarily surrendered on assurance I would be fully pardoned and allowed to live with my people at Standing Rock. I humbly request that I and those who came with me be sent back to Standing Rock. I will conduct myself peacefully and obey the rules of the Indian Service.[20]

There was no response. He did not give up, enlisting sympathetic visitors who called on him to intercede with Washington; the reports of his conduct were always favorable.

Yet, as diligently as Sitting Bull polished his new image, he still held firm to his core beliefs. Captain Richard Henry Pratt, who had established an Indian Industrial School in Carlisle, Pennsylvania, paid a visit. His purpose was to urge Sitting Bull to send the youngsters at Fort Randall to his school.[21] The chief knew Pratt's scholastic approach was one of regimented assimilation: students' hair was cut, native clothing was forbidden, and not a word of native language was permitted at any time. The students were indoctrinated to a new life, removed from

Sitting Bull with family at Fort Randall
LIBRARY OF CONGRESS (LC-USZ62-62749)

their families.[22] Pratt, the military man turned schoolmaster, recruited children from parents, then stripped his charges of their Indianness—shipping them to boarding school and literally scrubbing the prairie off them the day they arrived at his institute to clothe them in uniforms. Then the teaching of the white man's ways began with classes in academics and trades. The programmed schedule was punctuated by the ringing of a bell throughout the day. Attendance at Sunday school and church in town was demanded. For good measure, students were assigned work details to support the school. Discipline was constant. Punishment, abuse, and illness were frequent. There were runaways and deaths. The invitation was rejected out of hand: "I have seen the results of school. The children who return are neither white nor Indian. Nothing is done for them. I love my children too much to let anything like that happen to them. I will not approve this request."[23] Sitting Bull, while he did not know the full extent of the program, clearly understood the school's purpose of native cultural cleansing.

In September 1882, Lieutenant George P. Ahern, a recent graduate of West Point, was assigned to Fort Randall.[24] He was charged with managing the Sioux prisoners. Based on the conduct of the Indians over the prior year, this was not a difficult assignment. More significantly, because Ahern was sympathetic to the troubles of these people, he established a rapport with Sitting Bull. He assisted the chief with a growing volume of correspondence from persons in various American cities and even foreign countries.[25] The two men frequently talked, and the chief confided to the army man.[26]

"I came back from the Grandmother's Country, promised a reservation, but I am held prisoner here. Your government never keeps its promises."

"There are people in Washington who strongly dislike you. These feelings take time to go away. Right now, all you can do is behave."

"Behave, you mean submit. You make reports. What do you say about me?"

"My reports are to my commander. And he sends them up the chain of command. But I have no problem with you and your people. I report things as I find them. You cause no trouble here."

"Then your chain of command does not listen to you."

"Maybe you're right; this is an outpost. But I believe that what I report is read. Everything in the military takes time."

"Your government is strange. Many white men write to me. I have visitors. Newspaper men ask me questions. Men with camera boxes come to take my picture. Why all this attention? Does your government think Sitting Bull no longer exists?"

"They know who you are. The government knows the Lakota consider you to have strong medicine. Frankly, you are too important for your own good."[27]

—◆—

Upriver at Standing Rock, Gall, Crow King, Running Antelope, and John Grass received far different treatment. They were considered progressive Indians. They agreed to learn the way of the white man. Moreover, they were each cultivated to displace Sitting Bull's standing among his people.

While Sitting Bull was marking time, Agent McLaughlin was earnestly implementing the Department of Indian Affairs' program at his agency.[28] He was aware of resentment toward the government; he knew rations were not as plentiful as promised. He did not hesitate to address the Indians' concerns, calling them to a council to explain his approach to managing Standing Rock. Some old chiefs refused to attend. McLaughlin was not put off. He recognized where these people had come from— "starved into submission" and "recently surrendered."[29] Running Antelope urged the other chiefs to listen. Even former hostiles came to size up the agent. He won over most, by showing a sincere intent to work for his charges. With more than a touch of paternalism, James McLaughlin told them that he occupied the same relation toward them that "a father does toward his children." He told them he had confidence in them. "If the whole Sioux nation joins hands they can be as comfortable and as wealthy as the whites. I am not here to work for one or two of you, but to protect all."[30] He stressed the basic tenants of farming and schooling. Then he invited the chiefs among the assembly to tell him their concerns. This was not exactly standard operating procedure for an agent. John Grass gave an endorsement—"Take a look at the new father. His words are very good and it is your duty to think that his tongue is straight. Father, our forefathers before us suspected the white man, but I think your heart is good and you are my friend."[31] Because he was plainspoken and willing to listen, the Indians were disposed to accept him at his word. Still, Grass asked that the new agent swear to the Great Spirit that he did not come to steal from the Indian. To extend good relations, James McLaughlin invited all to a dinner at agency expense. Mostly, he showed them respect.

Agent McLaughlin was an active manager of all aspects of reservation life. He established new farming practices, assigning plots of land to individuals and district supervisors, to make over his Indians from their nomadic, hunting ways.[32] He did not favor cattle-raising; it was too symbolic of Sioux life as roamers.[33] Besides, farming kept the Indians afoot.[34] (Thomas Jefferson's agrarianism held strong in the West.) The agent invited the Catholic Church to send missionaries and establish schools at the agency; children were to learn the ways of the white man.[35] His Catholic faith did not deny welcome to Episcopalians and Congregationalists to the agency.[36] Families were proselytized. It was a reculturalization process.

It did not take him long to discourage old traditions. The Sun Dance and many cultural ceremonies, including the Buffalo and Horse Dances, were eliminated as pagan rituals. Only the Grass Dance was permitted, provided it was celebrated on Saturdays.[37] Sunday was the Sabbath, which meant adhering to Christian religious traditions. Assisted by the evangelism of missionaries, McLaughlin discouraged polygamy.[38] He may have been authoritarian, but McLaughlin was a strong protector of his wards—he kept drifters away from the Indian camps, and soldiers were not allowed to mingle with Indian women.[39] He beseeched Washington when rations ran short. Those who accepted the McLaughlin way got along.

Because of summer droughts, wicked winds, and early frost during the first two years of McLaughlin's tenure, farming produced an abundance of failure and scant success. Certainly the Sioux did not become self-sufficient. Rations became all important. The dependency built into the reservation system would not go away.

A new Indian police force was established.[40] Each policeman was assigned to supervise a certain district and patrol it. They were to keep the peace, discourage the old ways, and enforce regulations now prohibiting traditional tribal practices. The time necessary to tend to these duties left little for other occupation; and each man was required to furnish and keep a horse at his own expense. McLaughlin recognized the financial burden and recommended higher pay, advising the Commissioner of Indian Affairs that the men's service was of "importance to the government."[41] The agent carefully maintained fidelity with the police. Tribal courts were put in place, and McLaughlin selected leaders of the reservation Sioux to sit in judgment of Indian offenses.[42] There were no courts or commissions to review Indian grievances against the bureau. There is no question that these two institutions were extensions of Agent McLaughlin, but they acted ostensibly as Indian to Indian.[43] Their purpose was to undercut the authority of the old chiefs and consolidate the control of the agent.[44]

While Running Antelope was early promoted as a reservation chief, he was not all that the agent demanded. He was a person who wished to please everyone; while in the main progressive, he still had ties to the conservatives, most of whom were his longtime friends.[45] His followers were what McLaughlin termed "loafers"—those who would not work hard.[46] The major needed leaders who were both articulate and strong in accepting of the new ways. Two men especially met his standards. McLaughlin advanced the standing of Gall and John Grass among the people at Standing Rock.

Gall, an acknowledged leader from his days as a warrior, had credibility with his people. His physical stature matched his leadership. The man was robust and striking in appearance. Although a former hostile, he occasionally had lived on reservation land, moving between reservation and the prairie as he chose.[47] Thus, he more easily understood the need to adapt to the changing circumstances. McLaughlin, of course, knew that Gall had broken with Sitting Bull in Canada. Further enhancing his credentials, he was articulate and willing to work with McLaughlin. At McLaughlin's prompting, Gall told stories about Sitting Bull's cowardice at Little Big Horn. While Gall, Crazy Horse, and others were carrying the fight to the 7th Cavalry, "Sitting Bull was running with the women and children." Another old ally, Shell King, was similarly outspoken: "Sitting Bull led his people into misfortune and many hardships."[48]

John Grass (his Sioux name was "Field of Grass") was a long-established reservation man and fluent in a number of Siouan dialects and English. He never fought against the whites and was quick to appreciate the old ways would not work. His communication skills allowed him a wide audience. Simply put, he became a mouthpiece for his agent and was rewarded with trips to Washington.[49] Sitting Bull did not find Grass a deep thinker; he thought the man vain and easily influenced by those playing to his standing in the reservation community. Yet the man took himself seriously. He accepted farming, but urged stock raising as the better agricultural endeavor at Standing Rock.[50]

These two, in particular, were given preferential treatment and encouraged by McLaughlin to take the lead with certain other progressives at Standing Rock. Sitting Bull unknowingly was put in a struggle for the leadership of his people if ever he were allowed to return from Fort Randall.

In summer of 1882, the improbable happened. A herd of buffalo was discovered grazing in the western reaches of the reservation.[51] Excitement at the report ran through every camp and enclave. Major McLaughlin thought to use this to his advantage. As a reward for Indians' earnest efforts of undertaking farming, putting children in school, and listening to the word of Christian missionaries, the major and another agent, Leonard Love at neighboring Cheyenne River Agency, gave permission to organize a hunt.[52] The Indians may well have gone anyway; the hunger for buffalo had not been farmed out of them. McLaughlin later observed: "I was inspired . . . to show my faith in the Indians and give them the healthful exercise and natural food they were pining for."[53] More probably, the inspiration was prompted as a distraction from two years of drought, hot winds, and early frost, all to the detriment of efforts to farm.[54] In any event, he had the good sense to let Gall, Crow King, Grass, Gray Eagle, and others organize the hunt.[55] Firearms were broken out and ammunition issued. The Indians were days out on the Plains, riding ponies with rifles in hand, just as in their roaming life. The sky was broad and the undulating grasslands stretched forever. There was not a hint of white settlement. The ancient prairie land was still in place. The sullenness of reservation life evaporated. Running Antelope, Long Soldier, Red Horse, and Crazy Walking, all chosen for their hunting skills and prominence, directed hunters, scouts, skinners, and their families on the hunt. McLaughlin, who brought his son on the hunt, got caught up in the adventure.[56] There was exhilaration in just being guided by Sioux hunters and listening to and watching their preparation.

When the herd was located by scouts in the Hidden Wood Creek area, mounted Hunkpapa, Blackfeet and Yanktonai were at the ready.[57] They divided into two columns, and the lead hunters circled the animals. The buffalo bolted and ran. Riders drew their horses alongside and discharged their guns into animal after animal. Then another wave of hunters took over.[58] The pattern of attack continued into the late afternoon. Several buffalo whirled and gored the flanks of horses running beside them. Some riders were thrown to the ground. But the frenzy went on. The buffalo fell hard and often. Five thousand buffaloes were killed in two days.[59] McLaughlin shot five,[60] and his son took down seven.[61] The slaughter was as harsh as any at the hands of white sharpshooters. When it was done, the night camps were full of feasting and storytelling; a large celebration at Standing Rock was held on the return of the hunters. The new agent had advanced his relationship with the Indians of Standing Rock.[62] (Long Soldier made the event his winter count of 1882–1883—the pictograph depicts a white man wearing a black suit and hat sitting astride a horse, running beside a buffalo.[63])

Actually, James McLaughlin was participating in the final elimination of the herd, although it would take another hunt for the Standing Rock Lakota to see their last buffalo run. That fall, two thousand more were killed.[64] Subsequently, to provide a substitute hunting experience and as an appeasement, what were called "killing days" were instituted—government-issued cattle were released from agency corrals and designated Indians were allowed to shoot the animals with others assigned to butcher the beef.[65]

Equally threatening to the Lakota were emissaries sent from Washington. These white men came to Standing Rock in November 1882, with a specific mission—ostensibly for more efficient management of the great reservation, but intent on a land grab.

Congress had accepted a rider to an appropriations bill from a Dakota Territorial delegate to provide for a commission to negotiate a land deal with the Sioux. Local boosters seeking rail extensions pressured for more land to be made available to settlers.[66] The Secretary of the Interior appointed a commission to do the job.[67] Former Governor of the Dakota Territory Newton Edmunds led the delegation. With him were Peter Shannon and James Teller, as well as an interpreter by the name of Rev. Samuel Hinman, a long-standing colleague.[68] Edmunds was a strong promoter of treaties and in the mid-1860s had advocated negotiations over military action, fearing the effect of war on whites coming to his territory. However, as a treaty man he knew how to confuse the matter at hand. He was on the Manypenny Commission that forced the Black Hills from the hands of the Sioux. In 1882, he was acting at best with mixed motives. His primary intent was to make still more land available to settlers coming into the Dakota Territory. He took the position that no Indian could till all this land; there was just too much dirt made available by the coerced amendment of 1876. The proposal was that each of the six agencies then within the Great Sioux Reservation be assigned a separate tract to serve the Indians administered by that agency, instead of all Sioux sharing in the grand reservation.[69] This governmental reorganization had some practical appeal, but in dividing the lands, 14,000 square miles, or nearly 9 million acres[70] (approximately one half of the reservation), were to be withheld from the boundaries of any new reservation.

In other words, those lands would be open lands. The reservation reorganization was not simply an efficiency move. By 1878, the economic recovery from the Panic of 1873 spurred anew westward expansion. At the same time, the weather had cycled to years of more favorable rainfall. Farm machinery was significantly improved to better plow the prairie. Self-binding reapers and flour milling improvements increased grain production. Wheat farming in central and northern Dakota demanded better transportation to markets. Real estate agents joined the railroad corporations in publicizing the advantages of prairie living. In 1880, the Dakota Boom was at a roar; several new settlements had sprouted east of the Missouri River during the 1870s.[71] More farmland just across the river was eyed to meet the demand. No one seemed to pay attention to prior cycles of drought; certainly the railroads extending lines and establishing new towns did not mention it.

When the agreement was submitted to Congress the following February, the *New York Times* reported matter-of-factly:

> *Another great Indian reservation, marked upon the Land Office map by a green spot, surpassed in size only by the reservations of the Indian Territory, is to be thrown open to settlers. This is the great Sioux Reservation in Southern Dakota. The area to be thrown open is about 11,500,000 acres, or an area greater than the combined area of Massachusetts, Connecticut, Rhode Island and Delaware.*
>
> *. . . In this case, however, the Indians are not to be removed to other Territories, but are to be gathered into small reservations within the limits of the large one. These smaller reservations will, taken together, cover as much ground as is given up to the white settlers.[72]*

The *Times* knew the transaction was of great magnitude yet noted that it had not attracted much public attention.

Article II of the prepared "Agreement with the Sioux of Various Tribes" stated:

> *The said Indians do hereby relinquish and cede to the United States all of the Great Sioux Reservation reserved to them by the treaty of 1868, and modified by the agreement of 1876, not herein specifically reserved and set apart as separate reservations for them. The said bands do*

severally agree to accept and occupy the separate reservations to which
they are herein assigned as their permanent homes, and they do hereby
severally relinquish to the other bands respectively occupying the other
separate reservations, all right, title, and interest in and to the same
reserving to themselves only the reservation herein set apart for their
separate use and occupation.[73]

This may have been classic legal writing for conveying "all right, title, and
interest" in what was not reserved, but Hinman translated the parts about
the separate reservations being granted to the different bands of Sioux
and left out the part about giving back land to the United States. Somehow he forgot to mention an essential point. The headline of an article in
the *New York Times* characterized the act as: "NEW LANDS FOR SET-
TLERS."[74] The Indians never understood that the six new reservations
did not equal the whole.

To sweeten the deal, the recently made Indian farmers were now
promised 25,000 cows and 1,000 bulls, bearing the brand of the Indian
Department, based on the proportion of the population of each reservation to total Indians bound by the agreement. Second, to each lodge or
family who selected land within the reservation to which they belonged
and began cultivation, the United States would provide "one good cow,
and one well broken pair of oxen, with yoke and chain" within a reasonable time of settling the selected land.[75]

The Indians were told they had to work hard to earn their way and
better management of the land was the means to do that. The Indians'
heads buzzed with a bombardment of words of good intentions for the
betterment of their reservation lives. They were not told that their reservation would be divided and sold.[76] No one gave them a lesson in the
mathematics of simple subtraction. The gentlemen from Washington
were flimflammers with congressional credentials.

The commission had already taken its message to the Sioux at Santee Reservation[77] in Nebraska (just outside the southeastern tip of the
Great Sioux Reservation and home to Dakota relocated in 1863 after
the Minnesota War), then to Pine Ridge and Rosebud Agencies, where
it obtained marks.[78] Now the commissioners called on the leading men

selected by McLaughlin at Standing Rock. Grass and Gall, having been assigned farming plots and living in family clusters about the Standing Rock agency, believed the making of a specific reservation for Standing Rock had logic. Both McLaughlin and Bishop Martin Marty of the Dakotas in their own way endorsed the proposal.[79] The agent was not about to contradict the men from the nation's capital at his new post. Besides, he understood the importance of land; even though stretched on an Indian agent's salary, he was able by selling previously purchased property in Minnesota to speculate in two northern Dakota tracts along the Pembina River.[80] The bishop appreciated the invitation to attend as a means of furthering the Catholic Church's standing with the government. He warned that not to sign would displease God.[81] Grass and Gall and other prominent leaders signed on November 30, 1882.

But many more were indifferent or were suspicious enough not to sign on. Some Indian leaders at the various agencies were able to obtain permission to travel to Fort Randall; there they sought the counsel of Sitting Bull.[82] He was heartened by those seeking his advice. The chief, while not cognizant of the specifics of the document, instinctively knew that allowing the white man to carve up Indian land had no good purpose. The reservation was created for the Lakota; all were now on the reservation either voluntarily or by force, but they considered this government promise was written in blood. Their losses were too recent to buy what the government men were selling. The commissioners asked for no audience with Sitting Bull. They never came to Fort Randall for marks.

As required by the Laramie Treaty, a large number of signatures were necessary. The requirement of three-fourths signatures of consent for modification was not met at any of the agencies. This was of small consequence to Edmunds, who took the agreement back to Washington for acceptance. He well knew that the prior takeover of the Black Hills was not held to this prerequisite.[83]

But on this occasion, there were no grounds to fabricate a state of national emergency. The Indian wars were over; there was peace across the Plains. When the newspapers began reporting that reservation lands were to be opened to settlement, the reservation youngsters schooled in English translated for their elders. The Indians realized they had been deceived.[84] Providently, there were persons looking out for the Sioux people. Various groups in the East, considering themselves friends of the Indians, were beginning to speak out for the Native American. Reverend T. L. Riggs, a Congregational missionary at Oahe Station near the mouth of the Cheyenne River, south of Standing Rock, and other local religious persons, gave voice to the deceptions of the Edmunds Commission.[85] Herbert Welsh, one of the founders of the Indian Rights Association, organized in December 1882, had toured the Great Sioux Reservation during the summer of that year and was looking for a cause.[86] Hearing of these misdeeds, he went to Washington to lobby against acceptance of the agreement.[87] Reverend Hinman beat a retreat back to the reservation to secure additional signatures. He gathered marks from whomever, even from underage Sioux, some as young as three. When confronted, he explained that signatures of young Sioux were on the document only because their elders asked that they be allowed to sign.[88] The explanation was of no matter; there were enough questions as to the dishonesty in presenting the agreement to disturb the Capitol lawmakers.

Perhaps the Laramie Treaty did mean something. Senator Henry L. Dawes of Massachusetts, an Indian rights advocate, thought so. He took the lead in killing the approval of the treaty, when it was presented for ratification to Congress in February 1883.[89] Still, he favored division into smaller reservations and the concept of allotment, that is, the taking away lands from common ownership of tribes and transferring plots to individuals. He believed this would contribute to assimilation. Nor were the Indian reform organizations opposed to doing away with tribal ownership; they just insisted on a measure of due process.[90] The Senator let confidants know that he intended to repackage the Edmunds plan with some modification; and in this he was supported by the reformers. For now he was squarely on the side of the Indians who had been taken in. Indeed, he portrayed himself as a friend of the Indian. Later in 1883 he would lead a congressional investigation of the commission's actions, with site visits to the agencies within the Great Sioux Reservation.

Downriver, the conversations between Ahern and Sitting Bull continued. He maintained his theme that he was an important man to his people and that he belonged with them. There is no doubt that his notoriety gave him influence; what Sitting Bull refused to realize is that it also undercut him with those in charge of his destiny. The lieutenant could only attempt to provide a dose of reality: "The government does not want you with your people."[91]

Sitting Bull told Ahern that he appreciated his friendship and confided that true white friends were hard to come by. Yet, there were other supporters. Andrew De Rockbraine, an old soldier at the fort, lobbied Colonel Andrews on behalf of the chief.[92] "We know he is not Custer's killer. The man has handled himself well. Why is he here?"

"You know my sympathies. I agree he should be at Standing Rock, but I am not the War Department. Andy, I can only make him as comfortable as Fort Randall allows. I have to stand on orders."[93] (Early on, Andrews had written a letter requesting a trip to Washington be arranged for Sitting Bull to visit the president to discuss his status; it went unheeded.[94])

In December, a Yanktonai Sioux—Strike the Ree—with the assistance of Rev. John Williamson, another Congregational missionary, intervened.[95] They put together a letter sent directly to Secretary of War Lincoln, the man who had consigned Sitting Bull to Randall.[96] "What has Sitting Bull been convicted of doing that you hold him as a prisoner? When was he ever tried and condemned?"[97]

Of course, everyone knew that there had been no charges and no trial.

At last Lincoln reconsidered; he was satisfied that Sitting Bull could cause no further trouble. In April 1883, he directed the Secretary of the Interior to make arrangements for a transfer to Standing Rock.[98]

McLaughlin was informed. He quickly took a lead role, suggesting that the prisoner be sent in sufficient time to get crops in the ground for the spring growing season.[99] He was the man to manage Sitting Bull.

Within days the chief and his imprisoned band were allowed to board the Behan, another of the steamboats working the Missouri River. He was leaving center stage at Fort Randall[100] to go to Standing Rock where the high ground was commanded by someone intent on assuring he would acclimate to reservation existence. Old alliances had shifted. There was no intent to provide him a leadership position. Nevertheless, rival chiefs would see him as a threat.

CHAPTER FOURTEEN

On the Reservation

1883–1884

The Behan on its passage upriver made a stopover at Pierre. Just as in Bismarck two years earlier, a reception of townspeople wanted to see Sitting Bull. He was obliging, mingling with the locals and giving autographs.[1] The town residents' reaction reinforced that he was a person of importance. When acknowledged as chief, he was usually magnanimous.

On his journey to Standing Rock, a home that he was yet to know, his mind ran fast with thoughts. He remembered all the promises made to him and his people over the years.[2] He was coming to reclaim his role as head chief. To him agency chiefs were compromised men. He intended to demand his due. When asked by a reporter from Chamberlain if he knew that a federal commission was treating with the Sioux to sell land, he snapped that he knew nothing about it. Then in his next utterance, he acknowledged being told about "three rascally white men going around, but they cannot have my land."[3] He remained steadfast in protecting his Lakota.[4]

He well knew the several tribes and bands that had gathered at Greasy Grass were dispersed and nearly all were under reservation control. The militant Crazy Horse was dead. His own Hunkpapa band was broken. Most had left Canada before him, although some remained and had integrated with other northern tribes. Even his daughter had left him. (He might have comforted himself that bands always morphed as individuals quarreled, married in or out of the band, or took exception to the group's direction.) These were the thoughts that should have concerned him. But he was too much in a hurry to return to former leadership. He ran his own camp at Randall; he believed Standing Rock would be his to run. The trip against the current could not move fast enough.

Sitting Bull was about to discover he had been gone too long.

This time there was no organized large welcoming at Fort Yates. When the steamboat approached, only a few more people than usual gathered at the river landing.[5] Running Antelope was not among them. Nor was Gall. And the agent was not present. Sitting Bull and his band disembarked on the afternoon of May 10 and were told that they could set up temporary camp on the bank of the river. The first order of business was to seek out Agent James McLaughlin. He did not have to; the major sent word for Sitting Bull to come to the agency office the next afternoon. This was a man as strong willed as Sitting Bull; but here the agent held the upper hand. Equally important, he was more adept at scheming; McLaughlin intended to set the tone.

Fort Yates
DENVER PUBLIC LIBRARY, WESTERN HISTORY COLLECTION

Sitting Bull had heard through visitors at Fort Randall of abuses at some agencies, and he carried his own perceptions from the years of resisting reservation life. He knew there had been little rain and farming was marginal for the Indians of Standing Rock. At the same time, he continued to hear Lakota voices saying James McLaughlin was a good agent.[6] The man was not cut from the spoils system that long dominated agency work.[7] Because of this, he was inclined to accept the agent, although McLaughlin had not been helpful in their last meeting. The chief believed he had something to contribute.[8] What he did not comprehend was that agency chiefs owed their allegiance to James McLaughlin; and the agent was committed to remaking the Sioux into white Indians. There were no chiefs other than those the agent recognized. Sitting Bull did not have the right stuff.

When Sitting Bull appeared at the office the next day, McLaughlin was not there. Sitting Bull and his entourage were obliged to wait. In due time, the agent arrived.[9] Following an exchange of greetings, including McLaughlin's introduction of his wife, the major told Sitting Bull that he was pleased to be of assistance in his release.[10] Not distracted by the pleasantries, Sitting Bull immediately outlined a code of regulations he believed would best serve his people. He said that he did not want his people having to individually draw rations; rather the supplies were to be given to Sitting Bull for distribution. Provision for his people would be managed by him. This was the way it had always been for chiefs. He brought a list written for him by Lieutenant Colonel Swain of Fort Randall, specifying 24 chiefs and head men to manage the Indians affairs at the agency (of course, these names did not include the chiefs McLaughlin had put in place over the last 21 months). He asked the agent to confirm his choices.[11] Knowing that there was a farming program established for the Indians, he said that he did not desire to plant this season, but would watch what others were doing and then consider whether to do so at a later time.

Sitting Bull was a proud man. He demanded an element of independence. He advised the agent that he was the chief of all Indians at the agency, endorsed by letter of the president in Washington. Thus, his name should be first on the agency rolls. He asked to gather together from the reservation all Lakota who had followed him over the years.[12] He was entitled to this respect. He was ready to take on stewardship of the reservation Lakota.

McLaughlin grew impatient listening to demands (he knew there was no letter from the president and he had the last word). He did not aim to show any deference to this man. His intent was to mold or break the man. He fixed a hard gaze on the former prisoner of war, and his response was a lecture:

> *Let me give you some sound advice. The Great Father had not written any such letter and you will not be the biggest chief. You will be treated just like any other Indian at Standing Rock. You will receive rations individually as does everyone else. You will follow regulations. And you will farm the land assigned to you.*[13]

The old system of the chief overseeing provision for his people had been deconstructed. Expectation met reservation reality. It was James McLaughlin who ruled Standing Rock. He concluded what he had to say by pulling his watch from his vest pocket; Sitting Bull understood the meeting was over.

The major's purpose was to take the arrogance out of Sitting Bull. McLaughlin saw before him a man who was diminished physically, in part from years in exile and otherwise simply getting older.[14] These frailties the agent hoped would make it easier to manage Sitting Bull. It was clear the man was living in the past. McLaughlin was prepared to push him into the new realities of life prescribed by the Indian Bureau. The alternative was to become a forgotten man.

Sitting Bull did not expect a confrontation, but that is what he got. Although treated with disrespect, Sitting Bull pulled back to take measure. For the first time, he was an agency Indian. At this point, life at Standing Rock did not appear to offer any more freedom than his prisoner-of-war status at Randall; actually he was treated better there. Here he was insulted. Sitting Bull withdrew, with increasing wariness of Agent McLaughlin.

McLaughlin did not wait for further reaction; within days he had a 12-acre plot plowed for Sitting Bull's band.[15] Surprisingly, Sitting Bull did not turn his back on what was presented; the new agency ward took up the hoe. When McLaughlin came to inspect the plot and found Sitting Bull at work, he asked whether the planting was difficult. "No," replied Sitting Bull slightly arching an eyebrow: he "was now determined to become a farmer in earnest."[16] A cynical remark, but it satisfied the agent. McLaughlin suppressed a wry smile. It seemed that the chief humbled himself, dropping his previous demands of entitlement. To the contrary, he was biding his time, while observing the behavior and manner of his overseer. He knew he could choose where he would comply and where he would hold firm. If change was in order, it had to produce something better. It was not enough to tell the Lakota how to live. He took to the field to show he was not lazy, as was his view of so many reservation Indians. The two men were already jockeying for position.

Major McLaughlin wanted to believe that his I-am-in-charge approach had set Sitting Bull on the right path. At the same time, caution told him that the man needed close watching. In a report to the Commissioner of the Indian Affairs on August 15, McLaughlin wrote:

> *Sitting Bull is an Indian of very mediocre ability, rather dull, and much inferior to Gall and others of his lieutenants in intelligence. I cannot understand how he held such sway over or controlled men so eminently his superiors in every respect, unless it was by his sheer obstinacy and stubborn tenacity. He is pompous, vain, and boastful, and considers himself a very important personage, but as he has been lionized and pampered by the whites since the battle of the Little Big Horn, I do not wonder at his inflated opinion of himself. I however, firmly believe that Sitting Bull will never cause any trouble, he having been thoroughly subdued; moreover, his influence is very limited now, and I hope to be able to turn what little he has towards the advancement of his people.*[17]

From Sitting Bull's perspective, he had been pardoned by Major Brotherton in 1881, and he expected the pardon to be fulfilled. A reservation, although limited by boundaries, should allow one to feel the earth, sun, wind, and rain and live comfortably with family. In his mind, he was not trading one prison for another. He would resist any rules of the agent that conflicted with such freedoms. He had no reason to be a friend of the agent. His attitude only stiffened, when others told him that McLaughlin had a hand in his being sent to Fort Randall.

During the same month of August, a Select Committee of the Senate came to Standing Rock, with the task of investigating the conditions of the tribes of Montana and Dakota Territories and the administration of their agencies. The missteps of the Edmonds Commission had opened the door to a broader inquiry. At least the assignment was characterized that way. The chairman was Henry Dawes of Massachusetts, who was intent on advancing his role as a protector of Indian rights. With him were John Logan of Illinois, Angus Cameron of Wisconsin, John Morgan of Alabama, and George Vest of Missouri.[18] They had just come from Pine Ridge where Red Cloud told them of the misdeeds of the Edmonds Commission. In reply to Dawes, who asked whether the Rev. Hinman was an honest man, Red Cloud was direct: "Hinman lies."[19] He fooled both the Indians and the big men back in Washington. Red Cloud wanted the paper that had been signed torn up. He would not sell any of his reservation. Others at Pine Ridge Agency lined up to testify they were never advised that the agreement gave away any reservation land. Dawes was well aware that back home the uproar over the commission's actions shouted "scandal."[20] The old Oglala chief had been pointed down too many wrong paths. Prior willingness to take the government's word turned to disapproval. Senator Dawes appeared open-minded. In the end, Red Cloud was satisfied with the investigation; more precisely, he got caught up with the opportunity the committee provided him to stand for his people.[21] The chairman would redefine his approach as the hearings moved to other agencies.

When the committee came to Standing Rock, McLaughlin sought his own conversation with commission members, warning them to be mistrustful of Sitting Bull. The man was not honorable and did not appreciate agency ways. "You really do not want to hear from him. He is a habitual liar and schemer."[22] The agent himself thought the reduction of the size of the Great Sioux reservation made sense. There was too much land for the Indian. He advised the commissioners that handouts of food and clothing should be phased out as rapidly as possible and that the way to make the Indian self-sufficient was through farming.[23] Bishop Marty came down from Bismarck to have his own conversations with the commissioners, assuring them there were no abuses at Standing Rock.[24] Then the agent sent out invitations to the adult men to come to meet with the commission.

Despite the committee's defined mission, it was more interested in control and appearance than fact-finding. McLaughlin arranged for the speakers on behalf of the agency Indians at the sessions. He wanted the investigation directed toward Washington and not his management. He chose two lead speakers in Running Antelope and John Grass.[25] Even though they had often appeared before white men such as these, it did not go as expected. They were sharply interrogated rather than asked to provide testimony of their experiences on the reservation. Other Indians who came forward to tell of grievances were peppered with questions about earning their keep and applying themselves to productive use of tools, machinery, and seed, which the government intended to supply. These questions were puzzling to the speakers. The purpose was to fill the record with diversions. Still, Running Antelope advised those speaking not to offend these important men. "Talk quietly and in friendly terms."[26]

John Grass, however, managed to get on record his criticism of the Edmunds Commission:

> *Those men talked a great deal, and we were bewildered. It was not with willing hearts that we signed. . . . Those men fairly made my head dizzy, and my signing was an accident. . . . The white men talked in a threatening way, and the crowd of Indians behind me got frightened and rushed up and signed the paper. . . . Bishop Marty stood before us and told us if we did not sign it, we might as well take a knife and stab ourselves. . . . And he told us also if we did not sign we would be displeasing God.*[27]

When an elderly Lakota known as Red Fish rose to speak, an Indian Police sergeant came up and told him that he "looked as if he had been drinking whiskey, and had better sit down."[28] Intimidated, the man did not give testimony. The charge was false, but many agency Indians had grown dependent on alcohol secured from nearby storekeepers and whiskey traders to numb reservation life. Outwardly silent and submissive, these men were suppressing resentment against the controlled conditions of their new life. Sitting Bull positioned himself to the rear of the audience watching how the proceedings unfolded. His quiet observation would not last. The real problems affecting the agency were not being addressed.

A murmuring in the meeting hall among the Indians standing near Sitting Bull reached the front table. The chairman commented to the assembled: "Ask Sitting Bull if he has anything to say to the Committee."[29]

The chief came forward. He stood for a moment to be certain that he had the attention of the panel behind the table and replied: "Of course I will speak if you desire me to do so. I suppose it is only such men as you desire to speak who must say anything."[30] He garnered the spotlight by not seeking it. Because others stepped forward with criticism, he had stood down. The longer-residing reservation leaders had not asked him to speak. But to those around him he gave a running commentary; this undertone was just noisy enough to invite attention.

Dawes quickly underscored that this was an investigating committee as Sitting Bull came forward: "We supposed the Indians would select men to speak for them. But any man who desires to speak, or any man the Indians here desire shall talk for them, we will be glad to hear if he has anything to say." (The committee was confident it could handle Sitting Bull.)

Sitting Bull was not any man: "Do you know who I am, that you speak as you do?"

"I know you are Sitting Bull, and if you have anything to say, we will be glad to hear you."

"Do you recognize me; do you know who I am?"

"I know that you are Sitting Bull."

Sitting Bull pressed harder: "You say you know I am Sitting Bull, but do you know what position I hold?" He was reclaiming his status as chief in reservation life; if McLaughlin would not acknowledge this, he would proclaim it to the committee.[31]

"I do not know any difference between you and the other Indians at this Agency."

"I am here by the will of the Great Spirit, and by his will I am chief. My heart is red and sweet, and I know it is sweet, because whatever passes over me puts out its tongue to me; and yet you men have come here to talk with us, and you say you do not know who I am. I want to tell you that if the Great Spirit has chosen anyone to be the chief of this country, it is myself."

"In whatever capacity you may be here today, if you desire to say anything to us we will listen to you; otherwise we will dismiss the council."

The lack of recognition of his standing and the intolerant tone of chairman drew a comeuppance: "Yes, that is right. You have conducted yourselves like men who have been drinking whiskey, and I came here to give you some advice." The men at the head table were aghast.

Having verbally scourged the distinguished government men, the chief turned his back to the head table and made a hand gesture toward the door. He was saying "conference over." There was nothing more to say. The Indians in the room withdrew and the committee had no audience to dismiss or chastise. For the moment, he was in command of his people. His oratory had stoked the suppressed resentment of the Indians at Standing Rock.

The committeemen fumed. Logan called Agent McLaughlin forward: "What the hell kind of agency are you running here? We were sent to investigate grievances and your Sitting Bull comes to insult us. Who is running this agency—you or a renegade who calls himself a chief? He should never have been released from Fort Randall."[32] As an experienced politician, Senator Logan was quick to invoke righteous outrage.

McLaughlin responded stiffly that he was in charge. Taking his leave, he sought out Running Antelope, calling him forward for a private tête-à-tête. Major McLaughlin pushed his hat back on his head—a reflex action that signaled his displeasure.[33] The lecture was pointed: "You get that son of a bitch straightened out and those damned Indians back here."[34]

Running Antelope had already realized the gravity of the situation. He wisely told Sitting Bull that everyone knew he was chief and called him aside for further conversation.[35]

We want your guidance; but you come back from prison and throw your standing against the men sent to help us. We were here last year when the Edmunds men came; you were not. The people withdrew from the meeting as you directed; but when they consider the consequences, they will feel betrayed. The government is not living up to providing enough rations. These men need to understand that.

Sitting Bull responded: "Look how these men in the meeting room treat us. They are not good listeners."

Running Antelope, better schooled to reservation life, counseled: "These men come from Washington. They were sent to help us. Senator Dawes could be the Grandfather one day. No one tells them they've been drinking whiskey; you have to make amends."

For once, Running Antelope made sense.

Agency chiefs intercepted the dispersing crowd with admonitions that offending the government men would produce harsh consequences. "Sitting Bull is a hot head who does not understand how things work around here and only knows how to make insults." "You all need to go back to the meeting." Others also came forward to urge Sitting Bull to be contrite. Some of the Yanktonai reentered the meeting room to tell the commission that Sitting Bull did not speak for them. Sitting Bull realized that he did not have sufficient support and recognized his lack of understanding of reservation politics. He acknowledged to Running Antelope that he may have acted rashly and would counsel with his immediate supporters. It did not take long for him to say he would make amends. He knew he had not shown respect to the important men on the commission. Running Antelope promptly advised McLaughlin, and the agent asked the committee to reconvene.

Sitting Bull, tactfully, opened his remarks with an altered tone:

I came in with a glad heart to shake hands with you, my friends, for I feel that I have displeased you; and I am here to apologize to you for my bad conduct and to take back what I said.

I heard that you were coming from the Grandfather's house some time before you came, and I have been sitting here like a prisoner waiting for someone to release me. I was looking for you everywhere, and I considered that when we talked with you it was the same as if were talking with the Grandfather; and I believe what I pour out from my heart the Grandfather will hear.

What I take back is what I said to cause the people to leave the council, and I want to apologize for leaving myself. The people acted like children, and I am sorry for it. I was very sorry when I found out that your intentions were good and entirely different from what I supposed they were.

Now I will tell you my mind and I will tell you everything straight. I know the Great Spirit is looking down upon me from above and will hear what I say, therefore I will do my best to talk straight; and I am in hopes that someone will listen to my wishes and help me carry them out.

I have always been chief, and have been made chief of all the land. [Sitting Bull may have been making amends, but the committee men stiffened at these words.] Thirty-two years ago I was present at councils with the white man, and at the time of the Fort Rice council I was on the prairie listening to it, and since then a great many questions have been asked me about it, and I always said, 'Wait.' And when the Black Hills council was held, and they asked me to give up that land, I said they must wait. I remember well all the promises that were made about that land, because I have thought a great deal about them since that time.

Whatever you wanted of me I have obeyed and I have come when you called me. The Grandfather sent me word that whatever he had against me in the past had been forgiven and thrown aside, and he would have nothing against me in the future, and I accepted his promises and came in; and he told me not to step aside from the white man's path, and I told him I would not, and I am doing my best to travel in that path.

I feel my country has got a bad name, and I want it to have a good name. It used to have a good name, and I sit sometimes and wonder who it is that has given it a bad name. You are the only people who can give it a good name, and I want you to take good care of my country and respect it. When we sold the Black Hills, we got a very small price for it, and not what we ought to have received. I used to think that the size of the payments would remain the same all the time, but they are growing smaller all the time. I want you to tell the Grandfather everything I have said—that we want some benefit from the promises he has made to us. And I don't think I should be tormented with any talk about giving up more land until those promises are fulfilled. I would rather wait until that time, when I will be ready to transact any business he may desire. I consider that my country takes in the Black Hills, and runs from the Powder River to the Missouri, and that all of this land belongs to me. Our Reservation is not so large as we want it to be, and I suppose the Grandfather owes us money now for land he has taken from us in the past.

You white men advise us to follow your ways, and therefore I talk as I do. When you have a piece of land, and anything trespasses on it, you catch it and keep it until you get damages. I see doing the same thing now, and I want you to tell all this to the Grandfather. I am looking into the future for the benefit of my children [the Sioux] and that is what I mean when I say I want my country taken care of for me. My children will grow up here, and I am looking ahead for their benefit, and for the benefit of my children's children, too; and even beyond that. I sit here and look around me now, and I see my people starving. I want the Grandfather to make an increase in the amount of food that is allowed us now, so that they may be able to live. We want cattle to butcher—I want to kill three hundred cattle at a time. That is the way you live, and we want to live the same way. Tell the Grandfather when you get back home. If we can get the things we want, our children will be raised like the white children.

When the Grandfather told me to live like his people, I told him to send me six teams of mules, because that is the way the white people make a living, and I wanted my children the Sioux to have these things to help them make a living. I also told him to send me two spans of horses with wagons, and everything else my children would need. I asked for a horse and buggy for my children; I was advised to follow the ways of the white man, and that is why I asked for those things. I never ask for anything that is not needed. I asked for a cow and a bull for each family, so that they can raise cattle of their own. I asked for four yokes of oxen and wagons with them. . . .

It is you own fault that I am here; you sent me here and advised me to live as you do, and it is not right for me to live in poverty![36]

He spoke for the people with both a request and a scold:

I want to tell you that our rations have been reduced to almost nothing, and many of the people have starved to death. Now I beg you to have the amount of our rations increased so that our children will not starve, but will live better than they do now. I want clothing too. Look at the men around here and see how poorly dressed they are. We want some clothing this month, and when it gets cold, we want more to protect us from the weather. That is all I have to say.[37]

Mollification was mixed with sting from the Chief of the Hunkpapa.

Senator John Logan quickly demanded of the chairman "a word with that man before he sits down."[38]

The Senator rose from his seat as would a preacher taking the pulpit:

This committee has the best interests of the Indian before it. You have insulted us. You have a reputation for showing disrespect to representatives of Congress. God did not make you a chief; appointments are not made that way.

You are not a great chief; you have no following, no power, no control,
and no right to any control. You are on an Indian reservation merely
at the sufferance of the government. You are fed by the government,
clothed by the government, your children are educated by the govern-
ment, and all you have and are here today is because of the govern-
ment. If it were not for the government, you would be freezing and
starving today in the mountains. I merely say these things to you to
notify you that you cannot insult the people of the United States or its
committees. . . . The government feeds and clothes and educates your
children now and desires to teach you to become farmers, and to civilize
you and make you as white men.

This ignored that rations were forever short and of poor quality throughout the reservation system. (The committee should have been looking for
evidence of the many agents who diverted money intended for rations to
their own pocket.[39])

The senator from Illinois (hereafter known as "High Hat"[40] to the
Indians in attendance both based on his tall black hat and his haughty
attitude) was not finished with his rant to put down the chief. He snarled
a final affront: "You are a beggar."

Logan resumed his position at the table. Sitting Bull remained standing in place before the committee. "I wish to say a word about my not
being a chief, have no authority, am proud, and consider myself a great
man in general."

The senator cut him off: "We do not care to talk anymore with you
tonight."

"I would like to speak. I have grown to be a very independent man,
and consider myself a very great man." He was insulted, but checked
his ire.

Logan snapped: "You have made your speech. And we do not care to
have you continue any further."

"I have just one more word to say. Of course, if a man is a chief, and
has authority, he should be proud, and consider himself a great man."[41]
The great chief was not lacking in oratorical force. He would not cower
before a United States senator. The frock-coated, bat-wing-collared

gentlemen were dressed down by someone they viewed as a common a blanket Indian.

Logan wanted Sitting Bull arrested for disrupting the meeting. Major McLaughlin cautioned that could have repercussions, but inside he was seething. Sitting Bull was undermining what McLaughlin was trying to accomplish at Standing Rock. His early assessment of the man held true—Sitting Bull was divisive in reservation life. The agent stammered assurance that he would take care of Sitting Bull under reservation rules.

In the face of Senator Logan's bluster, Sitting Bull countered with advocacy for the Lakota people. To him, reservation Indians should not be subservient to the government; they were owed respect as well as retribution. The United States had used its might to take from them, but it needed to recognize their dignity. This resonated with many who were afraid to speak for themselves. But to the progressive faction of the Standing Rock Indians, Sitting Bull was a disgruntled, out-of-touch old man.[42] He refused to walk toward the future. He was challenging the system to which these Indians had adjusted in order to get along. There would be repercussions. The agency chiefs knew better than to embarrass James McLaughlin. To government officials, Sitting Bull was an egotistical firebrand.

The agency Lakota were aware of the tension between the chief and agent, and there was frequent talk of deteriorating relations. Talebearers reported overhearing a conversation of Sitting Bull and McLaughlin in the agent's office. It was rumored that when McLaughlin offered Sitting Bull a drink of whiskey, the chief grabbed at the major and stammered: "Don't you ever offer me anything like that, to make a fool of me?"[43] (While the chief may have drunk whiskey in the past, he was a critic of its bad influence throughout his life.[44]) For his part, Sitting Bull claimed (notwithstanding the first visit) never to have entered the agent's office, insisting that any conversation be held outside: "I do not care to go inside a white man's house. Under the roof of a white man's house are lies and intrigue. I wish to remain out in the open air. The air outside is pure, inside impure."[45]

The talebearers continued to gossip at the agency, and word of one of the principal's alleged criticism or ill remark would reach the other second or third hand. No one sought to move the two to better relations. They thought it more interesting to see the matter play out.

One month later McLaughlin had to make a critical decision about Sitting Bull. The City of Bismarck, after a close campaign, was designated as the new capital of Dakota Territory. A celebration was planned to coincide with the opening of the Northern Pacific Railroad to the West Coast. Former President Ulysses Grant agreed to come; the city wanted a delegation of Native Americans, and of course it wanted the most famous of America's Indians. An invitation was sent in care of Agent McLaughlin. The former and current Secretaries of the Interior were on the list of invitees.[46] It was a significant event and important to James McLaughlin's standing in the Territory. Though displeased with Sitting Bull's outspokenness, the agent did recognize the public's interest in the man.

While still assaying how best to deal with Sitting Bull, McLaughlin was confident that he could manage him in this setting. Certainly, the people serving the former president knew of the invitation and no word had come from Interior advising restraint. Delivering the chief could only enhance McLaughlin's position with the Indian Bureau. He decided Sitting Bull could attend.[47] And just maybe the excursion could buy a more cooperative Sitting Bull for the agency.

Sitting Bull made McLaughlin court him. First, he said he had no interest in the ceremony, but after further discussion, he gave in. It would get him off the reservation. As the events unfolded, he brightened up. This time he accepted his first locomotive ride, from Mandan over the river to Bismarck; the Northern Pacific, a former nemesis, provided passes for his entourage. He led the Indian delegation in the parade. When asked to speak, he dutifully stepped forward.[48] His words, as translated by a young army officer, were amiable.[49] The newspapers reported of a far different man than had addressed the Dawes investigatory commission. However, later some said that Sitting Bull actually castigated the audience as representatives of the whites who took Lakota land and made his people outcasts. (The chief was not above playing his white audience as fools for his own amusement. He was not bought off by the excursion.) Once again, he basked in the outside world's interest. While most of the Indian delegation camped near the railroad tracks, he was provided a room at the Sheridan House.[50] Life was not so bad on tour, off reservation.

CHAPTER FIFTEEN

Chief on Tour (Standing Rock Star)

1884

Following the Bismarck trip, McLaughlin reported to the Commissioner of Indian Affairs that Sitting Bull was settling into his new life. In other words, the agent had matters well in hand. As relations eased, the agent no longer stood as the strict overseer.

Another opportunity to travel soon presented itself, and McLaughlin again had to consider whether to allow Sitting Bull off the reservation. There were pluses. The man exhibited good behavior when he visited a metropolis; and the agency chiefs were happy to see him away. An invitation for Sitting Bull's appearance at an exhibition came from a Major Newell; and an old friend, Reverend Brother Taliour of St. Mary's Training School in Illinois sent a letter of endorsement of the request.[1]

On the downside, the agent worried about any action that advanced Sitting Bull. In a letter of February 14, 1884, McLaughlin responded to Taliour:

In reply I desire to say that such could not be permitted for obvious reasons, but the positive refusal of Sitting Bull to place himself on public exhibition leaves further explanations unnecessary. I will add however that I do not believe that either the Hon. Secretary of the Interior or Comr. of Indian Affairs would grant the request, neither would I recommend it knowing that such would be detrimental to the Indian Service, to see that the most noted disaffected Indian leader of modern times was being paraded around the country and lionized by the

public for no commendable action, but for his persistent obstinacy in
holding out so long against the Government and commission of law-
less actions, which would certainly be prejudicial to the best interests of
the Government in the management of Indians.[2]

McLaughlin definitely thought this way, but perhaps he was stage managing. He did not believe the best presentation of Sitting Bull lie with
Newell, and he had an ulterior motive. His agent's salary made it difficult
to care for his family.[3] He believed that he could legitimately make money
by merchandizing the Hunkpapa chief, but such an endeavor had to be
carefully planned.

In March, James McLaughlin made an extraordinary move. Acting
both in the role of tutor and tour guide, he took Sitting Bull and One Bull
to Minneapolis-St. Paul, staying at the Merchant's Hotel.[4] McLaughlin
said he was testing his premise that firsthand experience with civilized
America would move Sitting Bull and his nephew toward assimilation.
The agent offered an attentive hand throughout the trip. Sitting Bull saw
a printing press operation and even talked over a telephone line to One
Bull. He threw a switch to turn on electric lights. He visited a shoe fac-
tory and watched over the making of a pair of shoes that were given to
him; next he toured a warehouse stacked with food products. Later he
went to a firehouse to observe a demonstration of firemen responding to
a call.[5] In the whirlwind of big city life, he attended a show that featured
a young woman sharpshooter—Annie Oakley.[6] He was fascinated with
her performance and asked to see her afterward; she responded with an
autographed photograph. At the same time, the legendary chief was a hit
with the locals; the press and the curious vied for the opportunity to see
and possibly talk with the man. McLaughlin caught the spillover recognition of the man at the chief's elbow at every appearance.[7] Each was using
the other. And neither would drop a cautious regard of the other. James
McLaughlin was at his cordial best but still set the agenda.

To some degree, Sitting Bull was impressed, but as a keen observer he
also saw the raw edge of urban life while he was supposed to be taking in
the highlights. He did not understand how a wealthy country could have so
many poor; he was deeply troubled at seeing children begging in the streets.

Alvaren Allen, the proprietor of the hotel the two travelers stayed at in St. Paul, took note of the celebrity chief and how McLaughlin controlled the visit. In a private meeting, Allen discussed with McLaughlin the monetary potential of using the famous Lakota in show business. McLaughlin reacted favorably yet warned that close management was needed. He suggested that his wife should be signed on as an interpreter.[8] He understood that fame could be translated to financial reward. Agent McLaughlin intended to work to make that happen when he returned to the agency.

In the meantime, William "Buffalo Bill" Cody was also making inquiries for his touring "Wild West" show; he sent his assistant, John Burke, to personally meet with McLaughlin.[9] Next, the former agent of Standing Rock, Reverend Joseph Stephan, came forward with a proposal, endorsed by the Secretary of the Interior.[10] Each was put off, as had been Newell. The first was easy to dismiss. Stephan did not have the business expertise to undertake a traveling show.[11] There was no money there. The Cody solicitation, while tempting, required a carefully crafted reply. In April, a letter reached Buffalo Bill's North Platt, Nebraska, address, commenting on several inquiries:

> *I desire to say that I have received so many propositions of the kind that it has become considerable of a bore as I could not endorse the putting of Sitting Bull in an exhibition, especially at "dime museums" or second class entertainments and therefore replied in the negative to some and paid no attention to others.*[12]

The letter acknowledged that John Burke was a gentleman who well-presented Colonel Cody's proposal, then added:

> *I cannot now entertain any such proposition at the present time when the late hostiles are so well disposed and are just beginning to take hold of an agricultural life. I would say in conclusion that you need have no fear of any of the "cheap John" shows or dime museums getting possession of Sitting Bull or any other Indians from this agency, and if they would be permitted to join any traveling company, in conjunction*

with other attractions, I would prefer to have them in your troupe to any other now organized that I have any knowledge of.[13]

James McLaughlin was now considered the Indian agent who managed Sitting Bull. He was the American boss of Sitting Bull. But the chief maintained a cool distance.

Upon his return to Standing Rock from the Minnesota trip, Sitting Bull received permission to move his family away from the agency complex and Fort Yates.[14] He settled on the Grand River about 40 miles west of the Missouri. He said he selected this location in part because he was born on the Grand. He never liked his designated agency plot. He disapproved of what most agency Lakota had become. He strongly believed in keeping families together, and here he was able to cluster family and allies about him.[15] His new residence was a log cabin in which his brother-in-law, Gray Eagle, had lived.[16] Gray Eagle moved to a cabin across the creek and even provided the chief a horse and some cattle. Relations eased between the two; however, Gray Eagle remained a progressive. He was mainly motivated to assist his sisters, who were married to Sitting Bull. Other longtime supporters, such as Crawler, Catch the Bear, and Black Bull, also moved to the Grand River.[17] Running Antelope had a log house just to the east, and Jumping Bull and One Bull set up nearby.[18] Sitting Bull settled into farming his own spread; he grew oats, corn, and potatoes, and he acquired a few cattle and horses.[19] For Sitting Bull, there was insulation from the authoritarian McLaughlin. At the same time, he was suffering from periodic illness[20] and continued to be bothered by the affliction to his eye.[21] He felt the Grand River plot would be restorative. From the agent's standpoint, the chief was out of the way. He only came to the agency on ration days, and that seemed to work for James McLaughlin. Seeking further autonomy, the chief asked for a subagency on the Grand. That was denied, but a request for a day school was granted.[22]

With the chief aging and life quieter around agency headquarters, McLaughlin hoped Sitting Bull may be mellowing. The agent reported that Sitting Bull came by the agent's house on occasion and spoke of his pleasure in traveling outside the reservation and learning of big city ways.[23] (This, of course, contradicted Sitting Bull's distain for the white man's house. No one could recall such sociability on the part of Sitting Bull.) He had not been disruptive for some time. In May, the major thought, "What influence he has is being turned in the right direction; the recent trip to St. Paul has been instrumental in bringing this about."[24] There were other factors at work. The 40 miles of separation between the two served both well. More significantly, Sitting Bull lost his mother in 1884.[25] She had always been his sounding board.[26] With her death, at times he appeared lost in thought and closed off much of the outside world.

Yet the chief still could be contrary. In July, McLaughlin got back to Alvaren Allen of St. Paul that Sitting Bull had to be "manipulated and managed as you would eggs"[27] to get his commitment to go on tour. The agent fashioned an approach to Sitting Bull. As incentive, the chief was told that the trip would include the primary cities in the East and he would be given an opportunity to meet the president. The inducement worked; Sitting Bull gave his assent. A 15-city tour was arranged for the fall, with St. Paul as the gathering point. The show was billed as "Sitting Bull Combination" and was presented as a repertory company emphasizing Indian life on the Plains.[28] He was the drawing card; Allen was to hold him in check. Traveling with the chief were Crow Eagle, Flying By, Gray Eagle, Long Dog, Spotted Horn Bull, and their several wives.[29] Whether there was any fear of the locomotive at the Bismarck on his first stopover in 1881, as observed by one reporter, Sitting Bull was comfortable moving by rail on this tour. The iron horse now was accepted as advanced transportation, even though overnight travel required sleeping in the passenger seats. The railroad was apparently forgiven its role in the elimination of the buffalo.

The first show was held in New York City and ran for two weeks; then it moved to Philadelphia. Sitting Bull made what had become his typical appearance and spoke to the crowd in his own language that he intended to go to Washington to visit the Great Father. The problem was the tour did not have Washington on its schedule. Moreover, Allan in his role as impresario translated the chief's words with great flourish, describing how Sitting Bull set a trap for General Custer and swooped in to kill him and his men at the Little Big Horn. When the audience was told that the savages annihilated the 7th Cavalry, it booed the villain. A young Lakota who was educated at the Carlisle Indian School in Pennsylvania sat in the audience; he sought out the chief after the show and told him what was offered as Sitting Bull's words. Incensed at how he was used, Sitting Bull quit. He demanded that Allan return him to the reservation.[30] It was reported to the public that he had suffered chest pains.[31]

The outsourcing of Sitting Bull increased jealousies back at Standing Rock, as McLaughlin suspected it might. But this also served another of the agent's purposes. The travels drew comments on the reservation: "He did not stop the white man with his call to unite at Greasy Grass, but now he has embraced him." "He does not take to agency life, but dines with white people in cities." "He is a two face." "How can he be a chief when he is away all the time?" The criticism may have been based on envy, but there was some justification as Sitting Bull dallied in the white world. Certainly, the Hunkpapa chief enjoyed the recognition and the experience at a white man's expense.

McLaughlin knew well how to use others for his own purposes. In personal interaction with Sitting Bull, the agent's prior strictness seemed to have lessened. Behind the scenes, McLaughlin encouraged his agency chiefs to undercut the old chief. Gall, an ally at the Little Big Horn, continued to speak of Sitting Bull's cowardice; "the man hid behind the dresses of women."[32] The major often drew on such testimony to fill the ears of those who asked his assessment of the great chief. Because he did not want his view to appear subjective, he backed-filled it with testimony of others. Progressives like Gall and Glass were agency chiefs, but when visitors came to Standing Rock, the desire always was to meet with Sitting Bull. In his absence, the others extended their influence among the agency Indians and, of course, supported the agent's rule. They were jealous and wanted more than McLaughlin's encouragement and respect.

Sitting Bull returned home to the Grand River. He drew comfort from his family and supporters. But he had to realize that his larger influence was fading. Those drawn to him were the elderly, those unable or unwilling to work, and the disaffected.[33] They looked to the old chief for protection. This was not the burden he wanted. In trying to find his purpose, Sitting Bull again would succumb to the escape of the outside world.

At the end of the year and into the first of 1885, Buffalo Bill Cody pressed hard to make the chief a part of his show tour for the coming season. This time McLaughlin indicated he was supportive, but approval had to come from Interior. Cody worked his connections; he got endorsements from Generals Sheridan, Miles, and Terry, all former adversaries of Sitting Bull. But the Secretary of the Interior said no. The showman then wired Commanding General William Sherman, who applied backroom pressure.[34] On May 18, a telegram went to McLaughlin formally advising the major to make it happen. Sitting Bull was put under contract to the Cody Wild West production, receiving $50 per week, with a signing bonus of $125 and an advance of $100, together with all traveling expenses.[35] Sitting Bull was also allowed to charge the solicitous public for autographs and photographs.[36] Other Lakota were hired at $25 per week.[37]

The entourage from Standing Rock joined the show in Buffalo, New York, in June 1885. One of the headliners in the show was Annie Oakley, whom Sitting Bull called "Little Sure Shot";[38] her presence was one of the reasons he signed on. His first favorable impression of the show woman from the prior year progressed to fondness on the tour. Part of her image was the young girl making her way on the frontier; she symbolized family values.[39] But she was genuine and someone who the chief found easy to converse with.

Buffalo Bill portrayed the Indians as a noble race about to vanish,[40] while at the same time he burnished his image as an Indian scout and friend of Custer.[41] His shows often concluded with an Indian attack on a settler's cabin to which Cody came to the rescue. A strange juxtaposition of images. Nevertheless, because he accepted the Indians for whom they were, the Indians in his troupe worked without complaint. Besides, there was a comfortable life outside the reservation—money, regular meals, ability to continue many of their cultural ways during the run of the show, and the opportunity to see the outside world.[42] Even laughter returned to the touring Lakota.

Sitting Bull was given a starring role, but other than appearing at the beginning of the program, he did not have to partake in any of the staged Western vignettes that made up the action parts of the Wild West show.

Cody showed him respect; he was not introduced as the slayer of Custer, but the renowned chief of the Sioux Nation.[43] This was exactly how Sitting Bull thought of himself; it was the image he wanted to project to the American public. (Paradoxically, as a performer representing the noble Indian, he wore a full headdress; as chief to the Lakota, he affected a simpler appearance of one or two feathers rising from the back of his head.) Actually, he was minstrel entertaining in Indian face. Vanity got in his way, and for a time, the Lakota chief unwittingly was a caricature of himself. He wanted to believe he was burnishing an image to take back to the reservation.

Buffalo Bill spoke of the Plains Indians he showcased: "Their lands were invaded by gold seekers and when the government failed to protect them, they thought it was time to do it themselves."[44] William Cody certainly had the ability to adapt to the circumstances of the day. In 1873, he favored the taking of the Black Hills.[45] Now Cody walked the inconsistent line of presenting the taming of the frontier, while portraying the first citizens of the Plains as only trying to defend their land.[46] Yet, the public did not forget that winning the West meant subjugating the Indian.

The producer and director directed his productions to create a mythic view of the frontier and at the same time feature himself in key roles.[47] Since the 1850s, easterners had been fed stories of the making of the West through newspaper accounts and dime novels of larger-than-life men. Buffalo Bill was such a person. The West had been won; it was now time to show urban dwellers the way it had been. Millions wanted just that. They came to experience the adventure from their bench-side seats, watching the staged presentations by real-life cowboys and Indians. The Indian may have been a dependent of the reservation system, but he was showcased in the cities of America.

Because of his drawing power, Sitting Bull's image was featured on poster advertisements. ("Foes in '76, Friends in '85."[48]) Announcement of his name at the shows often drew boos and hisses, common to melodramas of the time. Philadelphia was the site of a particular incident. A representative of the Indian Rights Association sought a private visit after a show. Through an interpreter, the man directed: "Ask Sitting Bull, if he ever had any regret for his share in the Custer massacre." A so-called reformer friend or not, Sitting Bull, on hearing the question, shot a finger toward the man's face: "Tell this fool that I did not murder Custer; it was a fight in an open day. He would have killed me if he could. I have answered to my people for the dead on my side. Let his friends answer for the dead on his side."[49]

In performance, he offset accepting the role of villain by furtively twisting the tail of the American public. Sometimes, Sitting Bull mocked the show's audiences by swearing oaths at them in his native tongue. When these remarks drew applause, he evidenced a sardonic smile. He understood he was on display, and he exacted his own form of price. It was fun for a while. As a counterbalance, his travels extended his fame throughout the country. He received even greater recognition at shows in Canada.[50] Mayors and some members of Parliament sought him out and acknowledged him as an Indian general and statesman. Four years earlier, they virtually ran him out of the country, now they embraced him. All of this would prompt Buffalo Bill to seek to re-sign him in 1887 when the show would travel to England.[51]

On tour he was the subject of many interviews by the press. He took advantage of these occasions to make the case for his people; and he frequently complained about America's stealing of the Black Hills. Cynics said he was justifying his absence from the reservation and a more comfortable life on tour. Show business was both an opening to the larger world and a platform to reach out. While in Washington, D.C., for a show, Sitting Bull was finally able to visit the White House, but President Grover Cleveland was not there to receive him.[52] It was a slight not to be forgiven. And it contributed to the realization that he had to use his influence from the inside out. His voice had to speak from the prairie, not urban America. It was time to reclaim his relevance after dallying as a Wild West performer.

When the season closed in October, the chief went home, saying he was tired of the crowded cities, and looked forward to a return to the openness of the prairie.[53] Still, it was unclear how he intended to handle himself back on the reservation—whether he had either the desire or drive to assert direction. And he knew McLaughlin remained an obstacle.

It did not take James McLaughlin long to turn critical. He concluded that the touring experience was not productive; instead of appreciating

Sitting Bull and Buffalo Bill

civilization, "he is inflated with the public attention that he received." "He tells preposterous stories to the other Indians."[54] Moreover, Sitting Bull had not saved any of the money he earned, instead giving it to street urchins and spending it on dinners for friends.[55] "He squandered his money." The man did not learn from the opportunity given him. Sitting Bull had a different perspective. He confided to Annie Oakley on tour that "[t]he white man knows how to make everything, but he does not know how to distribute it."[56]

The Indian celebrity walked away from show business, but he would not go unnoticed by the U.S. government. Presentation to the American public had restored some of his clout after all.

McLaughlin began to question himself on the advantage of having this Indian on parade.

CHAPTER SIXTEEN

Reservation Disrupted

1884–1886

Once back at Standing Rock, the differences between the two men ran to the surface. McLaughlin remained intent on deconstructing the chief. Sitting Bull believed he now had America's renewed affirmation that he was the great chief of the Sioux. He did not need McLaughlin's acknowledgment, except in the odd way that snipping attacks can tell a targeted person that he has meaning. To the agent, Sitting Bull was as ever an obstructionist to achieving the bureau's goals for the Indians.

In his heart, Sitting Bull considered himself and the Lakota as one—he was his people's protector. He had too much hubris to think otherwise. Born to the prairie, he did not forget his heritage. He learned at his father's side. He became a warrior. He was chosen by his people to be chief and given wisdom by the Great Spirit to guide his people. He fought the white man for his people. For this, he was hunted down and made to surrender to the white man. Now he saw himself being removed as chief for lesser men. This was wrong.

Although Sitting Bull had moved out of the daily view of McLaughlin, the agent did not let distance dim vigilance. McLaughlin had spies and informants living nearby; and Sitting Bull's people kept him aware of the agent's latest machinations. Ration days at the agency store house provided opportunity for gossip.

Important to McLaughlin's diminishing of Sitting Bull's station were men that the agent had promoted at Standing Rock—rival chiefs and policemen.[1] These were his "progressives." Gall and John Grass were the type of new Indian that McLaughlin wanted the outside world to see. Gall symbolized the great warrior who had converted to the new path and was able to understand the white man. Grass always articulate appeared strong minded; but he was easily influenced. To McLaughlin he was an effective speaker to be used to the agent's advantage.

Gall and Grass were willing to adapt. Each understood that they could ascend in power by association with McLaughlin. A codependency was at work; the agent needed men like this to maintain his position. Gall and Grass owed McLaughlin their roles in the inner circle of agency management.[2] They were district farmers; later they were made judges over Indian offenses.[3] These rewards were not just to increase their standing; they were effective in holding the peace at Standing Rock. James McLaughlin expressed the importance of the reservation court this way: "The general influence of the court tends to reduce crime amongst Indians and is a means of settling many vexatious differences between members of the tribe; it promotes good government and civilization."[4] Most important to the agent was the willingness of these men to accept Christianity. Gall attended Episcopal services with his family; John Grass became a member of the same church and later converted to Catholicism. These men were treated as friends of the agent.

McLaughlin kept up relations with the Fort Yates brass. He did not quarrel with the post officers as his predecessor Father Stephan had, but his strength lay in not needing the soldiers. A well-run reservation had to come from within, not from military control. The police and court system served to maintain his strong hand. The overall Lakota populace tolerated the police but never forgot the military was stationed next door.

Another of McLaughlin's inner circle was Crow King. A former warrior leader and close ally of Sitting Bull, he, too, became a part of the progressive camp.[5] He first broke with the chief in Canada and held him responsible for an ill-guided exile that brought the Lakota misery and death. Crow King was a point dog in attacking Sitting Bull as a coward and an old man, out of touch with the new way. He taunted his old chief openly and invited others to do so as well. When Crow King died suddenly in 1884, the more vocal snipping and goading subsided among the progressives.[6] Still, whether out front or behind the scenes, jealousies played hard against the chief. He had to realize that the Lakota who carried McLaughlin's endorsement had more power than he did.

Sitting Bull's relationship with the Indian Police was always strained, even though his nephew, One Bull, joined the force early on. Predictably, he saw the police as serving McLaughlin, similar to the former guard, called akicita, who served the old chiefs when the prairie was theirs.[7] Their purpose was to keep the people in line. Those McLaughlin appointed were often officious and played favorites. Moreover, many on the force had specific biases against Sitting Bull and they had standing to intrude in the affairs of his followers.

Bull Head, one of the top police officers, took up residence near Sitting Bull in the Grand River area. His assignment was to provide surveillance of the chief's activities; and Sitting Bull knew this. An incident between the two arose during a visit to the Crow Reservation in Montana that gave an additional negative edge to their relationship. The trip was at the invitation of the Crow and intended to be an opportunity for reconciliation and sharing experiences of reservation life.[8] The Crow reservation was located immediately north of the Little Big Horn battlefield. The year was 1886, 10 years after the battle with Custer. The Standing Rock and Cheyenne River Lakota petitioned the Commissioner of Indian Affairs to attend. The Crow Indian agent objected to the visit, but surprisingly permission was granted. Of course, Sitting Bull was expected to attend; and McLaughlin included Bull Head and other Indian Police ("metal breasts," or ceska meza, so called because of the badges worn on their coat jackets[9]) in the Standing Rock delegation to keep watch. Some representatives from Pine Ridge came as well. While in route, there was a stopover at the reservation of the Northern Cheyenne at Lame Deer, just to the east of the Crow's land. At the agency store, Bull Head quarreled with a close friend of Sitting Bull. The argument seemed trivial; it was over a sack that Catch the Bear had just filled with provisions. Bull Head thought the sack when empty had been given to him and then misappropriated while he was preoccupied. He accosted Catch the Bear, grabbed the bag and dumped its contents on the ground; then taking the sack, he slapped Catch the Bear on the backside. Catch the Bear gave no physical retaliation, but hard words were shouted: "You will pay for what you have done."[10] Sitting Bull, when told of the affront, seemed to give it passing notice.

Entering the Crow camp, the visiting Lakota were subjected to boasts from their old enemy. Sitting Bull bore the brunt of the boorish behavior. As a warrior and guest, he understood such activity and knew that the rites of bad-mouthing would be followed by gestures of goodwill and a feast. The policemen for the most part were forever reservation Indians, not former hostiles, and they took the boasts as a challenge to Sioux manhood. One of the Crow men pulled back his breechcloth and thrust his pelvis toward the face of Sitting Bull. Shave Head, who took his name because he cropped his hair as a white man, stiffened at what he considered to be high offense to the Lakota. The disrespect drew no reaction from Sitting Bull. He let it play out. Later the Lakota and Cheyenne made their own boasts of their past adversarial times with the Crow; then the former enemies settled down to the business of council.[11]

Sitting Bull's discretion produced results. At the conclusion of the gathering, 30 gift horses were presented to Sitting Bull as a sign of peace from the hosts. Sitting Bull proposed to share the horses among the Lakota who traveled with him. Bull Head came forward when the horses were to be sorted out; he asserted his position as a policeman and threw a lariat around the neck of a fine black and white spotted pony. Sitting Bull stepped forward, removed the lariat, and motioned to Catch the Bear to take the horse. Bull Head was told that he could have a buckskin that the chief chose for him. This was his reprimand for embarrassing Catch the Bear earlier on the trip.[12]

During the several days of council, boasting, and feasting, the Lakota learned that the Crow were being pressured to take allotments of individual parcels within their reservation. Many already had accepted title. The allotment program was built into Article 6 of the 1868 Laramie Treaty but generally had not been implemented. It was intended to break the communal hold on land and place smaller plots into the hands of individual families. This was not a program that Sitting Bull could accept.[13]

No one made a record of the conversations at the council, but after the Sioux returned home, the Crow became resistive of the allotment program. Agent Henry Williamson of the Crow Agency reported: "During this talk several of the Crow chiefs, who had never uttered a word against allotment, took the same stand as Sitting Bull said he had taken at his agency."[14] Sitting Bull had returned to the land of the Greasy Grass and again was made the rogue in the eyes of the government. But he was rediscovering his purpose as chief.

The trip also set key members of the Indian Police firmly against Sitting Bull. The insulted Bull Head held hard to his grudge; Shave Head joined the chorus of agency dissenters who proclaimed Sitting Bull a coward and looked for reason to cite him for offenses on the reservation.[15]

Shell King was another agency Indian with whom Sitting Bull had differences; and the chief was quick to denigrate the man. One day at agency headquarters, Sitting Bull berated his adversary for abandoning the traditional life. In a flare of temper, Shell King drew a knife; Sitting Bull brandished a hatchet. There was no bloodshed; both were cited and the Court of Indian Offenses confiscated the weapons as punishment.[16] Sitting Bull shouted a curse at Shell King. About one week later, lightning struck the man dead.[17] Sitting Bull was seen as still possessing strong medicine.[18] He could not be written off as a has-been by the Standing Rock population.

While disparaged for living in the past, Sitting Bull did not reject all that the white man had to offer. He understood the need for schooling: "We must teach the children to read and write, so the white man cannot cheat us, and we must hang onto our land until the young folks can speak English and look out for our interests."[19] Knowledge of the English language was a means to an end. While Sitting Bull only achieved a limited familiarity with English,[20] he understood the manner of the white man very well. "When you find anything good in the white man's road, pick it up; but when you find something bad, or that turns out bad, drop it, leave it alone."[21]

The religious men and women who came to work the reservations were most often involved in education as well. A Congregational missionary, Mary Collins, established a station near Running Antelope's lodge in 1885.[22] She was bright and strong minded and burned with a religious fervor. Miss Mary Collins was a teacher and preacher and had some knowledge of medicine; and she could speak Lakota.[23] She carried herself more like a schoolmarm. She was always truthful;[24] and her straightforward manner of dealing with the Indians gave her respect. Sitting Bull approached the woman: "I want you to teach my people to read and write, but they must not become white people in their ways; it is too bad a life. I could not let them do it."[25] Fundamentally, he would not give mastery to the white man. He underscored his position: "I would rather die an Indian than live a white man."[26] Sitting Bull's children attended the day school McLaughlin had authorized near Grand River, and he encouraged others in his settlement to send their children. However, the parents remained in charge, and, invariably, there were days when children were kept out of school. Focusing on such absences, McLaughlin charged that Sitting Bull "prejudiced" his neighbors against school. He was "working against our schools and will not send any of his children, and tries to influence others, and is very pompous and insolent; it may therefore be necessary for me to adopt stringent measures with him."[27]

There was never an effort to look at the context.

Mary Collins balanced her zeal to make converts with a common touch. She earned great respect with all the Lakota whom she came to know; she was affectionately called Wenonah (Princess).[28] She and Sitting Bull became friends and conversed frequently.[29] She complimented him to others: "He had an indefinable power which could not be resisted by his own people or even others who came into contact with him."[30] McLaughlin saw the man in a very different light.

Missionary Collins learned much about the Sioux people through her friend. All the while she carried the Bible's message to him. And although he trusted her, Sitting Bull would not accept her religion.[31] Sitting Bull listened to her and certainly came to some knowledge of Christianity. But his view was straightforward: "What does it matter how I pray, so long as my prayers are answered?"[32] He would not give up his people's religious beliefs: "The Sioux were better Christians before they heard of Christ, than the white men are now."[33] The more it was preached to him, the more he found criticism: "White men say it is not right for Indians to worship skulls of buffaloes who gave us the meat of their bodies, but that we should worship the pictures and statues of white men who never gave our ancestors anything."[34]

McLaughlin considered the rejection of Christianity to be pigheaded. He felt that this was the fundamental problem with Sitting Bull. He was frustrated that the chief rejected all reasonable approaches to show him a better path. Sitting Bull, when confronted with the agent's aversion to polygamy and demand that he put one of his wives out of his house, responded: "I like both; I do not wish to treat them differently."[35] Such rectitude riled McLaughlin.

In a detailed report on many matters, James McLaughlin set forth his implementation of the Indian Bureau's policy and commented on those who resisted it:

The Indians of this Agency, with a few exceptions, show steady progress and wholesome advancement in civilization.

Increased interest and efforts to provide permanent habitations and more comfortable homes are manifest from year to year, also better care of stock, more intelligent cultivation of fields and accumulation of property is very apparent, as is also an acceptance and increasing knowledge of the precepts of Christianity with less opposition to placing their children in school and a gradual abandonment of Indian customs. Some of the older persons however cling tenaciously to the old Indian ways, are jealous of seeing their former power pass from them and cannot be brought to accept the new order of things, but this retarding influence is gradually losing its weight and as the old non-progressive Indians pass away there will be none among the rising generation found to be "obstructionists" as some of the old men of the present day do. The chiefs who live in the past do not appreciate what is being done for the amelioration of the Indian race by a beneficent government. The young men are beginning to think for themselves and to do business as individuals regardless of the interference of tribal relations of chiefs; and the industrial education coupled with the patient missionary teaching that is now being pushed forward among the rising generation, if continued, insures their Christianization without which there can be no true civilization.[36]

Of course, Agent McLaughlin's reports to the Commissioner of Indian Affairs were crafted to demonstrate his good management of Standing Rock. The Indian agent was forever making reports.

Both adversaries manifested inconsistencies in their reaction to one another at times. When McLaughlin thought that he could get the man's cooperation, he wrote reports that Sitting Bull was applying himself. He offered the hand of ostensible goodwill. Gestures of friendship were the currency of the moment. When McLaughlin's efforts were spurned, he reported the man was a troublemaker. He went so far as to threaten the chief with time in the guardhouse. Sitting Bull most always stood aloof; he would not be McLaughlin's friend.

Whenever he chose, Sitting Bull could strike a dissident note to cause the major to push his hat back on his head. Or he could appear to go along. Sitting Bull understood how the agent operated, and he picked his time to agitate. Because the agent did not know when this might occur, periodic détente was forever on the edge of dissolution. There were times when the chief may have had no other purpose than provocation of the agent.

But Sitting Bull did not have to speak to irritate. Silence or a sharp look signaled McLaughlin that the chief viewed himself superior to the agent. Sitting Bull knew sarcasm and the major's imperious ways. He could mimic McLaughlin's mannerisms, which at times he would do to the entertainment of friends.[37] To the chief, James McLaughlin was like a "jealous woman."[38]

When Buffalo Bill wanted Sitting Bull for his 1887 London tour, McLaughlin showed some interest. He was willing to reconsider his restriction on travel because it presented an opportunity for his wife to go abroad as interpreter. Now it was Sitting Bull who decided it was best that he stay at home. "It is bad for our cause for me to parade around, awakening the hatred of white men everywhere. Besides, I am needed here; there is more talk of taking our lands."[39] The temptation placed before Sitting Bull was rejected. His duty was at Standing Rock.

Again McLaughlin was upstaged by his ward—that Indian was just "perverse." Foreigners arriving in America were quick to embrace the new country. Men from England, Ireland, Germany, and other European countries seized the opportunity to volunteer for the army in the West for a job and citizenship.[40] To McLaughlin, it did not make sense to resist the path to a better life offered by the bureau to Native Americans.

It was the dominant clashing with the defiant. The unrelenting McLaughlin against the unbowed Sitting Bull. Neither carried respect for the other.

Strong convictions directed both men. McLaughlin's was shaped by his religion, his belief in his adopted country, and the role assigned to him by his government. Sitting Bull's was grounded in his heritage and his people's relationship to the great prairie. Even his silence could not be taken as a statement that all was right with the Indian Bureau. The dramatic change in his people's lives became his burden. The Lakota were struggling to survive in a new world.

In the chief's view, Agent James McLaughlin symbolized what was wrong with America's approach to the Indian. He manifested the American attitude of arrogance that only the white man knew what was best for the Indian. Sitting Bull could not excuse the man based on his good reputation with others. Each thought the other adverse to the well-being of the Lakota people. As divided as they were, neither could forget that Sitting Bull held power as a chief. Ironically, that common touchstone fueled their cross-purposes.

CHAPTER SEVENTEEN

Bait and Switch Legislation

1887–1889

Washington was forever rewriting the rules.

In 1887, Senator Henry Dawes succeeded in passing his version of allotment. The stated purpose of the new act was to serve as an effective means to implement the broad intent of Article 6 of the Laramie Treaty of 1868, which first recognized the possibility of the head of a family both being a farmer and homesteader on land within the reservation. But the lawmakers created a scheme, by which after their unilateral determination of a sufficient amount of acreage for allotted parcels there still would be land unaccounted for. The act had the corresponding and more significant objective of taking the excess land from the reservations to make available to white settlers. The justifying principle of removing common ground from the Indian was to hasten his reculturation.

Specifically, the Indian General Allotment Act (generally known as the Dawes Act) granted the right to the head of an Indian family to apply for a patent to receive 160 acres from the reservation.[1] The size of the parcel for the family mirrored the Homestead Act for settlers. The federal government was to hold the patent in trust for 25 years. At the end of this time, title would transfer to the Indian or his heirs.[2] Citizenship awaited those who completed the patent process or who voluntarily took up residence separate from the tribe and adopted the habits of civilized life.[3] Having applied himself diligently during the 25 years, the Indian was expected to be fully assimilated. An Indian working the land could request a patent. For those who did not come forward within four years, the government would select a plot.[4] Presumably, the uncooperative Indians would not be granted citizenship.

For Congress, the intent of the General Allotment Act was to break up the reservations.[5] Individual title had to supplant the collective ownership. This was the road to self-sufficiency. And the legislation had the strong endorsement of the Indian Rights Association. The Congressional Record described the proposed legislation:

> *The bill provides for the breaking up, as rapidly as possible, of all tribal organizations and for the allotment of lands to the Indians in severalty, in order that they possess them individually and proceed to qualify themselves for the duties and responsibility citizenship.*[6]

Senator Dawes put it more colloquially—to be civilized was to "wear civilized clothes, cultivate the ground, live in houses, ride in Studebaker wagons, send children to school, drink whiskey and own property."[7]

Clearly, the provision to grant land not needed for allotment to settlers was an essential part of the bill. There always had been congressional complaints about the cost of maintaining the reservations; this was a means of cutting expenses and satisfying the unquenchable demand for land by America's citizens. The third proviso of Section 5 set out language to implement the same plan which the Edmunds Commission had hidden from the Sioux five years earlier:

> *And provided further, That at any time after lands have been allotted to all the Indians of any tribe as herein provided, or sooner if in the opinion of the President it shall be for the best interests of said tribe, it shall be lawful for the Secretary of the Interior to negotiate with such Indian tribe for the purchase and release by said tribe, in conformity with the treaty or statute under which such reservation is held, of such portions of its reservation not allotted as such tribe shall, from time to time, consent to sell, on such terms and conditions as shall be considered just and equitable between the United States and said tribe of Indians, which purchase shall not be complete until ratified by Congress . . .*[8]

Of course, this act promoted for the benefit the Indian was not based on any discussion with any of the nation's several tribes. While some humanitarian groups compared the act to the Emancipation Proclamation,[9] at least one saw it as a measure to seize native lands under the banner of looking out for the Indian. The National Indian Defense Association was the only reform group that raised its voice in opposition.[10]

The 1887 measure set out the plan but further legislation was necessary to apply it to specific reservations in the form of agreements with the tribes who occupied the land. Congress did not take long to set its sights on the Great Sioux Reservation. On April 30, 1888, the Sioux Act of 1888 was authorized by Congress. To oversee allotment more efficiently within the Great Reservation, six units corresponding to the agencies within the reservation were described as distinct reservations. These were not collectively the sum of the whole. Vast amounts of land—more than 9 million acres, were unassigned. These lands were to be made available for purchase by the United States.[11] The act did not specify beyond general terms how this would be accomplished: the Secretary of the Interior was authorized to negotiate for these lands in conformity with past treaties or statute under which the reservation is held and on terms that were just and equitable. It was not that there was a shortage of land for settlers, but boomers in the Dakota Territory agitated for more land to attract people. Increased population both boosted the opportunity for statehood and provided more customers for the railroads.

Acknowledging the requirement of the Laramie Treaty, the act specified the terms of an agreement for which the reservation Indians had to vote their acceptance.[12] The General Allotment Act required a survey of the reservations in order to divide the arable lands into sections for allotments. But the government was in a hurry. The ratification vote as proposed included both the consent to sell and setting of the price for the excess lands.[13] Surveying and allotment could come later.[14] Besides the presence of surveyors tramping the reservation land with magnetic compasses, chains, leveling rods, and transits could spook the entire effort.

McLaughlin knew early on that the legislation was not acceptable to his constituents at Standing Rock. On successive days in early April, the agent wrote to two different parties who had inquired of Sitting Bull's availability for another tour, expressing concern about the chief's reaction to the legislation from Washington. To E. D. Comings of St. Paul he wrote that because Sitting Bull is "bitterly opposed to the ratification of the Sioux Bill, although no more so than others of the Sioux," there are those who would encourage getting him away from his people for a few months.[15] The same day, he wrote to his friend, Paul Blum of Cincinnati, Ohio:

> *Regarding Sitting Bull I hardly know what to say. His behaviour for the past few months has been all that could be desired, but he is such a strong composition that he is liable to change at any time. He is very much opposed to the ratification by the Indians of the "Sioux Bill," recently passed both houses of Congress and therefore the friends of that measure would doubtless be pleased to get him out of the way this summer where his influence would not be so strongly felt as if present on the reservation. I, however, do not know what view the Department might take of it.*[16]

The major, however, did not even inquire of Sitting Bull's interest in traveling that summer.

Richard Henry Pratt, the superintendent of the Carlisle Indian Training School, was selected to sell the implementation of the allotment plan to the residents of the Great Sioux Reservation.[17] Imperious and self-righteous, he headed a commission sent from Washington. Before he even reached the reservation, he was disliked for who he was. There had been too many sons and daughters uprooted and shipped to his school in Pennsylvania; "the domestication of wild turkeys"[18] was the description given to Pratt's approach to Indian education. Other members of the commission were Rev. William Cleveland, a cousin of the president and Dakota missionary, and Judge John Wright of Tennessee.[19] All were certain they could obtain the necessary signatures.

This time the Indians understood what was happening.

The commission came first to Standing Rock on July 21. The terms of negotiation were predetermined in Washington. The price on the lands to be acquired was set at 50 cents per acre, to be paid as settlers bought the land. The proceeds would be placed in a permanent fund, which the government guaranteed would be no less than $1 million, and half of the interest was to be used to fund education and agriculture. The other half would be paid out in cash each year. It was just a matter of convincing the Indians that this was just and equitable. Of course, there would be expenses in administering the fund for which the government would be reimbursed.[20] As added incentive, the Sioux would finally get the 1,000 bulls and 25,000 cows that Edmunds had earlier promised (actually, this was a routine promise in numerous prior treaties).[21] At least there appeared to be some recognition that the ground assigned to the Sioux Reservation was more appropriate for grazing than farming.

On July 23, the commission was ready to go to work. They invited all the men of the Standing Rock to their meeting. James McLaughlin extended a gracious welcome, observing that the gentlemen "were not strangers to this country."[22] He was really talking to two audiences. For the reservation men the message was that the commissioners came with good intentions. Running Antelope, as was his custom, played the role of diplomat, asking the Sioux to listen to what the men have to say.[23] The commission offered copies of the agreement for study. It was expected that those who could read English would understand the legal document; for those who could not read, their children who had attended school could translate. Only a few took copies.[24] They were not interested in the words on paper, whatever they may say. Sitting Bull made a token appearance. Later he counseled that the commission should be approached cordially, even though he knew they would seek to exhaust the Indians with talk.[25] He was either tactful beyond his usual manner or confident of the Standing Rock Lakota's desire to hold onto all their reservation lands.

McLaughlin had been solicited by the Secretary of the Interior to assist in securing the necessary signatures. An ex officio seat on the commission was offered to him, but he recused himself because it put him in a difficult position with the people of Standing Rock.[26] Although he approved reducing the size of the reservation, he considered the amount of compensation offered to be unfair.[27] Out of earshot of the commissioners, the agent told his wards he questioned what was proposed. He gave every impression of being on their side.

On the second day, Commissioner Wright directly challenged the virility of the reservation Indians, telling them that they could either continue to look to the government for handouts or they could make a living for themselves.[28] They had best chose the latter, he told them, because the president does not control the money in the national treasury.[29] Rejection of the plan to make the Indians self-sufficient "may well result in people electing men who will close the door to the treasury."[30] The Indians must sign.

The Indians held their own councils at night. Working behind the scenes, Sitting Bull secured pledges not to vote in favor.[31] The old chief felt he had regained a measure of command. The Indians decided not to argue. Let the white men talk themselves out. Pratt implored the Lakota not to reject the hand that came to help. Their land only had value because the white man made the towns and brought the railroads to the Plains.[32] The chairman advised that the $1 million was a minimum; the sale of all lands ceded could yield $5 million.[33] Then he preached the importance of allotment to them. The Sioux heard day after day what the act could do for them.

At some point a few Sioux felt they needed to respond. John Grass asserted himself, giving the commissioners a lesson in math. He told the commission that 5 percent of the permanent fund of $1 million meant $50,000 each year.[34] About half of the annual interest was to be directed to education and industrial purposes. With the number of reservation Indians, the remaining one half would produce $1.00 cash to each reservation Indian.[35] He said the government already owed for land taken. He argued that Manypenny had deceived the Sioux about the boundaries of the reservation. He reviewed past unkept promises. Gall, too, was outspoken, declaring the "Great Father was guilty of lying and stealing."[36] With these strong words, the Sioux had nothing more to say. Gall was championing the position of his old collaborator, Sitting Bull. And for this occasion, John Grass was not an agency mouthpiece. Sitting Bull believed he was again surrounded by like thinking men.

Pratt responded that they needed to focus on this measure not the past.[37] Agent McLaughlin endorsed looking only to the future.[38] The commission's constant theme was that to refuse to sign was "like slapping your Great Father in the face."[39] Grass pulled back from further debate; he told the commissioners that they talked too much. All of their words were "enough to crush us down."[40] Richard Pratt would not give up. He continued the meetings into August, sometimes using coercive tactics and threats.[41] He insisted the Indians had to vote and offered two ballots: red for no and black for yes.[42] The Indians were suspicious of even making a mark on the red form. John Grass took the point. He told the commissioners that if they sold at 50 cents an acre, that was "too cheap." Then he told them that the Indians had come from various parts of the reservation, neglecting their stock, while the commissioners are paid by the government every day of the talks.[43]

While most listened at the urging of Agent McLaughlin, they decided minimal response served them best. Finally on August 21 Gall rose to advise that the meetings had gone on too long:

> *We are through now. We have gotten entirely through, and have brought this matter to a conclusion in a good humor. We have spoken to you pleasantly, and we have got much to do at home, and we are going home today.*[44]

With that, Gall threw up his hands and the Indians stirred to leave. McLaughlin was on his feet, calling the Indians back.[45] It would not do for the Indians to walk out on the Washington representatives. But the commissioners knew the meetings were over. Reverend Cleveland seized the moment to allow the commission to adjourn the meeting on its own terms:

> *My friends, we have heard what you say, and we agree with you that your crops ought to be attended to. So we have come to the conclusion that it is better for you to go home and attend to your crops now, and we ourselves will wait here until we get instructions from the Great Father as to what he wishes us to say further to you.*[46]

No further instructions came. Pratt recognized the commission could not obtain the necessary signatures here. He took the 22 favorable black ballots that had been cast at Standing Rock and the commission south to the Lower Brule Agency.[47] There he got 244 signatures.[48] At Crow Creek Agency a few positive votes were obtained, but the majority refused to commit. Frustrated, the commission went back to Washington and published a report critical of the Lakota it sought to help by the allotment plan. It even suggested they should be forced to take the measure's medicine for their own good.[49] In other words, implement the act without the three-fourths signatures. But there were too many reformers to countenance the same tactics utilized by the 1882 Edmunds Commission. Senator Dawes knew there must be another answer.

A different tact was in the making. The agencies were invited to send delegates to Washington. The trip was intended to sell the Indians on the Pratt plan that they had resisted all summer. There were 61 delegates, one of whom was Sitting Bull.[50] James McLaughlin considered the principal delegates of his agency to be John Grass, Gall, Mad Bear, and Big Head.[51] All of these men had been outspoken at meetings with the commissioners; but they were also men that the agent could reason with.

It was curious that Sitting Bull was included within the Standing Rock delegation. Perhaps, the agent did not trust leaving him home; equally important was his recent good conduct—he had not been disruptive during the month the Pratt Commission had been at the agency. But McLaughlin's reconnaissance had failed him; he appeared not to realize that Sitting Bull had been working behind the scenes or otherwise discounted his effectiveness. In any event, it was better to have him in view and James McLaughlin intended to manage the trip. Red Cloud, the other most recognized chief of the Sioux Nation, was not chosen as a delegate from the Pine Ridge Agency; he was considered too effective in such matters.[52] He had been at the point in stymieing Pratt at Pine Ridge.[53] With strong friends in the East who could lobby for him, the articulate Red Cloud was considered capable of manipulating the conference. He knew how to play to the press and the reformers. Although not having experience in the political arena, Sitting Bull stepped into the power vacuum.[54] Nonetheless, always the dissident, he could not assume the role a leader of the delegation. And if he tried, McLaughlin was prepared to undercut him with the other delegates. Sitting Bull knew not to take on his agent in this situation. But he was prepared to act within the delegation. The opportunity to influence was his to seize.

The Hunkpapa chief may have broken with Red Cloud in 1868, but on the reservation their attitudes toward their respective agents and limits on their chiefdoms were markedly similar. The great Oglala chief soon discovered he had been deceived by the Fort Laramie Treaty. First, he and Spotted Tail were deemed head chiefs of the Sioux by the government; subsequently in 1876, General Crook deposed him in favor of Spotted Tail. He was forced to live on the reservation. The agency named for him was dissolved, and he was moved to Pine Ridge.[55] Thereafter, he was replaced as agency chief by Agent Valentine McGillycuddy with progressives, Young Man Afraid of His Horses (his full name was Young Man Whom His Enemies are Afraid of His Horses) and American Horse.[56] By the mid-1880s, Red Cloud was in constant argument with the agent and sought to have him removed for mismanagement of funds and other misconduct.[57] Despite his rivalry with the reservation progressives, Red Cloud held a high profile among the Oglala. He was smarter in working the system than was Sitting Bull; because of contacts he had in Washington and New York, he had influence with the outside world. His white acquaintances carried his objections against the agent to Washington; an investigator was sent to the Pine Ridge. McGillycuddy was called before the bureau on charges.[58] The campaign to displace him made matters difficult for McGillycuddy, but it took a new administration to remove Red Cloud's nemesis.[59] A new agent finally came to Pine Ridge in 1886.[60] Red Cloud reconciled with Young Man Afraid; and the two of them became leaders in resisting the sale of excess lands of the reservation through the allotment plan.[61] The Pratt Commission had not been able to gather sufficient votes at Pine Ridge, and Red Cloud was held responsible.[62]

The Indians traveled by train, arriving at the nation's seat of government on the evening of Friday, October 12 (none of them gave any significance to the date as the anniversary of day on which Columbus was said to have discovered America).[63] They were entertained with tours of the Smithsonian and the National Zoo.[64] Several went to churches in the city on Sunday. The pastor of St. Matthew's extended an invitation for lunch to Major McLaughlin and the Indians who accompanied him.[65] While

Washington hospitality was accepted, they were not distracted from protecting their interests at the reservation. On this trip, Sitting Bull maintained a distance from his agent; he would accept no shepherding about town by McLaughlin as he did in 1884 in Minneapolis-St. Paul.

The *Washington Post* on October 13 described the purpose of the trip: The Indians "now hold possession of about 22 million acres of land in southwestern Dakota, the greater part of which they have no use for."[66] Their trip was categorized as a negotiation session by the newspaper. The Indians only came to see how much they could get for their land. The allotment scheme simply had been put in a new box; the plan remained a means to the release of land back to the United States. It was another land grab from the Indian.

Sitting Bull focused on a wound to the heart, reminding the delegation that the Black Hills still belonged to the Lakota. Everyone understood him to mean that the government had illegally seized these lands.

The Great Father has proven himself a trickster in our past dealings.

When the White People invaded our Black Hills country our treaty agreements were still in force but the Great Father has ignored it— pretending to keep out the intruders through military force, and at last failing to keep them out they had to let them come in and take possession of our best part of our tribal possession. Yet the Great Father maintains a very large standing army that can stop anything.[67]

The business of the trip commenced on Saturday with a gathering at the Interior Department. The Indians attired in white man's clothes were ushered into the secretary's office.[68] Secretary William Vilas offered a perfunctory welcome and made quick introductions of attending officials. Then he invited immediate discussion. The Indians begged off, saying they were tired from the trip. Vilas persisted, speaking of the federal government's interest and desire to properly provide for the Sioux. The General Allotment Act was for their benefit. The Indians insisted they wanted some time to collect themselves from the trip east and caucus. The secretary let them know that he was a busy man. The delegation did not give in. Rebuffed, he dismissed the meeting.[69] Secretary Vilas, impatience showing, could only brusquely admonish the Indians to consider their position and come back for discussion.[70]

The Indians held their own meetings over the weekend to formulate their response. There were factions within the ranks. Some delegates were ready to accept the proposal; others were adamant that no deal could be made. The trip was not to be a buy-off of votes. Sitting Bull took over; he spoke for two hours against acceptance. Then he proposed the tactic of setting a high price.[71] (He should have known better. This approach was used by Red Cloud and Spotted Tail when the government wanted to buy the Black Hills in 1874; in response to their demands, the government provoked a war to get what it wanted.) The price was put at $1.25 per acre, the same price as the government sold its own land on the frontier.[72] Sitting Bull sought to hold back those delegates who were ready to give in. The compromise was setting a price the majority believed was not acceptable. All of the Standing Rock delegates held firm. On Monday, Vilas and his bureaucrats continued to advocate the benefits of the act. Sitting Bull announced: "I am now one of your people. I have plenty that I could say myself, but I wish the other men here to speak for me."[73] Gall came forward and was a spokesperson. John Grass, American Horse from Pine Ridge, and others gave their reasons for not accepting the measure. Grass proclaimed: "Look at our people; we are poor and we ought not be poor. We ought to be rich. You are the cause of our being poor."[74] He borrowed the words from Sitting Bull. The three primary players at Standing Rock at last were united in a common cause. The always deliberative Sitting Bull clearly understood the importance of giving others the speaking roles in this setting. While generally categorized as a lone wolf, he still was capable of leading the pack when he had other reservation Indians to himself. He knew of all the dissonant chords; he played off of past grievances and deceits. Sitting Bull had not lost his persuasive powers. The problem was that the others were vulnerable to being co-opted by an able agent backed by an overriding government program. McLaughlin was just as convinced of the bureau's mission; and his job was to guide his charges along the proper path. And the arguments put forth by the speakers from the delegation carried a general message of lack of fair treatment. It did not take much to parse the words to hear "dollars."

Extended discourse was something the Lakota refused to do with Pratt; this time the delegates explained their position, and the government representatives saw an opening. The dominant objection was that 50 cents per acre was an insult and yet another instance of the United States attempting to take advantage of the Indian.

The talks having moved to numbers, the secretary decided to put an offer on the table. He said he would ask Congress to consider $1.00 per acre, which price would hold for three years. The price would then go to 75 cents per acre for two years and thereafter to 50 cents.[75] He asked them to formulate their response in writing.[76] Of course, to do so meant that they had to work with their agents. Forty-seven signed onto a statement setting the price at $1.25 per acre.[77] Most felt this was a tactful response that would hold their land in place. Fourteen were of the minority view that the deal should be made as presented.[78]

The delegation formally submitted its demands on Wednesday, October 17. The secretary was not pleased but deliberately withheld a verbal response. He would review the matter with the president. By the Indians finally setting a price and the minority showing a willingness to sell, there was evidence that the government could accomplish its goal. These were interpreted as signs of flexibility. The delegates had created the perception that the deal could be made. Some time was needed for Washington to figure it out.

On Friday, Secretary Vilas flatly rejected the counteroffer. He saw no need for further talks.[79] The meeting was over. The hardliners of the delegation were not disappointed. All were ready to go home. But the Sioux would find that this business was not finished.

James McLaughlin insisted on a promised meeting with President Grover Cleveland; for the president to refuse, he advised, would insult the Indians. What he achieved was simple political formality. There was a shaking of hands and saying a few words; then it was done.[80] That was just fine with the Indians; they wanted no more talk.

Of course, there could be no trip to Washington without documenting it with a photograph. All the delegates assembled on the steps of

U.S. Commissioners with Delegation of Sioux Chiefs, 1888. Sitting Bull is far left in third row; opposite end of same row are McLaughlin and Gall.
LIBRARY OF CONGRESS

the Capitol Building on October 15.[81] Included were the Pratt commissioners, the commissioner of Indian Affairs, and other officials and interpreters. The camera's lens caught Sitting Bull at the far right side of the gathered group, leaning away from the third row of other Indians. James McLaughlin is in the same row at the opposite end, standing military straight; close to him are his favorites—Grass and Gall. All the Indians were dressed in dark suits ("citizen's dress"), with only their moccasins and long hair true to their culture. Sitting Bull's stance infers either his discomfort or independence. Probably both. When there was a request for another photograph with the Standing Rock delegation, the chief walked away.[82]

The Indians went home convinced of a stalemate in their favor.

Whether Vilas was absolute in drawing the line or thought he had succeeded in opening the door to compromise can be debated. No matter, the topic would remain on the government's agenda. In the meantime, there was a national election. The Republican Party, whose long political grip over the presidency had loosened when Democrat Grover Cleveland was elected in 1885, took back the White House and Congress in the 1888 election. The Republicans and big business needed Republican states to hold power. A lame duck Congress was forced to divide the Dakota Territory into two prospective states in early 1889 so that the Democrats would come away with at least one new state out of the four that were to be admitted.[83] The new Republican president—Benjamin Harrison from Ohio—took office on March 4, 1889, and appointed a new Secretary of the Interior as part of his cabinet.[84] Two days earlier, outgoing President Cleveland signed legislation admitting North Dakota and South Dakota, together with Montana and Washington, as states of the union.[85] It was clear that South Dakota representatives especially required additional available land to attract settlers.[86] Pressure from cattlemen and the railroad interests was intense.[87] Farming had come to dominate the area east of the Missouri River; the prevailing thinking said land to the west should be used in the same way.[88] All of this meant less Indian land. The incoming Harrison administration committed itself to the sale of land within the Great Sioux Reservation. It reviewed the Sioux negotiations with Secretary Vilas and determined the quickest way to its objective was to meet the last price stated. Senator Dawes, the Republican from Massachusetts, was at the ready, steering a new Sioux bill through Congress. Red Cloud, petulant from his adverse reservation experiences, heard of the pending legislation and demanded a meeting in Washington. The new Secretary of Interior, John Noble, would hear none of it. While Red Cloud managed to go to Washington anyway, his conversations with the acting commissioner of Indian Affairs amounted to nothing. Outgoing President Cleveland signed the legislation on March 2.[89]

The legislation set the price per acre at $1.25, which was to hold for three years. For land sold during the succeeding two years to homesteaders, the price dropped to 75 cents per acre; thereafter the price became 50 cents per acre.[90] The administration had met the demand of the Sioux on price. In return, the Sioux would receive title to the land the government chose to allow to them.

There were other modifications to make the package appear more attractive. The minimum amount from the sale of the lands was guaranteed at $3 million to be placed in trust;[91] and the expenses of surveying and sale of the ceded lands were not to be deducted from the proceeds.[92] The allotment of 160 acres was increased to 320 acres for family heads,[93] recognizing that the small homestead square did not work on the prairie. The Laramie Treaty provision for educational benefits would be extended another 20 years (the 1888 bill also indicated extension but was less specific).[94] The act also provided compensation to the Red Cloud and Red Leaf bands for the horses the military confiscated in 1876.[95] Finally, none of this would happen without the assent of three-fourths of the adult males living on the Sioux Reservation, as required by the Fort Laramie Treaty of 1868.[96]

Within weeks of passage, Harrison executed the authorization given him by the act to establish another commission to obtain the necessary signatures for ratification. An appropriation of $25,000 had been included within the measure for the commission to assure sale of the plan.[97] On May 19, the president named the men who were charged to deliver the Indians' consent.[98] It was not going to be an easy task; there had been too many times that the United States backtracked on its word and too much shoddy management of agencies. The chairman—Charles Foster, former governor of Ohio—was joined by William Warner, a former congressman from Missouri and commander of the Grand Army of the Republic (a fraternal organization of veterans of the Union army who served in the Civil War), and General George Crook, the Indian war campaigner.[99] It was Crook who had the experience and was the key to the negotiations. There is no question that this was his commission. Although an old military adversary, he had gained the reputation among the Indians as a straight talker. Crook intended to get the job done and had all the time he needed to do so. His approach was one of patience over outright pressure.[100] But on occasion, he would prod the Sioux with appeals to their responsibility of providing for their families.[101] The open meetings were more for show; the real work was done behind the scenes. The general in a report to the Secretary of the Interior described his approach:

It was soon discovered that it was impossible to deal with the Indians as a body in open sessions. The matter had been already decided as the result of their tribal councils; and, when all were present, each one sustained the other in opposition to which each had pledged himself. It was therefore determined to endeavor to convince individuals that substantial advantages to the Indians as a whole would result from acceptance of the bill.[102]

The commission began its meetings at Rosebud, Cheyenne River, and Lower Brule and had gotten approval from all except Pine Ridge.[103] An aging and nearly blind Red Cloud dug in. With the support of Little Wound and Young Man Afraid of His Horses, all that could be secured at Pine Ridge were signatures of a bare majority of adult males.[104] Crook did not start by haranguing the Sioux. Instead he drew from the budgeted funds to provide grand dinners and time for informal discussion.[105] He even permitted dances that had been outlawed by the agents. He hired squaw men and mixed-bloods to lobby their relatives and acquaintances.[106] Divisions over votes set Lakota against Lakota throughout the reservation.

Sitting Bull was aware of what was taking place throughout the reservation and rightly worried that the commission would win support from lesser chiefs at the lower agencies. For the moment, he was not in a position to do anything about it. Suffering from lung congestion, an annoyed Sitting Bull confided to a visiting Bismarck photographer: "The white is wise in books. He can read and write and we cannot. We know nothing about books and, the whites have fooled us."[107]

In June, help from outside the reservation came from a woman member of the National Indian Defense Association. (The NIDA was at the extreme of groups supporting the Indians; it did not agree with assimilation and focused on the unhappy state of reservation life.[108] It was the only Indian reform organization that held to the principle that Indian tribal life had value.[109]) Mrs. Catherine Weldon of Brooklyn, New York, had corresponded with Sitting Bull and other key agency Indians from the time of the Sioux visit to Washington the prior October.[110] Now she traveled to Bismarck and made her way to the Parkin Ranch located on the Cannonball River, the northern boundary of Standing Rock.[111]

She was a widow with a school-age son in boarding school when she came to Standing Rock.[112] She was refined, something of an artist, and, more importantly, an ardent reformer. She certainly had more courage than the usual Eastern Native American sympathizer; she put herself in the Dakotas among the Sioux during a critical time. Her plan was to join with Sitting Bull to shore up Indian opposition to the Sioux Act of 1889.[113] She naively assumed cooperation from the Agent McLaughlin. She knew he was on record against the Sioux Act of 1888 and had a good reputation for running his agency. James McLaughlin quickly was informed of her arrival at Parkin Ranch and rode up to Cannonball to meet her.

She was not to be missed. She dressed the part of a society lady from the East, in finery and jewelry.[114] She was not of pioneer stock and better clothed than the officer's wives McLaughlin knew living at the fort. Either as a comment on her fashion or more personally directed to her character, the chatter among these women was that her bustle was too small.[115] In her late forties when she arrived at the edge of reservation, she appeared younger. Of course, the woman was attractive. She was educated and independent; she also was considered something of a bohemian.[116] Probably she looked on herself as a blue-stocking woman. Not particularly religious, she had no interest in Christianizing the Indian.[117] Her primary friends in the East were Dr. Thomas Bland and his wife, Cora, of the NIDA.[118] Catherine Weldon was a liberal who fully embraced the cause of working with the Indian against the intrigues of the U.S. government.[119] Catherine was not even her true name; she was born in Switzerland as Caroline Schlotter.[120] She came to America in 1871 and a few years later married a carpenter by the name of Richard Weldon.[121] When he died, she was left with modest family money, but people thought her to be rich.[122] There was no question that she was on a nonreligious mission. She strongly believed in the philosophy of her organization that Indians should hold to their culture and have the right of local self-government.[123] She was as certain of her purpose as Mary Collins, but otherwise distinct in her need for an emotional identity with the Indian. But, unlike so many others, she came to assist the Lakota help themselves.[124] She combined forward thinking and earnestness all wrapped in a fervent desire to serve. To many she was a dilettante, impressed with her own importance.

Having intercepted letters she had written to Sitting Bull, McLaughlin knew who she was and her intended business.[125] At first he seemed solicitous. But within a few minutes, without the woman mentioning the chief's name, he sought to disabuse her of dealing with the man she had come to help. "He is a coward, a selfish man, no one's friend, of no importance, and a heavy burden on the younger men who are more progressive."[126] She sat puzzled as to why the conversation had turned to disparaging Sitting Bull. The major became more direct, commenting on her organization and its president: "I am not sure what you intend to accomplish but you need to know that Dr. Bland has no foothold or influence at Standing Rock."[127] The agent would accept no interference with his supervision of Standing Rock. Dr. Bland's association recently had been criticized in the Yankton Daily Press for the association's efforts "to neutralize in advance the work of the commission" at the Rosebud Agency.[128]

James McLaughlin continued his lecture: "You do not know life on the reservation. I have worked here for eight years. These people are my friends. I too understood that last year's Sioux bill was not fair for the Indians. But, now the government is more generous; it is giving the Sioux exactly what they asked for."[129] She was not put off, and McLaughlin saw no good way to exclude her from the reservation. Rather he hoped she would be nothing more than a minor annoyance. She had said one of her purposes for the visit was to paint a portrait of Sitting Bull.[130] She asked to see him. Strategically, he thought it better to let her exhaust her quest in the discomfort of a Dakota summer.

McLaughlin heard that Sitting Bull was seriously ill with pneumonia.[131] Knowing the chief was in no position to respond, the agent allowed Weldon to dispatch a letter inviting Sitting Bull to the agency headquarters for a meeting. Perhaps, the woman would tire of waiting; or the chief would never come. She held onto her expectation for weeks. When a recovered Sitting Bull finally arrived, he stood before her dressed in workaday clothes and wearing a hat.[132] She wore a tailored jacket over a long skirt, and a bonnet wrapped her hair and shaded her face. Beneath this fashion statement were sensible boots covered by gaiters. He exhibited no accoutrements of chiefdom. This was not the appearance she imagined. He was slightly hesitant, probably still affected by his illness. He removed his hat to greet her, and her gaze was met by soulful eyes. The eyes were the most noticeable feature of the man. As he stood before her, she found him beguilingly noble. She greeted him with the few words she had learned in Lakota. Her "Hau" was met with his "Hello."[133] Mrs. Weldon reaffirmed that she came with support from her organization and was prepared to work with him in stopping the commission's breakup of the reservation. Letters expressing the Defense Association's offer to assist the Sioux also had gone to chiefs at some of the other agencies.[134] She would champion his cause.[135] Here was a woman who appreciated what he represented; Mrs. Weldon gave no indication of designs to change him. Obviously, she got his attention. And as their conversation continued, Sitting Bull did not fail to charm her, as he did with most white women who met him.

Mrs. Weldon immediately attempted to organize a trip to the lower agencies for the chief to campaign with her against the Sioux Bill. Sitting Bull returned to Grand River to make preparations for the trip.[136] Mrs. Weldon knew that for Indians to travel, an agency pass was necessary. She made the request. McLaughlin forbade it.[137] Weldon was furious. She shrieked at the agent: "I have friends in Washington."[138] Her words had no effect; McLaughlin had his own friends in Washington. For insurance, he directed an associate to discourage Sitting Bull, threatening him with prison if he traveled anywhere with the white woman.

When Mrs. Weldon said she would go alone to other agencies, he told her she could travel on any road that she wished but not on reservation roads. She initiated a letter campaign to urge the agent's removal.[139] McLaughlin knew the power was with the commission and that the Indian Bureau would not listen to this woman. He decided to let gossip do its mischief against her.[140] It was quick in coming. The white women of the agency offered no hand of friendship. The press, when advised of her presence, viewed her as a crank and wrote that the woman was crazy enough to think she could become Sitting Bull's wife.[141] There is no question she viewed him as charismatic. And he was chief of the Lakota. He epitomized the cause she came to fight for. As a crusader she was filled with purpose. Sitting Bull called her "Woman Walking Ahead."[142]

The *Bismarck Tribune* of July 2 characterized her as a foolish woman:

No sooner had the agent refused than Mrs. Wilder (sic) flew into a rage, and declared her intention to see her political friends in Washington and secure Major McLaughlin's removal. Those who came from Standing Rock state that she used the most scathing and abusive language to the Major and accused him of using the Indians as prisoners. So abusive and threatening was her language that the agent politely ordered her to leave the reservation.

Mrs. Wilder (sic) is a widow and is visiting the reservation. She is a great admirer of Sitting Bull, and it is gossip among the people in the vicinity of the Agency that she is actually in love with the cunning old warrior.[143]

Mrs. Weldon, having previously met Red Cloud through her national association,[144] asked for his advice. In a letter of July 3 she complained about the overbearing Agent McLaughlin:

He fears Sitting Bull's influence among his people and therefore pretends to his face that not politics were the reason for refusing the pass, but my welfare, and he took this opportunity to humble the old chief and make his heart sad.

In order to lessen my influence as a member of the N.I.D.A., he makes me ridiculous by having the story printed in which it is stated that I should have said that I came all the way from N. York to marry Sitting Bull. Red Cloud is there no protection for a defenseless woman?[145]

She continued her missive, advising that Sitting Bull would never sign, but was apprehensive that some of the other chiefs might break ranks. The letter never left the agency; it was intercepted and forwarded to James McLaughlin.[146] Her charge that the agent "fears my presence & did all he can to destroy me"[147] went nowhere.

The commission arrived at Standing Rock by Missouri steamboat from the southern agencies on July 23. Everyone knew the significance of this visit. Men from every section of Standing Rock came for the convocation, camping just below Fort Yates. Six hundred signatures were necessary to carry the measure. An outdoor assembly hall was fashioned by placing large tree limbs on three sides to form a square with a wall of the agency warehouse.[148] The commissions and officials sat on a slightly raised stage area built in front of the doors to the building.[149] General Crook did not begin with the usual presentation of the government's good intentions; instead he invited comment. Ostensibly, he wanted open discussion; in reality he did his best work in private conversations. The common meetings drew quick opposition to what the government representatives came to sell; but behind the scenes lobbying of progressives and factions and outright buying of votes aimed to change this. The operative tactic created the impression that those who failed to sign would not receive the benefits being offered through the bill.[150]

Again, Sitting Bull chose to work beyond the commission's sight.

Friends and Relatives: Our minds are again disturbed by the Great Father's representatives, the Indian Agent, the squaw men, the mixed-bloods, the interpreters, and the favorite ration chiefs. What is it they want of us at this time? They want us to give up another chunk of our tribal land. This is not the first time or the last time. They will try to gain possession of the last piece of ground we possess. They are again telling us what they intend to do if we agree to their wishes. Have we ever set a price on our land and received such a value? No, we never did. What we got under former treaties was promises of all sorts. They promised how we are going to live peaceably on land we still own and how they are going to show us the new ways of living—even told us how we can go to heaven when we die, but all that we realized out of the agreements with the Great Father was, we are dying off in expectation of getting things promised us.

One thing I wish to state at this time is, something tells me that the Great Father's representatives have again brought with them a well-worded paper, containing just what they want but ignoring our wishes in the matter. It is this that they are attempting to drive us to. Our people are blindly deceived.

Therefore, I do not wish to consider any proposition to cede any portion of our tribal holdings to the Great Father. If I agree to dispose of any part of our land to the white people I would feel guilty of taking food away from our children's mouths, and I do not wish to be that mean. There are things they tell us that sound good to hear, but when they have accomplished their purpose they will go home and will not try to fulfill our agreements with them.

My friends and relatives, let us stand as one family, as we did before the white people led us astray.[151]

The Indian leadership of the agency rejected the dictated terms of the act. The last position they had taken in Washington was no longer on the table.[152] Gall, Grass, Mad Bear, and Big Head were outspoken.[153] Grass argued that white settlers would not take land at the higher price of $1.25 per acre and instead wait for the price to go down.[154] Therefore the benefits of sale were illusory. Again, the Indians retreated to complaints about how they had been manipulated by the government in the past.

Crook commented on the vagaries of Washington lawmakers and offered practical advice:

Last year when you refused to accept the bill, Congress came very near opening this reservation anyhow. It is certain that you will never get any better terms than are offered in this bill, and the chances are that you will not get so good. And it strikes me that instead of your complaining of the past, you had better provide for the future.[155]

This time the Indians asked to see the agreement papers; they wanted to study them. They asked for their own stenographers.[156] But the papers contained legal terms and concepts that were beyond comprehension. The feasts continued and bribes were strategically offered to certain individuals. The plan was to whittle away the organized opposition. When worry was expressed that rations (beef provisions were already in short supply) would be cut as soon as the land was secured, Crook gave his personal assurances that would not happen. And he made promises beyond the scope of the bill, saying he would use his influence in Washington to obtain additional concessions.[157]

Meanwhile Mrs. Weldon served as private secretary to Sitting Bull, writing to other key reservation Indians, translating letters he received, and explaining various government documents.[158] At the same time, she kept up her own contacts with reformers back East.[159] She provided money to organize opposition and supplied maps showing the size of the lands to be taken and identified parcels which the government sought, as well as price lists.[160] The chief was getting the type of information that had been missing in past dealings with government envoys and commissions. Sitting Bull, in turn, sent schoolboys to the meetings to observe the commission and bring him word of what was taking place.[161]

Ultimately, Catherine Weldon could not help him hold the agency chiefs and head men in place. The alliance of reservation resistance forged in 1888 began fraying. Questions were raised: "Who was the white woman who said she came to aid Sitting Bull?" Crook was sure McLaughlin would work his people in the right direction.

James McLaughlin was in a delicate position; he agreed with the government plan but had to be careful with his agency chiefs who had advocated opposition the prior year. He was up to the task. The day after the commission's arrival, he stopped by Crook's quarters at Fort Yates to discuss how his Indians could be won over.[162] "Give me some time, but let the Indians talk as much as they want at your meetings."[163] Taking a mediator's stance, he advised that some additional concessions may be necessary. A particular sticking point was the army's confiscation in 1876 of the surrendering Hunkpapa horses; McLaughlin urged compensation of $200,000, a generous price.[164]

The break in the opposition came three days after the conference opened. The agent and his wife were entertaining the commissioners at a reception and dinner. McLaughlin had requested a meeting with Grass that same night to privately discuss the proceedings to date. Grass knew what was coming. He insisted the meeting be in an out-of-the-way place, and it was set at Nick Cadotte's house, five miles from the agency. Cadotte was a brother-in-law to John Grass.[165] The dinner host politely excused himself from the reception with the explanation that some unexpected, but relatively minor, trouble had come up. It was best that it not wait until morning. "There is nothing for the commissioners to concern themselves with; just agency business. I should be back relatively soon. I want to be sure there is nothing to distract the Indians from meeting with you gentlemen"[166] No apology was needed; Crook knew that it was time for the agent to turn his agency chiefs around. Louis Primeau, the reservation interpreter, was already outside waiting with a wagon. When they got to the destination, Cadotte told McLaughlin that Grass was afraid someone may observe him with the major at the house. The man was tucked out of sight in a nearby barn.[167]

The conversation took a while; McLaughlin did not get back for dinner. But he succeeded in getting Grass's commitment to support the measure.[168] The two schemed on how Grass could reposition himself and then carefully formulated the words for a speech that would draw in the reservation Indians.[169] McLaughlin had his collaborator. However, John Grass was adamant that he would not take on the burden of convincing Gall.[170]

It was left to McLaughlin to approach Gall and others.[171] The agent was not above using his own scare tactics: "If the Act were not concurred in, a worse thing might happen: legislation might be enacted without requiring the consent of the Indians."[172] He emphasized this was their last chance. He reminded them that they had committed in writing to sell at $1.25 per acre in Washington; they must honor their word. He was certain that Crook could secure compensation for the horses taken from the Standing Rock Lakota, just as compensation was made available to the bands at Pine Ridge.[173] The agent came to collect on the promotion of his agency chiefs; without his friendship each was just another Indian on the reservation.

When the commission meeting resumed, John Grass subtlety changed direction. He did not say he favored anything, instead he requested concessions, which he made sound like complaints. He said that maintenance of schools provided for in the act should be chargeable to the 1868 Treaty at Fort Laramie for 20 more years. He sought increases in food provisions. When the commission pledged to meet these requests, Grass had the basis to reconsider his announced opposition.[174] He had played the role of the statesman, as scripted by James McLaughlin.[175] Once there was debate instead of cries of protest, Crook knew the commission would get the votes it came for. Others now turned positive.[176]

Word of defections in the Standing Rock opposition reached Sitting Bull at his Grand River village. An irate chief called on longtime associates to join him in a run on the commission, but the momentum had already shifted. McLaughlin anticipated such a play; his eyes and ears at Grand River told him that Sitting Bull was about to come to the agency. The Indian agent would not be embarrassed on his own ground this time. Some of the Lower Yanktonai were placed in an outer semicircle around the meeting place to intercept any attempt to storm the assembly. The Indian Police were instructed to protect speakers and break up any demonstration.[177] The next day, when Sitting Bull led a charge of 20 supporters on horseback, they were met and held back by Lieutenant Bull Head and his police force just beyond the meeting area. "You cannot threaten these proceedings." Sitting Bull only shot the man a quick look of disregard and shoved his way into the meeting, leaving his supporters and Indian Police in a standoff.

General Crook was presiding and about to take signatures:

Now we understood that there have been some threats made against the Indians who sign this bill. You need not be alarmed, because no one will be allowed to interfere with you. And if any damage or injury is done those who have signed, we will ask to have it paid for from the rations of those who do not sign. So there will be no trouble.[178]

He asked attendants to move the tables at which the commissioners were seated forward in order to facilitate the Indians approaching. No dissent was expected.

Sitting Bull called out: "I would like to say something, unless you object to my speaking. If you do, I will not speak. No one told us of this council today, and we just got here."

Crook turned to McLaughlin with a parliamentary tactic: "Did Sitting Bull know we were going to hold council?"

And the major dutifully replied: "Yes, sir. Everybody knew it."[179]

Sitting Bull had been outmaneuvered. He was not allowed to open debate. He was out of order and escorted away by Bull Head's men. The signing went forward.

Grass, Mad Bear, and Big Head stepped up to provide their affirmation.[180] Gall, who was designated to sign third, held back, alarmed by shouting around him; he feared someone from Sitting Bull's outfit may do him harm.[181] Seeing the commotion, McLaughlin hastened forward to secure the rolls of those who had signed. When all quieted down, Gall signed.[182] Then signature after signature of acceptance was entered on the register books. Over 600 signatures were secured before the commission left in early August.[183] When all the votes were finally gathered, 803 had approved.[184] Even close allies of the chief, including One Bull, his nephew and adopted son, signed. Indians in Buffalo Bill's Wild West show on tour in Europe were approached by representatives of the government to sign. Away from the pressure, they refused.[185]

Sitting Bull was undone. He had not been able to keep the opposition coalition together. He was not present when Grass orchestrated the change of position. He had misjudged the resolve of the reservation Indians. He felt betrayed. He could never lend his name to sale of Lakota land. When asked by a newspaper man what the Indians thought of the Sioux Act of 1889, he snapped back: "Indians, what Indians. There are no Indians but me."[186]

His view was not as simple as an aversion to settlers on the Plains. It ran much deeper. He understood that physical separation from the land was part of the diminishing of Lakota culture and spirituality.

Not even the woman reformer from Brooklyn stayed to pick up the pieces. By the end of the summer, she was gone, returning to the East Coast to rejoin her son. Mrs. Weldon felt she had accomplished nothing more than further straining relations between Sitting Bull and McLaughlin. The agent was glad to be rid of her meddling. But she did not entirely let go; through ongoing correspondence she remained in touch with the chief. Either she or the man himself enrolled Chief Sitting Bull in the National Indian Defense Association; that fall he was listed as contributing $2.00 and holding membership together with other reservation Indians whom Weldon had befriended.[187]

Sitting Bull went home. Sensing the chief to be exhausted and emotionally down, the agent sent an intermediary, Gray Eagle, to encourage him to come to terms with the reality of the new way. "Brother-in-law, we have settled on the reservation now. We are under the jurisdiction of the government. We must do as they say."[188] Gray Eagle welcomed the opportunity to direct his brother-in-law. Sitting Bull acknowledged that all Gray Eagle said was true. "But I cannot give up my Indian race and habits. They are too deeply seated in us. You go ahead and follow the white man's road, and do as he says. But for me, leave me alone."[189] He was older and slower, but still leaning into the wind.

Gray Eagle, not appreciative of such indifference, raised his voice: "Well, if you are not going to obey, and do as the whites say, you are going to cause a lot of trouble and lose your life. I have sworn to stand by the government."[190] Then reflecting on their relationship, he added: "We have been friends for a long while, but if you will not obey the orders of the agent, we shall not be together anymore."[191] Gray Eagle understood that continued resistance would not be tolerated. The ratification of the Sioux Act of 1889 was the final nail in the crate to which the old life had been consigned. So again Gray Eagle broke with the chief.

The old prairie man felt his identity as chief was lost. It was the agency chiefs, willing to take the white man at his word, who were depreciating the Lakota people. He could not stop them. He could no longer carry the fight. Yet he would not bend to the will of McLaughlin. Resigned to live out his life at Grand River, he looked for escape from the rigidity of the reservation. Only away from the agency, next to the river of his birth, did some semblance of Lakota identity seem to hold.

Conditions only worsened.[192] Crops withered over two successive years of drought, during the time Indians met with two different commissions.[193] With only traces of spring and summer rains falling to earth, a hot sun seared the ground. The prairie was parched brown. Before that, the winter of 1886–1887 had produced a great freeze. Thousands of cattle, owned by white and red men alike, were caught in a sudden and steep arctic drop in temperature coupled with snowdrifts; the animals solidified in place waiting their time to turn to bones.[194] The hundred days of severe freeze in Montana was known as the "Great Die Up." The weather took back what the land had offered. In 1889, black leg disease, an acute infection that leads to blood poisoning and rapid death, afflicted the cattle on the Plains.[195] Still the Indians were criticized for not making themselves self-sufficient. To the government all they wanted was the dole.

One of General Crook's most effective promises in getting consent was that rations would be extended. Such assurance was still born; Congress, in an economy move,[196] prior to the commission leaving Washington for the Great Sioux Reservation, reduced appropriations for all reservations.[197] The Indian Bureau executed this budget decision in the fall by cutting beef rations by 20 percent.[198] In a matter of months, bitterness at being forced into another land reduction ran throughout the reservations.

President Harrison on February 10, 1890, declared the Agreement of 1889 formally accepted and announced the ceded land open.[199] There was no survey of the lands and no allotments. Seven weeks later, word came that George Crook died; no one carried forward his personal promises to win further concessions from the government.[200] Nor was there a race to pay $1.25 per acre for excess land. The prospective settlers knew of the recent weather cycles affecting these lands and were not rushing to the Dakotas.[201] The so-called scientific principle of the rain following the plow evaporated in the heat of the prior two summers. The dissenters to the Sioux Act now chastised those signing for having again been duped. Indian stood against Indian, and the government sat on the sidelines. Divisions between progressives and conservatives hardened.[202]

The system had not worked. While trying to lift the long-term well-being of the Indian with legislation, no attention was paid to actual conditions on the Sioux reservations. Despair was rampant. Disease had been afflicting the people for some time. Throughout reservation villages, there were children hacking with cough and children burning with fever. Children undernourished and in ragged clothes.[203] Adults sick. Indians, young and old, dying. Bodies of dead relatives to bury and mourn. These were daily occurrences, repeated month after month.[204] The Plains people were in severe distress. The allotment plan held no promise for relief.

James McLaughlin obviously witnessed these same misfortunes. Twenty years later, he wrote:

The day the Indian moved out of his airy tepee into the closed-up house in which no provision was made for ventilation of any sort, he reduced his chance of surviving by a considerable percentage. When he was compelled to change his diet to conform to that of the whites, to eat food improperly cooked by women who knew nothing of cookery, giving up his substantial meat food and living on materials for which he was unfitted by a thousand years of training, he further lowered his chances of sustaining life. The Indian was ignorant of the laws of sanitation, but when he lived in the open, he provided against bad sanitary conditions instinctively; he moved his camp so often that the matter of sanitation never had to be considered. In his new house, he lived amidst filth because he was ignorant that it was filth. He never had a cold and his lungs were sound, in the old days. When he moved into a house from which all fresh air was excluded, he wore the same clothing indoors as in the open—as he had always been used to. He became the prey of colds and fevers; bad sanitary conditions brought their train of disorders, and his blood was impoverished, because he was badly nourished by his new diet.

. . . Pulmonary disorders followed close on colds that were not treated at all, and tuberculosis in its varied forms beset the wretched people. They were quite hopeless in the presence of epidemic disorders.

. . . His children died of disorders he had never heard of, and his parents died in the long winter nights. He was a probationer in the school of civilization, and he was having a hard time of it..He was by turns browbeaten and cajoled, bribed and punished, threatened and rewarded, and all of the worst elements in his character developed for want of firm, consistent, and honest treatment.[205]

Reservation realty was subsumed by orders from the Indian Bureau. Certainly, James McLaughlin recognized the physical problems affecting the Indians, and many times he wrote his superiors asking for relief. But fundamentally he was the dutiful agent, accepting what he had to work with. The Bureau's policies simply did not allow the Indian to become self-sufficient.

Sitting Bull saw the situation in simpler terms: "With whiskey replacing the buffaloes, there is no hope for Indians."[206] Most Lakota had no ears for what he had to say.

He would not be given the opportunity to speak for his people again.

CHAPTER EIGHTEEN

Ghost Dance and Disobedience

1889

By the late 1880s, so many Indians had died of war and disease on the Plains that the Sioux could hear their ghosts whispering in the prairie winds.

Conditions on the reservation were never good. Each year they further worsened. Farming did not fulfill the intent of making the Indian self-reliant.[1] The Indians were always dependent on government rations and always shortchanged.[2] Health care was either ignored or inadequate.[3] Basically reservation Indians prescribed their own medicines from whatever they saw on the shelf; doctors were little more than dispensing pharmacists. The medicine man was still influential. Christian religion found ready converts largely because churches supplied food. Alcoholism was prevalent. Apathy ruled the day. The Sioux and all Indians were in great duress. The decade would close with drought to make conditions worse.

All activity was under the dominance of the white man. There was forced agrarianism, proselytization by Christian preachers, confinement and supervision by agents. To America, the Indian was vanishing. The choice was either become a part of the melting pot or face extinction. There were those who could not accept the alternatives.

In the far West came forward a mystic preaching a new type of religion for the Indian. It mixed native religion with Christianity, and it was mesmerizing.[4] Word of mouth and written correspondence advanced the news across the country's Western reservations. The holy man's native name was Wovoka.[5] He was a Paiute from Mason Valley, Nevada.

Wovoka, Paiute Prophet
NEVADA HISTORICAL SOCIETY

He was a broad-shouldered man, standing nearly six feet in height, who wore a three-piece dark suit, kerchief around his neck, and civilized shoes. On his head there was either a black or white hat, each with the same tall, rounded crown rising from a flat wide brim, which shaded his full cheeked face. His hair was cut blunt.[6] When he removed his jacket for relief from the heat, he usually tucked an eagle feather into a band around one arm. Wovoka commanded attention. But it was what he said that had effect. His words came on with a rush—like a summer rainstorm crossing the dry prairie. His voice was that of an evangelical preacher, and people responded. However, because he would sometimes display magic tricks, some viewed him as a huckster

The foundation of what Wovoka preached was laid in the 1870s by a Northern Paiute religious man called Tavibo, who was his father.[7] The father was known as a weather doctor, having the power to predict and even control the weather. Orphaned at about age 14, Wovoka was taken in by the family of a white man—David Wilson—in northern Nevada, and the young man was given the name Jack Wilson.[8] At the Wilson ranch he learned English and became familiar with the teachings of the Bible. He was already a recognized native preacher when during the eclipse of the sun on January 1, 1889, he lay ill with a fever and fell into a dream.[9] While unconscious, Jack Wilson was taken into the spirit world, where he said that he saw all Indians who had died. A vision came to him of the second coming of Christ.[10] This coming, Wovoka proclaimed, held special significance for the red man. A new earth would be created.[11] It was a reach forward to make the past return.

To the red man who had seen his way of life so drastically change within a generation, the message was seductive.

The white man had spent his God-given graces; the Messiah's message of salvation had been ignored. Christ now was coming to raise up the Indian as the chosen people. The Indians would be taken up to the sky to rejoin their ancestors, and the earth would swallow the white man. Then the Indian would come back to earth, finding buffalo reoccupying the Plains. That message may have sounded strident to whites, but the Paiute holy man did not advocate violence. He stressed: "You must not hurt anybody or do harm to anyone. You must not fight. Do right always. It will give you satisfaction in life."[12]

To hasten the arrival of the red millennium, he told his followers to dance.

> *All Indians must dance, everywhere, keep on dancing. Pretty soon in next spring Great Spirit come. He bring back all game of every kind. The game be thick everywhere. All dead Indians come back and live again. They all be strong just like young men, be young again. Old blind Indian see again and get young and have fine time. When Great Spirit comes this way, then all the Indians go to mountains, high up away from whites. Whites can't hurt Indians then. Then while Indians way up high, big flood comes like water and all white people die, get drowned. After that, water go way and then nobody but Indians everywhere and game of all kinds thick. Then medicine man tell Indians to send word to all Indians to keep up dancing and the good time will come. Indians who don't dance, who don't believe in this word, will grow little, just about a foot high, and stay that way. Some of them will be turned into wood and be burned in fire.*[13]

The Messiah was said to already be on earth and his revelation would occur soon. "When the earth shakes, do not be afraid. It will not hurt you." The Indians were to dance and dance. "Make a feast at the dance and have food that everybody may eat. Then bathe in the water."[14] It was as though the medium was the message. The more there was dancing, the greater the fervor. The dance was an opiate sometimes producing hallucinations.

If Christianity had anything to offer to the Indian, it was a Red Messiah. The message began to take hold in certain reservations in the far West.[15] Its obvious appeal was the promise of being lifted from the despair of reservation life. Each tribe that accepted the religion provided their own adaptation.[16] But the promise was always one of restoration. People who suffered much and saw only a bleaker future on the reservation were told their Indianess would be rewarded.

The Ghost Dance had reached eastward to the Great Basin by mid-1889.[17] While most of the Sioux were engaged in the discussions with the Crook Commission over the allotment and severalty plan, word of the movement was heard at Pine Ridge and other Sioux reservations. That fall certain Lakota, including Short Bull of the Brules, traveled by rail to Wind River Agency, a Wyoming reservation home of former enemies—the Arapaho and Shoshone—then on to visit the Bannocks in Idaho, and finally to the land of the Paiute to meet with Wovoka. They were taken to a mountain where the man spoke to them. There they were introduced to the dance and taught the religious doctrine that supported it. With them were Cheyenne and Shoshone.[18] All heard the words of Wovoka in their own language.[19] They were ready converts and full of fervor to return home. Wovoka promised to protect them along their journey. Kicking Bear, an Oglala at birth but now a Miniconjou chief, and Short Bull would become the most dedicated disciples to instill the message among the Sioux at Standing Rock.[20]

On the return trip, the Sioux were surprised to find a small herd of buffalo grazing in their path. They shot just one and ate of its meat. Then while they were resting, they saw the buffalo carcass rise and walk away.[21] They interpreted this to be a sign that Wovoka's medicine was strong.

Returning home the following March, they brought the teachings of the Paiute Shaman to Pine Ridge, Cheyenne River, and Rosebud reservations.[22] Another delegation was send to Nevada; and when they returned they confirmed the report of the first travelers.[23] News spread to the other Sioux reservations.[24] As James McLaughlin would later say, the movement reached distant locations "with the speed of the telegraph."[25]

Central to the expression of the religion were group dancing and song. The activity went on for hours. Before the dance, men usually fasted and purified themselves in a sweat lodge.[26] The dance would start in the afternoon, interrupted by a dinner meal, and then resume in the evening. Both women and men participated, joining hands and moving in a circle (also symbolic of the sacred hoop), inward in a back and forth motion.[27] Faces were painted with symbols; red was the dominant color.[28] There could be no white manufactured items worn by the believers.[29] Exhausted by the rigors of continual dancing, some fell into unconsciousness and said they saw apparitions of relatives from the dead.[30] There was often a prayer tree, with bits of cloth attached, placed in the middle of the dancers. The dance was repeated and repeated. Wailing called out to the dead. The ground was stomped over and over and over, enveloping the dancers in dust. The name given to this frenetic exercise was the "Ghost Dance" because its purpose was to pray for resurrection of dead ancestors. This was a new form of the previously agency outlawed Sun Dance. The agents did not know what to make of it. They knew that in the summer before, General Crook had allowed some traditional dances as part of his commission's campaign to sell the Sioux Bill of 1889. This new practice of religious expression hopefully was of little consequence, but some officials saw sparks of defiance. There was no Father De Smet to sort things out.

At the same time, Thomas J. Morgan, an ardent Indian rights reformer and now the commissioner of Indian Affairs, spelled out the government's goals:

> *It has become the settled policy of the Government to break up reservations, destroy tribal relations, settle Indians upon their own homesteads, incorporated them into the national life, and deal with them not as nations or tribes or bands, but as individual citizens. The American Indian is to become the Indian American.*[31]

As the movement attracted followers among the Lakota, the Sioux provided their own adaptation to the dance in the form of a distinct garment known as a ghost shirt.[32] These shirts and dresses were simple muslin or cotton, but painted with symbols and frequently had sewn against the material pieces of dead animals—feathers, claws, wings, teeth.[33] It was the purpose of the sack-like garment, however, that raised concern to the whites. These shirts, the religious leaders said, allowed no bullet to pass.[34] Kicking Bear told his followers that the Father in heaven would see that the guns of the white man would do no harm. "The sacred garments are bullet proof."[35] No matter whether intended as a symbol of immortality or actual defense, nearby settlers saw the shirts as an indication of new militancy.[36] Within the Sioux reservations, Wovoka's doctrine of peace was undergoing a transformation antagonistic to whites. Kicking Bear declared:

> *My brothers, I bring to you the promise of a day in which there will be no white man to lay his hand on the bridle of the Indian's horse; when the red men of the prairie will rule the world and not be turned from the hunting grounds by any man. I bring you word from your fathers the ghosts, that they are now marching to join you, led by the Messiah who came once to live on earth with the white men, but was cast out and killed by them. I have seen the wonders of the spirit land, and have talked with the ghosts. I traveled far and am sent back with a message to tell you to make ready for the coming of the Messiah and return of the ghosts in the spring.[37]*

He went further, becoming more inflammatory:

> *And while my children are dancing and making ready to join the ghosts, they shall have no fear of the white man, for I will take from the whites the secret of making gunpowder, and the powder they now have on hand will not burn when it is directed against the red people, my children who know the songs and dances of the ghosts. But that powder which my children, the red men, have, will burn and kill when is directed against the whites and used by those who believe.[38]*

When the settlers living near understood the religion also offered prophesy to reclaim the land, alarm began to spread. Were the Sioux about to go off reservation? Weren't these the same Indians who overwhelmed

Custer? Questions were raised whether the Indian Bureau had failed in its efforts to bring progress to the reservation. The Lakota were reclaiming their old ways. Everyone knew there was smoldering Indian resentment. Was it about to flash? As early as April, McLaughlin asked the commissioner to permit expansion of the Indian police for better surveillance of the malcontents in the Grand River camps.[39] He knew of Sitting Bull's embittered attitude over the 1889 Act and heard that he was urging resistance to any surveys on the reservation.

A Sioux attending the Presbyterian College confided to his friend, Charles Hyde of Pierre, South Dakota, that he thought an uprising was coming. Hyde felt he had received an important warning. On May 29, he wrote to the Secretary of the Interior: "[T]he Sioux or a portion of them are secretly planning an outbreak in the near future."[40] This message, coupled with others to the bureau about the Ghost Dance invading the reservations, prompted Acting Commissioner of Indian Affairs Robert Belt to call for investigation from his Sioux agents.[41] Commissioner Thomas Jefferson Morgan, a strict assimilationist, was frequently away from the capital, but his directive was uniformly followed. Reacting to the noise reaching Washington, the commissioner wanted to know what was happening on the Western Plains. In June, all the agents reported back that there was nothing to worry about.[42] The Ghost Dance had hardly gained a foothold at the reservations. At best, the religion was a fringe movement. In fact, it never was adopted by the majority of Indians at any of the reservations. But the nonprogressives were drawn to it. It was a protest to white subjugation. Many whites began to take it as a serious threat to their place on the prairie.

McLaughlin's June 18 response told that all was in good order at Standing Rock; and he was right. But he was upset that there was any question of the management of his reservation. His reaction was to point a finger at Sitting Bull:

There are, however, a few malcontents here, as at all of the Sioux Agencies, who cling tenaciously to the old Indian ways and are slow to accept the better order of things, whose influence is exerted in the wrong direction, and this class of Indians are ever ready to circulate idle rumors and sow dissensions to discourage the more progressive, but only a very few of the Sioux could possibly be united in attempting any overt act against the Government, and the removal from among them of a few individuals (the leaders of disaffection) such as Sitting Bull, Circling Bear, Black Bird & Circling Hawk of this Agency; Spotted Elk [aka Big Foot] and his lieutenants of Cheyenne River; Crow Dog & Low Dog of Rosebud, and any of like ilk of Pine Ridge, would end all trouble or uneasiness in the future.[43]

The modicum of tolerance toward Sitting Bull was slipping away. But the chief's concern was not with reaction to the Ghost Dance, but retaliation against him for frustrating the survey of reservation lands. He sent word to Mrs. Weldon to inquire through her friend, Dr. Bland, whether McLaughlin has been given orders from Washington to invoke sanctions against noncooperating Indians. Sitting Bull had not given up his fight after all.[44]

This was a time of universal dire conditions across the Plains. Even white settlers in the Dakotas and Nebraska were abandoning farms under economic duress from the ongoing draught.[45] Nothing the Indian farmers planted survived the summer; and as always, rations were short.[46] With the miserable state of reservation life, more converts came forward to a gospel of hope. Big Foot and Hump at Cheyenne River and Short Bull at Rosebud became leading advocates. Kicking Bear assumed the role of prophet to the Sioux; and Pine Ridge attracted the largest number of followers.[47] Song rang out a rhythmic message:

> The whole world is coming,
> A nation is coming, a nation is coming,
> The eagle has brought the message to the tribe.
> The Father says so, the Father says so.
> Over the whole earth they are coming,
> The buffalo are coming, the buffalo are coming,
> The crow has brought the message to the tribe,
> The Father says so, the Father says so.[48]

By early August, the dance had taken firm hold of certain Indians at Pine Ridge; and in September it was in place at Rosebud.[49] A new agent, Perain P. Palmer, was appointed to Cheyenne River. In taking charge, he advised that the Interior Department was displeased with Indians pursuing the dance; the Sioux responded that they were displeased with the Department of the Interior.[50] He sent his police to break up dance ceremonies at the camps of Hump and Big Foot. The Indians brandished Winchesters, intimidating the police.[51] The police were sent back once again only to suffer the same humiliation. Soon, members of the force were turning in their badges. Palmer concluded that the hostile Indians were preparing to defy the government.[52]

The prairie pulsed with excitement—feet pounded the earth below into dusty powder; song rang out. People were alive again. This was the way it used to be; and this is the way it should be for the next generation. The Lakota, having been prohibited from dancing by reservation rule, were taking back their traditions. They were remaking their time-honored religion. Camps were established with tipis erected for the ghost dancers to live in common within the reservations. The agents of the various Sioux reservations did not know how to handle it. Wovoka, who started as a prophet, within a year was viewed by the Sioux as the Messiah himself. The newspapers labeled the movement the "Messiah Craze."

Initially, the Standing Rock Lakota stood at a distance. Sitting Bull was put off by the Christian elements of the religion but inquisitive.

Then, during the late summer, Sitting Bull made several requests to travel south to the Cheyenne River Reservation in order to learn about the religion.[53] Every request was denied by Major McLaughlin. "That man is going nowhere. I want him watched carefully; I want to know every move he makes at Grand River."[54] Sitting Bull had other ideas. If he could not leave Standing Rock, then he would invite Kicking Bear to come to him. In October, the Sioux prophet visited Sitting Bull seeking support for the movement. He quoted Wovaka to the chief:

I will cover the earth with new soil to a depth of five times the height of man, and under this new soil will be buried the whites. The new

land will be covered with sweet grass and running water and trees,
and herds of buffalo and ponies will stray over it, that my red children
may eat and drink, hunt and rejoice.[55]

The dance lasted for days. A newspaper reporter from Chicago was present and took a Kodak photograph of the dancers.[56]

Of course, McLaughlin heard what was taking place at Grand River. He was outraged. "How did that sacrilegious crackpot get on my reservation? Damn Sitting Bull!"[57] He sent policemen to break it up.[58] He was upset, as always, with Sitting Bull and offended that Christian principles were being subverted to advance a pagan religion. McLaughlin called Sitting Bull a "fake spiritualist."[59] The real issue was that Sitting Bull again appeared in ascendancy with his people. If the Ghost Dance afforded Sitting Bull an opportunity, it also would provide the reason for James McLaughlin to finally rid himself of a rival.[60]

The agent dispatched Crazy Walking, the captain of the police, and several policemen to put a stop to the activity at Grand River.[61] Crazy Walking was overwhelmed by the dancers. Sitting Bull told him: "The dance is not the most important undertaking. They will eventually stop."[62] (No one thought to follow up on this enigmatic statement; but it did not square with targeting Sitting Bull as a leading advocate.) Crazy Walking could only summon the courage to tell Kicking Bear that McLaughlin wanted the Ghost Dance apostle off Standing Rock Reservation.[63] He accepted the word of Kicking Bear that he was leaving in a matter of days. Why create a disturbance?

When the captain returned to the agency, his report was hardly good enough. McLaughlin dispatched Lieutenant Chatka and two other men to force Kicking Bear off the reservation. Chatka was not intimidated and pushed his way through a circle of dancers to confront Kicking Bear.[64] "The Ghost Dance must stop!" Kicking Bear said he was planning to leave in a day or so. The lieutenant said now was the time to leave.[65] The religious man and six supporters from Cheyenne River mounted their horses, and Chatka escorted them to the common border with their own reservation.[66] No one interfered with the police. Within a few days, the dancing resumed at the Grand River camp.

The real issue was control. The reservation always had factions. Good management played them off against each other. For the agent at Standing Rock, the dissident faction was located at the Grand River, home of Sitting Bull. The Ghost Dance created an energizing cohesiveness that pulled the dancers together. This rattled nerves and set off alarm that there could be a spillover effect. James McLaughlin's command of his reservation was threatened. He put his expanded police force to work for closer surveillance of the Grand River camps.

Mary Collins, the Congregationalist missionary, offered the intervention of Christian prayer, which she took directly to Grand River. She made her point by having an organ hauled to one of the dances, countering the chants of the dancing Indians with Christian hymns.[67] The missionaries who had worked so long for the souls of the Lakota were upset with the Messiah Craze as a misdirection of key tenets of Christianity— Jesus, the Son of God, come to earth, the resurrection, and salvation from tyranny of the temporal life all were co-opted. Jesus was coming only to save the Indian. This had particular appeal to recently converted Roman Catholics on the reservation. Collins was not afraid to tell the disciples they were wrong. She talked and argued with Sitting Bull. No one intimidated Mary Collins. And no one tried.

Certain agents began complaining to Interior, prompting the military to show interest. Word moved through the ranks that the tedium of peacetime service may be cut loose. The army was far in advance of the Indians in any thought of an outbreak.[68]

CHAPTER NINETEEN

White Squaw

Spring 1890

During the winter of 1889–1890, Catherine Weldon corresponded with Sitting Bull from her home on Liberty Street, Brooklyn.[1] She also persisted in her plea to those who would listen in New York that the Sioux Act was a mistake that needed correction.

Mrs. Catherine Weldon was a lady ahead of her Victorian time. She certainly dressed fashionably and was capable of using the ploy of the defenseless woman.[2] But she had grit. She withstood the gossip and slights of the proper white women residing at the agency and fort who could not accept her way of life among the Indians. The more charitable referred to her as a "misguided crank" and a "meddlesome busybody."[3] The barracks talk was that a common whore who works for her money commanded greater respect.

Weldon felt she could best serve the Sioux people by returning to Standing Rock. She intended to live among them. Not at the agency but at Grand River. More particularly, she knew Sitting Bull was at ease with women, and she intended to become his personal aide. He was an incandescent personality, and she could not resist drawing near the flame. On April 5, 1890, she wrote Major McLaughlin:

> *It is with reluctance that I humble myself to address you, knowing that you cannot feel friendly disposed towards me. I do so however out of love for my Indian friends and because you are probably the only person who can furnish me with some necessary information and possible*

permission. Even enemies can act magnanimous towards each other, and I hope you will extend to me the courtesy of a gentleman to a lady, and answer my questions with a frank yes or no.[4]

She told him of her aspiration to live among the Dakota people and even claimed she was willing to buy ceded land, but there was too much uncertainty to pursue that course straightaway.[5] While candid about her purpose, she tactfully said she would not come to the reservation without the major's consent.

I suppose it is needless to state that I have no intention to become either Sitting Bull's wife or a squaw, as the sagacious newspapers editors surmised. I honor and respect S. Bull as if he was my own father and nothing can ever shake my faith in his good qualities and what I can do to make him famous I will certainly do and I will succeed, but I regret that at the present time he is so universally misjudged:— I would be under great obligations to you if you could conquer your dislike for me sufficiently to answer me regarding my intended removal to Dakota and possible short stay at the reservation if you approve or disapprove.[6]

The major did not think this deserved a reply, and he definitely did not welcome the possibility of having her again interfering with his Indians.

Catherine Weldon took matters into her own hands and returned in May, first setting up at Parkin Ranch just outside the reservation. Her 14-year-old son, Christie, arrived in early summer after finishing his school term.[7] Word was sent on to the chief that she was staying a few miles north of the reservation. Sitting Bull made several visits to her;[8] after a few weeks' time he invited her and her son to the Grand River settlement.[9] McLaughlin was disturbed at this turn of events. When she offered to teach, he advised that "no vacancy" presently existed at the Grand River schools and the nearby training schools "afforded ample facilities."[10] This woman could not be trusted to educate Indian children. He was not about to endorse any work by this woman. While he did not make it comfortable for her, he took no direct steps to remove her. At least she was in concert with him that the Messiah Movement presented a false message.

Sitting Bull allowed the dancers to camp near his settlement, and he was often seen observing the ceremonies from a tent overlooking the dancers.[11] It was Shave Bear who led the dancers at Grand River.[12] There was conflicting testimony of whether Sitting Bull actually participated in the dances. No government official saw him do so; and he was quoted as both saying he did and did not.[13] He knew the dead did not rise again. Yet, there is no question that he encouraged the dancers. His position was similar to what Little Wound of Pine Ridge would later tell General Miles: the Indians should quit acting like whites and reclaim their identity. Secondly, the dancers were loyal to him and he was not going to reject them. Because his band embraced the movement, he showed considerable interest.

Catherine Weldon saw the Ghost Dance as a fraud that could only bring harm to the Lakota. She even offered to debate Kicking Bear,[14] intending to challenge him to produce the Messiah. She called Kicking Bear a "false prophet."[15] He had no interest in talking with her. She saw him as having the power of a strong mind over weak minds. Because he evaded her, she turned her attention to the dancers. They did not listen either. It was not the role of Lakota women to lecture their men, and a white woman espousing friendship was entitled to no more deference. While Sitting Bull remained communicative, he deflected her admonishments.

Even in the face of the Grand River Indians being unreceptive to her criticisms, Weldon offered them a barrage of advice. She told Sitting Bull's people about hypnotism and argued that the Kicking Bear's converts were predisposed to the suggestive power of the repetitive message of the dance. She showed them the work of magnets and explained there were scientific answers to the supposed magic of the bent piece of metal.[16] "What makes the telegraph wires speak? It is the same power of the lightning."[17] She believed in science and not superstition.[18] When science did not work, her rhetoric turned ridicule: "If Kicking Bear is sent by the true God, then may he strike me dead."[19]

Weldon and Sitting Bull had their own dustup.[20] First, she took a temperate approach:

I understand the Ghost Dance and even see some Christian overtones in it, because it predicts a messiah coming for the Indian people. This is a false message. The government fears how your people react to it. You must council your people to reject the Ghost Dance. Your children go to Christian schools, why is this so difficult for you?

Sitting Bull was equally forthcoming: "Missus Catherine, I have always prayed to the Great Spirit. Does only your god have ears?"

Catherine Weldon was quick to point out that she was not one of the reservation's religious missionaries:

I am not here to make you Christian. I am here to tell you the Ghost Dance is not any religion; and because it is viewed as militant, your people are at risk. The Ghost Dance frightens the white man. Because you will not denounce Kicking Bear, he gathers strength. Because you allow the dance in your camp, you appear to lead it. Your medicine is still strong. Do not misuse it. You know the soldiers can destroy your people.

He responded with questions:

Why, Missus Catherine? We have done nothing to them. Am I so strong that all I need is shirts? Where are my warriors? I do not wear a ghost shirt. I know cloth shirts will not stop bullets. I was born Lakota. Why do I have to change? I have submitted to the reservation. Is that not change enough?

When she said: "You do not want this fight," he told her he had no intention of fighting. Then he found ground on which they could agree.

My people were hunters, not farmers; they lived off the buffalo when there were always buffalo. Your people sent shooters to kill the buffalo. We tried farming. The summer winds and poor ground makes that impossible. We are prisoners on our own land and your government always wants more.

The newspapers were unrelenting in undermining Catherine Weldon,[21] certain that she was abetting the Ghost Dance.[22] Most of the time, it was enough to know that she was championing Sitting Bull. On the other hand, followers of the chief could not understand the influence of the woman. She was against the Ghost Dance. She made him indecisive. Without her interference, Sitting Bull would surely advocate the new Gospel. Talebearers were undercutting him at every opportunity. They said he offered her marriage. "She has passed a poison over his eyes." "What is wrong with him? He tells us to resist the white man's ways; and yet he wants this white woman." His conduct was confusing to his supporters and gave currency to his enemies. McLaughlin could only smile at the chief's predicament.

Sitting Bull invited Mrs. Weldon to become a part of his household.[23] While she may have undertaken domestic chores at his house during the summer, it was work intended as part of earning her keep.[24] Her drive was to accomplish much more for the Lakota. She bristled at being asked to be a part of his household. She was far superior to that role; she was his partner in working for the betterment of his people, not a housemate. He already had two wives—Four Robes and Seen by the Nation. Moreover, it would give validation to a vicious rumor. She was irate at any suggestion that she was a "white squaw." From Sitting Bull's perspective, he was tendering the protection of his home. She served him, and he offered the gift of the hearth.

Still, Weldon thought Sitting Bull to be a great chief and viewed him in heroic terms. She well may have had aspirations to write his biography.[25] She bestowed gifts on him and paid for feasts with his retinue.[26] She read to him from the biographies of Napoleon and Alexander[27] so that he might understand that other great men were beset by adversity. When he would not accept her enlightened views about the Ghost Dance, she felt spurned. She saw him as wrong-minded. And it became obvious that she could not turn her Lakota friends away from the Ghost Dance. She realized that she created discord for the chief among his peers. She was conflicted.

In the meantime, McLaughlin dropped Sitting Bull from the list of district farmers because he ignored work.[28] The agent discussed with

Louis Primeau, the agency's mixed-blood interpreter, what to do about the growing crisis at Grand River. Informants reported that Sitting Bull was conducting séances at his lodge. When Primeau offered assurance that the information was an exaggeration—"[J]ust some sniveling Indians chanting prayers,"—McLaughlin ranted: "I tell you that Sitting Bull is behind the Ghost Dance. Never forget the man is a cunning snake. And, the snake has to be put out of the tent."[29] Primeau could only reply that no good Indian listened to the chief anymore.

Sitting Bull
STATE HISTORICAL SOCIETY OF NORTH DAKOTA (1952-1857)

McLaughlin did not want to be reassured. In an October 17 report to the commissioner of Indian Affairs, he complained that Sitting Bull was "continually agitating and fostering opposition" to government surveys to implement severalty. He labeled the man an "intriguer" who "will not commit an overt act or open offense himself," and instead worked from the shadows to direct others to do his "mischief." In later section of the dispatch to Washington, this characterization was contradicted. There the chief was accused of being the "High Priest" of the Ghost Dance movement at Standing Rock. It was a 13-page handwritten position paper to justify the removal of Sitting Bull. The opening paragraph emphasized McLaughlin's reputation as a responsible agent, not "an alarmist." Then the report turned to Sitting Bull's growing discordant behavior, Weldon's infatuation and interference, the agent's demand that the Ghost Dance be discontinued, and the need for a close watch of the chief's activities.[30] This harangue intensified in further correspondence to Indian Affairs during the month of November. McLaughlin's ire was showing. He had difficulty maintaining his usual calm and controlled demeanor.

Catherine Weldon knew that her mission had failed. She confessed to Sitting Bull: "I have made enemies for you. McLaughlin does not trust me, and your own people hate me."

"I do not fear the agent. The Grand River people still listen to me. You are the one who must stop attacking our beliefs."

"That, I cannot do. I do not believe in the Ghost Dance, and neither do you. But you will not tell your people to stop."

"Of course I cannot tell them to stop. You are telling me to say there is no future for my people."[31]

She always had been open in her opinions; in return he was purposefully guarded.[32]

Catherine Weldon came to the Dakotas as an idealist seeking to make a difference. Her purpose was to assist Sitting Bull, but she could not turn him away from a destructive course. She told him that he was "deceived by your prophets."[33] She was continually quarreling with the ghost dancers. They became acerbic in their attacks on her; they did not understand Sitting Bull's and his immediate family's tolerance of the woman. Sitting Bull was seeking to have it both ways. The situation challenged his chieftaincy. She was in a dither. Denounced by the ghost dancers and not getting the support she wanted from Sitting Bull, she foolishly reached out to McLaughlin.[34] She wrote as one trying to protect her Indian friends, with the knowledge that they were bringing trouble upon themselves. Her words tumbled onto the writing paper as frantic, fearful, and full of alarm. More telling was her correspondence alleging that Sitting Bull was in a distressed position to hold his followers. She said the chief was under the "evil influence of Kicking Bear." Kicking Bear is "a vile imposter." She asked for "pity on our poor Unkpapas & Sitting Bull." "[D]o not send the police or Soldiers." Yet she was not ready to give up, saying she would "stay for several days & see what my influence can do." Let me "induce him to come of his own accord."[35] Clearly she had heard word of the police moving against Sitting Bull.

The situation was untenable, and everyone knew it. Sitting Bull was urged to get rid of her—since she was against the ghost dancers, she had to be a collaborative of McLaughlin.[36] This white woman could not continue living at Grand River. Everyone knew it. Miss Carignan, sister of the new schoolmaster, and One Bull were the first to come forward, offering to take her to the agency; this she could not accept.[37] Even Gall came by, saying he would take her to Fort Yates. She knew this would be an insult to Sitting Bull, and she demurred.[38] But she was at the breaking point; beset by collision of emotions, she was unnerved. Criticism of her had grown so bitter she was afraid for her child. Her mind was in a muddle. She no longer knew how to help Sitting Bull. And he was not willing to accept her advice. She had to get out. Within days she demanded Sitting Bull take her to the Parkin Ranch, just north of the agency on the Missouri.

On October 22, he drove her and young Christie by wagon to Cannonball.[39] The weather was pleasant enough, but long silences set a chill between the chief and his woman passenger. They spoke little along the way. Perfunctory comments, not conversation. On arrival, she stepped down on the arm of her son; then Christie helped the chief unload the baggage. Mrs. Weldon properly extended her hand, saying she hoped to see him again under better circumstances. Sitting Bull took her hand fully into his own (for a white man, he usually would only take two fingers of the hand, if he chose to shake hands at all). This was his only hint of caring.[40] Because he did not ask her to return, the gesture was not comforting. She felt a shiver run across her back. He would not see her again. Both had to realize that, although each quietly hoped her absence from Grand River would be temporary. He was stoic; she remained confused and hurt.

On his return to Grand River, he stopped at the agency to pick up rations. This would be his last time there. Alone and vulnerable, he headed home. Soldiers at the fort heard talk that three agency Indians were waiting to intercept him at a bridge crossing on the primary road to Grand River and said nothing.[41] But after passing through Fort Yates, in a random turn of fate, he took a different route than expected to go home.[42] His mind was not on the road but jumbled with thoughts of past conversations with Catherine Weldon and where the Ghost Dance might take his people. The traces were not taut; he let the horses chose the path. No one knows the actual intent of the men supposedly lying in wait, but everyone knew that McLaughlin wanted to separate Sitting Bull from the Messiah Movement. There was neither an ambush nor confrontation; he returned home without incident. But when scuttlebutt of the intrigue reached him, Bull Head was identified at the lead of those out to get him.[43] Hearsays of possible arrest came to him more frequently. He became suspicious of all but family and close associates.

Sitting Bull raised the question to friends:

> *Why should the Indian police come against me? We are of the same blood, we are all Sioux, we are relatives. It will disgrace the nation, it will be murder, it will defile our race. If the white men want me to die, they ought not put up the Indians to kill me. I don't want confusion among my own people. Let the soldiers come and take me away and kill me wherever they like. I am not afraid.*[44]

At Pine Ridge, Daniel J. Royer, a political appointee, was assigned as the new agent that October. He knew nothing about Indians and quickly earned the derisive tag of "Man Afraid of His Indians."[45] Walking into a hotbed of the Ghost Dance religion and not equipped to deal with it, he sent a letter to the commissioner of Indian Affairs asking for military help to suppress the Ghost Dance.[46] Red Cloud, although no advocate of the movement, did nothing to stop it. An employee at Pine Ridge by the name of Phillip Wells wrote to McLaughlin on October 19: "Dr. D. F. Royer our new agent took charge this week, but I think he has got an elephant on his hands, as the craze had taken such a hold on the Indians before he took charge. As yet I have all hopes he will be able to stop it without any serious trouble."[47] He asked the Standing Rock agent for his confidential opinion on handling the situation.

Royer's mismanagement of his new charges ultimately would propel his problem into military response. But he was not alone; Agent Palmer at Cheyenne River had been warned by friendly Indians that Big Foot was gathering weapons to assure that his people could stay together and pursue the dance.[48] Surely they were preparing to fight.

Harper's Weekly of October 20, 1890, warned:

> *The delusion of the coming of the Messiah among the Indians of the Northwest, with the resulting ceremony known as the ghost dance, is indicative of greater danger of an Indian war in that region that has existed since 1876. Never before have diverse Indian tribes been so generally united upon a single idea.*[49]

In the same article, as if the lines were lifted from one of McLaughlin's reports (actually they were; his report to Commissioner Morgan of October 17 had been released to the press[50]), Sitting Bull was singled out:

> *Sheer obstinacy, stubborn tenacity of purpose, and low cunning, with an aptitude for theatrical effect and for working on the superstitions of his people, are the attributes by which he has acquired and retained influence among the Northwest tribes. Personally he is pompous, vain, boastful, licentious, and untrustworthy. He has constantly been a disturbing element at the agency since his return from confinement as a military prisoner seven years ago, and has grown worse in this respect as he has felt his authority and importance departing.*[51]

There was no question to the white world that Sitting Bull's involvement with the Ghost Dance meant trouble. The press fanned what should have been considered minor camp fires into a fast-moving conflagration across the northern grasslands.

Thunder launched its artillery over the Grand River camp, but the rain that followed was short-lived. It had been a dry summer and would stay relatively mild into late fall, just as Sitting Bull had predicted.[52] The cadenced dance chants continued:

> The father says so,
> The father says so.

You shall see your kindred!
You shall see your kindred!
The father says so,
The father says so.[53]

James McLaughlin was not one to try to understand the frustration of the nonprogressive Indian. To him, if the Ghost Dance was viewed a threat to the whites, that was all he needed to know. The old mischief-maker, Sitting Bull, was fomenting insurrection. Yet, Gall and Grass were able to discourage any reception of the new religion in their settlements.[54] All was quiet in the more populous eastern section of the reservation. It was known that most Indians at Standing Rock did not widely partici-pate in the Ghost Dance, as was happening at Pine Ridge and Cheyenne River. McLaughlin, in a calmer moment, assessed that not more than 10 percent of the Indians on his reservation were suspected followers.[55]

Catherine Weldon at first remained close by at Parkin Ranch. On October 24, she wrote to McLaughlin, complaining that she had turned her former friends into enemies and said she believed they were ready to fight. She continued to be preoccupied with rejection: "If I had known what obstinate minds I had to contend with, I would not have undertaken this mission to enlighten & instruct them."[56] She may have embraced the culture, but she had her own ideas of change. A week or so later, Cath-erine Weldon and her son, who was suffering from infection from a rusty nail that had pierced his foot, boarded a steamer to Pierre, South Dakota. Before they landed young Christie died of severe muscle contractions induced by tetanus infection.[57] Lockjaw, they said. When she arrived on November 13, the papers were full of stories about Pierre being selected as the new state capital.[58] Still Mrs. Weldon attracted enough attention to be mentioned in the *Daily Free Press*, coupled with the observation that the Messiah Craze continued to burn hot.[59] In mourning, she did not want the attention.

On November 20, from Kansas City, she wrote Sitting Bull to tell him of her son's death and ask for forgiveness for being so harsh in her criticism of the Messiah Movement while reminding him she was a true friend.[60] She was distraught with grief, writing again on November 23, berating herself: "I gave my heart & my soul to you & to the Dakotas, & their welfare alone was my care; & my poor boy was motherless."[61] Finally, on December 1, she sent another letter to Sitting Bull asking him to write as "comfort to me in my great troubles." Still, she could not ignore the danger of the Ghost Dance to her Dakota friends. She closed with "Oh, my friend, may the Good God who used to watch over both of us, open your eyes to the truth."[62]

Sitting Bull had always been in a struggle to regain leadership on the reservation. As his influence waned, he needed the support of this Eastern woman activist.

Catherine Weldon could no longer serve him. She was lost in her own circumstances and caught in the cross fire of criticism from every quarter. To the local citizenry, she was a femme fatale living in scandal in Sitting Bull's cabin and neglecting her child. To the agency establishment, she was a radical stirring up Indian unrest. To the Lakota ghost dancers, she was a former friend who turned against them. Derided at every turn, she turned to the religion she had long ignored. She thought of serving God through the sisterhood.[63]

Sitting Bull was pained by the loss of this woman. At 59 years of age, he was an uncertain chief. Weldon was right that he succumbed to pressure—involved in the Ghost Dance as a watchful bystander, he was forced by station and tradition to the front. He could not accept losing his people. He was grasping for relevancy.

In that in between time where fall nights begin to chill from soft days, Sitting Bull rode his horse into the countryside along the Grand River to look for a couple of missing ponies. Somehow the river on which he was born provided a message. He mused on the earlier times of his life. He worried about the state of the Lakota now confined to the boundaries of Standing Rock. A few miles out, his horse broke its gait at the warble of a lone gray bird with yellow markings on its throat in a tree near the stream. It was a meadowlark, but the bird's call was startling sad. The chief understood the resonances of birds. He could imitate many sounds of this bird and had taken note of messages he had received before in the voice of a meadowlark. The meadowlark always had been a good totem; the bird was known among the Lakota to speak their language.[64] This time what he heard was not the bird's trill. Rather, the chief was told: "Lakotas will kill you."[65]

The message was unambiguous; it cut knife sharp. He took it as a word of warning, with no ability to avoid its fulfillment. Sitting Bull knew he had enemies within his own people. When he returned to the settlement, he looked for his nephew, One Bull, and told him of the admonition. One Bull did not lightly brush it off, but tried to place the message in the context of the heavy burden of being a Lakota chief. "Your responsibility is great; we all look to you. You have carried us so long; you are tired."[66] Afflicted by periodic maladies and older age, Sitting Bull appeared to accept this interpretation for the moment.

Nevertheless, the haunting words continued to trouble Sitting Bull. He told his other nephew, White Bull: "Great men are usually betrayed by those who are jealous of them."[67] He appreciated with greater intensity his family and immediate supporters who lived nearby. A week later, he confided to Crow Foot, his son, who was a most serious young man of about 17: "I have been forewarned that my life will be taken by Lakota men. I do not know when. I fear for my people; I fear for my family. You need to prepare yourself to serve them."[68]

But there were those on the reservation who considered him a remnant of the past. Most of the Standing Rock Sioux were pragmatists and had chosen accommodation. Sitting Bull was out of touch, yet brought trouble to all because he challenged the system providing for the Indian. Crow Foot did not understand: "How can I help people who want to kill you?"

"You know there are good people who live among us. Seek them out, they will help you. I want your brothers and sisters to grow with you. There is much that is not good in the white man's world, but that is the world around us. Be careful.

"Son, I have done nothing wrong. The white man does not care what is inside us, what makes us who were are. They tell us 'change.' They say 'Listen to us—live here, farm there, become a Christian.'" The chief considered the use of the word "Christian" and added a harsh postscript: "White men love their whores more than their wives."[69]

He wrapped his arms around Crow Foot and quietly said: "Live well."

Left to himself, the chief reflected on former close associates who were now deceased. Four Horns died in 1887, and Black Moon died the following year.[70] They were friends, warriors, and allies; they were with him throughout all their lives—on the prairie, in battle, in exile, and on the reservation. He witnessed measles, whoping cough, and influenza all devastate reservation children and adults.[71] He himself had suffered the loss of children of his own from various maladies. Just a couple of years earlier, his 19-year-old daughter, Walks Looking, died shortly after giving birth to a son.[72] No one could say what illness took her.

More often he thought about what he now considered a premonition. His mind could not shake the words of the meadowlark. Perhaps the death reserved for him was losing his Lakota people to the white man and agency-made chiefs. His efforts at leadership had come to nothing.

The meadowlark had been a friend. But now its words produced dark thoughts that would affect his mood over the months to come. He was physically and mentally drained. He questioned whether Wakan Tanka was talking to him or his own doubts were shouting in his head. He felt the breath of disloyalty. Enemies were coming for him. He used the Ghost Dance to hold position.

CHAPTER TWENTY

The Plot

Autumn 1890

Alarmed at reports from Pine Ridge and Rosebud reservations, Commissioner Morgan called for updated information from all the Sioux agencies.[1] Somehow the United States was perceived at risk from a few hundred Indians in scattered reservation camps, chanting in pursuit of a trancelike religious experience. At the same time the Indians were delusional to believe that an apocalypse was about to come for the white man. The Ghost Dance was really a prayer for restoration of the Lakota spirit.

In McLaughlin's October 17 report to the commissioner, he clearly was aware that the Messiah Craze was affecting other reservations, but said that it had not reached an alarmist state at Standing Rock.[2] In fact he dismissed it as "absurd nonsense." Royer may not have known how to handle reservation Indians, but James McLaughlin was managing quite well. There was no uprising coming. However, he vilified Sitting Bull as the "leading apostle of this latest Indian absurdity; in a word he is the chief mischief maker at this agency and if he were not here this craze so general among the Sioux would never have gotten a foothold at this Agency." The seed was sown that Sitting Bull was the problem; a few pages later McLaughlin directly warned that his "removal sooner or later will be necessary." The major further pressed his point, saying that the man was adept at "influencing ignorant henchmen." Then he alleged that Sitting Bull attacked the allotment plan by telling those who would sign that they would be relegated to a small corner of the reservation and told to maintain themselves, while those who did not would command all the common land and enjoy the old Lakota ways.

James McLaughlin concluded his account with the avowal that he intended to "exhaust all reasonable means" to quiet the movement by inviting Sitting Bull to the agency for a one-on-one conversation away from the dancers.[3] The major always protected his reputation of a conscientious agent whose first imperative was to work with the Indians. But he provided a telling alternative recommendation of "confinement in some military prison some distance from the Sioux Country." Acting Commissioner Robert Belt reinforced McLaughlin's first direction with a response on October 29, instructing that Sitting Bull needed to know that he would be held to "strict accountability for the misconduct of any of his followers."[4]

In a follow-up letter of November 13, the agent warned that his prior letter had been given to the press (he did not explain how) and quoted in part. Because several on the reservation were now literate in English and read newspapers, they were aware of the state of affairs at Sitting Bull's camp. The dissemination of this news on the reservation was now "causing unnecessary alarm."[5] James McLaughlin was approaching the tipping point.

The major was receiving regular reports from John Carignan, the new teacher at Grand River School and another set of eyes for the agent.[6] Carignan's accounts carried no embellishment or invective as contained in reports from Lieutenant Bull Head. He simply reported that school attendance was dropping as the weeks progressed, with parents keeping their children from classes to attend Ghost Dances.[7] Sitting Bull was blamed.[8] The worshipers camped closed to his cabin.[9] He did not distance himself from the dancers; he put himself at the center of the action. He had no intention of discouraging these people. There was some suspicion that there was a McLaughlin mole inside Sitting Bull's key council of supporters.[10] The dancers only attracted more attention.

Mary Collins continued her efforts to intercede. Interestingly, she never felt in danger; her view was that the Indians were distorting Christian beliefs and she had to bring them the true word. She always considered herself a friend of Sitting Bull's despite their religious differences. Collins directly confronted Sitting Bull at his tent overlooking the Grand River encampment of dancers. "Brother, you are ruining your people. You are deceiving them and you know it."[11] Sitting Bull dismissed her, saying that the movement had gone too far. She persisted: "The people are neglecting their homes and their property. There will be great suffering."[12] It was to no avail. On departing she saw an Indian that she knew in an apparent trance, lying in the dirt. She bent down telling him he was a faker and ordered him to arise; he quickly obeyed.[13] A few dancers who witnessed this intercession broke from the dance; and some even packed up their wagons.[14] Yet she barely caused a ripple in attempts to quell the movement.

More importantly, the military's attention was drawn to reports of growing reservation unrest.

General "Bear Coat" Miles became the commander of the Division of the Missouri, headquartered in Chicago, in September.[15] On October 31, President Harrison requested the Secretary of War to conduct an investigation of the Indian Messiah Movement and "crusade upon the whites."[16] Concern had reached a new state of anxiety. Miles always considered the military had a better perspective of the situation than the civilian agents. The commander put troops in the field in case of a disturbance.

Military buildup was fortified by newspaper speculation and sensationalism, not reconnaissance. No one tried to understand the movement; they reacted from misinformation and preconceived notions. But there was an element of militancy in the Lakota version of the Ghost Dance. Or was it just cultural pride? The potential of outbreak from the managed confinement of the reservations was now the talk of the day.

Brigadier General Thomas Ruger, commander of the Department of the Dakota, went to Standing Rock to investigate. He found it no disturbance and Agent McLaughlin unruffled. Ruger filed a report that there was "no probability of an outbreak at present, nor during the winter" and further observed that the craze gave no indication of consequence in the coming spring.[17] But in conversation with the agent and commander of adjacent Fort Yates, Lt. Colonel William Drum, the general accepted McLaughlin's opinion that it was prudent to remove Sitting Bull from the reservation when the winter months set in.[18] Next, he went to Cheyenne River.[19] There were more signs of confusion than danger. As a precaution,

Ruger decided to call up infantrymen from a neighboring post to support the company at the fort on the reservation and calm Agent Palmer.[20]

President Harrison called up troops in a move to impress the reservation Sioux that the army was at the ready.[21] The United States was talking itself into trouble.

Royer, meanwhile, was in a state of panic at Pine Ridge. He continued to telegraph dire messages to the bureau and pleas for help.[22] To the agent's surprise, Valentine McGillycuddy, Red Cloud's old adversary and now on the staff of the South Dakota governor as assistant adjutant general, visited Pine Ridge.[23] Despite his past problems, McGillycuddy was well received by the Indians. It was Royer who was not welcoming. The adjutant general declared the dance harmless. The real problem was a shortage of beef rations and resulting hunger at the reservation.[24] Royer fired off a telegram to the commissioner: "McGillycuddy is here abusing the administration, inciting the Indians to disturbance, and doing me dirt and I want him removed."[25] The former agent had a rejoinder: "When the Seventh Day Adventists get up on the roofs of their houses, arrayed in their ascension robes to meet the 'second coming,' the U.S. Army is not rushed into their field."[26] McGillycuddy favored letting the Indians dance themselves out.

Red Cloud chose not to interfere with the ghost dancers at Pine Ridge, sure that the movement would soon fade. "If it is false, and there is nothing in it, it will go away like the snow under the hot sun."[27] General Miles, during his own visit to Pine Ridge, advised Red Cloud to calm his people, but he seemed satisfied there was no cause for alarm.[28]

In fact, Miles observed that the problem on the Sioux reservations was not the dancing. Rather just as McGillycuddy concluded, the blame lay with rations running short and Congress delaying appropriations.[29] These circumstances would not lessen the military's role; the general knew hungry people became malcontents. At the same time, the War Department and Interior quarreled over which was in charge. Popular sentiment was in favor of the military. And the general took the opportunity to voice again his criticism of civil management of the agency system.[30] Agent McLaughlin was not pleased.

McLaughlin finally decided to visit Grand River to see for himself the goings on and to intercede with Sitting Bull. On November 16, he

and Louis Primeau observed the dancing from afar.[31] That night they
went to Bull Head's house, about three miles to the northwest. The next
day McLaughlin returned, meeting the chief outside his cabin. At first,
the agent took a conciliatory approach. He said that he had always looked
to Sitting Bull's best interests and reminded him that "I was the one who
was responsible for your return to Standing Rock from Fort Randall."[32]
Sitting Bull knew this was revisionist history,[33] yet he held back any
word of contradiction. As a crowd began to gather about the two men,
McLaughlin got to the point:

*I want to know what you mean by your present conduct and utter
disregard of department orders. Your preaching and practicing of this
absurd Messiah doctrine is causing a great deal of uneasiness among
the Indians of the reservation and you should stop it at once.*[34]

Sitting Bull countered:

*White Hair, you do not like me personally. You do not understand this
dance. But I am willing to be convinced. You and I will go together
to the tribes from which this dance came, and when we reach the last
one, where it started, if they cannot produce the Messiah, and if we do
not find all the nations of the dead coming this way, then I will return
and tell the Sioux it is all a lie. That will end the dance. If we find the
Messiah, then you are to let the dance go on.*[35]

McLaughlin said he had neither inclination nor agency funds for
such a journey.[36] He was not about to spend his time with Sitting Bull
on a religious chase—"to catch the wind that blew last year."[37] Instead,
he urged him to come to the agency to discuss the matter in a reasoned
manner. The verbal jousting was over. Of course, Sitting Bull was not
going to put himself at the agent's base of operation. Yet he did not say no.
He tactfully responded that he could not go "without the consent of his
people. I will talk to the men tonight, and if they think it advisable I will
go to the agency next Saturday."[38] When necessary, Sitting Bull could put
on a good face. He knew how to phrase a conciliatory comment that had

no real commitment. The agent expected to see Sitting Bull on the next ration day, but the chief sent word that he could not come because one of his children was sick.[39] There would be no talk; he need not further suffer McLaughlin's advice. His allegiance was to his family and the Lakota of his camp.

The agent had his own view of winning over the ghost dancers through their stomachs. On his visit to Sitting Bull's camp, he saw that the number of dancers was not as great as his spies had described earlier.[40] He intended to push the decline further and concocted a strong-arm measure. On November 19, he wrote to the commissioner that a notice should go to the Grand River camp inviting those who questioned the new religion and were friendly to the government to register at the agency. Only those giving up the dance would be issued food supplies.[41] He would strip off the bystanders and hangers-on. The bureau did nothing with this request.[42] A week later, in a letter to his friend with the IRA, Herbert Welsh, he said that "the fanatical dance could be suppressed without military intervention," had he been permitted to withhold rations.[43] The captain of the Indian Police, Henry Bull Head, recommended a variation of this in a letter to the agent; his plan was to force the ghost dancers at Grand River to come to the "good chiefs" for rations.[44]

By mid- to late November, General Miles shifted his position.[45] He now believed that false prophets were turning the movement toward violence. Sitting Bull was singled out as a principal organizer; a Ghost Dance camp was at the front door of his Grand River village. An outbreak was considered very possible, and the general ordered more troopers into the field.

Sitting Bull symbolized the heart of the resistance. He always was good newspaper copy; the press did not waste time in having him at the lead of the Ghost Dance activity on the Sioux Reservation. This, together with his widely accepted reputation as an agitator, put him in the government's sights. Yet he was a dissident, not a militant organizing a rebel force. He was not even leading the Messiah Movement. He was the wrong target. He was using the movement to augment his own support among his people and at the same time remind the Indian agent of Standing Rock that Sitting Bull was his own Indian. He walked a dangerous course.

General Nelson Miles was a military man in the process of remaking the army of the West to keep it relevant. His career required that he show the capacity of the modern army to respond to Indian insurrection. There were those who cautioned that Miles was exaggerating the threat of potential hostilities for presidential aspirations.[46] Such commentary was brushed aside.

Within the same timeframe, Colonel Drum served notice that there were growing signs of rebellion and that all white people at Standing Rock should come into the garrison. Even Mary Collins went to the fort.[47] This was particularly noticed by both Indian and white residents because she had never feared living among the Indians. Did she think an outbreak was coming? Apparently not, because she soon asked permission to return home and did so, unafraid to drive her buggy out over the prairie.[48]

Catherine Weldon was now in Kansas City, Missouri, and reading reports in the press. On November 20, she wrote a letter of warning to Sitting Bull:

The papers are full about the Indians, and that they may make war upon the white people. I have nothing more to say and advise that (sic) what I always said. I always advised you & your people for their own good and the day will surely come when you will know it. War can do no good, only hasten your destruction. Oh, my friend, and my Unkpapas, you are deceived by your prophets, and I fear some bad white men who are leading you into endless troubles. I said enough when I was among you, you ought to remember my harsh words. If I spoke harsh to you sometimes, forgive me; a true friends (sic) warning is not always pleasant to hear. I meant it for the best.

Plenty of soldiers surround you now, on all sides; Should the Indians make trouble, it will be bad for them. Be reasonable & take care.[49]

That same day, troops invaded both Pine Ridge and Rosebud. Five days earlier, Agent Royer had telegraphed that "the Indians were dancing in the snow and are wild and crazy."[50] He demanded protection. On

November 17, he got his answer. General Miles ordered Brigadier General John Brooke, Commander of the Division of the Platte, to send in the troops.[51] One hundred seventy cavalry and two hundred infantry men entered Pine Ridge at daybreak; Brooke personally came to guide the operation at Pine Ridge.[52] Simultaneously, 110 cavalry men and 120 infantry men were sent to Rosebud.[53] The blue coats were back in large numbers. But the Indians had no intention of making war. Still the ghost dancers at Pine Ridge said they would not give up the dance. If attacked, they would defend themselves.[54] At Rosebud, dancers fled; many of them heading to Pine Ridge.[55]

Brooke did not attack. Washington had said it wanted a bloodless campaign.[56] The army was there to show force. The general's goal was to separate the believers from the friendlies. Then emissaries approached the dissidents to reason with them. Kicking Bear and Short Bull were not waiting on the army's arrival; they were at an elevated plateau, known as Cuny Table, in rough terrain in the northwest area of Pine Ridge Badlands. To the Indians this was the "Stronghold," affording a natural fortified landform against any invader.[57]

The southern Badlands are a distinct area of the Dakotas. They are a landform that rises above the Plains in southwest South Dakota. The name is descriptive of the perception of the place as a harsh landscape. Here one finds gullies and washes, cliffs and buttes, jagged sandstone formations, eroding claystones, soft sedimentation deposits, and broken terrain. The French artist E. de Girardin, on an expedition in 1849, described it as a "city in ruins . . . surrounded by walls and bulwarks, containing a palace crowned with gigantic domes and monuments of the most fantastic and bizarre architecture."[58] Some of the most truculent of the ghost dancers holed up within its Stronghold.[59]

But others were gathered at Big Foot's redoubt on Deep Creek and Hump's camp about 30 miles away on Cherry Creek. Big Foot entered into ongoing discussions with Lieutenant Colonel Sumner at Camp Cheyenne. The chief was mild-mannered and said he was not looking for trouble; yet he had told his ghost dancers to arm themselves a few weeks earlier.[60] Hump, who had served Bear Coat as a scout in the Nez Perce war, was convinced to cooperate within a few days. He accepted a position of scout, in return for the promise of food and being allowed to keep weapons. Hump brought most of his band to the agency on December 9.[61] This was a serious defection from the Ghost Dance movement. None of the camps put forward a threatening stance.

Yet the newspapermen clamored for stories of the coming invasion. There were at least 21 correspondents gathered at Pine Ridge.[62] Even Frederic Remington, the Western artist, was sent out by *Harper's Weekly* to make sketches.[63] General Brooke cultivated no rapport with the press and issued no releases;[64] disappointed correspondents had no attacks to write about. Nevertheless, reporters had to send their publishers stories. Unverified rumors and even conversations with other reporters provided words fit to print.[65]

What was published spread panic among nearby ranchers and settlers.[66] The *Rapid City Journal* in South Dakota on November 20 reported the Sioux were "on the warpath."[67] The governor activated the South Dakota Home Guard. The *Buffalo Echo* in Wyoming, on November 22, went so far as to put out an extra, screaming: "THE MASSACRE BEGUN," based on the word of a person traveling in the area.[68] A woman stage passenger had seen nothing and merely, when asked, passed on hearsay conversation that she had heard during her trip.[69]

To meet the demands of the press, wires from General Miles about the situation were made public. On November 22, several newspapers across the Plains and in the East carried similar stories, based on these wires.[70] The *New York Tribune* in a subheadline, under the primary headline, "THE DANCES CONTINUE," declared: "Sitting Bull communicates with all the Sioux, even in Canada, urging them to aid his party—many braves supposed to have taken refuge in the Big Horn Mountains."[71] Nothing was happening in the Big Horns, and Sitting Bull's communications with anyone outside of his own reservation were nonexistent. The article picked up datelines from Minneapolis and Chicago of November 21, indicating "Indians are dancing with rifles strapped upon their backs."[72] The situation was termed "critical." "'Nothing but a miracle could save us from Custer's fate,' said a prominent officer. 'And I hope to God,' he added, 'that reinforcements will arrive before the red devils make their break.'"[73] Settlers were reported to be flocking from the countryside in South Dakota to cities based on the "well defined rumor that the Sioux will take the warpath tomorrow."[74] Such reports were at odds with what was actually happening. Settlements nearby the reservations were quiet.

James McLaughlin even received adverse press based on a report from a correspondent at Mandan, North Dakota:

> *Sitting Bull would (sic) be arrested and put in irons, but the agent is afraid that this would precipitate trouble. Agent McLaughlin has lost control of Bull and the other leaders. At Bull's camp, the dance of 200 braves keeps up day and night. All reports that come by wire from Fort Yates are colored. Military censorship is exercised on every message.*[75]

In truth, McLaughlin, while feeling some heat, was timing his move; and he held a firm hand on his reservation. While the agent was reporting to the Indian commissioner that all was quiet at Grand River, he was telling others that Sitting Bull was the prime advocate of the Ghost Dance and "his aggressiveness had assumed proportions of open rebellion against constituted authority."[76] The case that the man had to be removed was building. It did not matter that Sitting Bull was not a leader of the movement;[77] his reputation and association was sufficient to make him the target of suppressing the movement. McLaughlin was not going to suffer the embarrassment of the chief giving prominence to the Ghost Dance at his agency.

The *New York Tribune*'s article, to bolster its speculative reporting, included a quote from an undisclosed army officer:

> *Miles is predicting a general Indian war and virtually asks that the command of the entire Army be turned over to him. He wants to create a scare and pose as the saviour of the country. In fact, he is almost in the attitude of a political Messiah, such as the Indians themselves are looking for.*[78]

The general was not the only one to act for his own self-interest. The *Mandan Pioneer*, with its community currently facing the closure of its military base at the southerly edge of town, described Fort Lincoln as an essential garrison to respond to any disturbance at Standing Rock.[79] The purported crisis was too convenient not to embellish. The fort, once the home post to George Custer, was 60 miles north of Fort Yates. Both the *Chicago Tribune* and *New York Times* of November 28 continued fanning the flames with stories of potential immediate hostilities. A few newspapers on the prairie saw things differently. On the same day, the editor of the *Sturgis Weekly Record* published a broadside against such yellow journalism:

> *This ghost dance has been worked up into a very wonderful and exciting manner by pinheaded "war correspondents" and other irresponsible parties until they have succeeded in massing nearly half of the United States army to be spectators to an Indian pow wow.*[80]

In this setting, Nelson Miles put in motion a bizarre strategy. Buffalo Bill Cody was in New York in the late fall, having just returned from Europe. The general summoned him to Chicago for dinner and asked Cody whether he would travel to the Dakotas and talk Sitting Bull out of promoting the Ghost Dance. Cody welcomed the opportunity to put himself back on the ground in the West and was certain that he was the man for the job of dealing with his former friend.[81]

General Miles had more in mind than to have Cody just meet with the chief. He gave Cody a directive on November 24 authorizing him "to secure the person of Sitting Bull and deliver him to the nearest com'g officer of U.S. Troops, taking a receipt and reporting your action."[82] Miles believed that the showman could affect the arrest without incident. But, just in case, Cody was handed one of the general's calling cards, on the back of which was written that the military should supply any assistance requested by the special envoy.[83] Cody accepted the assignment and departed by train. Before leaving, he played the task to the press as the old Indian scout, saying that his former friend was the worst of the bad Indians: "[H]is conduct now portends trouble."[84] Ever the promoter, he even speculated that the Ghost Dance might flare into the greatest Indian uprising yet known.[85] Such statements were self-aggrandizing. Buffalo

Bill arrived at Mandan, North Dakota, on Thanksgiving Day, November 27. A telegram was sent to the post saying Cody's party would pull in that night. With him were Dr. Frank Powell, Robert "Pony Bob" Haslam, G. W. Chadwick, and a couple of newspaper reporters out of Bismarck.[86] They only got as far as the Cannonball River that day, stopping at Parkin Ranch for a layover.[87]

Twenty-five miles away, James McLaughlin was not pleased at the pending arrival of Cody. He ran Standing Rock, not the military; and he did not need Miles sending a showman to do the job. He did not want a spectacle on his reservation. A messenger was dispatched to Jack Carignan to ascertain the temperament of the Indians at Grand River. Carignan replied that he foresaw no trouble, unless the Indians were forced to defend themselves.[88] But he added advice that was more meaningful to McLaughlin—"[K]eep all strangers, other than employees, who have business among the Indians away from here, as Sitting Bull has lost all confidence in the whites, since Mrs. Weldon has left him."[89] Appearing at Fort Yates on the afternoon of November 28, Cody presented his credentials advising the commander to provide whatever support might be requested. This was not what Colonel Drum wanted to hear, insulted that a civilian could direct the military. Although Cody also carried the title "colonel," it was an honorary title given to him by the governor of Nebraska. While Drum tried to tactfully work through how assistance may be provided, it was not clear that Buffalo Bill was asking for assistance. In short order, Major McLaughlin came over to greet the old Indian scout. Adopting a concerned tone, he warned William Cody of the danger of going into the Ghost Dance camp at Grand River. Cody was not dissuaded. But he was going nowhere that day. He and his party were invited to the Officers' Hall and shown the hospitality of unlimited pours of hard whiskey.[90] The old man proceeded to drink his military hosts under the table. The interruption of Cody's mission gave more time to McLaughlin to maneuver. He hurried a telegram at 6:00 p.m. to the commissioner of Indian Affairs. There was no hesitancy in seeking to preempt General Miles:

William F. Cody (Buffalo Bill) has arrived here with commission from Gen. Miles to arrest Sitting Bull. Such a step at present is unnecessary and unwise as it will precipitate a fight which can be averted. A few Indians still dancing but does not mean mischief at present, I have matters well in hand and when proper time arrives can arrest Sitting Bull by Indian police without bloodshed. I ask attention to my letter of November 19. Request Gen. Miles's order to Cody be rescinded and request immediate answer.[91]

When the telegram reached the capital, it was carried from the commissioner to the Secretary of the Interior, then to the president.[92] There was no immediate response.[93] And the next morning Cody announced he was ready to go. If Cody ever thought the mission dangerous, he did not prepare for it. He was all show and no Indian fighter, dressed in one of his tailored performance suits, patent leather shoes, and silk stockings.[94] He declined the dutiful offer of Drum for a military escort.[95] Buffalo Bill set out for Grand River with two haul wagons filled with gifts.[96] In his mind, he still viewed his relationship with Sitting Bull well-bonded from their touring days together. His disparaging remarks to the press a few days earlier were a showman's swagger. His intent was to talk Sitting Bull into agreeing to meet with Miles. Accordingly, he set out about 11:00 a.m. armed with presents not weapons, only asking for directions. The order rescinding Cody's mission did not arrive at the fort telegraph station until 3:00 p.m. Urgency replaced whatever the reason for initial hesitancy. It was sent from the highest level, the president's office.[97] But the old Indian scout was well underway toward Grand River.

McLaughlin was not done. He had a backup plan in place to delay Buffalo Bill on the road. Louis Primeau had been sent to Oak Creek Crossing the day before and arranged what appeared to be a chance meeting with the Cody entourage on the road to Sitting Bull's cabin.[98] Primeau, primed to feign surprise in meeting up with the famous showman, inquired what Cody was doing in this part of the country. When his purpose was stated, Primeau told Cody: "It's too bad you came all this way; because I saw Sitting Bull on another trail a couple of miles northwest of here, heading to Fort Yates just yesterday in a buggy with one horse shod and the other not."[99] The tracking detail was intended to play to Buffalo Bill's pathfinder reputation. (Primeau had fabricated the tracks the day before.[100]) Cody asked for directions and turned about to head back toward Yates. Later that evening, the telegraphed order rescinding William Cody's directive from Miles was delivered to Cody while he was still on the false trail about four miles out from Fort Yates.[101] He had one word of reaction: "Damn!" In short order, Buffalo Bill was headed back to Mandan. McLaughlin claimed that his action to intercept Buffalo Bill saved the man's life.[102] The fiction of imminent danger of a white man going into Sitting Bull's camp remained in place. McLaughlin knew otherwise. But there is no question that he outsmarted Miles.[103] Now, McLaughlin put his plan of arrest in motion.

The warm fall weather finally began to turn cold on December 5.[104] The more customary temperatures of a Dakota winter were settling in. The next day, the agent wired Acting Commissioner Belt for authorization to arrest Sitting Bull, notwithstanding that all was quiet.[105] In fact, that was just the situation he wanted to exploit. He said the arrest needed to be made by the Indian Police without advance word to avoid bloodshed. Belt wired back to wait for the military. The major turned to Inspector Gardner of the bureau, who was on a visit to the fort, and requested 20 more policemen in order "to watch the movements of Sitting Bull and ghost dancers."[106] Again, he told the military that he had the matter in hand. He wired General Ruger in St. Paul that there was no need for immediate arrest: "Every day of cold weather cools the ardor of the dancers." He further advised that Sitting Bull could be "kept on the reservation by the Indian Police without fear of escape before arrest is required."[107] Reassuring the outside world that all was calm, McLaughlin remained committed to arrest. In a word, he did not need nor want the military to command the removal of Sitting Bull. Agent McLaughlin would pick the time to act.

The Secretary of the Interior granted only the request for additional men and instructed Belt to inform all reservation agents that there were to be no arrests, except by instruction of Interior or order of the military.[108] The existing agency police force knew of the talk of arresting Sitting Bull; and some expressed reluctance, either in the belief it was not a good idea or because they had relatives at Grand River. McLaughlin took the occasion to reconstitute the police force. He discharged One Bull, the chief's nephew, and others whom he considered sympathizers.[109] Henry Bull Head, who had been advocating arrest, was granted the opportunity to recommend men he knew were loyal and had no such misgivings about the charge that lay ahead.[110]

James McLaughlin knew from the army's intervention at the other reservations that his management of the pending arrest was at risk. With the turn of the weather, it was clear that there would be no sudden run to Pine Ridge or Cheyenne River. He took this time to work out a means to snare Sitting Bull, without a military operation on his reservation. He already had authorized the construction of a shelter 18 miles northeast of the Grand River settlement, next to the Oak Creek bridge crossing.[111] This, he said, was to protect winter travelers, but it really was a means of having the police closer at hand to a trouble spot. He asked Carignan for increased surveillance.[112] And he was not closed mouth about his strategy, releasing to the newspapers a report of his intentions. His plans were published in the *St. Paul Pioneer Press* on December 10 to answer critics:

> *There is no reason why Sitting Bull should not be arrested as soon as he comes within reach of the agency. He has broken his promise to send his children to school, and he did not come in last ration day as ordered. I expect him on Saturday, and we may get him before that time.*[113]

Now his reasons were couched as violations of agency rules. McLaughlin was positioning the situation as a disciplinary matter.

Close-by settlements were in a state of confusion. On November 21, a petition was sent to McLaughlin by V. E. Parr on behalf of the residents of La Grace, South Dakota, stating that the townspeople were fearful and no Indians should be allowed to leave the reservation.[114] Ten days later, six citizens (undoubtedly storekeepers) of La Grace sent their own petition that the Indians be allowed to cross the river for trading, observing that the Indians always have been well behaved.[115] Word had spread so far that an unnamed man from Augusta, Georgia, expressed concern in a December 8 letter warning Sitting Bull to stop dancing. "If there is any more moon-light hops, you will be swept away like the chaff before jimmeykane."[116]

Based on suspicion of arrest coming, Sitting Bull's followers took up guard duty to watch the settlement. In discussions with these old confederates, the chief questioned why McLaughlin would have him arrested:

Why does he keep trying to humble me? Can I be any lower than I am? Once I was a man, but now I am a pitiful wretch—no country, no fast horses, no guns worth having. Once I was rich, now I am poor. What more does he want to do to me? I was a fool ever to come down here. I should have stayed with the Red Coats in the Grandmother's country.

I did not start this Ghost Dance; Kicking Bear came here of his own accord. I told my people to go slow, but they were swept into this thing so strong nothing could stop them. I have not joined the sacred dance since I was told to stop, away back.[117]

With the McLaughlin-induced collapse of the Cody mission, General Miles stepped up his own stratagem.[118] On December 10, General Ruger received a telegram from Miles, ordering him to have the commanding officer at Fort Yates arrest the chief.[119] Word was dispatched to the assistant adjutant general to the Department of the Dakota, M. Barber, to issue a coded telegram with the order. Dated December 12, the wire went from St. Paul, Minnesota, to Colonel William F. Drum of Fort Yates; it was deciphered as follows:

The Division Commander has directed that you make it your special duty to secure the person of Sitting Bull. Call on Indian agent to cooperate and render such assistance as will best promote the purpose in view. Acknowledge receipt and, if not perfectly clear, repeat back.[120]

There was no intent to give the assignment to anyone but the military.[121] But James McLaughlin discerned some leeway in the second sentence and interpreted it to fit his purpose.

General Miles had not reckoned on James McLaughlin's command of his reservation. Agent McLaughlin and Colonel Drum conferred. The agent construed the call for cooperation to mean that he should manage the arrest. McLaughlin counseled that the army taking the lead would only provoke the strongest reaction; Drum acquiesced. The situation was delicate and best handled by the Lakota policemen.[122] James McLaughlin knew how to play the Sitting Bull card better than anyone; the army would be back up. Drum became a collaborator in the McLaughlin intrigue. The Indian police force was responsible only to the agent, and there was no friend of Sitting Bull in the ranks. James McLaughlin had long waited for this opening, and he was certain the police would not fail; this could not be put in the hands of the military. The roles Miles intended were reversed. The arrest was planned for December 20, the next ration day, when it was expected that most of the Indians in Sitting Bull's settlement would at the agency.[123]

This strategy changed almost immediately. Earlier that month, Short Bull invited Sitting Bull to Pine Ridge, saying that he had a revelation that the Messiah was coming early.[124] Sitting Bull should be present; and his people agreed.[125] Spies got word back to McLaughlin, and the agent made a countermove. As early as December 10, he had a letter dispatched to Grand River, ordering the dancers back to their farms.[126] The agent's messenger warned the chief that those who remained were to be disarmed and dispersed and their ponies would be taken from them.[127] The intent was to cause a break between those camping at Grand River and Sitting Bull. Fireworks were about to be set off. James McLaughlin knew the danger; he promised pensions to the policemen or their families, if they were injured or killed in a fight with Sitting Bull's ghost dancers.[128]

The next day, he followed with a letter to Sitting Bull, carried by the chief's close friend, Bull Ghost. The letter appealed to Sitting Bull's chieftaincy, saying that it was up to older, wiser men to advise the ignorant to give up the Messiah Craze. "My friend, listen to this advice. . . Do not attempt to visit any other agency."[129] This was mere paperwork. The agent offered a measure of contrived friendship at the same time that he was formulating a plan of action. On December 12 and 13, the agent positioned his police nearer Sitting Bull's cabin under the pretext of finishing construction of the shelter at Oak Creek Crossing.[130] Sergeant Shave

Head was ordered to take his men and report to Bull Head's house on the Grand River.[131] The time was near.

Sitting Bull, too, felt a sense of urgency. On the night of December 11, he dictated a letter for Agent McLaughlin to his son-in-law, Andrew Fox, a reservation-educated man but not highly proficient in English. The letter was talked out while Sitting Bull sat conversing and smoking with advisors and Andrew sat near with pencil in hand. To these men he said that the agent thinks they had originated the Ghost Dance, but it came from another reservation. On the evening of December 12, the same day as the order for arrest had been wired, Sitting Bull's letter was brought to McLaughlin.[132] The letter rambled and was poorly constructed. Apparently attempting to establish some commonality, early on, it said that they both prayed to the same God. Further, since the Lakota said nothing against his religion, he should say nothing about his. Near the end of the missive appeared the words: "I got to go, & to know This Pray."[133] (The letter did not give a destination. Perhaps Fox did not stumble in his use of English; Sitting Bull on occasion was purposely enigmatic.) The major read this clause to mean that Sitting Bull was going to join forces with the ghost dancers at Pine Ridge.[134] It seemed plausible since all of the agent's sources stated Sitting Bull was preparing to leave, although there was only hearsay regarding the invitation of Short Bull. Puzzlingly, the letter closed with the request for a reply "soon."[135] (If it was intended as asking for permission to leave the reservation, it would have been in deference to agency rules, which even Kicking Bear and Short Bull had ignored the prior year in visiting Wovoka in Nevada.[136]) The sentence that preceded the request for a reply advised that Sitting Bull had heard that the agent planned to take the camp's ponies and guns. Perhaps confirmation or denial was requested. In any event, it appeared that nothing at Grand River would happen until McLaughlin first responded to Sitting Bull.

But it was James McLaughlin's construction of the letter that set the course—Sitting Bull was ready to bolt from the reservation. The major immediately dispatched two messages. The first, on December 12, was via a courier letter from Louie Primeau to his cousin at Grand River, Charles DeRockbrain, to tell Bull Head to watch Sitting Bull closely and if he attempted to leave, "stop him." On the back side of the letter there was a note stating that it was sent under direction of the "U.S. Ind. Agt."[137] The second, on December 13, was McLaughlin's response to Sitting Bull telling him not to ask to visit any other agency "at present."[138] Another curious phrase, perhaps intended to stall Sitting Bull from his supposed journey.

Word spread among the Indian Police that within two days Sitting Bull would be arrested.[139] On the evening of December 13, the chief's loyal guard spent the night at his cabin in reaction to rumors they had heard that the agent was ready to move against Sitting Bull.[140] At the same time, on McLaughlin's order One Bull was sent north along the agency road to Cannonball to haul freight from Mandan.[141] Either this assignment was intended to remove a would-be ally of Sitting Bull from the scene of the coming arrest[142] or a cover for an informant whom McLaughlin wanted to protect.[143] By the afternoon of the following day, Hawk Man, one of the special police assigned to watch what was happening at Grand River community, brought another letter to McLaughlin at 4:00 p.m.[144] This letter was from Jack Carignan at Grand River School; he wrote that Lieutenant Bull Head had information that Sitting Bull was preparing to leave on December 15:

> It seems that St. Bull has received a letter from the Pine Ridge out-fit, asking him to come over there, as God is to appear to them. S.B.'s people want him to go, but he has sent a letter to you asking your permission, and if you do not give it, he is going to go any way. He has been fitting up his horses, to stand a long ride and will go a horseback in case he is pursued.

> Bull Head would like to arrest him at once before he has the chance of giving them the slip, as he thinks that if he gets the start, it will be impossible to catch him.[145]

It was not certain whether Sitting Bull intended to join Short Bull and Kicking Bear or, perhaps, seek out the great chief of the Oglala, his former ally—Red Cloud. (Catherine Weldon had told Sitting Bull of her contacts with Red Cloud and the similar positions each held on the Sioux

Act. From this perspective, it made sense that he might be interested in conferring with Red Cloud; but, based on years of strained relations, this was not to be expected.) Where Sitting Bull was not specific, Carignan was exact. The truth was that McLaughlin extracted what he wanted from the letter.

Colonel William Drum concurred with James McLaughlin that the time for arrest was now.[146] There was no need to check with the command in St. Paul or Miles in Chicago; the two men operated from the prior directive. That was all that they needed.

Ultimately, James McLaughlin could no longer abide the man. Over the years, every effort at friendship and persuasion had failed. Sitting Bull was a cantankerous Indian filled with self-importance. He was a continual disturbance to agency administration. He was promoting militancy among the ghost dancers. Now McLaughlin had documentation to show that the man was working to incite rebellion. Major McLaughlin would not stand down any longer. He had staved off the embarrassment of General Miles sending a drunken showman to remove Sitting Bull from the reservation. He was not going to suffer military preemption at Standing Rock. Sitting Bull was a problem on McLaughlin's turf. The arrest would be handled by the reservation's own police force.

The remark of Bull Head, a dedicated enemy of Sitting Bull,[147] to Carignan sparked the long-anticipated apprehension. (Not unexpectedly, conversations days earlier among the police about the timing of the arrest proved on the mark.) The major took full command. McLaughlin first prepared a letter of written instructions, both in English and Lakota, directing Bull Head and Shave Head to arrest Sitting Bull:

Lieut. Bull Head or Shave Head,
Grand River

From report brought by scout "Hawk Man" I believe that the time has arrived for the arrest of Sitting Bull and that it can be made by the Indian Police without much risk.—I therefore want you to make the arrest before daylight tomorrow morning and try and get back to the Sitting Bull road crossing of Oak Creek by daylight tomorrow morning as soon after as possible. The Cavalry will leave here tonight and will reach the Sitting Bull crossing of Oak Creek before daylight tomorrow (Monday) morning, where they will remain until they hear from you.

Louis Primeau will go with the Cavalry Command as guide and I want you to send a messenger to the Cavalry Command as soon as you can after you arrest him so that they may be able to know how to act in aiding you or preventing any attempt at his rescue.[148]

I have ordered all the police at Oak Creek to proceed to Carignan's School to await your orders, this gives you a force of 42 Policemen for to use in the arrest.[149]

After his signature, McLaughlin added finality to the order: "You must not let him escape under any circumstances."[150] It was placed in a Department of the Interior official business envelope[151] and special couriered to Grand River, where the police were already in position. Gray Eagle, the brother-in-law, was in on the plan. His house, only a short distance from Sitting Bull's cabins, was selected as a rendezvous point. Word was also dispatched to Jack Carignan that the time was at hand and he was to assist the police. There was no order given for the arrest of Shave Bear or other ghost dancers at Grand River. Nor were militant threats coming from the Grand River Ghost Dance camp. Sitting Bull was set up.

Colonel Drum gave orders that the one hundred men of the 8th Cavalry, under the command of Captain E. G. Fechet, were to leave Fort Yates at midnight with anticipated arrival at Oak Creek Station by 6:30 on the morning of December 15 to back up the Indian Police.[152] Their job was to take delivery of the prisoner from the police. The major knew there must be some role for the army, but he put his chosen people in the lead.

Gall and Grass also knew the time was at hand; they jointly signed a letter to Major McLaughlin asking for arms in the event that the dancers advanced on their camp near Oak Creek.[153] Their letter said they had heard about the soldiers going to Grand River and they would camp at Oak Creek to protect their children's teachers.

After the conclusion of Ghost Dance sessions, Catch the Bear and others usually drew together at Sitting Bull's house and stayed until morning. Sitting Bull told them he did not need their watch that night. He was waiting on word from McLaughlin and there was nothing to worry about.[154] He seemed to think there was security in his correspondence. If so, he misjudged the agent. By the time McLaughlin's instructions arrived at Bull Head's house around 10:00 p.m., there was a force of 28 policemen assembled under direction of the lieutenant.[155]

Red Tomahawk of Indian Police
STATE HISTORICAL SOCIETY OF NORTH DAKOTA (1952-7304)

CHAPTER TWENTY-ONE

Arrest at Grand River

December 15, 1890

The predawn of Monday, December 15, came with sporadic shivers of sleet.[1] No one was about to fall asleep in the saddle. The morning sky to follow was certain to be masked in gray.

Lieutenant Bull Head's home was just three miles distant on a northwest line from Sitting Bull's two cabins.[2] While the police waited there, others were at Carignan's school to the east; more police were coming from Oak Creek Crossing.[3]

In the morning darkness, Jack Carignan and three men set out, crossing above the Ghost Dance camp.[4] Camp dogs barked a preliminary alarm. When a voice from the camp called out, Carignan responded in Lakota that he was getting an early start on a trip to the agency.[5] It apparently was a satisfactory answer; he proceeded without further interruption to join Bull Head.[6] At about 4:00 a.m., Bull Head's and Carignan's groups banded together and set out to Gray Eagle's house, two miles away, west of the Grand River but not far from Sitting Bull's cabins.[7] The group from Oak Creek Crossing caught up a short time later. The policemen tied white handkerchiefs about their necks to distinguish themselves from other Indians who may come to the aid of Sitting Bull.[8] When the strike force gathered for final instructions, the lieutenant led them in a Christian prayer, asking the white man's god to provide protection for this undertaking.[9] Then, at 5:30, the police took the final steps to execute their mission. They were uneasy, but committed to the assignment. Each bolstered the other, and they counted on surprise to assure success. They were now 43 strong under the command of Bull Head and Shave Head.[10] The plan was to seize Sitting Bull while the Grand River camp was asleep.

The route taken was not direct. Puffed up with venom, these men slinked through the shivery murkiness when snakes should be in winter sleep.

They purposely had positioned themselves west of Sitting Bull's settlement, so that there would be no appearance of anyone approaching from the northeast, the direction of Fort Yates.[11] From Gray Eagle's place they circled southward on horseback, ghosting through the bottoms along the west riverbank with its tree cover, and then crossed over the stream to Sitting Bull's cabins.[12]

As the horses traversed the river, dogs yipped; and there was stirring within the larger settlement ahead of the police force.[13] But the icy rain muffled any unusual sound in crossing the creek bed, and no one detected the police movement. Now dismounted, Bull Head and Shave Head hurried a small detail to the door of Sitting Bull's main house and silently motioned another group to the second cabin just a short distance to the north.[14] A greater number of police surrounded the two cabins several yards back. All had their revolvers ready.

The door to the main house was thrown open.[15] Sitting Bull's name was called out. The pre-dawn threw a dim shaft of light across the threshold. A match flared, then lit a kerosene lamp; shadowy figures rushed in.[16] "I come after you to take you to the agency. You are under arrest, come with us,"[17] barked Bull Head. Sitting Bull pushed his body up from a floor mat, covered with a couple of agency-issued woolen blankets. Leaning on one elbow, his eyes squinted to see the intruders. His wife, Four Robes, and Crow Foot were there as well, but they were either of no concern to the police or shoved aside as they awakened. Two older men who had stayed the night and the pregnant wife of One Bull ran out from the cabin.[18] Nobody tried to stop them. One of the police found a revolver, two rifles, and some knives tucked under bed matting.[19] None of the occupants had attempted to reach for a weapon. Only one weapon was loaded; a policeman pulled a cartridge from the chamber and broke the rifle against the ground.[20] Outside dawn began to throw light on the stealth mission. The police had mistimed the arrest that was intended to spirit Sitting Bull away while the camp slept.

The chief was grabbed by the arms, pulled to his feet, and told to dress. Startled, he was at first confused. He asked Four Robes to go to the other cabin to gather proper clothing.[21] He appeared compliant; but when the police grew impatient and threw garments found in the cabin at him, telling him to hurry, Sitting Bull scolded them for their lack of respect.[22] Fully aware of the circumstances, he played for time. The policemen got caught up with talk and taunts. In the exchange, the chief still wielded some measure of intimidation. Apparently the special operation did not have a precise plan on how to deliver him to the army, because when he asked that his own horse be secured and saddled, two policemen were dispatched to the task. More time ran. Four Robes gave the alarm to the other household.[23] In moments, the entire camp came to high alert and supporters scrambled toward Sitting Bull's dwelling.[24] About 20 minutes had elapsed since the metal breasts first entered the cabin. During the delay, several other policemen entered the cabin to see what was holding up departure. "Take him and let's go!" The furtiveness used in approaching the arrest no longer held.

With time running against them, the policemen took hold of Sitting Bull. When the chief was pushed out ahead of his captors, several of his supporters were just outside.[25] The shouting crowd was admonished not to interfere.[26] Catch the Bear cursed the police; he called for Bull Head, his old adversary, to come forward.[27] The police with Sitting Bull in tow now resorted to bluster against the gathering. Gray Eagle told the chief "to do as the agent says. Go with the police."[28] While Gray Eagle may have been trying to defuse an impending blowup, the words stung Sitting Bull. Crow Foot called out: "You always called yourself a brave chief. Now you are allowing yourself to be taken by the metal breasts."[29]

At these words, Sitting Bull fumed before police and followers:

My own children now come as agents of the government to arrest me and stand ready to shoot down their own flesh and blood to assist that government.

*You have no right to do this. You are cowards to come to my house
in the nighttime. You are dogs to raise your hands against your own
people, and you do not deserve to be called Lakota or to live.*[30]

Sitting Bull turned defiant: "I will not go."[31]

Lieutenant Bull Head urged him to keep moving. Loneman snapped
a meaningless encouragement: "No one will harm you. The agent wants to
see you and then you are to come back, so please do not let others lead you
into any trouble."[32] With a revolver pressed against his back, the police
attempted to move the chief through the crowd.

Anger fractured any restraint. The throng became belligerent, pushing back at the police. Commanded to stand back, shouting erupted from
everywhere. Someone called out: "You will not take away our chief!"[33]
A growing number of outraged ghost dancers and allies of Sitting Bull
bunched forward in a semicircle confronting the police.[34] Fiery talk ran at
both sides: "Let him go."

"Let our chief go."

"Stand back."

"Move away and no one will be hurt."

"Let go of the chief."

"Cut them down."

"Get out of our way. Stand back, we are only here for Sitting Bull."[35]

Bull Head yelled: "No one will be killed. We came after Sitting Bull.
The agent wants him. The agent is going to build the chief a house near
the agency, so that, whenever any of his people need anything, the chief
can get it right of way."[36] A preposterous statement.

These words only fueled the building tension. "Lies, Lies." The crowd
drew closer and more threatening. Catch the Bear shoved against the
police line. Taunts and retorts collided.

Sensing the confrontation about to explode, Gray Eagle stammered that he had tried to save Sitting Bull, but the man was too obstinate.[37] He pulled back from the front, and then slipped away from the line of the policemen. He was washing his hands of the police action. Concerned for his sisters, he hastened to the second cabin. Upon entering, he urged the wives of Sitting Bull to go to his house to avoid harm. They chose to stay.[38]

Catch the Bear, menacing a rifle, moved front and center of Sitting Bull's followers and commanded: "Come on now. Protect our chief." He levered a shell into the chamber of his Winchester. Bull Head and Shave Head were on either side of Sitting Bull dragging him forward, and Red Tomahawk was prodding from the rear. The situation was at a flash point. In rapid succession, there were three sharp bursts of gunshots. Catch the Bear had pulled up his rifle and fired[39]—CRR-AACK. Instantly there was another CR-ACK, followed by a third CR-ACK. At the opening shot, there was no way Sitting Bull would walk another step.

Catch the Bear's shot hit Bull Head in the leg. Falling, the police chief reflexively pulled the trigger on his revolver. That shot struck Sitting Bull in the chest. Standing behind, Red Tomahawk, afraid that he was about to be overwhelmed, put his pistol to the back of the head of the slumping Sitting Bull and squeezed hard on its trigger. A scream of lead tore through the skull. If Sitting Bull's mind attempted to assess the damage of the first bullet entering his body, his mental process could not outpace the second shot. Blood ran from the back and front of his head, and his body immediately collapsed.[40] Sitting Bull lay still on the earth.

A determined Red Tomahawk was hardwired that Siting Bull had to be taken. His shot putting a bullet in the chief's head was driven by commitment to mission and survival instinct.

This was not a special force prepared to respond to what-ifs. With Sitting Bull cut down, panic took hold. The cold morning ignited. Gunshots raced to find flesh. The intended clandestine mission spun out of control. Shave Head went down. The three fallen bodies lay close together on the ground, but only the chief was dead. Catch the Bear turned his rifle toward policeman John Loneman. When the weapon misfired, Loneman grabbed the barrel and pried the rifle loose. He swung the butt of the rifle at Catch the Bear and caught him in the midsection, knocking him down. Catch the Bear was shot while doubled over gasping for air.[41] Some Grand River Indians assaulted policemen with clubs.

Wailing from Sitting Bull's wives and daughters at the second cabin cut through the chilled air. Men shouted and ran. Shooting now came from all directions. Each side scattered for cover. More bullets found the unprotected bodies of Bull Head and Shave Head.[42] Sitting Bull's comrades pulled back to the trees along the river, leaving the police to take refuge at the two cabins and adjacent corrals.[43] The wounded policemen were dragged inside the first cabin.[44] Policemen on the inside were caught in a trap, dependent on their comrades scattered outside to take control of confused cross fire.

Crow Foot, alone and without a weapon, had pulled back into the protection of the cabin. With the police commanding the door, he saw no way to escape. Frightened, he took cover in a darken corner behind some canvas wall covering. He did not avoid notice long. Loneman grabbed the boy—"There is another one here. What should we do with him?"[45] The fallen Bull Head, propped up with bed coverings, told them: "Do with him what you want."[46] Crow Foot was slammed with a rifle to the head and thrown toward the door. He grabbed at the door post to stop his fall. Gunfire from outside cut him down.[47]

In the face of shots discharging in all directions, a second Indian with the same name of Hawk Man was dispatched on horseback to summon Captain Fechet.[48] The army detail had not held up at Oak Creek as originally proposed, but pushed on toward Grand River.[49] They were three miles away, when Hawk Man reached them, telling the captain that all of the police were dead. The cavalry charged out at a gallop with the artillery wagons following. Minutes later, another messenger came up and said the police were surrounded. Upon arrival at 7:30, Fechet positioned his troops on a rise overlooking the fight at the settlement and called up the Hotchkiss artillery.[50] There now was light enough to survey the scene of the calamity. Two rounds exploded near the cabins.[51] Red Tomahawk, who had assumed command, sent Loneman with a white flag to warn of the policemen's location.[52]

A few miles away at Grand River, One Bull returned before the time of the arrest from his freight hauling trip after midnight and went to bed. He was awakened by the distant crackling of gunshots.[53] Heading toward Ghost Dance camp, he was intercepted by the Indian Police and told Sitting Bull was dead. He was warned away. When he inquired about the women who were with Sitting Bull, he was informed they were not harmed. He was directed to gather up his wife and go home.[54] One Bull did as he was told.

As the army swept onto the scene, the Grand River Indians retreated across the river, seeking cover in the trees. Not one shot was taken at the soldiers.[55] If the Indians wanted to cut and run, that suited Fechet.[56] His forces pursued them only a short distance; and when assured the Indians were scattered, Fechet ordered a return to Fort Yates.[57]

The guns fell silent. A hundred voices cried across Standing Rock: "Tatanka Iyotake is dead. They have killed Tatanka Iyotake." Within hours, several hundred Hunkpapa hurried toward the Cheyenne River Reservation and the Badlands further south.[58] They believed that ghost dancers were still strong to the south and would offer protection. But those scattering were running against a hard wind. All had to realize that the white man held the land and their lives.

In retrospect, the Cody intervention directed by Miles in November may have been the better course, but it probably would have only been a temporary stay of the violence coming.

The body of Sitting Bull lay on the frozen earth, stained red with congealing blood. There were no more storms to weather. There were seven bullet holes in his corpse.[59] This was not enough. Holy Medicine, a brother of one of the slain policemen, came forward to view the body. He took up a wooden yoke lying nearby and smashed it against the dead man's head.[60] Crow Foot's body lay a few feet away.

Captain Fechet and attendants surveyed the immediate area of the shootout. Inside, Lieutenant Bull Head and his sergeant, Shave Head, were still alive but with bodies badly broken by multiple wounds.[61] There was one other injured policeman, known as Middle.[62] Four policemen were found dead. On Sitting Bull's side there were eight dead;[63] near the stable two horses had been taken down by random shots.[64] Those of the Grand River people who were wounded were not officially accounted for. However, there were no reports of women killed in the shootout.

Sitting Bull's cabin
STATE HISTORICAL SOCIETY OF NORTH DAKOTA

An ambulance wagon was summoned to take the three wounded Indian police to Fort Yates for immediate care; it hastened back and arrived that night.[65] Shave Head would die the next day in the hospital; Bull Head lingered for a few days.[66] While waiting for the ambulance, Bull Head wanted it known that he was the one who killed the chief of the Hunkpapas: "Look after my family in the future and advise them. Never forget, I killed Sitting Bull."[67] Shave Head and Red Tomahawk also claimed credit.[68]

In the afternoon, a haul wagon was brought up to gather the dead. Certainly, the body of Sitting Bull would be carried back to Yates (Red Tomahawk viewed his orders to return with Sitting Bull, dead or alive). The chief's dead supporters were dragged into one of the camp cabins and left.[69] The bodies of the four slain Indian police also had to be brought back. It was decided that Sitting Bull's body would be put on the bottom of the wagon's floor bed, wrapped in a blanket; the other dead were placed on top as a measure of respect.[70] The wagon moved out at noon.

The settlement of log houses belonging to Sitting Bull and his family was plundered, with objects either stolen or smashed.[71] His wives were held for a short time by Captain Fechet's men and then released.[72] Other family members were taken to the fort as prisoners, and some went into hiding.

News of these events at Grand River had reached McLaughlin as soon as the early afternoon of December 15, and he quickly dispatched a telegram to the commissioner, tersely summarizing the events of the arrest:

His followers attempted his rescue and fighting commenced. Four police were killed and three wounded. Eight Indians killed including "Sitting Bull" and his son "Crow Foot" and several others wounded.[73]

Protecting his role in the incident, he added that the Indian Police had performed "nobly" and promised "particulars by mail."

CHAPTER TWENTY-TWO

The Report

December 16, 1890

The wagon carrying the dead from Grand River stopped overnight at Oak Creek Crossing and reached Standing Rock about 4:30 p.m. on December 16. Agent McLaughlin had approved the early closing of school so that families could show respect at the arrival of those who had died.[1] Youngsters talked about the shootout and told each other the soldiers were coming. They were bringing in the body of Sitting Bull with the slain Indian police.

The bodies of the policemen were placed in the agency meeting house, and Sitting Bull's corpse was taken to the dead house at the fort.[2]

Curiously that morning, the major found time to respond to a letter of December 5 from the members of Troop F of the 7th Cavalry Association, at Fort Supply, Indian Territory (Oklahoma), inquiring whether Sitting Bull was at the Custer massacre. McLaughlin advised that Sitting Bull was in camp, but, "As soon as Reno opened fire Sitting Bull fled with his family and was several miles away from the field of action." The old chief immediately returned when he heard the Indians were victorious "and arrogantly proclaimed himself leader of the battle by having gone into the hills nearby where he propitiated the evil spirits...."[3] Apparently it was a good day to work on unfinished business.

Later in the day, when the agent was briefed on more particulars of the incident (he debated whether that was the proper term), he composed a statement of the police action. Major McLaughlin carefully chose the right words to elaborate on the telegraph message sent the previous afternoon.

. His report on lined paper of the United States Indian Service, written
in Palmer cursive, was addressed to the commissioner of Indian Affairs,
Thomas J. Morgan. The opening paragraph declared the agent's action in
the matter was "governed by Department Instructions." The details were
as follows:

> *The troops left Fort Yates at 12 P.M. on the night of Sunday the 14th
> instant for Grand River with Louis Primeau as guide and my Indian
> police who were then at Grand River, or enroute, were instructed to
> arrest Sitting Bull, when the troops were sufficiently near to afford
> them protection in case of resistance to the arrest.*
>
> *At Day Break on Monday morning the 15th the Police went to
> Sitting Bull's camp direct to his house and surrounded the house; a
> detail was sent into the house where Sitting Bull was sleeping on the
> floor, the remainder staying outside, they aroused him and announced
> their purpose, and he at first seemed inclined to offer no resistance and
> they allowed him to dress, during which time he changed his mind
> and they took him forcibly from the house. By this time the police were
> surrounded by Sitting Bull's followers, members of the "Ghost Dance,"
> and the first shot was fired by "Catch the Bear" one of the hostiles and
> the Lieutenant of Police, Henry Tatankapah, (Bull Head), who was
> in command of the detachment of 42 men, was struck; the fighting
> then became general, in fact it was a hand to hand fight. Sitting Bull
> was killed, shot through the body and head in the early part of the
> fight by Bull Head and Marcelus Chankpidautah (Red Tomahawk)
> who each shot at him. Four Policemen were killed outright and three
> wounded, one of the latter dying at the Agency Hospital this morning
> after his removal there.*
>
> *Bull Head, the Lieutenant of Police is dangerously wounded but
> may recover. The hostile Indians lost 8 killed and several wounded and
> were driven from the field by the police; they fled up Grand River leav-
> ing their wives and families & all their property and dead behind them.
> Two Troops of the U.S. Cavalry (100 men) arrived on the ground
> immediately after the fight which had occupied less than half an hour
> and took possession of the camp, its inhabitants property and dead.*

Burial of Indian Police
MINNESOTA HISTORICAL SOCIETY

The Military did not pursue the fleeing hostiles and the latter will no doubt fall into the hands of some one of the commands moving at the different points west or south of the reservation.

The dead policemen will be buried tomorrow at the Agency with Military honors. Sitting Bull's remains are in the possession of the Military at Fort Yates.

The details of the battle show that the Indian Police behaved nobly and exhibited the best of judgment and bravery, and a recognition by the Government for their services on this occasion is richly deserved and should be promptly given with a substantial allowance for the families of those who are dead and also for the survivors to show them that the Government recognizes the great service that has been done for the Country in the result of yesterday's fight.[4]

In conclusion, the report noted that "the loss of the some of our best policemen . . . is to be very much regretted, yet the great good accomplished by the ending of Sitting Bull's career whose influence has been of such a retarding nature and the determination of the police in maintaining the will of the Government is most gratifying."

The tone was one of a man in earnest service of his government, and the complimentary close was subservient as fit the custom of the time: "I am, Sir, very respectfully your obed't Serv't," signed James McLaughlin. The report was posted immediately, and note of receipt at the Office of Indian Affairs six days later was entered on the cover packet as "Dec. 22."

James McLaughlin had no qualms about the death of Sitting Bull. But there was no way to dismiss the man as irrelevant. Sitting Bull was always known as a dissident and disturber. He skirmished with the U.S. military during the 1860s and refused to sign treaties of peace. He masterminded the Battle of Little Big Horn, commonly known as the "Custer Massacre," then fled into Canada and kept five thousand of his people in exile for four years. He returned the United States to surrender without contrition and when released as a prisoner of war he refused the good intentions of reservation life. He argued against the government's sale of reservation land that the United States said was intended to make the Indian more self-sufficient. He encouraged the militancy of the Ghost Dance movement and supposedly connived insurrection, which precipitated the order for his arrest.

Sitting Bull was a bad Indian. James McLaughlin was unequivocal in a follow-up report:

> *I desire to say that "Sitting Bull" who was constitutionally a bad man, without a redeeming quality, has been growing worse during the past year, so that his aggressiveness had assumed proportions of open rebellion against constituted authority notwithstanding that every honorable means to change him from his imprudent course had been resorted to.*[5]

The December 16, 1890, report seemed complete but was without reference to specific witness collaboration. None of the Indian police were interviewed, and certainly no one sought information from Sitting Bull's camp. The army's official account, made the next day, recited the same story with additional emphasis on the actions of the soldiers. There were no formal charges made against Sitting Bull. Nor would there be a court of inquiry.

Yet questions persisted. McLaughlin, 20 years later, was still defending his role in the killing of Sitting Bull:

> *I stood for peace, the peace of the community and welfare of the well-disposed Indians, and thought that the arrest would be made without bloodshed. It was not the shedding of Sitting Bull's blood that I regretted so much as I did the killing of the loyal Indian policemen who were shot down by crazed fanatics on Sitting Bull's order. And he brought on the trouble which ended in his death and also the killing of much better men than he was.*[6]

CHAPTER TWENTY-THREE

Burial

December 17, 1890

December 17 was the day set for the burial of the slain Indian policemen. The morning broke clear, but it had a raw edge.

During the noon hour, well over a hundred mourners attended services at the Congregation Church just south of the agency complex.[1] From there, they slowly proceeded to the nearby Catholic cemetery, bearing five caskets.[2] A tall, slender white wooden cross, about 20 feet high, cast the barest of shadow over the assembly. Darkly clothed family members and observers pulled close in a circle around freshly dug graves. A Catholic priest and Congregational minister intoned prayers, commending the spirits of the fallen to Almighty God. At the internment of the four policemen killed at the Grand River shootout and Shave Head, who died from his wounds on the next day, a military guard gave a rifle salute.[3] Major James McLaughlin, impeccably dressed in a three-piece suit and a black overcoat, with a bowler hat in hand, remarked that the policemen died in the service of their country and thanked the families of the fallen for their commitment to duty.[4] These were brave and honorable men. No one spoke of walking a tortured white man's road that put the Indian Police at conflict with their Lakota brothers at Standing Rock.

There certainly was no place for Sitting Bull at this cemetery.[5] He was not Christian; he had chosen to put himself at odds with the forward movement of his people. The mourners of the killed policemen pronounced him guilty of those deaths. They were outraged that his body was carried in the same wagon as their family members and friends from Grand River shootout to the agency. To them, he and his ghost dancers had turned away from their people. To the family and associates of Sitting Bull, the infidelity belonged to the Indian Police.

A coffin 2 by 2 by 6 feet 4 inches had been made for Sitting Bull in the fort carpenter shop on December 16 and taken over to the dead house.[6] His body was rewrapped in canvas and placed in the wooden box.[7] A few military personnel came by that night, but no one talked about what took place.[8]

As services for the policemen concluded, McLaughlin left the assembled mourners, opening the gate of the cemetery enclosure, and walked toward Fort Yates.[9] He had one more obligation—the burying of the man responsible for all the sorrow at Standing Rock. Overhead, thin clouds now defused the winter sun. An anxious wind snapped the flag above the fort parade grounds. The weather's temperature was dropping.

A single teamster manned a wagon carrying the body of the old chief, with four soldiers from the Fort Yates stockade following behind. It was not a funeral procession. And it was not going to take long. The wagon simply went to the far northwestern corner of the fort, where it was met by the acting post surgeon, assistant post surgeon, and post quartermaster.[10] These three officers were present to provide the military's attestation that the burial took place.

James McLaughlin quickened his step as he entered the grounds of the fort. The coffin was unloaded next to an open grave. One of the soldiers pulled back the cover of the coffin and poured chloride of lime and then acid over the canvas shrouded body.[11] (Reportedly, this was to prevent grave robbers from later seeking relics; others claimed it was to mask the mutilation already done to the body while at the post.[12]) The lid was quickly nailed in place and the box lowered. It was already below the ground by the time McLaughlin arrived.[13] The assembled men had not come to show respect; they were there to see the Lakota chief buried. The agent was fulfilling the professional duty of his office. It only took a few minutes to attest that Sitting Bull's resistance was at an end. McLaughlin's gray mustache and sharply cut beard accented his resolute look. He was too dignified to turn up the collar on his overcoat against the coldness. With the first shovels of dirt by the four prisoner-soldiers, fumes from the chemicals vented upward. James McLaughlin turned away. It was now late afternoon, and the sky ran gunmetal gray, hastening toward nightfall. One of those attending observed: "It is pretty hard for a dead Indian to lead an uprising." McLaughlin pulled his timepiece from his vest pocket, looked at it, and gave the rejoinder: "It was never going to happen on my reservation." That statement would stand as an amen to the funeral.

There was no slow beat of drums; there were no funeral words. There was no meadowlark's trill. With the grave closed, McLaughlin and the officers walked toward the warmth of the fort's headquarters. A quick current pushed against a nearby tree and ruffled the few remaining leafs.

Those who would grieve Sitting Bull were either under guard at Fort Yates or some 40 miles removed, in hiding at the cluster of cabins along the Grand River. Although most of his supporters had fled, anticipating reprisals from the violence surrounding his death, it was at the Grand River that the chief and spiritual leader of the Lakota was remembered. By the day of his burial, wailing cries from his two wives had subsided. Any trace of a funeral lament had been swallowed two days earlier by the winter quiet between Sitting Bull's cabin and the river.

Sitting Bull was buried beside the graves of soldiers and not among his own people, who would not have him. He was a champion who his people failed to acknowledge.

The burial was neither Christian nor Lakota. His body was dropped into the ground and quickly covered. There was no ritual dressing and wrapping of the body, no lock of hair cut from the deceased to be secured in a bundle and kept by a family member for a year to honor the spirit and facilitate transition to the next life. (The religious traditions of spirit keeping and gathering of goods for a giveaway on behalf of the deceased had been outlawed since 1883.[14])

That night shreds of clouds attempted to hide a half moon over Fort Yates. It was an uncertain time for the Lakota.

The American people were told that Sitting Bull's remains were interred on December 17, 1890, below the Dakota prairie at the western edge of the Missouri River. The Western press did not mourn Sitting Bull; rather he was castigated. An editorial by L. Frank Baum of the *Aberdeen Saturday Pioneer* pontificated:

> *The proud spirit of the original owners of these vast prairies inherited through centuries of fierce and bloody wars for their possession, lingered last in the bosom of Sitting Bull. With his fall the nobility of the Redskin is extinguished, and what few are left are a pack of whining curs who lick the hand that smites them. The Whites, by law of conquest, by justice of civilization, are masters of the American continent, and the best safety of the frontier settlements will be secured by the total annihilation of the few remaining Indians. Why not annihilation? Their glory has fled, their spirit broken, their manhood effaced; better that they die than live the miserable wretches that they are.*[15]

Baum felt it expedient for the government to pursue extermination—it was mercy killing of a misplaced race.

In the East, however, some struck a different tone. The *New York Herald* on December 17 wrote:

> *It is stated today that there was a quiet understanding between the officers of the Indian and military departments that it would be impossible to bring Sitting Bull to Standing Rock alive, and that if brought in, nobody would know precisely what to do with him. He would though under arrest, still be a source of great annoyance, and his followers would continue their dances and threats against neighboring settlers.*[16]

Although it raised a question, the story appeared resigned to accepting the death and moving on. But on December 21, the *New York World* ran an opinion editorial by author and clergyman William Murray, a supporter of the National Indian Defense Association. "The lying, thieving Indian agents wanted silence touching past thefts and immunity to continued thieving."[17] Murray charged "murder" and decried that the great chief's body was buried "like a dog's."[18]

The execution of Sitting Bull was explained by those in charge—killed while resisting arrest.[19] Six Indian police were killed in the attempted capture. He and his supporters caused the altercation that led to deaths on both sides. The Indian policemen had properly done their duty. The Lakota dealt with one of their own.

There were later reports to come from Sitting Bull's people that the killing did not happen as set out in the McLaughlin and Fechet accounts. (No Zapruder film existed to reconstruct the killing scene.) His wife, Four Robes, claimed that upon the police bursting into the cabin, the chief was rousted. Then Crow Foot, lying in his bed, was shot before he could rise. There immediately followed the killing of Little Assiniboine, the adopted brother of Sitting Bull, also known as Jumping Bull.[20] The chief was grabbed and shoved out of the cabin naked, stumbling into a barrage of gunfire. Scarlett Whirlwind, wife to One Bull, emerging from the other cabin, also saw the chief shoved from his cabin naked. She said she saw a flash of a gun from behind, and Sitting Bull went down. Catch the Bear had not fired the first shot.[21]

Others said, rather than the chief being escorted from the cabin, Sitting Bull and Crowfoot walked out the door to be cut down by a hail of bullets.[22] The winter count of 1880–1891 by Long Soldier depicts Sitting Bull's cabin surrounded on three sides by hoof prints and bullet tips pointed inward,[23] suggesting a firestorm of gunshots aimed at the cabin. Complicating matters is the question of whether One Bull had a role in the arrest; some relatives of Sitting Bull later reported that his absence from Grand River was intentional and he had prior knowledge of the order to the Indian Police.[24] (Lending weight to this view is a January 6, 1891, letter from John Carignan to James McLaughlin on behalf of One Bull. The letter advised that One Bull wanted the agent to do something for him, but it would "cause dissatisfaction among certain parties who are down on him." His uncle was the cause of his disgrace and One Bull sought to prove he was a good Indian. Perhaps if he were chief of Sitting Bull's band, he said, his influence would be of some benefit to McLaughlin.[25])

Different witnesses, different points of view.

The Chief of the Lakota who had gathered the Sioux and Cheyenne at Greasy Grass was no more. He was never the irrational rebel.

He was not inclined to change course with the prevailing wind. He was a man bound to the land and his people. His friend, Catherine Weldon, wrote:

> *The great hope and purpose of his life was to unify the tribes, and bands of the Dakotas, and hold the remaining lands of his people as a sacred inheritance for their children. This fact made him unpopular with all who saw his policy and influence obstruction to their selfish schemes, hence they demanded him removed.*[26]

His journey ended where it began. He was born along the Grand River in 1831 and died there 59 years later. The tragedy was that he was killed because he resisted on behalf of the Lakota people. He had refused to fade into the shadows of reservation life.

McLaughlin made another report to Thomas J. Morgan, Commissioner of Indian Affairs, on December 24. This was a detailed account to answer "so many absurd reports and ridiculous accounts regarding the arrest and death of Sitting Bull,"[27] which were carried in the public press throughout the country. His description of the shootings was precise, based on his own interviews with witnesses and the Fechet report. He set forth the protection of general populace of the reservation as a key reason for the arrest:

> *The police officers and others of the progressive Indians had been urging me for several weeks to permit them to arrest Sitting Bull and other leaders of disaffection who were engaged in fomenting mischief and participating in the Ghost Dances, they, the Ghost dancers, having become so aggressive that the peaceably disposed Indians could not remain in that district or pass through the settlement without being subjected to insults from Sitting Bull or his followers.*[28]

Then he quoted Captain Fechet's report commending the Indian Police for the conduct of the operation. The dutiful agent closed his lengthy letter with the reassurance that the vast majority of the Indians on the reservation were loyal to the government and expressed "universal satis-faction at the result of the fight [which obliterates] the seeds of disaffec-tion sown by the Ghost Dance."[29] For McLaughlin, the "domination of the old regime among the Sioux" on his reservation was over.[30]

Afterword

By the end of 1890, the Ghost Dance craze was on the wane,[1] but the military would not let the winter months alone exhaust enthusiasm for the religion.

An Indian agent had taken preemptive action, and General Miles, commander of the army overseeing the Plains, was not pleased. The army always took precedence over the bureau in dealing with Indian disturbances. The general had troops on the move to clean up the mess.

In response to anticipated reaction to Sitting Bull's death, army patrols fanned out between the Cannonball and Grand Rivers within Standing Rock, looking for Indian trouble and found none.[2] Rather they located scattered bands of dispirited people.

Some of the Grand River Hunkpapas fled immediately after the shootings at Sitting Bull's cabin and sought out Ghost Dance camps in the Badlands area to the south.[3] McLaughlin had emissaries follow them with promises of no reprisals if the Indians returned to the agency.[4] Several did, while others hurried on to join Big Foot, who was camped near the fork of the Cheyenne and Belle Fourche Rivers.[5] Big Foot as a key leader of the Ghost Dance movement had been under military observation for some time and he knew it. With Sitting Bull disposed of, Big Foot, Kicking Bear, and Short Bull were marked as the remaining hostile leaders.

Hearing of the great chief's death, Big Foot took his people toward Pine Ridge, in search of Red Cloud.[6] Some of the Hunkpapa on the run caught up with him, and Big Foot had his hands full keeping them in line.[7]

Military reconnaissance picked this movement up, and word was dispatched to General Miles. He had previously deployed troops of the 8th Cavalry under Lt. Colonel Edwin Sumner to watch Big Foot. Miles wanted no uprising. Or maybe he did. At a minimum, he was sending a clear signal to the Indian agents that he was in charge; and he played to the hysteria of the whites that had been building.[8] A telegram to the commanding officer at Fort Meade, South Dakota, was sent on December 23 to be delivered in the field to Sumner:

> *Report about hostile Indians near Little Missouri not believed. The attitude of Big Foot has been defiant and hostile, and you are authorized to arrest him or any of his people and to take them to Meade or Bennett. There are some young warriors that run (sic) away from Hump's camp without authority, and if an opportunity is given they will undoubtedly join those in the Bad Lands. The Standing Rock Indians also have no right to be there and they should be arrested. The division commander directs, therefore, that you secure Big Foot and the 20 Cheyenne River Indians, and the Standing Rock Indians, and if necessary round up the whole camp and disarm them, and take them to Fort Meade or Bennett.[9]*

The military believed that Big Foot's band was headed to the Stronghold to join Short Bull and Kicking Bear. Sumner, who understood Big Foot was close to capitulating and had prior good relations with the man, did not press, allowing the chief time to come in on his own.[10] Miles thought that Sumner mismanaged his assignment.[11] Other units were sent from the 7th Cavalry to pursue the trail further south.[12] The Stronghold was found empty on December 27.[13]

Late morning of December 28, Major Samuel Whitside's scouts located the old chief along an icy Porcupine Creek, miles below the Badlands.[14] He was hardly in a position to make a fight. The scouts found him lying in the back of a wagon, sick with pneumonia, wrapped in blankets and attended to by a few braves.[15] Whitside and the 7th Cavalry were called forward, with the major riding directly to the wagon to take charge. Within a few minutes of conversation, Big Foot agreed to surrender.[16] He only asked for a brief respite to prepare his band for turning themselves over to the military.

It was arranged that he and his people would camp nearby that night and submit to the soldiers the next day. An army ambulance wagon was brought up at the major's order, and Big Foot was transferred into it.

He was sent ahead, and his band was moved out under escort.[17] That evening, Lt. Colonel Forsyth took command.[18] The colonel informed Whitside that once the Indians were disarmed, they were to be marched south across the state line into Nebraska and shipped by rail to prison in Omaha.[19] To insure delivery on Big Foot's promise, two Hotchkiss rapid-firing guns were positioned on a northerly knoll overlooking the camp and sentries were posted.[20] A show of intimidation was hardly necessary. The officers both pushed back the night's falling temperature and celebrated the anticipated next day's capture with whiskey.[21] Early the next morning, they moved into the Indian camp along the bank of a river, known as Wounded Knee, to gather weapons. Two more Hotch-kiss guns were placed on the knoll.[22] An extreme show of force against a docile camp.

The morning of December 29 was quiet, and the Indians were coop-erative as the troopers moved among them. The soldiers seemed not to care that several Indians were wearing ghost shirts.[23] A low murmur went through the ranks of those surrendering; but the soldiers did not concern themselves. It seemed like submissive wailing. Only one medicine man, Yellow Bird, was haranguing the captors.[24] In searching a deaf man known as Black Coyote, a soldier found a rifle hidden under the man's blanket and tore at the blanket to remove the weapon. Black Coyote resisted. The gun discharged.[25] The suppressed emotions of the surrendering Indians flared.

Indians pulled away from the soldiers and some drew knives; soldiers bashed and punched captives with rifles. A man known as Yellow Bird threw dust above his head, which was later reported as a signal for resis-tance.[26] A few sporadic gunshots popped among the submissive crowd. Without hesitation, artillery guns on the hill began firing. A fusillade shattered the early morning's stillness and ripped those massed below. The Hotchkiss guns disgorged two-pound shells at the rate of 50 per minute. Mothers fell to the earth clutching babies to protect them from gunfire. Women and children running to escape were hunted down up to three miles away. One hundred forty-six men, women, and children were killed.[27] There was no difference between the bodies clothed with ghost shirts and those without them; bullets pierced the flesh of all. The indiscriminate rapid fire from the guns even took out 25 soldiers. On this day, the 7th Cavalry was said to have exacted its revenge for the battle at Greasy Grass.[28] (The assignment of the 7th to this operation presented an eerie coincidence—11 of the 19 officers within the command had been at Little Big Horn in June 1876.[29])

By the afternoon, the sky went gray-white and a northern airstream sent a blizzard over the field of Wounded Knee. Dead Indian bodies were left where they had dropped to freeze in the night.[30] The corpse of Big Foot was later found sprawled on his back in the snow in a distorted shape, slightly inclined with elbows planted against the ground, as if he were trying to regain his feet; a blanket was hooded as a muffler around his head and extended out the bottom of his short coat to the upper portion of his leggings.[31] The earth was crusted with bloody snow. In this after stillness, ghosts from lifeless bodies screamed to the sky with no one to hear them.

Four days later—New Year's Day 1891—a mass grave was dug by hired civilians, and the corpses were thrown in.[32] Photographers documented the macabre scene. Eighteen of Forsyth's men would be awarded Medals of Honor for their outstanding conduct during this engagement.[33]

This time from the editor's desk of the *Aberdeen Saturday Pioneer* on January 3, 1891, Frank Baum aimed harsh words at Nelson A. Miles: "The peculiar policy of the government in employing so weak and vacillating a person as General Miles to look after the uneasy Indians, has resulted in a terrible loss of blood to our soldiers, and a battle which, at its best, is a disgrace to the war department."[34] Other newspapers saw it as unavoidable under the circumstances.[35] Miles was quick to decry the result and convened a court inquiry in an unsuccessful effort to censure Forsyth.[36]

Short Bull and Kicking Bear were in the valley of White Clay Creek, about 15 miles north of the agency and were ready to come in. But hearing of Wounded Knee they pulled back.[37] At the first of the year, General Miles took to the field, bringing 3,500 troops to Pine Ridge.[38] Then, through intermediaries like Young Man Afraid he sent out invitations to surrender.[39] The Sioux well remembered the relentless Bear Coat's reputation. The Indians were demoralized; defections occurred daily. Miles did

Chief Big Foot (Spotted Elk)
DENVER PUBLIC LIBRARY, WESTERN HISTORY COLLECTION

not even bother to have his men confiscate arms from those who gave up.[40] Kicking Bear at first was nowhere to be found. However, in late January, he presented himself with rifle in hand directly to the general at Pine Ridge and was taken prisoner without incident.[41] Miles took Short Bull and Kicking Bear to Chicago in late January with the intent to confine them at Fort Sheridan. But at the request of his friend Buffalo Bill, he released them to his custody for a European tour of the Wild West show.[42]

The last resistance from the mighty Plains Indians was extinguished.[43] Images on glass plate photographs taken during the 1870s and 1880s held only a glimpse of what Sitting Bull tried to preserve.

The Sioux legend that told of Iktomi, the Spider Man spirit or trickster, spreading word that a new man was approaching had come to pass. "You shall know him as washi-manu, steal-all, or better by the name of fat-taker, wasichu, because he will take the fat of the land. He will eat up everything, at least for a time."[44]

The prairie was lost.

The frontier was proclaimed closed in 1890 by the United States Census Bureau. Eight hundred miles southeast of the Standing Rock Agency sprawled Chicago, the Midwestern metropolis numbered according to that year's national census at over a million persons. It had recovered from the great fire of 1871 and rebuilt itself into America's second city. Chicago was the site of the nation's first skyscraper, supported on an iron frame, rising to nine stories; and a thousand trains came and went from the city each day. This was the industrial and commercial center of the heartland. In April 1890, President Harrison confirmed Chicago's selection as the host city for the 1893 world's fair, to be known as the "Columbian Exposition," commemorating the four-hundredth anniversary of the European discovery of America.[45] Twenty-seven-and-a-half million people visited the fair over a period of six months.[46]

The exposition was powered by alternating-current and illuminated at night by electric street lights. Various exhibits proclaimed the changes forthcoming in the next century, and Professor Frederick Jackson Turner lectured before a convocation of historians on the closing of the frontier. The fair's "White City" underscored the arrival of the modern industrial age.

For the amusement of the attendees along the midway there was the first Ferris wheel; nearby at the North Dakota Building Sitting Bull's log cabin on the Grand River had been relocated and reconstructed.[47] James McLaughlin was called on to authenticate the log structure, and in his writing he emphasized it was the place where the Indian Police in support of the government made a "gallant" stand against dissident Indians.[48] The reassembled cabin was showcased with the intent to put a period at the end of an era.

Just outside the fairgrounds, Buffalo Bill staged his Wild West show, celebrating life on the frontier that no longer existed.[49] Indians were in urban Chicago, and Custer's Last Stand was reenacted as entertainment.

The three great chiefs of the Sioux each had been forced into reservation life. Crazy Horse and Sitting Bull were killed at the hands of their own people on these enclaves. The third, Red Cloud, more willing to seek middle ground, continued to live out his years at Pine Ridge until his death in 1909.

Major James McLaughlin remained the agent at Standing Rock for an additional five years after Sitting Bull's death; he then became a U.S. Indian Inspector with broad authority over all reservations throughout the country, reporting directly to the Commissioner of Indian Affairs. He continued this employment for 28 years.[50] Ever loyal, his service was exemplary. A town on the reservation approximately 25 miles southwesterly of Fort Yates was named in his honor.

James McLaughlin devoted the full energy of his adult life to the transformation of the Indian. The only problem was he did not see the flaws in the reservation system.

Sitting Bull never gave up the influence of the Lakota's prairie earth.

Endnotes

Author's Preface: Perspective

1 - McLaughlin, My Friend the Indian (1910), p. 3.

Chapter One: Fort Yates, North Dakota

1 - In 1890, the superintendent of the U.S. Census Bureau announced Western settlement had broken America's frontier line. Three years later, Frederick Jackson Turner, a historian from the University of Wisconsin, delivered to colleagues in Chicago his thesis, "The Significance of the Frontier in American History."
2 - Pfaller, James McLaughlin: The Man with an Indian Heart, 368.
3 - The fort was decommissioned in 1893.
4 - Pfaller, James McLaughlin: The Man with an Indian Heart, 191.
5 - Id., 368.
6 - Constructed dialogue based on conflicting views of Sitting Bull within his own people.
7 - Palmer, The Dakota Peoples, 243.

Chapter Two: The Northern Plains

1 - McLaughlin, My Friend the Indian, 7.
2 - Meldahl, Hard Road West, 40.
3 - Savage, Prairie, A Natural History, 14.
4 - Id., 22; Isenberg, The Destruction of the Bison, 16–17, 19.
5 - The central and southern Great Plains were at the heart of a firmament that produced the dust bowl of the 1930s. Plowed earth from farming dislodged native grasses over millions of acres; then the pulverized, fallow dirt itself was blown away by winds during a prolonged drought. These same characteristics in varying degrees also struck the northern Plains. Sodbusters who had tilled the soil lost their homesteads. Egan, The Worst Hard Time, 2, 9, 153, 254–55.
6 - Adams, Sitting Bull, An Epic of the Plains, 22–23, referencing Washington Irving's description of the winds on the prairies.
7 - Savage, Prairie, A Natural History, 76–77.

8 - Utley, *The Lance and the Shield, The Life and Times of Sitting Bull*, 199; Isenberg, *The Destruction of the Bison*, 66–67.

9 - DeMallie, "Lakota Belief and Ritual in the Nineteenth Century," DeMallie and Parks (Ed.), *Sioux Indian Religion*, 32.

10 - The name "buffalo" is a corruption of the French "les boeufs," meaning beeves.

11 - McGee, *The Siouan Indians*, 189–90; Robinson, *A History of the Dakota or Sioux Indians*, 20–21.

12 - Meyer, *History of the Santee Sioux*, 1-5; Lazarus, *Black Hills White Justice*, 4.

13 - Palmer, *The Dakota Peoples*, 1–2, 29.

14 - Id., 12, 48; McGee, *The Siouan Indians*, 160–61. Robinson, *A History of the Dakota or Sioux Indians*, 15, makes the distinction between Dakota and Sioux: "The latter is the generic name for many tribes having a common origin and speaking a similar language. The former comprised an alliance of seven of the Sioux bands, closely related."

15 - Robinson, *A History of the Dakota or Sioux Indians*, 22.

16 - Marcy, *The Prairie Traveler*, "The Buffalo," Ch. 7.

17 - Carlson, *The Plains Indians*, 19 and 39.

18 - Page, *In the Hands of the Great Spirit*, 183; Marshall, *The Day the World Ended at Little Big Horn*, 40–41.

19 - Lazarus, *Black Hills White Justice*, 5.

20 - Carlson, *The Plains Indians*, 19, 39.

21 - President Th. Jefferson, Instructions to Captain Meriwether Lewis, June 1, 1803.

22 - Lewis and Clark may have been considered journeyers by the native inhabitants of the countryside, but the Treaty between the United States of America and French Republic of April 30, 1803 (known as "The Louisiana Purchase Treaty"), specifically provided in Article I, "the French Republic has incontestable title to the domain and to the possession of said Territory." That title was transferred to the United States pursuant to the treaty and two conventions of the same date. Article III declared that "The inhabitants of the ceded territory shall be incorporated in the Union of the United States." This did not mean Indians; a subsequent article exacted a promise by the United States to execute treaties previously agreed upon with "tribes and nations of Indians until by mutual consent of the United States and the said tribes or nations other Suitable articles Shall have been agreed upon."

23 - Ambrose, *Undaunted Courage*, 93–96.

24 - Buckley, *William Clark: Indian Diplomat*, 8, quoting from the Clark journals.

25 - Ambrose, *Undaunted Courage*, 206.

26 - Palmer, *The Dakota Peoples*, 123; Walker, *Lakota Society*, 131; Greene and Thornton, *The Year the Stars Fell*, 138, 142.

27 - Isenberg, *The Destruction of the Bison*, 21, quoting Stephen Long's description from exploration of the Plains in 1821–1820.

28 - Standing Bear, *My People the Sioux*, 30.

29 - See decision of Chief Justice John Marshall in Johnson vs. McIntosh (1823)21 U.S. 543, 591: "However extravagant the pretension of converting the discovery of an inhabited country into conquest may appear; if the principle has been asserted in the first instance, and afterwards sustained; if a country has been acquired and held under it;

if the property of the great mass of the community originates in it, it becomes the law of the land, and cannot be questioned. So, too, with respect to the concomitant principle, that the Indian inhabitants are to be considered merely as occupants, to be protected, indeed, while in peace, in the possession of their lands, but to be deemed incapable of transferring the absolute title to others. However this restriction may be opposed to natural right, and to the usages of civilized nations, yet, if it be indispensable to that system under which the country has been settled, and be adapted to the actual condition of the two people, it may, perhaps, be supported by reason, and certainly cannot be rejected by Courts of justice."

30 - Robinson, *A History of South Dakota*, from Earliest Times, 10.

31 - Palmer, *The Dakota Peoples*, 247

32 - Id., 246–47, Vestal, *New Sources of Indian History*, 186–88; Utley, *The Lance and the Shield*, 39.

33 - Ostler, *The Plains Sioux and U.S. Colonialism from Lewis and Clark to Wounded Knee*, 32.

34 - Marshall, *The Day the World Ended at Little Big Horn*, 110.

35 - Vestal, *New Sources of Indian History*, 1850–1891, 189.

36 - Adams, *Sitting Bull*, 42.

37 - Treaty of Fort Laramie (1851), Article 2.

38 - Id., Article 5.

39 - This is a frequently used description in negotiating with Indians in the 1800s, meaning forever or a very long time. It is stated to have been first documented in a U.S. treaty with the Seneca or Cherokee Nation and is referenced as a broken promise when the Indian Removal Act of 1830 caused the relocation of the Cherokee, resulting in the Trail of Tears.

40 - Treaty of Fort Laramie (1851), Article 7; Lazarus, *Black Hills White Justice*, 19.

41 - Adams, *Sitting Bull*, 44.

42 - Vestal, *New Sources of Indian History*, 200, 203–05.

43 - Id., 206; Adams, *Sitting Bull*, 46.

44 - Vestal, *New Sources of Indian History*, 44.

45 - Finerty, *War-Path and Bivouac, Historical Introduction*, xvii.

46 - Treaty of Fort Laramie (1851), Article 7.

47 - Treaty of Fort Laramie (1851), Article 5.

48 - Utley, *The Lance and the Shield*, 44.

49 - Vestal, *New Sources of Indian History*, 205.

50 - Vestal, *Sitting Bull, Champion of the Sioux*, 1850–1891, *A Biography*, 3.

51 - Id., 13.

52 - Id., 14.

53 - Utley, *The Lance and the Shield*, 15.

54 - Id., 22.

55 - Id., 19.

56 - Id., 21.

57 - Id., 35.

58 - Vestal, *Sitting Bull, Champion of the Sioux*, 23.

59 - Id., 23–24.

60 - Id., 25–26.

61 - Utley, *The Lance and the Shield*, 28, 33.

62 - Vestal, *New Sources*, 142–52; according to Robert Higheagle, Sitting Bull was "a man medicine seemed to surround," Utley, *The Lance and the Shield*, 33.

63 - Utley, *The Lance and the Shield*, 30; Vestal, *Sitting Bull, Champion of the Sioux*, 22–23.

64 - Utley, *The Lance and the Shield*, 22.

65 - Id., 70.

66 - LaPointe, *Sitting Bull, His Life and Legacy*, 42.

67 - Ibid.

68 - Utley, *The Lance and the Shield*, 35.

69 - Vestal, *New Sources*, 203.

70 - Vestal, *Sitting Bull, Champion of the Sioux*, 246–47 (statement made to the Select Committee of the Senate investigating the condition of the Indian tribes of Montana and Dakota in 1883, set forth in chapter 13, below).

71 - Vestal, *New Sources*, 194.

72 - Vestal, *Sitting Bull, Champion of the Sioux*, 83.

73 - Adams, *Sitting Bull*, 47.

74 - Id., 108.

75 - Gilpin, *The Central Gold Region*, 120.

76 - Id., 121.

77 - Larmar (Editor), *New Encyclopedia of the American West*, 282.

78 - A phrase used by some to describe the Plains; see Milton, *South Dakota, A History*, 185.

79 - Linklater, *Measuring America*, 28.

80 - Utley, *The Lance and the Shield*, 48.

81 - Id., 49–52.

82 - Id., 51.

83 - Utley, *Frontiersmen in Blue*, 276.

Chapter Three: Minnesota River Valley Uprising

1 - McLaughlin, *My Friend the Indian*, 17; Anderson and Woolworth, *Through Dakota Eyes, Narrative Accounts of the Minnesota Indian War of 1862*, 8.

2 - Anderson and Woolworth, *Through Dakota Eyes*, 26–27. The Cut Head band of Yanktonai who settled in the area of Devils Lake got its name when its leader suffered a scalp wound during a fight with the Sisseton. McLaughlin, *My Friend the Indian*, 25. Because years later these Indians were some of those who took up farming in the Minnesota River Valley, the terms "cut hairs" and "cut heads" sometimes are confused.

3 - Anderson, *Little Crow, Spokesman for the Sioux*, 113–22; Anderson and Woolworth, *Through Dakota Eyes*, 19–20.

4 - www.thinknd.org/resources/IndianStudies/spiritlake/historical_conflict.html, "The

Dakota Conflict."

5 - Anderson, *Little Crow*, 123.

6 - Id., 127.

7 - Id., 128.

8 - Anderson and Woolworth, *Through Dakota Eyes*, 35–36 and 38.

9 - Anderson, *Little Crow*, 138.

10 - Utley, *Frontiersmen in Blue, The United States Army and the Indian*, 1848–1865, 264.

11 - Wilson, *The Earth Shall Wee*p, 271–72.

12 - Anderson and Woolworth, *Through Dakota Eyes*, 40.

13 - Anderson, *Little Crow*, 138–39.

14 - Utley, *Frontiersmen in Blue*, 265.

15 - Anderson, *Little Crow*, 135–36.

16 - Id., 222, ftn. 3. But in Anderson and Woolworth, *Through Dakota Eyes*, 56 and 59, there are quotes of eyewitnesses that Myrick actually was found with a mouthful of grass.

17 - Utley, *Frontiersmen in Blue*, 264–65.

18 - Id., 266.

19 - Anderson, *Little Crow*, 164.

20 - Id, 165.

21 - Ibid.

22 - Anderson and Woolworth, *Through Dakota Eyes*, 14, 206–15.

23 - Utley, *Frontersmen in Blue*, 269.

24 - Id., 268 and 270; Anderson, *Little Crow*, 162–63, 169–71.

25 - Utley, *Frontiersmen in Blue*, 270–71.

26 - Ibid.

27 - Utley, *The Lance and the Shield*, 58.

28 - Anderson and Woodworth, *Through Dakota Eyes*, 268–69.

29 - Utley, *Frontiersmen in Blue*, 277–78.

30 - Utley, *The Lance and the Shield, The Life and Times of Sitting Bull*, 60.

31 - Vestal, *Sitting Bull, Champion of the Sioux*, 59.

32 - Id., 62.

33 - Utley, *Frontiersmen in Blue*, 280.

34 - Pfaller, *James McLaughlin: The Man with an Indian Heart*, 3.

35 - McLaughlin, *My Friend the Indian*, 1.

36 - Pfaller, *James McLaughlin: The Man with an Indian Heart*, 2.

37 - Calvert, *Standoff at Standing Rock*, 17.

38 - Pfaller, *James McLaughlin: The Man with an Indian Heart*, 3.

39 - Fenno, photograph (1864); State Historical Society of North Dakota. The photograph is a formal portrait of James and Louise McLaughlin in the year of their marriage. He is attired in a dark suit (the frock coat with velvet collar of his suit reinforces his drive to succeed), and she is in a checked dress with white collar.

40 - Pfaller, *James McLaughlin: The Man with an Indian Heart*, 3.

41 - Utley, *The Lance and the Shield*, 102; McLaughlin, *My Friend the Indian*, 8.

42 - Vestal, *New Sources of Indian History*, 287; Pfaller, *James McLaughlin: The Man with an Indian Heart*, 3.

43 - Pfaller, *James McLaughlin: The Man with an Indian Heart*, 4.

44 - Id., 3–4. In later life she would write a book about the legends and folk lore of the Sioux, entitled *Myths and Legends of the Sioux* (1916).

45 - McLaughlin, *Myths and Legends of the Sioux*, Foreword.

46 - Kelsey, *Tribal Theory in Native American Literature*, 21.

47 - McLaughlin, *My Friend the Indian*, 8.

48 - Id., 16–17.

49 - Utley, *The Lance and the Shield*, 249.

Chapter Four: Powder River War

1 - DeTrobriand, *Army Life in Dakota*, Introduction by Will, xxi.

2 - Adams, *Sitting Bull, An Epic of the Plains*, 100.

3 - Utley, *The Lance and the Shield, The Life and Times of Sitting Bull*, 62; Lazarus, *Black Hills White Justice*, 41.

4 - Bray, *Crazy Horse: A Lakota Life*, 78.

5 - Kelman, *A Misplaced Massacre, Struggling over the Memory of Sand Creek*, 8–9, 115–18, and 46.

6 - Connell, *Son of the Morning Star*, 177.

7 - Welch, *Killing Custer*, 143–44; Connell, *Son of the Morning Star*, 178.

8 - Greene and Scott, *Finding Sand Creek: History, Archaeology and the 1864 Massacre*, 46.

9 - Kelman, *A Misplaced Massacre*, 195; Lazarus, *Black Hills White Justice*, 29; Adams, *Sitting Bull*, 102.

10 - Senate Reports to the 38th Congress, the Joint Committee on the Conduct of the War (1865).

11 - Ibid.

12 - Sides, *Blood and Thunder*, 478–79.

13 - Utley, *Frontiersmen in Blue*, 307.

14 - Utley, *The Lance and the Shield*, 71; Finerty, *War-Path and Bivouac, Historical Introduction*, xxiii.

15 - Olson, *Red Cloud and the Sioux Problem*, 27–32.

16 - Id., 35.

17 - Id., 34.

18 - Id., 36; Adams, *Sitting Bull*, 147–55.

19 - Utley, *The Lance and the Shield*, 71.

20 - Sandoz, *Crazy Horse, The Strange Man of the Oglalas*, 196, 205.

21 - Olson, *Red Cloud and the Sioux Problem*, 36.

22 - Utley, *The Lance and the Shield*, 66.

23 - Id., 64–65.

24 - Id., 67, n. 4.

25 - Bray, *Crazy Horse*, 98.

26 - Ibid.

27 - Id.,99.

28 - Ibid.

29 - Ostler, *The Plains Sioux and U.S. Colonialism*, 45–46.

30 - Id., at 46–47.

31 - Ostler, *The Plains Sioux and U.S. Colonialism*, 47.

32 - Sandoz, *Crazy Horse*, 196, 205.

33 - Ostler, *The Plains Sioux and U.S. Colonialism*, 46.

34 - De Trobriand, *Army Life in Dakota*, xxii.

35 - Utley, *The Lance and Shield*, 64.

36 - Id. at 75, 78; Yenne, *Sitting Bull*, 56.

37 - Larson, *Red Cloud, Warrior-Statesman of the Lakota Sioux*, 67.

38 - Id., 115.

39 - Lazarus, *Black Hills White Justice*, 32.

40 - Adams, *Sitting Bull*, 157.

41 - Lazarus, *Black Hills White Justice*, 46.

42 - Ibid.

43 - Cozzens (Editor), *Eyewitness to the Indian Wars 1865–1890*, Vol. V, 3–4; Letter to O. T. B. Williams of Cheyenne, Wyoming, dated September 6, 1868, and published in the Cheyenne Star.

44 - Adams, *Sitting Bull*, 160.

45 - Larson, *Red Cloud*, 115; Adams, *Sitting Bull*, 165.

46 - Id., 164.

47 - Lazaurs, *Black Hills White Justice*, 46–47.

48 - Ibid.

49 - Adams, *Sitting Bull*, 166.

50 - Larson, *Red Cloud*, 108.

51 - Id., 120; Adams, *Sitting Bull*, 174.

52 - Ostler, *The Plains Sioux and U.S. Colonialism*, 46.

53 - Lazarus, *Black Hills White Justice*, 47.

54 - Larson, *Red Cloud*, 115.

55 - Id., 120–22; Olson, *Red Cloud and the Sioux Problem*, 77–88.

56 - Ostler, *The Lakota and the Black Hills*, 92.

57 - Adams, *Sitting Bull*, 195.

58 - Utley, *The Lance and the Shield*, 78.

59 - Id., 76. His missionary career in America had begun in 1838.

60 - Chittenden and Richardson (Editors), *Life, Letters and Travels of Father De Smet among the North American Indians*, 319.

61 - Id., 85, 113.

62 - Id., 13, 102, 105–06.

63 - Id., 2.

64 - Id., 119–20, 127, 128–29.

65 - Id., 85, 123.

66 - Id., 60–62, 84–86, 89, 91.

67 - Id., 89.

68 - Id., 118.

69 - Vestal, *Sitting Bull, Champion of the Sioux*, 105.

70 - Utley, *The Lance and the Shield*, 78–79; Vestal, *Champion of the Sioux*, 98.

71 - Chittenden and Richardson (Editors), *Life, Letters and Travels of Father De Smet*, 95.

72 - Utley, *The Lance and the Shield*, 79, 81.

73 - Vestal, *Champion of the Sioux*, 102.

74 - Id., 102–03.

75 - Id., 104.

76 - Id., 105.

77 - Vestal, *Champion of the Sioux*, 104–05.

78 - Adams, *Sitting Bull*, 171.

79 - This is a summary of a longer quotation found in Adams, *Sitting Bull*, 172–73, and Vestal, *Champion of the Sioux*, 106–07.

80 - Vestal, *Champion of the Sioux*, 108.

81 - Id., 108–09.

82 - Larson, *Gall: Lakota War Chief*, 17, 70–71.

83 - Vestal, *Champion of the Sioux*, 110.

84 - Id., 109.

85 - Id., 110.

86 - Vestal, *New Sources of Indian History*, 226, 229.

87 - Id., 230.

88 - Id., 111.

89 - Fort Laramie Treaty of 1868, Article 1.

90 - Lazarus, *Black Hills White Justice*, 56.

91 - Vestal, *New Sources of Indian History*, 326.

92 - Id., 327.

93 - Lazarus, *Black Hills White Justice*, 64.

94 - Utley, *The Lance and the Shield*, 84.

95 - De Trobriand, *Army Life in Dakota*, 292.

96 - Utley, *The Lance and the Shield*, 84.

97 - Fort Laramie Treaty of 1868, Article 2.

98 - Ibid.; Lazarus, *Black Hills White Justice*, 48–49.

99 - Lazarus, *Black Hills White Justice*, 55.

100 - Fort Laramie Treaty of 1868, Article 15.

101 - Yenne, *Sitting Bull*, 64.

102 - Fort Laramie Treaty of 1868, Article 16.

103 - Welch, *Killing Custer*, 67. The railroad lobby had applied pressure on the government to obtain this concession; railroads were refusing to extend track into new western lands without protection.

104 - Id., Article 11, 1st, 2nd, and 6th Provisos.

105 - Id., Article 11, 6th Proviso.

106 - Id., Article 2.

107 - Id., Article 16.

108 - Lazarus, *Black Hills White Justice*, 52.

109 - Welch, *Killing Custer*, 61.

110 - Knight, *Following the Indian Wars*, 72; Adams, *Sitting Bull*, 181.

111 - Lazarus, *Black Hills White Justice*, 54–55.

112 - Welch, *Killing Custer*, 62.

113 - Knight, *Following the Indian Wars*, 92–93.

114 - Custer, *My Life on the Plains*, 192.

115 - Knight, *Following the Indian Wars*, 63.

116 - Id., 101.

117 - Id., 95.

118 - Welch, *Killing Custer*, 64; Knight, *Following the Indian Wars*, 98.

119 - Warren, *Buffalo Bill's America*, 137; Connell, *Son of the Morning Star*, 200–01. Custer himself claimed that the sister of Black Kettle offered him a 17-year-old maiden in marriage, but he diplomatically refused. Custer, *My Life on the Plains*, 171–72. However, he mentions an "exceedingly comely squaw" (Id., 191) of 20 with long raven black hair—variously Mo-nah-se-tah or Mo-nah-see-tah—several times throughout his writing about the aftermath of the Washita Battle. He is consistently complimentary and gives her credit for assisting him with later negotiations with the Cheyenne.

120 - Welch, *Killing Custer*, 61.

121 - Id., 63; *Custer, My Life on the Plains*, 181.

122 - Adams, *Sitting Bull*, 191.

123 - *New York Tribune*, December 14, 1868.

124 - Custer, *My Life on the Plains*, 183.

125 - Connell, *Son of the Morning Star*, 202–03, attributing the statement to Chief Medicine Arrow; Utley, *Cavalier in Buckskin*, 193.

126 - Lazarus, *Black Hills White Justice*, 56; Adams, *Sitting Bull*, 194.

127 - Olson, Red Cloud and the Sioux Problem, 65–66, 72–73.

128 - Id., 83–89; Lazarus, *Black Hills White Justice*, 55–56.

129 - Olson, *Red Cloud and the Sioux Problem*, 83.

130 - Id., 84.

131 - Id., 119.

132 - Lazarus, *Black Hills White Justice*, 63; Robinson, *History of the Dakota or Sioux Indians*, 398–99.

133 - Olson, *Red Cloud and the Sioux Problem*, 84–93, 101.

134 - Id., 96–99; *Larson, Red Cloud*, 138.

135 - Olson, *Red Cloud and the Sioux Problem*, 102.

136 - Id., 114–43.

137 - Id., 105; Robinson, *History of the Dakota or Sioux Indians*, 396–97.

138 - Olson, *Red Cloud and the Sioux Problem*, 126–27.

139 - Lazarus, *Black Hills White Justice*, 139; Larson, *Red Cloud*, 144–45.

140 - Olson, *Red Cloud and the Sioux Problem*, 152.

141 - Id., 151–52.

142 - Larson, *Red Cloud*, 150.
143 - Olson, *Red Cloud and the Sioux Problem*, 168
144 - Lazarus, *Black Hills White Justice*, 61.
145 - Bray, *Crazy Horse*, 181.
146 - Yenne, *Sitting Bull*, 149; Utley, *The Lance and the Shield*, 207.
147 - Larson, *Gall: Lakota War Chief*, 95; Vestal, *Champion of the Sioux*, 115.
148 - Utley, *The Lance and the Shield*, 117.
149 - Id., 87. Others date his ascendancy to primary chief to prior to his encounter with Fr. De Smet in 1868 (see Vestal, *Champion of the Sioux*, 96); but this seems unlikely because at this time *Red Cloud* and the Oglala were at the forefront of the war over the Boseman Trail.
150 - Pfaller, *James McLaughlin: The Man with an Indian Heart*, 4–5.
151 - Id., 5.
152 - Ibid.
153 - McLaughlin, *My Friend the Indian*, 12.
154 - Id., 29.
155 - Id., 12.
156 - Id., 9
157 - Id., 5.
158 - Pfaller, *James McLaughlin: The Man with an Indian Heart*, 5.
159 - Id., 26.
160 - Photograph held by the State Historical Society of North Dakota.
161 - Pfaller, *James McLaughlin: The Man with an Indian Heart*, 12; McLaughlin, *My Friend the Indian*, 15.
162 - Pfaller, *James McLaughlin: The Man with an Indian Heart*, 6.
163 - Id., 19.
164 - Id., 24.
165 - Id., 25.

CHAPTER FIVE: PAPA SAPA

1 -Lazarus, *Black Hills White Justice*, 57–58; Larson, *Red Cloud*, 128.
2 - Textor, *Official Relations between the United States and Sioux Indians*, 38.
3 - Isenberg, *The Destruction of the Bison*, 128.
4 - Welch, *Killing Custer*, 67.
5 - Isenberg, *The Destruction of the Bison*, 128.
6 - Id., 84, 128, 152.
7 - Donovan, *A Terrible Glory*, 30. See also Smits, "The Frontier Army and the Destruction of the Buffalo," *The Western Historical Quarterly*, Vol. 25 No. 3, pp. 312–36.
8 - Isenberg, The Destruction of the Bison, 128–29, 143–52. See also Smits, "The Frontier Army and the Destruction of the Buffalo, "52, *The Western Historical Quarterly*, 312–36.
9 - Id., 128–40; Warren, *Buffalo Bill's America*, 53–55; Miles, *Personal Recollections & Observations of General Nelson A. Miles*, 134.

10 - Bray, *Crazy Horse*, 75. Adams, *Sitting Bull, An Epic of the Plains*, 39–40.

11 - Adams, *Sitting Bull*, 42.

12 - Diedrich, *Sitting Bull, The Collected Speeches*, 23. By 1888, there would be fewer than one thousand of the great animal in the United States. Isenberg, *The Destruction of the Bison*, 143.

13 - Utley, *The Lance and the Shield, The Life and Times of Sitting Bull*, 92–93.

14 - Id., 97.

15 - Lazarus, *Black Hills White Justice*, 66.

16 - Id., 57.

17 - Id., 106; Schell, *History of South Dakota*, 158–74, discusses the boom of population in the Dakotas from 1878–1886.

18 - Welch, *Killing Custer*, 130.

19 - Ibid.

20 - Connell, *Son of the Morning Star*, 234.

21 - Utley, *The Lance and the Shield*, 111.

22 - Robinson, *History of the Dakota or Sioux Indians*, 414.

23 - *New York Times*, September 19, 1873.

24 - Utley, *The Lance and the Shield*, 117–18.

25 - Adams, *Sitting Bull*, 248–49; Donovan, *A Terrible Glory*, 102–05.

26 - Utley, *The Lance and the Shield*, 115.

27 - Schell, *History of South Dakota*, 125–28.

28 - Schmidt (Editor), *General George Crook, His Autobiography*, 189.

29 - Lazarus, *Black Hills White Justice*, 8.

30 - Ostler, *The Plains Sioux and U.S. Colonialism*, 58–59; Marshall, *Crazy Horse*, 200.

31 - Ostler, *The Lakota and the Black Hills*, 4.

32 - Bray, *Crazy Horse*, 187.

33 - Utley, *The Lance and the Shield*, 115; Lazarus, *Black Hills White Justice*, 8.

34 - Schell, *History of South Dakota*, 128.

35 - Ibid.

36 - Adams, *Sitting Bull*, 257; Robinson, *History of the Dakota or Sioux Indians*, 413.

37 - Ostler, *The Lakota and the Black Hills*, 85.

38 - Robinson, *History of the Dakota or Sioux Indians*, 415.

39 - Sandoz, *Crazy Horse, The Strange Man of the Oglalas*, 287.

40 - Schmidt (Editor), *General George Crook, His Autobiography*, 189.

41 - Utley, *The Lance and the Shield*, 126–27.

42 - Lazarus, *Black Hills White Justice*, 80–81.

43 - Robinson, *History of the Dakota or Sioux Indians*, 420.

44 - Utley, *The Lance and the Shield*, 125.

45 - Robinson, *History of the Dakota or Sioux Indians*, 419.

46 - Marshall, *The Journey of Crazy Horse*, 208.

47 - Utley, *The Lance and the Shield*, 126.

48 - Robinson, *History of the Dakota or Sioux Indians*, 419.

49 - Id., 417.

50 - Id., 419–20; Ostler, *The Lakota and the Black Hills*, 92.

51 - Utley, *The Lance and the Shield*, 126.
52 - Ostler, *The Plains Sioux and U.S. Colonialism*, 61.
53 - Ibid.
54 - Ostler, *The Lakota and the Black Hills*, 88.
55 - Id., 343.
56 - Pfaller, *James McLaughlin: The Man with an Indian Heart*, 27–28.
57 - Id., 27–28.
58 - Id., 28.
59 - Ibid.
60 - Id., 29.
61 - Id., 30.
62 - Id., 29
63 - Id., 30–31.
64 - Id., 32.
65 - Id., 32–33.
66 - Id., 35.
67 - Id., 32.
68 - Id., 35.
69 - Id., 36.
70 - Ibid.
71 - Ibid.
72 - Ibid.
73 - Id., 36.
74 - Ibid.
75 - Id., 36.
76 - Id., 37.
77 - Ibid.
78 - Id., 38; Meyer, *History the Santee Sioux*, 231.

CHAPTER SIX: THE 1876 YELLOWSTONE CAMPAIGN

1 - Ostler, *The Plains Sioux and U.S. Colonialism*, 61.
2 - Fort Laramie Treaty of 1868, Article 16.
3 - Id., Article 11, Lazarus, *Black Hills White Justice*, 68.
4 - Vestal, *Sitting Bull, Champion of the Sioux*, 141.
5 - Utley, *The Lance and Shield, The Life and Times of Sitting Bull*, 120.
6 - Donovan, *A Terrible Glory*, 34.
7 - Utley, *The Lance and the Shield*, 128.
8 - Donovan, *A Terrible Glory*, 35.
9 - Vestal, *Champion of the Sioux*, 142.
10 - Ibid.
11 - Connell, *Son of the Morning Star*, 250.
12 - Utley, *The Lance and the Shield*, 176.

13 - Knight, *Following the Indian Wars*, 162.

14 - Lazarus, *Black Hills White Justice*, 52.

15 - Larson, *Gall, Lakota War Chief*, 105.

16 - Knight, *Following the Indian Wars*, 162; Utley, *Little Bighorn Battlefield (Official National Park Handbook)*, 27.

17 - Vestal, *Champion of the Sioux*, 142.

18 - Utley, *Little Bighorn Battlefield (Official National Park Handbook)*, 27.

19 - Robinson (Editor), *The Diaries of John Gregory Bourke*, Vol. 1, 217.

20 - Ibid.

21 - Robinson, *History of the Dakota or Sioux Indians*, 423.

22 - Id., 424. See Miles, *Personal Recollections & Observations*, 219, for description of soldiers in the field bundling themselves to protect from the cold of winter campaigns.

23 - Robinson, *History of the Dakota or Sioux Indians*, 423.

24 - Yenne, *Sitting Bull*, 78; Finerty, *War-Path and Biouvac*, 18.

25 - Vestal, *Champion of the Sioux*, 143.

26 - Yenne, *Sitting Bull*, 78.

27 - Utley, *The Lance and the Shield*, 131.

28 - Id., 136.

29 - Utley, *Little Bighorn Battlefield (Official National Park Handbook)*, 27, 32.

30 - Vestal, *Champion of the Sioux*, 155.

31 - Ibid.

32 - Ibid.

33 - Utley, *The Lance and the Shield*, 142; Yenne, *Sitting Bull*, 89–90.

34 - Vestal, *Champion of the Sioux*, 144–45.

35 - Utley, *The Lance and the Shield*, 102; Bray, *Crazy Horse*, 167.

36 - Vestal, *Sitting Bull, Champion of the Sioux*, 151–52.

37 - Maurer, *Visions of the People*, essay by Powell, "Sacrifice Transformed into Victory," 90–91.

38 - Vestal, *Champion of the Sioux*, 153.

39 - Ibid.

40 - Sandoz, *Crazy Horse*, 317; Marshall, *The Journey of Crazy Horse*, 72, 221; Bray, *Crazy Horse*, 61.

41 - Vestal, *Champion of the Sioux*, 155–56.

42 - Ibid.; Knight, *Following the Indian Wars*, 191.

43 - Schmidt (Editor), *General George Crook, His Autobiography*, 195 (Secretary of War, Annual Report, 1876, No. 500).

44 - Report of Brig. General George Crook to Lt. General Sheridan, June 19, 1876; Robinson, *The Diaries of John Gregory Bourke*, Vol. 1, 335.

45 - Utley, *The Lance and the Shield*, 142.

46 - Robinson (Editor), *The Diaries of John Gregory Bourke*, Vol. 1, 487.

47 - Id., Vol. 1, 319, n.1.

48 - Vestal, *Champion of the Sioux*, 156.

CHAPTER SEVEN: SOLDIERS FALLING UPSIDE DOWN

1 - Vestal, *Sitting Bull, Champion of the Sioux*, 158.

2 - Utley, *Little Big Horn Battlefield (Official National Park Handbook)*, 63–64.

3 - Marshall, *The Day the World Ended at Little Big Horn*, 134.

4 - Connell, *Son of the Morning Star*, 403; Marshall, *Little Big Horn*, 48–49.

5 - Welch, *Killing Custer*, 149.

6 - Donovan, *A Terrible Glory*, 175; Yenne, *Sitting Bull*, 85–86.

7 - Donovan, *A Terrible Glory*, 172–73.

8 - Utley, *Cavalier in Buckskin*, 177; Donovan, *A Terrible Glory*, 301; Yenne, *Sitting Bull*, 87; Finerty, *War-Path and Bivouac*, 206–07.

9 - Utley, *Cavalier in Buckskin*, 177–80; Donovan, *A Terrible Glory*, 196.

10 - Marshall, *Little Big Horn*, 134.

11 - Id., 132.

12 - Utley, *The Lance and the Shield, The Life and Times of Sitting Bull*, 147.

13 - Ibid.; Donovan, *A Terrible Glory*, 225.

14 - Yenne, *Sitting Bull*, 88, 97.

15 - Utley, *The Lance and the Shield*, 148–50.

16 - Id., 148.

17 - Vestal, *Champion of the Sioux*, 164.

18 - Yenne, *Sitting Bull*, 94.

19 - Vestal, *Champion of the Sioux*, 164–65.

20 - Donovan, *A Terrible Glory*, 228.

21 - Id., 225–26.

22 - Indians said the opening rounds were fired at Midday real time (probably about 1:00 p.m.), and the military reports generally put it at 3:00 p.m.; Welch, *Killing Custer*, 174–75. According to Connell, *Son of the Morning Star*, 304, time in the West in this era correlated to the nearest metropolitan center. Although a system of one-hour standard time zones was proposed for American railroads in 1863, it was never accepted. Instead the railroads implemented a version that fixed time zones borders that ran through stations in major cities and a guide was first published in 1868. Not until 1883 were standard time zones for the United States implemented by the railroads; but only when Congress adopted the Standard Time Act of 1919 did time zones become universal. Thus, it appears that the army searching for Indians in eastern Montana in 1876 related its time to that kept in eastern cities. Michno, *Lakota Noon, The Indian Narrative of Custer's Defeat*, 20, also tracks a two-hour difference in reported time. The Indians related to solar time.

23 - Vestal, *Champion of the Sioux*, 164.

24 - Utley, *The Lance and the Shield*, 150; Larson, *Gall*, 119.

25 - Palmer, *The Dakota Peoples*, 51; Dorsey, *Siouan Sociology*, 221.

26 - Michno, *Lakota Noon, The Indian Narrative of Custer's Defeat*, 49.

27 - Marshall, *Little Big Horn*, 70; Welch, *Killing Custer*, 159, said it was only one wife that was killed.

28 - Welch, *Killing Custer*, 95.

29 - Vestal, *New Sources of Indian History*, 322–23; De Trobriand, *Army Life in Dakota*, 51.

30 - Vestal, *Champion of the Sioux*, 181–82; Utley, *The Lance and the Shield*, 161–63.

31 - Utley, *The Lance and the Shield*, 150–51.

32 - Bray, *Crazy Horse: A Lakota Life*, 221–29.

33 - Welch, *Killing Custer*, 166.

34 - Utley, *Cavalier in Buckskin*, 188.

35 - Id., 267; Michno, *Lakota Noon*, 101.

36 - Vestal, *Champion of the Sioux*, 166–67; Yenne, *Sitting Bull*, 94.

37 - Vestal, *Champion of the Sioux*, 180–81.

38 - Vestal, *New Sources of Indian History*, 140, 322, and *Champion of the Sioux*, 147.

39 - Marshall, *Little Big Horn*, 40–41.

40 - Id., 102–04; Vestal, *Champion of the Sioux*, 149, challenges the notion that the Sioux were better armed.

41 - Finerty, *War-Path and Bivouac*, 211; Connell, *Son of the Morning Star*, 306–07. Knight, *Following the Indian Wars*, 187, reports that this was a common complaint of soldiers in the field. Welch, *Killing Custer*, 182–83, does not find support for the Indians being better equipped.

42 - Marshall, *Little Big Horn*, 71.

43 - Id., 73; Donovan, *A Terrible Glory*, 237.

44 - Welch, *Killing Custer*, 165.

45 - Dunn, *Massacres of the Mountains, A History of the Indian Wars of the West*, Vol. 2, 608.

46 - Donovan, *A Terrible Glory*, 229.

47 - Id., 274.

48 - Connell, *Son of the Morning Star*, 307–09; Donovan, *A Terrible Glory*, 239.

49 - Id., 174.

50 - Id., 178.

51 - Welch, *Killing Custer*, 205; Connell, *Son of the Morning Star*, 311.

52 - Vestal, *Sitting Bull, Champion of the Sioux*, 174.

53 - Welch, *Killing Custer*, 172; Michno, *Lakota Noon*, 289.

54 - The reaction to picking up a chronometer is loosely based on the accounts in Michno, *Lakota Noon*, 287, and Connell, *Son of the Morning Star*, 311.

55 - Connell, *Son of the Morning Star*, 303; Welch, *Killing Custer*, 35, based on time-motion studies of John Gray.

56 - Michno, *Lakota Noon*, 23–286, with the final stand at about 20 minutes, in midafternoon, 251–86.

57 - Donovan, *A Terrible Glory*, 290; Vestal, *Champion of the Sioux*, 175.

58 - Id., 177.

59 - Ibid.

60 - Finerty, *War-Path and Bivouac*, 216.

61 - Adams, *Sitting Bull*, 312.

62 - Vestal, *Champion of the Sioux*, 179.

63 - Utley, *The Lance and the Shield*, 160.

64 - Yenne, *Sitting Bull*, 101.

65 - Adams, *Sitting Bull*, 314.

66 - Vestal, *Champion of the Sioux*, 177.

67 - Welch, *Killing Custer*, 193.

68 - Finerty, *War-Path and Bivouac*, 216; Welch, *Killing Custer*, 186; Vestal, *Champion of the Sioux*, 186.

69 - Yenne, *Sitting Bull*, 103; Adams, *Sitting Bull*, 312.

70 - Vestal, *Champion of the Sioux*, 175.

71 - Id., 164; Connell, *Son of the Morning Star*, 285, 319–20.

72 - Vestal, *Champion of the Sioux*, 186; Connell, *Son of the Morning Star*, 285.

CHAPTER EIGHT: REACTION AND RETALIATION

1 - Knight, *Following the Indian Wars*, 213.

2 - Id., 218; Donovan, *A Terrible Glory*, 320–21.

3 - Pfaller, *James McLaughlin: The Man with an Indian Heart*, 46.

4 - Knight, *Following the Indian Wars*, 214.

5 - Id., 213.

6 - Id., 214.

7 - MacEwan, *Sitting Bull: The Years in Canada*, 72–73.

8 - *Bismarck Tribune*, July 6, 1876.

9 - Ibid.

10 - Knight, *Following the Indian Wars*, 195.

11 - Utley, *Cavalier in Buckskin*, 189. Yenne, *Sitting Bull*, 101, also opines that Custer died below the ridge. Michno, *Lakota Moon, The Indian Narrative of Custer's Defeat*, 251, 288, puts Custer at the last stand but also notes that the Indians did not know Custer was in command that day and there were several dead soldiers in buckskin jackets, the apparel by which Custer was known. All that is clear is that there had to be a last stand by some group of the 7th Calvary.

12 - Yenne, *Sitting Bull*, 95, 100; Vestal, *Champion of the Sioux*, 168–69; Connell, *Son of the Morning Star*, 308–09.

13 - Miles, *Personal Recollections & Observations of General Nelson A. Miles*, 293.

14 - *New York Herald*, July 7, 1876.

15 - Knight, *Following the Indian Wars*, 219.

16 - *Chicago Tribune*, July 7, 1876.

17 - www.spartacus-educational.com/WWplains.htm.

18 - Adams, *Sitting Bull*, 314, 317.

19 - Id., 317.

20 - Vestal, *Champion of the Sioux*, 186.

21 - Bray, *Crazy Horse: A Lakota Life*, 246.

22 - Vestal, *Champion of the Sioux*, 188.

23 - Hutton, *Phil Sheridan and his Army*, 319.

24 - Utley, *The Lance and the Shield*, 167–68; Knight, *Following the Indian Wars*,

223–24.

25 - Larson, *Red Cloud*, 109.

26 - Adams, *Sitting Bull*, 313–14.

27 - Knight, *Following the Indian Wars*, 219.

28 - Cozzens (Editor), *Eyewitness to the Indian Wars, 1865–1890*, Vol. IV, 336.

29 - Vestal, *Champion of the Sioux*, 195.

30 - Id., 37–38.

31 - Id., 47.

32 - Utley, *The Lance and the Shield*, 167–68.

33 - Calvert, *Standoff at Standing Rock*, 73.

34 - Finerty, *War-Path and Bivouac*, 231 and 244; Adams, *Sitting Bull*, 317.

35 - Finerty, *War-Path and Bivouac*, 248; Knight, *Following the Indian Wars*, 257.

36 - Knight, *Following the Indian Wars*, 258–59.

37 - Finerty, *War-Path and Bivouac*, 267.

38 - Knight, *Following the Indian Wars*, 258.

39 - Id., 266.

40 - Utley, *The Lance and the Shield*, 165.

41 - Id., 167–68.

42 - Lazarus, *Black Hills White Justice*, 98.

43 - Utley, *The Lance and the Shield*, 168.

44 - Bray, *Crazy Horse*, 245.

45 - Vestal, *Champion of the Sioux*, 194.

46 - Bray, *Crazy Horse*, 278.

47 - Id., 54, 202, 212; Larson, *Gall*, 148.

CHAPTER NINE: IN SEARCH OF INDIANS

1 - Vestal, *Sitting Bull, Champion of the Sioux*, 184.

2 - Id., 184–85; Utley, *The Lance and the Shield*, 180–81.

3 - Id., 185.

4 - Knight, *Following the Indian Wars*, 267.

5 - Id., 257, 269.

6 - Id., 253.

7 - Id., 270.

8 - Finerty, *War-Path and Bivouac*, 260.

9 - Adams, *Sitting Bull*, 319–20.

10 - Bray, *Crazy Horse: A Lakota Life*, 261.

11 - Finerty, *War-Path and Bivouac*, 259.

12 - Id., 276–79.

13 - Interpretative quotations based on events reported in Knight, *Following the Indian Wars*, 267–69, Adams, *Sitting Bull*, 369 ("Horsemeat Campaign"), and Finerty, *War-Path and Bivouac*, 263.

14 - Vestal, *Champion of the Sioux*, 191.

15 - Knight, *Following the Indian Wars*, 273.

16 - Vestal, *Champion of the Sioux*, 191.

17 - Larson, *Gall*, 146.

18 - Finerty, *War-Path and Bivouac*, 301.

19 - Strahorn, *Ninety Years of Boyhood (Strahorn Autobiography)*, 203–04.

20 - Knight, *Following the Indian Wars*, 275. Vestal, *Champion of the Sioux*, 189-191, reports that the couriers ran to Sitting Bull's camp, not Crazy Horse's.

21 - Knight, *Following the Indian Wars*, 275.

22 - Vestal, *Champion of the Sioux*, 193.

23 - U.S. Secretary of the Interior Report (1877), p. 724; Gitlin, *The Battle of the Little Big Horn*, 83.

24 - Utley, *The Lance and the Shield*, 167.

25 - Lazarus, *Black Hills White Justice*, 90.

26 - Ibid.

27 - Vestal, *Champion of the Sioux*, 288.

28 - Id., 208; Lazarus, *Black Hills White Justice*, 90.

29 - Lazarus, *Black Hills White Justice*, 91.

30 - Id., 146. It was not until 1891 that Oglalas met to discuss making a claim against the United States for having taken the Papa Sapa from them; and that claim was not filed until May 1923. Over 50 years later, the U.S. Court of Claims found: "The terms upon which Congress acquired the Black Hills were not the product of any meaningful negotiation or arm's-length bargaining, and did not reflect or show any considered judgment by Congress that it was paying a fair price. In the 'negotiations' the United States gave the Indians the Hobson's chose of ceding the Black Hills or starving." Sioux Nation of Indians v. U.S. (Ct. Cl. 1979) 601 F.2d 1157, 1167. Even in restoring food rations, there was a qualification that children between ages 6 and 14 regularly attend government schools and adults located on land suitable for cultivation perform labor. The Court of Claims ruled that the U.S. government had appropriated the property without payment of just compensation; this decision was upheld by the U.S. Supreme Court in United States v. Sioux Nation of Indians (1980) 448 U.S. 371.

31 - Lazarus, *Black Hills White Justice*, 93.

32 - Larson, *Red Cloud*, 208.

33 - Ibid.

34 - Ostler, *Plains Sioux and U.S. Colonialism*, 66.

35 - Id., 69.

36 - Utley, *The Lance and the Shield*, 165.

37 - Id., 169.

38 - Vestal, *Champion of the Sioux*, 195.

39 - Id., 197; Utley, *The Lance and the Shield*, 167.

40 - Vestal, *Champion of the Sioux*, 196.

41 - Id., 196–97.

42 - Ibid.

43 - Ibid.

44 - Adams, *Sitting Bull*, 330.

45 - Utley, *The Lance and the Shield*, 165.

46 - Vestal, *Champion of the Sioux*, 197.

47 - Ibid.

48 - Ibid.

49 - Miles, *Personal Recollections & Observations of General Nelson A. Miles*, 222.

50 - Yenne, *Sitting Bull*, 115.

51 - Vestal, *Champion of the Sioux*, 199; Miles, *Personal Recollections & Observations*, 225.

52 - Vestal, *Champion of the Sioux*, 200.

53 - Id., 206.

54 - Yenne, *Sitting Bull*, 114; Vestal, *Champion of the Sioux*, 186; Utley, *The Lance and the Shield*, 168.

55 - Vestal, *Champion of the Sioux*, 206–07.

56 - Utley, *The Lance and the Shield*, 171.

57 - Vestal, *Champion of the Sioux*, 201.

58 - Ibid.

59 - Miles, *Personal Recollections & Observations*, 221.

60 - Vestal, *New Sources of Indian History*, 258.

61 - Garland, *The Book of the American Indian*, 182–83.

62 - Utley, *The Lance and the Shield*, 172; Miles, *Personal Recollections & Observations*, 225.

63 - Yenne, *Sitting Bull*, 116.

64 - Utley, *The Lance and the Shield*, 172.

65 - Id., 173; Larson, *Gall*, 151.

66 - Vestal, *Champion of the Sioux*, 205–06.

67 - Id., 204.

68 - Miles, *Personal Recollections & Observations*, 227.

69 - Vestal, *Champion of the Sioux*, 206; Marshall, T*he Day the World Ended at Little Big Horn*, 183–84.

70 - Miles, *Personal Recollections & Observations*, 227.

71 - Vestal, *Champion of the Sioux*, 207.

72 - Bray, *Crazy Horse: A Lakota Life*, 89.

73 - Miles, *Personal Recollections & Observations*, 227.

74 - Id., 226.

75 - Utley, *The Lance and the Shield*, 173.

76 - Ibid.; Yenne, *Sitting Bull*, 117.

77 - Miles, *Personal Recollections & Observations*, 135; Vestal, *Champion of the Sioux*, 212.

78 - Garland, *The Book of the American Indian*, 185.

79 - Ostler, *The Plains Sioux and U.S. Colonialism*, 68.

80 - Miles, *Personal Recollections & Observations*, 228; Utley, *The Lance and the Shield*, 173.

81 - Vestal, *Champion of the Sioux*, 209.

82 - Larson, *Gall*, 153–54.

83 - Turner, *Across the Medicine Line*, 50.

84 - Ibid.

85 - Id., 49–50; *Anderson, Sitting Bull's Boss*, 123.

86 - Turner, *Across the Medicine Line*, 51–52.

87 - Anderson, *Sitting Bull's Boss*, 99.

88 - Utley, *The Lance and the Shield*, 175.

89 - Id., 177.

90 - Ibid.

91 - Id., 178; Yenne, *Sitting Bull*, 121.

92 - Utley, *The Lance and the Shield.*, 178; Yenne, *Sitting Bull*, 122.

93 - Ibid.

94 - Id., 179.

95 - Adams, *Sitting Bull*, 334.

96 - Sandoz, *Crazy Horse*, 347.

97 - Id., 349.

98 - Sandoz, *Crazy Horse*, 351–52.

99 - Pearson, *"Nelson A. Miles, Crazy Horse, and Wolf Mountain"*, 51; Montana, *The Magazine of Western History*, 53–67.

100 - Bray, *Crazy Horse,* 256.

101 - Id., 257–58.

102 - Id., 259; Miles, *Personal Recollections & Observations*, 237–38.

103 - Yenne, *Sitting Bull*, 122; Utley, *The Lance and the Shield*, 179.

104 - Sandoz, *Crazy Horse*, 354.

105 - Utley, *The Lance and the Shield*, 181.

106 - Ibid.

107 - Yenne, *Sitting Bull*, 122.

108 - Bray, *Crazy Horse*, 259–61.

109 - Id., 261.

110 - Id., 282–85.

111 - Adams, *Sitting Bull*, 336; Larson, *Red Cloud*, 210–11.

112 - Bray, *Crazy Horse*, 337–42.

113 - Bray, *Crazy Horse*, 302.

114 - Id., 308.

115 - Id., 284–85; Sandoz, *Crazy Horse*, 407–08.

116 - Sandoz, *Crazy Horse*, 411; Bray, *Crazy Horse*, 208.

117 - The Winter Count of 1877–1878 by American Horse depicts Crazy Horse with a soldier's rifle's bayonet thrust into his abdomen and blood flowing. Green and Thornton (Editors), *The Year the Stars Fell, Lakota Winter Counts at the Smithsonian*, 278.

CHAPTER TEN: NORTHERN SANCTUARY

1 - Turner, *Across the Medicine Line*, 57.

2 - Vestal, *Sitting Bull, Champion of the Sioux*, 212.

3 - Id., 211.

4 - MacEwan, *Sitting Bull: The Years in Canada*, 9.

5 - Anderson, *Sitting Bull's Boss*, 73.

6 - Utley, *The Lance and the Shield*, 197.

7 - Anderson, *Sitting Bull's Boss*, 10.

8 - Miles, *Personal Recollections & Observations of General Nelson A. Miles*, 125; Knight, *Following the Indian Wars*, 291.

9 - Ostler, *The Plains Sioux and U.S. Colonialism*, 120–21.

10 - Larson, *Gall*, 160; Anderson, *Sitting Bull's Boss*, 132.

11 - Utley, *The Lance and the Shield*, 191–92.

12 - Ostler, *The Plains Sioux and U.S. Colonialism*, 121.

13 - MacEwan, *Sitting Bull: The Years in Canada*, 112.

14 - Vestal, *New Sources of Indian History*, 1850–1891, 236–37.

15 - Yenne, *Sitting Bull*, 133; Utley, *The Lance and the Shield*, 197.

16 - Anderson, *Sitting Bull's Boss*, 137.

17 - Utley, *The Lance and the Shield*, 186-188; Turner, *Across the Medicine Line*, 94–95.

18 - Anderson, *Sitting Bull's Boss*, 137.

19 - Turner, *Across the Medicine Line*, 98–99.

20 - Utley, *The Lance and the Shield*, 188; Turner, *Across the Medicine Line*, 100.

21 - MacEwan, *Sitting Bull: The Years in Canada*, 105–06.

22 - Ibid.

23 - Turner, *Across the Medicine Line*, 121.

24 - Utley, *The Lance and the Shield*, 191.

25 - Id., 191.

26 - Anderson, *Sitting Bull's Boss*, 180, 189–90.

27 - Utley, *The Lance and the Shield*, 190.

28 - Anderson, *Sitting Bull's Boss*, 61.

29 - Utley, *The Lance and the Shield*, 186.

30 - Anderson, *Sitting Bull's Boss*, 110.

31 - Id., 109–10.

32 - Id., 111.

33 - Utley, *The Lance and the Shield*, 186.

34 - Id., 190–91.

35 - West, *The Last Indian War: The Nez Perce Story*, 123–263.

36 - Id., 267.

37 - Welch, *Killing Custer*, 233; Utley, *The Lance and the Shield*, 191; Anderson, *Sitting Bull's Boss*, 139.

38 - MacEwan, *Sitting Bull: The Years in Canada*, 137.

39 - Turner, *Across the Medicine Line*, 120.

40 - Id., 105.

41 - Utley, *The Lance and the Shield*, 183.

42 - Turner, *Across the Medicine Line*, 121.

43 - Vestal, *Champion of the Sioux*, 219.

44 - Adams, *Sitting Bull, An Epic of the Plains*, 337–38.

45 - Utley, *The Lance and the Shield*, 193.
46 - Ibid.
47 - Turner, *Across the Medicine Line*, 125.
48 - Anderson, *Sitting Bull's Boss*, 146.
49 - Id, 147.
50 - Turner, *Across the Medicine Line*, 130.
51 - Utley, *The Lance and the Shield*, 195.
52 - Vestal, *Champion of the Sioux*, 221.
53 - Ibid.
54 - Ibid.; Adams, *Sitting Bull,* 339–40.
55 - Vestal, *Champion of the Sioux*, 222; Turner, *Across the Medicine Line*, 133.
56 - Johnson, *Life of Sitting Bull and History of the Indian War of 1890–1891*, 150; Utley, *The Lance and the Shield*, 196.
57 - Turner, *Across the Medicine Line*, 134.
58 - Vestal, *Champion of the Sioux*, 221; Turner, *Across the Medicine Line*, 133.
59 - Welch, *Killing Custer,* 156.
60 - Turner, *Across the Medicine Line*, 195.
61 - Anderson, *Sitting Bull and the Paradox of Lakota Nationhood*, 131.
62 - Diedrich, *Sitting Bull: The Collected Speeches*, 109.
63 - Turner, *Across the Medicine Line*, 134.
64 - Id., 135; Vestal, *Champion of the Sioux*, 224.
65 - Anderson, *Sitting Bull's Boss*, 154.
66 - MacEwan, *Sitting Bull: The Years in Canada*, 112.
67 - Utley, *The Lance and the Shield*, 186.
68 - MacEwan, *Sitting Bull: The Years in Canada*, 14.
69 - Anderson, *Sitting Bull's Boss*, 159.
70 - MacEwan, *Sitting Bull: The Years in Canada*, 160.
71 - Miles, *Personal Recollections & Observations*, 306.
72 - Anderson, *Sitting Bull's Boss*, 154.
73 - MacEwan, *Sitting Bull: The Years in Canada*, 154–55.
74 - Diedrich, *Sitting Bull: The Collected Speeches*, 117.
75 - Anderson, *Sitting Bull's Boss,* 177.
76 - Ibid.
77 - Ibid.
78 - Ibid.
79 - Id., 179; Turner, *Across the Medicine Line*, 149–50.
80 - Anderson, *Sitting Bull's Boss*, 182; Yenne, *Sitting Bull*, 152; Utley, *The Lance and the Shield*, 203.
81 - Anderson, *Sitting Bull's Boss*, 183.
82 - Ibid.
83 - Id., 183.
84 - Id., 184.
85 - Id., 186–87.

Chapter Eleven: The Making of an Outlier

1 - Anderson, *Sitting Bull's Boss*, 158.
2 - Id., 181, 183; MacEwan, *Sitting Bull: The Years in Canada*, 156.
3 - Adams, *Sitting Bull, An Epic of the Plains*, 348.
4 - Anderson, *Sitting Bull's Boss*, 169.
5 - Id., 195.
6 - Turner, *Across the Medicine Line*, 85.
7 - Anderson, *Sitting Bull's Boss*, 196.
8 - Ibid.
9 - Larson, *Gall*, 167.
10 - Anderson, *Sitting Bull's Boss*, 198.
11 - Ibid.
12 - Turner, *Across the Medicine Line*, 106–07.
13 - Larson, *Gall*, 163–63.
14 - Turner, *Across the Medicine Line*, 220.
15 - Id., 212.
16 - Anderson, *Sitting Bull's Boss*, 192.
17 - Vestal, *New Sources of Indian History*, 246.
18 - Larson, *Gall*, 165.
19 - Anderson, *Sitting Bull's Boss*, 202.
20 - Vestal, *New Sources of Indian History*, 247.
21 - Id., 249.
22 - Larson, *Gall*, 170; Vestal, *New Sources of Indian 1*, 247, states that there was no quarrel.
23 - Anderson, *Sitting Bull's Boss*, 204; Utley, *The Lance and the Shield*, 218.
24 - Vestal, *New Sources of Indian History*, 249.
25 - Vestal, *Champion of the Sioux*, 233.
26 - Vestal, *New Sources of Indian History*, 255.
27 - Ibid.
28 - Utley, *The Lance and the Shield*, 219.
29 - Vestal, *New Sources of Indian History*, 252.
30 - Id., 253.
31 - Id., 252.
32 - Id., 254.
33 - Utley, *The Lance and the Shield*, 220.
34 - Vestal, *New Sources of Indian History*, 334.
35 - Vestal, *Champion of the West*, 234.
36 - Anderson, *Sitting Bull's Boss*, 207.
37 - Id., 201.
38 - Vestal, *Champion of the Sioux*, 235.
39 - Anderson, *Sitting Bull's Boss*, 209.
40 - Ibid.
41 - Vestal, *Champion of the Sioux*, 235.

42 - Vestal, *New Sources of Indian History*, 262.

43 - *Bismarck Tribune*, May 6, 1881.

44 - Vestal, *The Champion of the Sioux*, 234.

45 - Vestal, *New Sources of Indian History*, 255–56.

46 - Vestal, *Champion of the Sioux*, 233.

47 - MacEwan, *Sitting Bull: The Years in Canada*, 189.

48 - Adams, *Sitting Bull, 349*; Turner, *Across the Medicine Line*, 242.

49 - Turner, *Across the Medicine Line*, 242–43.

50 - Utley, *The Lance and the Shield*, 229–30; Hedren, *Sitting Bull's Surrender at Fort Buford*, 15–16.

51 - Turner, *Across the Medicine Line*, 244.

52 - Hedren, *Sitting Bull's Surrender at Fort Buford*, 3.

53 - Vestal, *Champion of the Sioux*, 236.

54 - Utley, *The Lance and the Shield*, 230.

55 - Vestal, *Champion of the Sioux*, 233.

56 - Id., 237.

57 - In 1889, the U.S. Court of Claims upheld that denial, ruling that although he had been encouraged and reassured of some payment by Major Brotherton of Fort Buford, the fort commander had no authority to bind his government to pay. Legare v United States (1889) 24 Ct. Claims 513.

58 - Id., 39.

59 - McLaughlin, *My Friend the Indian*, 32.

60 - Pfaller, *James McLaughlin: The Man with an Indian Heart*, 45.

61 - Vestal, *New Sources of Indian History*, 287. He was exonerated on a charge that he unfairly favored a supplier over others who presented lower bids. Pfaller, *James McLaughlin: The Man with an Indian Heart*, 57.

62 - Pfaller, *James McLaughlin: The Man with an Indian Heart*, 58; McLaughlin letter to Rev. Brouillet of the Bureau of Catholic Indian Missions, May 31, 1883.

63 - Id., 58.

64 - Ibid.

65 - Pfaller, *James McLaughlin: The Man with an Indian Heart*, 56.

66 - McLaughlin, *My Friend the Indian*, 32.

67 - Id., 30.

68 - Pfaller, *James McLaughlin: The Man with an Indian Heart*, 59.

69 - Id., 32.

70 - Id., 60.

Chapter Twelve: Surrender at Buford

1 - Utley, *The Lance and the Shield, The Life and Times of Sitting Bull*, 232.

2 - Vestal, *Champion of the Sioux*, 238.

3 - St. Paul and Minneapolis Pioneer Press, July 20, 1881.

4 - Hedren, *Sitting Bull's Surrender at Fort Buford*, 27, indicates the location of the

surrender was the residence, while Utley, The Lance and the Shield, 232, places it in the commander's office.

5 - Vestal, *Champion of the Sioux*, 237.

6 - Hedren, *Sitting Bull's Surrender at Fort Buford*, 29.

7 - Interpretative quotation based on circumstances of the surrender as indicated in Utley, *The Lance and the Shield*, 232.

8 - Vestal, *Champion of the Sioux*, 238.

9 - Id., 237; Anderson, *Sitting Bull and the Paradox of Lakota Nationhood*, 140.

10 - Utley, *The Lance and the Shield*, 233.

11 - Id., 233, 235.

12 - Vestal, *Champion of the Sioux*, 237.

13 - Vestal, *New Sources of Indian History 1850–1891*, 263.

14 - Id., 264.

15 - Utley, *The Lance and the Shield*, 237. There are other photographs of Sitting Bull with the goggles. Lindner, The Photographs of Sitting Bull, 3–4, Vol. 72, North Dakota History (2005).

16 - Yenne, *Sitting Bull*, 175.

17 - Id., 237.

18 - Yenne, *Sitting Bull*, 176.

19 - Ibid.

20 - Vestal, *New Sources of Indian History*, 264–65.

21 - Id., 264.

22 - Pope, *Sitting Bull, Prisoner of War*, 20.

23 - Yenne, *Sitting Bull*, 175.

24 - *Bismarck Tribune*, August 5, 1877.

25 - Yenne, *Sitting Bull*, 180; Warren, *Buffalo Bill's America*, 271.

26 - Vestal, *New Sources of Indian History*, 266.

27 - Ibid. But in New Sources of Indian History, 247, Vestal also remarks that when Sitting Bull came to Fort Yates Gall was the first to greet him.

28 - Calvert, *Standoff at Standing Rock*, 105.

29 - Larson, *Gall*, 182; *Utley, The Lance and the Shield*, 240.

30 - Interpretative comment based on circumstance of the expressed feelings of Sitting Bull toward Running Antelope. Utley, *The Lance and the Shield*, 238, 240; Anderson, *Sitting Bull and the Paradox of Lakota Nationhood*, 144.

31 - Pope, *Sitting Bull, Prisoner of War*.

32 - Utley, *The Lance and the Shield*, 240; Anderson, *Sitting Bull*, 144.

33 - Pope, *Sitting Bull, Prisoner of War*, 37–38.

34 - Utley, *The Lance and the Shield*, 240–41.

35 - Id., 249; Larson, *Gall*, 175. Pfaller, *James McLaughlin: The Man with an Indian Heart*, 60, puts the date of arrival by McLaughlin on September 10, 1881; but McLaughlin, *My Friend the Indian*, 182, states it was the September 8.

36 - Vestal, *New Sources of Indian History*, 289.

37 - In 1870, peace advocates had pushed through legislation that prevented the appointment of army officers as Indian Agents. The way around this in 1876 was to

restrict army officers' taking control of agencies as temporary. Olson, Red Cloud and the Sioux Problem, 223.

38 - Id., 290.

39 - The gesture of pushing his hat back was a telltale indication of McLaughlin's displeasure. Vestal, *New Sources of Indian History*, 290.

40 - Interpretative dialogue based on both McLaughlin's title of his book.

41 - Interpretative quotation based on observations of McLaughlin in his book, *My Friend the Indian*, 180, 182.

42 - Interpretative quotation based on McLaughlin's low regard for Sitting Bull. Nevertheless, a few days earlier, in a wire to the Commissioner of Indian Affairs, the new agent had openly questioned the removal of Sitting Bull as having the potential for unrest. Pope, *Sitting Bull, Prisoner of War*, 38.

43 - Vestal, *New Sources of Indian History*, 287, and *Champion of the Sioux*, 254.

44 - Larson, *Gall*, 177; Utley, *The Lance and the Shield*, 249.

45 - Deloria, *Vine, Custer Died for Your Sins*, 8; Deloria, Philip, *Indians in Unexpected Places*, 143.

46 - Indian Rights Association Papers; A Guide to Microfilm Edition 1864–1973 (1975), 1.

47 - Page, *In the Hands of the Great Spirit*, 311–12.

48 - Phaller, *James McLaughlin: The Man with an Indian Heart*, 39.

49 - Vestal, *Champion of the Sioux*, 255.

50 - Ibid.; *Vestal, New Sources of Indian History*, 288.

51 - Utley, *The Lance and the Shield*, 249.

52 - Deloria, *Ella, Dakota Texts*, 221–22.

53 - Larson, *Gall*, 174.

54 - Pope, *Sitting Bull, Prisoner of War*, 124–25. See McLaughlin Papers, Letter to Price, Commissioner of Indian Affairs, February 15, 1883.

55 - McLaughlin, *My Friend the Indian*, 286.

56 - Vestal, *New Sources of Indian History*, 267.

Chapter Thirteen: POW at Fort Randall

1 -Vestal, *New Sources of Indian History*, 1850–1891, 298.

2 - *Calvert, Standoff at Standing Rock, 105; Utley,* The Lance and the Shield, 241.

3 - Vestal, *New Sources of Indian History*, 298–99.

4 - Pope, *Sitting Bull, Prisoner of War*, 62–63.

5 - Vestal, *New Sources of Indian History*, 268–69.

6 - Garland, *The Book of the American Indian*, 202.

7 - Vestal, *New Sources of Indian History*, 280.

8 - Creelman, *On the Great Highway: The Wanderings and Adventures of a Special Correspondent*, 301.

9 - Id, 302–03.

10 - Id., 294.

11 - Utley, *The Lance and the Shield*, 242.

12 - Ibid.

13 - Photograph of Sitting Bull with members of his family at Fort Randall, Denver Library of Western History. Lindner, *The Photographs of Sitting Bull*, 7–8, Vol. 72, North Dakota History (2005), as well as other treatises, documents the names as stated in the text. But Ernie LaPointe, great-grandson of Sitting Bull, in his book Sitting Bull, His Life and Legacy, 83, identifies the white woman as Alice Quimby and the man on horseback as Captain Horace Quimby, her father. The same white woman and child together with the captain on the same horse appear in another photo with the same tipis in the background, but two other Indians in the foreground. That photograph is entitled "Minneconjou Sioux One bull and Black Prairie Chicken with early American tourists at Fort Randall." www.astonisher.com/archieves/museum/one_bull_big_horn.html.

14 - Turner, *Across the Medicine Line*, 251.

15 - Vestal, *New Sources of Indian History*, 271.

16 - Id., 269–70.

17 - Id., 270–71; Utley. *The Lance and the Shield*, 244.

18 - Vestal, *New Sources of Indian History*, 271.

19 - Id., 283. However, Pope, *Sitting Bull, Prisoner of War*, 124, tells about McLaughlin's claimed efforts to negotiate for release.

20 - Pope, *Prisoner of War*, 95; Utley, *The Lance and the Shield*, 245; Pfaller, *James McLaughlin: The Man with an Indian Heart*, 94.

21 - Vestal, *New Sources of Indian History*, 273; Utley, *The Lance and the Shield*, 244.

22 - Marshall, *The Day the World Ended at Little Big Horn*, 171.

23 - Vestal, *New Sources of Indian History*, 273.

24 - Id. 37, 271.

25 - Ibid.

26 - Id., 272.

27 - Interpretative dialogue based on the close relationship that formed between the two men. Vestal, *New Sources of Indian History*, 37, 280–81.

28 - Vestal, *Sitting Bull, Champion of the Sioux*, 254.

29 - McLaughlin, *My Friend the Indian*, 32.

30 - Pfaller, *James McLaughlin: The Man with an Indian Heart*, 64–67.

31 - Id., 68.

32 - Id., 75.

33 - Utley, *The Lance and the Shield*, 257.

34 - Vestal, *New Sources of Indian History*, 282.

35 - Pfaller, *James McLaughlin: The Man with an Indian Heart*, 80.

36 - Ibid.

37 - Id., 86.

38 - Id., 85.

39 - Id., 84.

40 - Anderson, *Sitting Bull*, 151.

41 - McLaughlin Papers, Report to T. J. Morgan, Commissioner of Indian Affairs, August 26, 1890.

42 - Pfaller, *James McLaughlin: The Man with an Indian Heart*, 85.

43 - Utley, *The Lance and the Shield*, 256.

44 - Utley, *Sioux Nation*, 27–28.

45 - Larson, Gall, 182.

46 - Marshall, *Little Big Horn*, 234, describes the term as deriving from "those who loaf about the forts."

47 - Vestal, *New Sources of Indian History*, 221.

48 - This interpretative quotation and the prior one are based on ongoing criticisms by Gall, noted by Utley, *The Lance and the Shield*, 251.

49 - Vestal, *New Sources of Indian History*, 341.

50 - Larson, *Gall*, 183.

51 - Ibid.

52 - McLaughlin, *My Friend the Indian*, 97.

53 - Id., 100.

54 - Larson, *Gall*, 174.

55 - McLaughlin, *My Friend the Indian*, 102.

56 - Id., 109.

57 - Typical buffalo chase or run described in Miles, *Personal Recollections & Observations of General Nelson A. Miles*, 123–25.

58 - Miles, *Personal Recollections & Observations*, 127; Isenberg, *The Destruction of the Bison*, 134.

59 - McLaughlin, *My Friend the Indian*, 114.

60 - Id., 113.

61 - Id., 101.

62 - McLaughlin, *My Friend the Indian*, 116.

63 - Green and Thornton (Editors), *The Year the Stars Fell, Lakota Winter Counts at the Smithsonian*, 282.

64 - Pfaller, *James McLaughlin: The Man with an Indian Heart*, 72. Ironically, in 1872, a great tract of land in the western reaches of the Territories of Montana and Wyoming, below the headwaters of the Yellowstone River, was set aside by an act of Congress as a national park. The Blackfoot Nation to which the area was assigned by the Fort Laramie Treaty of 1851 received no notice of this monumental declaration. This richly scenic and recreational reservation of over two million acres would become emblematic of the preservation of the American buffalo; although by 1890 the herd within the park was only two hundred. As of 1894, when all hunting within Yellowstone was prohibited, the population had declined to 25. See Isenberg, *The Destruction of the Bison*, 179.

65 - Utley, *The Lance and the Shield*, 271. Liberal interests within the Indian Office, calling the practice barbaric, finally terminated the activity in 1890. Utley, *Sioux Nation*, 22–23.

66 - Ostler, *Plains Sioux*, 217.

67 - Lazarus, *Black Hills White Justice*, 107.

68 - McLaughlin, *My Friend the Indian*, 271–72.

69 - Larson, *Red Cloud*, 237.

70 - Ibid. This number is reported at times as up to over 11 million acres, apparently

because it had not been surveyed.
71 - Schell, *History of South Dakota*, 158–74.
72 - *New York Times*, February 10, 1883.
73 - 1882 Agreement with the Sioux of Various Tribes, Article II (never codified).
74 - *New York Times*, February 10, 1883.
75 - 1882 Agreement with the Sioux of Various Tribes, Article IV (never codified).
76 - Ostler, *Plains Sioux*, 219.
77 - Kappler (compiler and editor), *Indian Affairs: Laws & Treaties*, Vol. II, p. 1066–67; seven members of the Santee Band had signed the Fort Laramie Treaty of 1869; in 1882, 21 Santee agreed to terms of the agreement carried by the Edmunds Commission, reserving their rights, "both collective and individual, in and to the Santee Reservation, in said Knox County and State of Nebraska."
78 - Ostler, *Plains Sioux,* 218.
79 - Utley, *The Lance and the Shield*, 257.
80 - Pfaller, *James McLaughlin: The Man with an Indian Heart,* 58–59.
81 - Larson, *Gall*, 198.
82 - Vestal, *New Sources of Indian History,* 280.
83 - Anderson, *Sitting Bull*, 153.
84 - Ostler, *Plains Sioux*, 219.
85 - Vestal, *Champion of the Sioux,* 244.
86 - Larson, *Gall*, 178–79.
87 - Ostler, *Plains Sioux*, 221.
88 - Ibid.
89 - Adams, *Sitting Bull, An Epic of the Plains*, 352.
90 - Larson, *Red Cloud*, 252.
91 - Interpretative dialogue based on reports of conversations between these men over several months, in Vestal, *New Sources of Indian History*, 272–73.
92 - Vestal, *New Sources of Indian History*, 283, and Champion of the Sioux, 243.
93 - Interpretative dialogue based on circumstances of the reported by Vestal, *New Sources of Indian History*, 283, and Utley, *The Lance and the Shield*, 241.
94 - Utley, *The Lance and the Shield*, 242.
95 - Anderson, *Sitting Bull*, 140.
96 - Vestal, *New Sources of Indian History*, 283.
97 - Utley, *The Lance and the Shield*, 245.
98 - Id., 246.
99 - Ibid. Pope, *Sitting Bull, Prisoner of War*, 124–25.
100 - Vestal, *New Sources of Indian History*, 284.

CHAPTER FOURTEEN: ON THE RESERVATION

1 - Utley, *The Lance and the Shield*, 246.
2 - Vestal, *New Sources of Indian History*, 286.
3 - Pope, *Sitting Bull, Prisoner of War*, 129–30, citing the Chamberlain Register.

4 - Vestal, *Sitting Bull*, Champion of the Sioux, 243.
5 - Vestal, *New Sources of Indian History*, 1850–1891, 286.
6 - Id., 290.
7 - Fritz, *The Movement for Indian Assimilation*, 219.
8 - Utley, *The Lance and the Shield*, 249.
9 - Pope, *Sitting Bull, Prisoner of War*, 132.
10 - Vestal, *New Sources of Indian History*, 283.
11 - Id., 292–94.
12 - Id., 294.
13 - Id., 295.
14 - Anderson, *Sitting Bull*, 154–55.
15 - Adams, *Sitting Bull, An Epic of the Plains*, 351.
16 - Vestal, *New Sources of Indian History*, 296.
17 - McLaughlin Papers, Annual Report to Commissioner of Indian Affairs, August 15, 1883.
18 - Vestal, *Champion of the Sioux*, 244.
19 - Olson, *Red Cloud and the Sioux Problem*, 292; Larson, *Red Cloud*, 239.
20 - Vestal, *Champion of the Sioux*, 244.
21 - Olson, *Red Cloud and the Sioux Problem*, 294
22 - Quotation is interpreted from context of McLaughlin's view of Sitting Bull as a troublemaker; see his excoriation of the man in his Report to the Commissioner of Indian Affairs, October 17, 1890.
23 - McLaughlin, *My Friend the Indian*, 273.
24 - Anderson, *Sitting Bull*, 153.
25 - Vestal, *Champion of the Sioux*, 244.
26 - Id., 246.
27 - Id., 245.
28 - Ibid.
29 - Ibid.
30 - The extended dialogue between Sitting Bull and the Commissioners that follows is found in Vestal, *Champion of the Sioux*, 245–53.
31 - Adams, Sitting Bull, 352.
32 - Interpretative quotation based on the anger demonstrated by Senator Logan.
33 - Vestal, *New Sources of Indian History*, 290.
34 - Interpretative dialogue based McLaughlin's embarrassment at the conduct of his agency Indians and desire to maintain good relations with the commissioners.
35 - The discussion that follows is interpretative dialogue, based on Running Antelope's reputation of wanting to do right by everyone and Sitting Bull's acquiescence to return to the meeting. Vestal, *Champion of the Sioux*, 248, notes that Running Antelope pled with Sitting Bull to make amends.
36 - Vestal, *Champion of the Sioux*, 248–50.
37 - Id., 251; source 48th Congress, Official Document 283, #2174, "Conditions of the Tribes in Montana and Dakota," 78–81.
38 - The Senator's remarks are found in Vestal, *Champion of the Sioux*, 251–52.

39 - Utley, Sioux Nation, 38–39, discusses the corruption of agents.

40 - Vestal, *Champion of the Sioux*, 252.

41 - Id., 253.

42 - Adams, *Sitting Bull*, 353.

43 - Vestal, *New Sources of Indian History*, 308. Pfaller, *James McLaughlin: The Man with an Indian Heart*, 395, ftn.25, contests Vestal on this point, saying would have been out of character for the agent to offer Sitting Bull whiskey.

44 - The record is not clear on whether Sitting Bull ever drank whiskey; he probably did. Vestal, *New Sources of Indian History*, 281, indicates he did not drink; Adams, *Sitting Bull*, 215, is equivocal; and Diedrich, *Sitting Bull, The Collected Speeches*, 46, states that he did so on occasion. What is certain is that he stood against its abuse.

45 - Vestal, *New Sources of Indian History*, 308.

46 - Utley, *The Lance and the Shield*, 261.

47 - Vestal, *Champion of the Sioux*, 255.

48 - Utley, *The Lance and the Shield*, 261.

49 - Ibid.

50 - Pfaller, *James McLaughlin: The Man with an Indian Heart*, 99.

CHAPTER FIFTEEN: CHIEF ON TOUR (STANDING ROCK STAR)

1 - McLaughlin Papers, Letter to Taliour, February 14, 1884. (Pfaller, *James McLaughlin: The Man with an Indian Heart*, 100, interprets the handwriting on the letter to indicate the last name of "Taliow.")

2 - Ibid.

3 - Pfaller, *James McLaughlin: The Man with an Indian Heart*, 167–69.

4 - Utley, *The Lance and the Shield*, 261.

5 - Yenne, *Sitting Bull*, 196.

6 - Id., 196–97.

7 - Utley, *The Lance and the Shield*, 262.

8 - Anderson, *Sitting Bull*, 137.

9 - Utley, *The Lance and the Shield*, 263.

10 - Pfaller, *James McLaughlin: The Man with an Indian Heart*, 101.

11 - McLaughlin Papers, Letter to Bishop Marty, September 16, 1884; Utley, *The Lance and the Shield*, 264.

12 - McLaughlin Papers, Letter to Wm. F. Cody, April 21, 1884.

13 - Ibid.

14 - Utley, *The Lance and the Shield*, 254; but in *New Sources of Indian History*, 1850–1891, 276, Vestal puts the year at 1887 and not 1884.

15 - Vestal, *New Sources of Indian History*, 276.

16 - Utley, *The Lance and the Shield*, 254.

17 - Id., 270.

18 - Id., 254–55.

19 - Id., 255.
20 - Id., 266.
21 - Anderson, *Sitting Bull*, 155; Pope, *Sitting Bull, Prisoner of War*, 8.
22 - Vestal, *New Sources of Indian History*, 277.
23 - Pfaller, *James McLaughlin: The Man with an Indian Heart*, 101.
24 - McLaughlin Papers, Letter to T. M. Stevenson, May 13, 1884.
25 - Utley, *The Lance and the Shield*, 252.
26 - Vestal, *Champion of the Sioux*, 77.
27 - Utley, *The Lance and the Shield*, 262.
28 - Id., 263.
29 - Ibid.
30 - Standing Bear, *My People the Sioux*, 184–87.
31 - Anderson, *Sitting Bull*, 157; Utley, *The Lance and the Shield*, 266.
32 - Interpretative quotation based on McLaughlin's encouragement of Gall's criticism.
33 - Vestal, *New Sources of Indian History*, 279.
34 - Yenne, *Sitting Bull*, 203.
35 - Id., 204.
36 - Vestal, *Champion of the Sioux*, 256.
37 - Warren, *Buffalo Bill's America*, 365–66.
38 - Id., 253.
39 - Warren, *Buffalo Bill's America*, 247–48.
40 - Id., 198, 202–03.
41 - Id., 135–36.
42 - Id., 358–59.
43 - Utley, *The Lance and the Shield*, 264–65.
44 - Warren, *Buffalo Bill's America*, 198.
45 - Ibid.
46 - Id., 200.
47 - Id., 217.
48 - Utley, *The Lance and the Shield*, 264.
49 - Yenne, *Sitting Bull*, 206.
50 - Turner, *Across the Medicine Line*, 253; Vestal, *Champion of the Sioux*, 256.
51 - Utley, *The Lance and the Shield*, 266.
52 - Utley, *The Lance and the Shield*, 265; Yenne, *Sitting Bull*, 205.
53 - Ostler, *Plains Sioux and U.S. Colonialism*, 215.
54 - McLaughlin Papers, Letter to Nate Salsbury, March 3, 1886; Utley, *The Lance and the Shield*, 265.
55 - McLaughlin Papers, Letter to John M. Burke, April 16, 1886; Vestal, *Champion of the Sioux*, 256.
56 - Vestal, *Champion of the Sioux*, 257.

CHAPTER SIXTEEN: RESERVATION DISRUPTED

1 - Vestal, *Sitting Bull, Champion of the Sioux*, 255.

2 - Utley, *The Lance and the Shield*, 251–52.

3 - Larson, *Gall*, 181.

4 - McLaughlin Papers, Report to T. J. Morgan, Commissioner of Indian Affairs, August 26, 1890.

5 - Vestal, *Champion of the Sioux*, 91–95.

6 - Utley, *The Lance and the Shield*, 251.

7 - Utley, *The Lance and the Shield*, 17.

8 - Id., 286.

9 - Vestal, *New Sources of Indian History*, 1850–1891, 51.

10 - Vestal, *Champion of the Sioux*, 259.

11 - Id., 259–60.

12 - Id., 260–61.

13 - Pfaller, *James McLaughlin: The Man with an Indian Heart*, 108; Utley, *The Lance and the Shield*, 266–67.

14 - Utley, *The Lance and the Shield*, 266–67.

15 - Anderson, *Sitting Bull and the Paradox of Lakota Nationalhood*, 166.

16 - Vestal, *New Sources of Indian History*, 148.

17 - Id., 149.

18 - Id., 150; McLaughlin, *My Friend the Indian*, 232.

19 - Vestal, *New Sources of Indian History*, 274.

20 - Johnson, *Life of Sitting Bull and History of the Indian War of 1890–1891*, 52. It was said that the chief had more knowledge of spoken English than he let on; and he knew some French from his trading with Metis and his time in Canada.

21 - Id., 273–74.

22 - Vestal, *New Sources of Indian History*, 61; Anderson, *Sitting Bull*, 149, places the date at 1883.

23 - Vestal, *New Sources of Indian History*, 61–62.

24 - Id., 63–64.

25 - Utley, *The Lance and the Shield*, 269.

26 - Ibid.

27 - McLaughlin Papers, *Letter to S. C. Armstrong*, November 9, 1885.

28 - Vestal, *New Sources of Indian History*, 63.

29 - Ibid.

30 - Id., 64.

31 - Ibid.

32 - Vestal, *Champion of the Sioux*, 263.

33 - Vestal, *New Sources of Indian History*, 283.

34 - Anderson, *Sitting Bull and the Paradox of Lakota Nationalhood*, 165.

35 - Vestal, *Champion of the Sioux*, 263.

36 - McLaughlin Papers, Report to T. J. Morgan, Commissioner of Indian Affairs, August 26, 1890.

37 - Ostler, *Plains Sioux*, 214.

38 - Vestal, *Champion of the Sioux*, 263, and *New Sources of Indian History*, 310.

39 - Id., 262.

40 - Agnew, *The Life of a Soldier on the Western Frontier*, 92.

CHAPTER SEVENTEEN: BAIT AND SWITCH LEGISLATION

1 - Indian General Allotment Act of 1887, Section 2.

2 - Id., Section 5.

3 - Id., Section 6.

4 - Id., Section 2.

5 - Warren, *Buffalo Bill's America*, 375. Lucy Textor in her paper, "Official Relations between the United States and the Sioux Indians," 45, published in 1896 stated: "[E]very allotment narrows the field, and ultimately [the reservation] will have to go. As citizens, the Indians must take their places in the current of civilization."

6 - 18 Congressional Record 191 (1886), 57.

7 - Flora and Flora, *Rural Communities*, Legacy and Chance, quotes Dawes with this statement and cites PPS Archives of the West, 1887–1914, and "The Dawes Act 1887." www.pbs.org/weta/thewest/resources/archieves/eight/dawes.htm.

8 - General Allotment Act of 1887, Section 5, Third Provision.

9 - Larson, *Red Cloud, Warrior-Statesman of the Lakota Sioux*, 252.

10 - Larson, *Red Cloud,* 253.

11 - Lazarus, *Black Hills White Justice,* 109.

12 - Utley, *The Last Days of the Sioux Nation*, 45.

13 - Id., 44.

14 - Ibid.

15 - McLaughlin Papers, *Letter to E. D. Comings,* April 9, 1888.

16 - McLaughlin Papers, Letter to Paul Blum, April 9, 1888.

17 - Utley, *The Last Days of the Sioux Nation*, 45.

18 - Fear-Segal, "Nineteenth Century Indian Education: Universalism Versus Evolutionism," 33 Journal of American Studies 329 (1999).

19 - Ostler, *The Plains Sioux and U.S. Colonialism*, 223.

20 - Utley, *Sioux Nation*, 44.

21 - Lazarus, *Black Hills White Justice*, 109. Utley, *The Last Days of the Sioux Nation*, 45.

22 - Larson, *Gall*, 202.

23 - Ibid.

24 - Ostler, *Plains Sioux,* 223.

25 - Utley, T*he Lance and the Shield*, 274.

26 - McLaughlin, *My Friend the India*n, 274.

27 - Id., 274, 276.

28 - Ostler, *Plains Sioux*, 224.

29 - Id., 223.

30 - Ibid.

31 - Vestal, *New Sources of Indian History, 1850–1891*, 301.

32 - Ostler, *Plains Sioux*, 225.

33 - Id., 224.

34 - Ibid.

35 - Ibid.

36 - Id., 227.

37 - Id., 225.

38 - Id., 226.

39 - Id, 227.

40 - Id., 225.

41 - Id., 227.

42 - Id., 224.

43 - Executive Documents of the United States for the Second Session of the Fiftieth Congress, and Special Session of the Senate Convened March 4, 1889, p. 131.

44 - Larson, *Gall*, 203.

45 - Ibid.

46 - Executive Documents of the United States for the Second Session of the Fiftieth Congress, and Special Session of the Senate Convened March 4, 1889, p. 132; Larson, *Gall*, 204.

47 - Ostler, *Plains Sioux*, 228.

48 - Larson, *Gall*, 204.

49 - Lazarus, *Black Hills White Justice*, 110.

50 - Yenne, *Sitting Bull*, 213–14.

51 - McLaughlin, *My Friend the Indian*, 277.

52 - Larson, *Red Cloud*, 254–55.

53 - Larson, *Red Cloud*, 254.

54 - Vestal, *New Sources of Indian History*, 302; Utley, *The Lance and the Shield*, 276.

55 - Larson, *Red Cloud*, 224; Utley, *Sioux Nation*, 20.

56 - Ostler, *Sioux Nation*, 28–29.

57 - Larson, *Red Cloud*, 217–48.

58 - Ostler, *Plains Sioux*, 206.

59 - Larson, *Red Cloud*, 246–47.

60 - Ostler, *Plains Sioux*, 211.

61 - Larson, *Red Cloud*, 259; Ostler, *Plains Sioux*, 211.

62 - Larson, *Red Cloud*, 253–54.

63 - Utley, *The Lance and the Shield*, 275.

64 - Yenne, *Sitting Bull*, 224.

65 - McLaughlin, *My Friend the Indian*, 278–79.

66 - *Washington Post*, October 13, 1888.

67 - Vestal, *New Sources of Indian History*, 304.

68 - Yenne, *Sitting Bull*, 218.

69 - Fletcher, *The Life of Sitting Bull and the Indian War of 1890–1891*, 234.

70 - McLaughlin, *My Friend the Indian*, 278.

71 - Utley, *The Lance and the Shield*, 276–77.

72 - Ostler, *Plains Sioux*, 228.

73 - Vestal, *New Sources of Indian History*, 302.

74 - Vestal, *New Sources of Indian History*, 302.

75 - Ostler, *Plains Sioux*, 228.

76 - McLaughlin, *My Friend the Indian*, 279.

77 - Utley, *Sioux Nation*, 47.

78 - McLaughlin, *My Friend the Indian*, 280.

79 - Yenne, *Sitting Bull*, 227.

80 - McLaughlin, *My Friend the Indian*, 280.

81 - Photograph, U.S. Commissioners and delegations of Sioux chiefs visiting Washington, October 15, 1888, U.S. Library of Congress.

82 - Pfaller, *James McLaughlin: The Man with an Indian Heart*, 115.

83 - Robinson, *Wounded Knee: Party Politics and the Road to an American Massacre*, 100–01.

84 - Yenne, *Sitting Bull*, 227.

85 - Utley, *Sioux Nation*, 48.

86 - Larson, *Red Cloud*, 256; Yenne, *Sitting Bull*, 228.

87 - Ostler, *Plains Sioux*, 217.

88 - Schell, *History of South Dakota*, 158–74.

89 - Olson, *Red Cloud and the Sioux Problem*, 312–13.

90 - The Sioux Act of 1889, Section 21.

91 - Id., Section 17.

92 - Id., Sections 25 and 26.

93 - Id., Section 8.

94 - Id., Section 17.

95 - Id., Section 27.

96 - Id., Section 28.

97 - Id., Section 29.

98 - Olson, *Red Cloud and the Sioux Problem*, 313.

99 - Ostler, *Plains Sioux*, 230.

100 - Utley, *Sioux Nation*, 49.

101 - Id., 50–51.

102 - Utley, *Sioux Nation*, 53.

103 - Larson, *Red Cloud*, 259.

104 - Id., 259–60.

105 - Ostler, *Plains Sioux*, 233.

106 - Id., 233–34.

107 - Pollack, *Woman Walking Ahead*, 25.

108 - Larson, *Gall*, 179.

109 - Page, *In the Hands of the Great Spirit*, 311

110 - Pollack, *Woman Walking Ahead*, 21.

111 - Id., 25.

112 - Vestal, *Sitting Bull, Champion of the Sioux, A Biography*, 271; Pollack, *Woman*

Walking Ahead, 42.

113 - Utley, *The Lance and the Shield*, 282.

114 - Vestal, *Sitting Bull Champion of the Sioux, A Biography*, 271;

115 - Pollack, *Woman Walking Ahead*, 28.

116 - Id., 42.

117 - Id., 56–57.

118 - Id., 57.

119 - Id., 87.

120 - Yenne, *Sitting Bull*, 232; Pollack, *Woman Walking Ahead*, 188.

121 - Pollack, *Woman Walking Ahead*, 321.

122 - Yenne, *Sitting Bull*, 232.

123 - Pollack, *Woman Walking Ahead*, 75.

124 - Id., 56–57.

125 - Vestal, *Champion of the Sioux*, 272.

126 - Pollack, *Woman Walking Ahead*, 26.

127 - Ibid.

128 - Id., 27.

129 - Interpretative quote based on McLaughlin's years in agency service and his stated positions taken on the two Sioux Acts to break up the Great Sioux Reservation.

130 - Pollack, *Woman Walking Ahead*, 80.

131 - Vestal, *New Sources of Indian History*, 93.

132 - Pollack, *Woman Walking Ahead*, 29.

133 - Ibid.

134 - Id., 27.

135 - Yenne, *Sitting Bull*, 233.

136 - Id., 44.

137 - Id., 46.

138 - Interpretative quotation based on statements in Weldon's letters in reacting to McLaughlin's attempt to stop her from traveling to Rosebud and southern agencies. Vestal, *New Sources of Indian History*, 97; Pollack, *Woman Walking Ahead*, 46.

139 - Pollack, *Woman Walking Ahead*, 46–47.

140 - Id., 49.

141 - Vestal, *New Sources of Indian History*, 97–98; Pollack, *Woman Walking Ahead*, 46, 48.

142 - Pollack, *Woman Walking Ahead*, 100.

143 - *Bismarck Tribune*, July 2, 1889.

144 - Larson, *Red Cloud*, 240–41.

145 - Vestal, *New Sources of Indian History*, 92–95.

146 - Vestal, *Champion of the Sioux*, 272.

147 - Vestal, *New Sources of Indian History*, 95.

148 - McLaughlin, *My Friend the Indian*, 285.

149 - Adams, *Sitting Bull*, 357.

150 - Lazarus, *Black Hills White Justice*, 112.

151 - Vestal, *New Sources of Indian History*, 303–04.

152 - Utley, *Sioux Nation*, 49.
153 - Larson, *Gall*, 207; McLaughlin, *My Friend the Indian*, 284.
154 - Ostler, *Plains Sioux*, 231.
155 - Utley, *Sioux Nation*, 50.
156 - Id., 51.
157 - Ostler, *Plains Sioux*, 234.
158 - Vestal, *Champion of the Sioux*, 273.
159 - Yenne, *Sitting Bull*, 241.
160 - Vestal, *Champion of the Sioux*, 273; Pollack, *Woman Walking Ahead*, 4, 21.
161 - Vestal, *New Sources of Indian History*, 306.
162 - McLaughlin, *My Friend the Indian*, 282.
163 - Interpretative quote based on McLaughlin now supporting the act but needing to work behind the scenes with his wards. McLaughlin, *My Friend the Indian*, 283.
164 - Adams, *Sitting Bull*, 356.
165 - McLaughlin, *My Friend the Indian*, 284.
166 - Interpretative quotation based on McLaughlin's solicitous relationship with the commission and a need to excuse himself from the reception.
167 - Vestal, *Champion of the Sioux*, 266.
168 - McLaughlin, *My Friend the Indian*, 285.
169 - Vestal, *Champion of the Sioux*, 276.
170 - McLaughlin, *My Friend the Indian*, 285.
171 - Larson, *Gall*, 208.
172 - Interpretive quotation based on the common theme used by Crook to lobby the Indians.
173 - Ostler, *Plains Sioux*, 234.
174 - Larson, *Gall*, 208.
175 - McLaughlin, *My Friend the Indian*, 285–86.
176 - Id., 286.
177 - Vestal, *Champion of the Sioux*, 269.
178 - Id., 268.
179 - Ibid.
180 - McLaughlin, *My Friend the Indian*, 286.
181 - Vestal, *Champion of the Sioux*, 269.
182 - Id., 269; Larson, *Gall*, 208.
183 - McLaughlin, *Champion of the Sioux*, 287.
184 - Id., 288.
185 - Warren, *Buffalo Bill's America*, 375.
186 - Vestal, *Champion of the Sioux*, 269.
187 - Pollack, *Woman Walking Ahead*, 79.
188 - Vestal, *Champion of the Sioux*, 270.
189 - Ibid.
190 - Id., 270–71.
191 - Ibid.
192 - Yenne, *Sitting Bull*, 234–35.

193 - Utley, *Sioux Nation*, 77.
194 - Rielly, Sitting Bull, A Biography, 127.
195 - Larson, *Red Cloud,* 263–64.
196 - Id., 261.
197 - Utley, *The Last Days of the Sioux Nation*, 55; Ostler, *Plains Sioux,* 237.
198 - Ostler, *Plains Sioux*, 237–38. Utley, *Sioux Nation*, 55.
199 - Utley, *Sioux Nation*, 57.
200 - Id., 58–59; Yenne, *Sitting Bull,* 229.
201 - Utley, *Sioux Nation*, 77; Ostler, *Plains Sioux*, 239; Vestal, *Champion of the Sioux*, 276.
202 - Lazarus, *Black Hills White Justice*, 112; Ostler, *Plains Sioux*, 279.
203 - Vestal, *Champion of the Sioux*, 275–76; Utley, *Sioux Nation*, 57; Lazarus, *Black Hills White Justice*, 113; Ostler, *Plains Sioux*, 239.
204 - These desperate conditions are described in Episcopal Bishop Hare's letter to Interior Secretary Noble, January 7, 1891, quoted by Mooney, *The Ghost-Dance Religion and Wounded Knee*, 840.
205 - McLaughlin, *My Friend the Indian,* 394–95.
206 - Ostler, *Plains Sioux*, 215.

CHAPTER EIGHTEEN: GHOST DANCE AND DISOBEDIENCE

1 - Lazarus, *Black Hills White Justice*, 113.
2 - Vestal, *New Sources of Indian History*, 1850–1891, 85–86.
3 - Utley, *Sioux Nation*, 56–57, 77; Vestal, *Champion of the Sioux*, 275–76.
4 - Lazarus, *Black Hills White Justice*, 113–14.
5 - Mooney, *The Ghost-Dance Religion and Wounded Knee*, 764.
6 - Spindler and Spindler, *The Ghost Dance: Ethnohistory and Revitalization*, 3.
7 - Mooney, *The Ghost-Dance Religion and Wounded Knee,* 701.
8 - Id., 765.
9 - Spindler & Spindler, *The Ghost Dance: Ethnohistory and Revitalization*, 5.
10 - Mooney, *The Ghost-Dance Religion and Wounded Knee*, 771–72.
11 - Id., 777.
12 - Id., 780.
13 - Id., 784.
14 - Id., 781.
15 - Smith, *Moon of Popping Trees*, 69–70.
16 - Id., 784–91; Utley, *The Last Days of the Sioux Nation*, 68.
17 - Utley, *The Lance and the Shield*, 281.
18 - Ostler, *The Plains Sioux and U.S. Colonialism*, 251.
19 - Id., 251–52.
20 - Mooney, *The Ghost-Dance Religion and Wounded Knee,* 817.
21 - Id., 797; Utley, *Sioux Nation*, 72.
22 - Mooney, *Ghost-Dance Religion and Wounded Knee*, 843; Ostler, *Plains Sioux*, 256,

states that the Lakota delegates returned in late 1889.

23 - Mooney, *Ghost-Dance Religion and Wounded Knee*, 819.

24 - McLaughlin, *My Friend the Indian*, 185–89.

25 - Id., 198.

26 - Mooney, *Ghost-Dance Religion and Wounded Knee*, 822.

27 - Id., 920–21.

28 - Id., 823.

29 - Utley, *Sioux Nation*, 87; Vestal, *New Sources of Indian History*, 43–44.

30 - Mooney, *Ghost-Dance Religion and Wounded Knee*, 917, quoting Mrs. Z. A. Parker, a teacher at Pine Ridge.

31 - Ostler, *Plains Sioux*, 194. See No. 107, Annual Report of the Commissioner of Indian Affairs, October 1, 1889.

32 - Mooney, *Ghost-Dance Religion and Wounded Knee*, 789–91.

33 - Id., 916.

34 - Id., 798.

35 - McLaughlin, *My Friend the Indian*, 188.

36 - Smith, *Moon of Popping Tree*s, 90.

37 - McLaughlin, *My Friend the Indian*, 185.

38 - Id., 188.

39 - Pfaller, *James McLaughlin: The Man with an Indian Heart*, 123.

40 - Vestal, *Sitting Bull, Champion of the Sioux, A Biography*, 276–77; Smith, *Moon of Popping Trees*, 82.

41 - Smith, *Moon of Popping Trees*, 82; Utley, *Sioux Nation*, 76.

42 - Utley, *Sioux Nation*, 81.

43 - McLaughlin Papers, Letter to R. V. Belt, Acting Commissioner of Indian Affairs, June 16, 1890.

44 - Pfaller, *James McLaughlin: The Man with an Indian Heart*, 127.

45 - Vestal, *Champion of the Sioux*, 277.

46 - Utley, *The Lance and the Shield*, 283; Utley, *Sioux Nation*, 94.

47 - Ostler, *Plains Sioux*, 277, 327.

48 - Mooney, *The Ghost-Dance Religion and Wounded Knee*, 1072. The crow is the messenger of the spirit world "because its color symbolizes death and the shadow land." Id. 982.

49 - Id., 846–47.

50 - Utley, *Sioux Nation*, 96.

51 - Ostler, *Plains Sioux,* 277.

52 - Utley, *Sioux Nation*, 97.

53 - Ibid.

54 - Interpretative quotation based on actions of McLaughlin in monitoring Sitting Bull's conduct and his distrust of the man.

55 - Smith, *Moon of Popping Trees*, 105.

56 - Vestal, *New Sources of Indian History*, 1850–1891, 2.

57 - Interpretative quote based on Pollack, *Woman Walking Ahead*, 146.

58 - McLaughlin, *My Friend the Indian*, 191

59 - Id., 198.

60 - Vestal, *Champion of the Sioux*, 276, 294.

61 - McLaughlin, *My Friend the Indian*, 191; Utley, *Sioux Nation*, 77.

62 - Vestal, *New Sources of Indian History*, 341.

63 - McLaughlin, *My Friend the Indian*, 191.

64 - Utley, *Sioux Nation*, 97–98.

65 - Utley, *The Lance and The Shield*, 284.

66 - McLaughlin, *My Friend the Indian*, 191.

67 - Vestal, *New Sources of Indian History*, 68; Utley, *The Lance and the Shield*, 291.

68 - Ostler, *Plains Sioux*, 292, 297.

CHAPTER NINETEEN: WHITE SQUAW

1 - Pollack, *Woman Walking Ahead*, 5, 100.

2 - Id., 87.

3 - Yenne, *Sitting Bull*, 230–31; Vestal, *Champion of the Sioux*, 275.

4 - Vestal, *New Sources of Indian History*, 1850–1891, 98.

5 - Id., 99.

6 - Id., 100.

7 - Pollack, *Woman Walking Ahead*, 94, 100.

8 - Id., 95.

9 - Id., 100.

10 - Pfaller, *James McLaughlin: The Man with an Indian Heart*, 126.

11 - Utley, *The Lance and the Shield*, 285; there is a photograph of the ghost dancers at Grand River, in Pollack, *Woman Walking Ahead*, 117.

12 - Vestal, *Champion of the Sioux*, 294.

13 - Vestal, *Champion of the Sioux*, 279, 281 (affirmative), Utley, *The Lance and the Shield*, 285 (negative), and *Plains Sioux*, 98 (he acts the part of an apostle).

14 - Vestal, *Champion of the Sioux*, 282.

15 - Utley, *The Lance and the Shield*, 286; Vestal, *New Sources of Indian History*, 102.

16 - Vestal, *Champion of the Sioux*, 282.

17 - Vestal, *New Sources of Indian History*, 111.

18 - Pollack, *Woman Walking Ahead*, 42.

19 - Vestal, *New Sources of Indian History*, 116.

20 - Pollack, *Woman Walking Ahead*, 5. The discussion between them that follows is interpretative dialogue based on the close relationship of Catherine Weldon and Sitting Bull and their differing views on the Ghost Dance. Her comments are based on letters she wrote as reported by Vestal, *Sitting Bull, New Sources of Indian History*, 104, 108.

21 - Utley, *Sioux Nation*, 99.

22 - Vestal, 108.

23 - Pollack, *Woman Walking Ahead*, 111.

24 - Utley, *Sioux Nation*, 99.

25 - Pollack, *Woman Walking Ahead*, 89.

26 - Vestal, *Champion of the Sioux*, 273.

27 - Id., 274.

28 - Pfaller, *James McLaughlin: The Man with an Indian Heart*, 126.

29 - The conversation between McLaughlin and Primeau is interpretative dialogue based on McLaughlin's professed concerns over Sitting Bull's role in the Ghost Dance movement at Standing Rock. McLaughlin, *My Friend the Indian*, 190–91.

30 - Pfaller, *James McLaughlin: The Man with an Indian Heart*, 130. McLaughlin Papers, McLaughlin to Hon. T. J. Morgan, October 17, 1890.

31 - The conversation between Weldon and Sitting Bull is interpretative dialogue based on their reported positions regarding the Ghost Dance.

32 - Vestal, *New Sources of Indian History*, 116.

33 - Id., 104.

34 - Vestal, *Champion of the Sioux*, 282.

35 - Vestal, *New Sources of Indian History*, 101.

36 - Fletcher, *The Life of Sitting Bull and the Indian War of 1890–1891*, 319.

37 - Pollack, *Woman Walking Ahead*, 135.

38 - Id., 135.

39 - Vestal, *Champion of the Sioux*, 282–83.

40 - Id., 283.

41 - Ibid.

42 - Ibid.

43 - Utley, *The Lance and the Shield*, 286; Anderson, *Sitting Bull and the Paradox of Lakota Nationhood*, 180.

44 - Vestal, *New Sources of Indian History*, 309–10.

45 - Utley, *Sioux Nation*, 103.

46 - Ibid.

47 - Vestal, *New Sources of Indian History*, 6.

48 - Smith, *Moon of Popping Trees*, 96.

49 - *Harper's Weekly*, October 20, 1890.

50 - Pfaller, *James McLaughlin: The Man with an Indian Heart*, 134.

51 - *Harper's Weekly*, October 20, 1890.

52 - Vestal, *Champion of the Sioux*, 285.

53 - Mooney, *The Ghost-Dance Religion and Wounded Knee*, 1061.

54 - Pfaller, *James McLaughlin: The Man with an Indian Heart*, 134.

55 - Ibid.

56 - Vestal, *New Sources of Indian History*, 102–03.

57 - Ibid.; Pollack, *Woman Walking Ahead*, 141.

58 - Pollack, *Woman Walking Ahead*, 263.

59 - *Pierre Daily Free Press*, November 13, 1890.

60 - Id., 103–05.

61 - Id., 106.

62 - Id., 110.

63 - Id., 105.

64 - Vestal, *Champion of the Sioux*, 22; Standing Bear, *My People the Sioux*, 39.

65 - Utley, *The Lance and the Shield*, 290.

66 - Quotation interpreted from probable support from a longtime ally.

67 - Vestal, *New Sources of Indian History*, 310.

68 - This quotation and what follows is interpretative dialogue based on Sitting Bull's special relationship to Crowfoot and the rumors that his enemies were closing around him.

69 - Ostler, *Plains Sioux*, 214.

70 - Utley, *The Lance and the Shield*, 252.

71 - Id., 280.

72 - Id., 270.

CHAPTER TWENTY: THE PLOT

1 - Utley, *The Lance and the Shield: The Life and Times of Sitting Bull*, 282.

2 - McLaughlin Papers, Report to T. J. Morgan, Commissioner of Indian Affairs, October 17, 1890. This is the report that was the basis of the *Harper's Weekly* article mentioned in the prior chapter.

3 - Ibid. McLaughlin, *My Friend the Indian*, 199–200.

4 - McLaughlin, *My Friend the Indian*, 200.

5 - McLaughlin Papers, Report to T. J. Morgan, Commissioner of Indian Affairs, November 13, 1890.

6 - Vestal, *New Sources of Indian History*, 1850–1891, 1–4.

7 - Id., 2.

8 - Utley, *Last Days of the Sioux Nation*, 98.

9 - Adams, *Sitting Bull, An Epic of the Plains*, 361.

10 - LaPointe, *Sitting Bull, His Life and Legacy*, 95.

11 - Utley, *The Lance and The Shield*, 291.

12 - Id., 292.

13 - Ibid.

14 - Vestal, *New Sources of Indian History*, 69.

15 - Utley, *Sioux Nation*, 104; Ostler, *Plains Sioux*, 289.

16 - Ostler, *Plains Sioux*, 292.

17 - Id., 293.

18 - McLaughlin, *My Friend the Indian*, 214–15; Utley, *Sioux Nation*, 110.

19 - Utley, *Sioux Nation*, 110.

20 - Ibid.

21 - Ostler, *Plains Sioux*, 293; Pfaller, *James McLaughlin: The Man with an Indian Heart*, 134. Utley, *Sioux Nation*, 115.

22 - Utley, *Sioux Nation*, 110.

23 - Vestal, *New Sources of Indian History*, 82.

24 - Id., 85–87.

25 - Id., 84.

26 - Id., 89.

27 - Ostler, *Plains Sioux*, 291.

28 - Ibid.
29 - Id., 290.
30 - Ibid.
31 - Utley, *Sioux Nation*, 101.
32 - Interpretative quotation based on Pfaller, *James McLaughlin: The Man with an Indian Heart*, 95.
33 - Vestal, *New Sources of Indian History*, 267.
34 - McLaughlin, *My Friend the Indian*, 205.
35 - Vestal, *Champion of the Sioux*, 285.
36 - Ibid.
37 - McLaughlin, *My Friend the Indian*, 207.
38 - Ibid.
39 - Utley, *The Lance and the Shield*, 289.
40 - Pfaller, *James McLaughlin: The Man with an Indian Heart*, 138.
41 - Ostler, *Plains Sioux*, 316.
42 - Pfaller, *James McLaughlin: The Man with an Indian Heart*, 138.
43 - McLaughlin Papers, Letter to Welsh, November 25, 1890.
44 - Vestal, *New Sources of Indian History*, 11 (quoting a letter of 12/9/90).
45 - Ostler, *Plains Sioux*, 302.
46 - *New York Tribune*, November 22, 1890, under the sub-headline—"DISPATCHES FROM GENERAL MILES."
47 - Vestal, *New Sources of Indian History*, 67–68.
48 - Id., 68.
49 - Id., 104.
50 - Utley, *Sioux Nation*, 111.
51 - Ibid.
52 - Id., 113–14.
53 - Ibid.
54 - Id., 117.
55 - Id., 118.
56 - Smith, *Moon of Popping Trees*, 128.
57 - Utley, *Sioux Nation*, 122.
58 - Zarki, *Badlands: The Story Behind the Scenery*, 13.
59 - Ostler, *Plains Sioux*, 317; Utley, *Sioux Nation*, 122.
60 - Smith, *Moon of Popping Trees*, 164.
61 - Utley, *Sioux Nation*, 132.
62 - Beck, *The Ghost Dance: Ethnohistory & Revitalization*, 19.
63 - Smith, *Moon of Popping Trees*, 175.
64 - Utley, *Sioux Nation*, 119.
65 - Ibid.
66 - Ostler, *Plains Sioux*, 308.
67 - *Rapid City Journal*, November 20, 1890.
68 - *Buffalo Echo*, November 21, 1890.
69 - From *The Ghost Dance, Wounded Knee*, www.wyomingtalesandtrails.com/

woundedk.html.

70 - Smith, *Moon of Popping Trees*, 132.

71 - *New York Tribune*, November 22, 1890.

72 - Ibid.

73 - Ibid.

74 - Ibid.

75 - *New York Tribune*, November 22, 1890, under the subheadline "SITTING BULL CALCULATING CHANCES," with Minneapolis, Minnesota, dateline of November 21, citing concerns from Mandan, North Dakota.

76 - McLaughlin Papers, Letter to T. J. Morgan, Commissioner of Indian Affairs, December 24, 1890. This quote is taken from McLaughlin's postmortem report recounting the evidence supporting arrest. See Ch. 23.

77 - Vestal, *New Sources of Indian History*, 44.

78 - *New York Tribune*, November 22, 1890.

79 - Smith, *Moon of Popping Trees*, 111–12.

80 - *Sturgis Weekly Record*, November 28, 1890.

81 - Ostler, *Plains Sioux*, 313.

82 - Utley, *Sioux Nation*, 124, ftn. 17.

83 - Warren, *Buffalo Bill's America*, 378; Utley, *Sioux Nation*, 124.

84 - Warren, *Buffalo Bill's America*, 378.

85 - Id., 379.

86 - Utley, *Sioux Nation*, 124.

87 - Pfaller, *James McLaughlin: The Man with an Indian Heart*, 142.

88 - Vestal, *New Sources of Indian History*, 8–9.

89 - Id., 10.

90 - Vestal, *Champion of the Sioux*, 287.

91 - McLaughlin, *My Friend the Indian*, 210.

92 - Utley, *Sioux Nation*, 125.

93 - Pfaller, *James McLaughlin: The Man with an Indian Heart*, 143.

94 - Smith, *Moon of Popping Trees*, 147.

95 - Yenne, *Sitting Bull*, 254.

96 - Warren, *Buffalo Bill's America*, 379.

97 - Utley, *Sioux Nation*, 125.

98 - Ibid.

99 - Interpretative quotation based on a report of the encounter between Primeau and Cody and the direction to Primeau to decoy Cody. Ostler, *Plains Sioux*, 315; Utley, *Sioux Nation*, 125.

100 - Utley, *Sioux Nation*, 125.

101 - McLaughlin, *My Friend the Indian*, 211.

102 - Utley, *The Lance and the Shield*, 294.

103 - Ostler, *Plains Sioux*, 315.

104 - Utley, *The Lance and the Shield*, 295.

105 - Ibid.

106 - Pfaller, *James McLaughlin: The Man with an Indian Heart*, 148.

107 - McLaughlin Papers, McLaughlin to Gen. T. H. Ruger, December 6, 1890; McLaughlin, *My Friend the Indian*, 213.

108 - McLaughlin, *My Friend the Indian*, 212.

109 - Vestal, *Champion of the Sioux*, 280.

110 - Ibid.

111 - Utley, *The Lance and the Shield*, 295.

112 - Vestal, *New Sources of Indian History*, 8–9; Utley, *Sioux Nation*, 150.

113 - St. Paul Pioneer Press, December 10, 1890; Pfaller, *James McLaughlin: The Man with an Indian Heart*, 146.

114 - Vestal, *New Sources of Indian History*, 74.

115 - Id., 76.

116 - Id., 77.

117 - Id., 310.

118 - Utley, *The Lance and the Shield*, 295.

119 - Utley, *Sioux Nation*, 152.

120 - McLaughlin, *My Friend the Indian*, 214.

121 - Welch, *Killing Custer*, 269.

122 - McLaughlin, *My Friend the Indian*, 215.

123 - Ibid.

124 - Vestal, *Champion of the Sioux*, 289.

125 - Utley, *Sioux Nation*, 152.

126 - Ibid.

127 - Vestal, *Champion of the Sioux*, 289; Ostler, *Plains Sioux*, 315–16.

128 - Vestal, *Champion of the Sioux*, 311.

129 - McLaughlin Papers, Letter to Sitting Bull, December 13, 1890; Pfaller, *James McLaughlin: The Man with an Indian Heart*, 150.

130 - Vestal, *New Sources of Indian History*, 12.

131 - Utley, *The Lance and the Shield*, 295.

132 - Utley, *Sioux Nation*, 152.

133 - Vestal, *Champion of the Sioux*, 292; Ostler, *Plains Sioux*, 322. The letter as written did not reference any specific agency or location, but it is often quoted as saying that Sitting Bull was requesting permission to go to Pine Ridge.

134 - Utley, *Sioux Nation*, 152; Ostler, *Plains Sioux*, 321–23.

135 - Vestal, *Champion of the Sioux*, 291–92, n. 2, sets out Andrew Fox's writing in English:

"I want to write a few lines to day & to let you know Some thing. I meeting with all my Indians to day, & writing to you this order. God made you all the white race & also made the Red race & even give they both Might & Heart to know everything on the whold; but white High then the Indians; but to day, our father is halp us the Indians. So we all the Indians knowing. So I thing this way. I wish no one come to in my pray with they gund or knife: so all the Indians Pray to god for life & try to find out good road and do nothing wrong. in they life: This is what we want & Pray: because we did not Say nothing, about your pray. because you preay to god: So we all Indians, while; we both to Pray only one god to make us: & you my friend to day. you think I am foll: I you take some wise man amongs my people. & you let them know back East. the white people. So I knowing that. but I thing that is all right. because I am foll to pray to God. So you don't like me: My Friend. I dont like my self, when some one is foll: I like Him; So you are the same, you don't like me because I am foll; and if I did not Here, then the Indians will be civilization: but because I am Here. & all Indians foll, & I know this is all you put down on newspapers back East. So I seeing the paper but I thing it is all right: & when you was Here. in my camp. you was give me good word about. my Pray. & to day you take all back from me: & also I will let you know something. I got to go to [here the words "Pine Ridge Agency" are supplied by the reader] & to know This Pray: So I let you know that & the Police man. Told me you going to take all our Poneys, gund, too; so I want you let me know that. I want answer back soon."

136 - Vestal, *Champion of the Sioux*, 290.
137 - Vestal, *New Sources*, 11–13; Utley, *The Lance and the Shield*, 296.
138 - McLaughlin Papers, Letter to Sitting Bull, December 13, 1890; Utley, *The Lance and the Shield*, 296.
139 - Vestal, *Champion of the Sioux*, 295.
140 - Id., 296.
141 - Id., 310–11.
142 - Ibid.
143 - LaPointe, *Sitting Bull, His Life and Legacy*, 95–101.
144 - McLaughlin, *My friend the Indian*, 216.
145 - Vestal, *New Sources of Indian History*, 13–14.
146 - Utley, *The Lance and the Shield*, 297.
147 - Pfaller, *James McLaughlin: The Man with an Indian Heart*, 153.
148 - Yenne, *Sitting Bull*, 265–66; Vestal, *Champion of the Sioux*, 300.
149 - McLaughlin, *My Friend the Indian*, 217–18.
150 - Id., 218.
151 - Vestal, *Champion of the Sioux*, 299; reproduced envelope opposite 301.
152 - McLaughlin, *My Friend the Indian*, 217, Vestal, *New Sources of Indian History*, 25.
153 - Vestal, *New Sources of Indian History*, 56–57.
154 - Vestal, *Champion of the Sioux*, 297.
155 - Utley, *The Lance and the Shield*, 298.

CHAPTER TWENTY-ONE: ARREST AT GRAND RIVER

1 - Utley, *The Lance and the Shield: The Life and Times of Sitting Bull*, 299.
2 - An illustration is provided in Mooney, *The Ghost Dance-Religion and Wounded Knee*, 859, figure 78, showing the locations of Bull Head's house and the camp of Sitting Bull, as well as the paths of the converging police forces from Carignan's school and Oak Creek Station.
3 - Utley, *The Lance and the Shield*, 298–99.
4 - Utley, *The Last Days of the Sioux Nation*, 156. Vestal, *Sitting Bull, Champion of the*

Sioux, 299, indicates there were four men accompanying Carignan.

5 - Vestal, *New Sources of Indian History*, 4.

6 - Pfaller, *James McLaughlin: The Man with an Indian Heart*, 154.

7 - Utley, *Sioux Nation*, 156, and *The Lance and the Shield*, 299.

8 - Vestal, *Champion of the Sioux, A Biography*, 299.

9 - Vestal, *New Sources of Indian History, 1850–1891*, 49.

10 - McLaughlin, *My Friend the Indian*, 218.

11 - Utley, *The Lance and the Shield*, 298.

12 - Pfaller, *James McLaughlin: The Man with an Indian Heart*, 154; Vestal, *New Sources of Indian History*, 49.

13 - Vestal, *Champion of the Sioux*, 300.

14 - Vestal, *New Sources of Indian History*, 50.

15 - Ibid.

16 - Vestal, *Champion of the Sioux*, 300.

17 - Vestal, *New Sources of Indian History*, 50.

18 - Utley, *The Lance and the Shield*, 300.

19 - Robinson, *History of the Dakota or Sioux Indians*, 477; Vestal, *Champion of the Sioux*, 300; Mooney, *The Ghost-Dance Religion and Wounded Knee*, 857.

20 - Pfaller, *James McLaughlin: The Man with an Indian Heart*, 155.

21 - Robinson, *History of the Dakota or Sioux Indians*, 477.

22 - Ibid.

23 - Vestal, *Champion of the Sioux*, 301.

24 - Vestal, *New Sources of Indian History*, 51.

25 - Vestal, *Champion of the Sioux*, 302–03.

26 - Ibid.

27 - Id., 306–07; Utley, *The Lance and the Shield*, 300.

28 - Vestal, *Champion of the Sioux*, 305.

29 - Vestal, *New Sources of Indian History*, 51.

30 - Crummett, *Tatanka-Iyotanka, A Biography of Sitting Bull*, 43. Smith, *Moon of Popping Trees*, 152–53, has a similar but not exact quote.

31 - Vestal, *New Sources of Indian History*, 51.

32 - Utley, *The Last Days of the Sioux Nation*, 159.

33 - Vestal, *New Sources of Indian History*, 51.

34 - Robinson, *History of the Dakota or Sioux Indians*, 477.

35 - Verbal confrontations between police and Sitting Bull supporters based on Vestal, *Champion of the Sioux*, 303–04, and *New Sources of Indian History*, 41–52.

36 - Vestal, *Champion of the Sioux*, 305.

37 - Ibid.

38 - Pollack, *Woman Walking Ahead*, 151.

39 - Police statements made to the military and Captain Fechet's reconstruction of the shootout upon arrest conclude that Catch the Bear fired first. Vestal, *New Sources of Indian History*, 30. Policeman Loneman provided the same information in a later interview published in *New Sources of Indian History*, 51–52.

40 - McLaughlin, *My Friend the Indian*, 221; Vestal, *Champion of the Sioux*, 307.

41 - Vestal, *New Sources of Indian History*, 52.

42 - Utley, *The Lance and the Shield*, 301–02.

43 - Id., 302.

44 - Pfaller, *James McLaughlin: The Man with an Indian Heart*, 159.

45 - Vestal, *Champion of the Sioux*, 308–09.

46 - Vestal, *New Sources of Indian History*, 53.

47 - Ibid.

48 - Ibid.

49 - Id., quoting Captain Fechet's report of December 17, 1890, to the post adjutant.

50 - Robinson, *The History of the Dakota or Sioux Indians*, 478; Vestal, *New Sources of Indian History*, 28.

51 - Ibid.

52 - Utley, *The Lance and the Shield*, 302.

53 - Vestal, *Champion of the Sioux*, 311.

54 - Ibid.; Utley, *The Lance and the Shield*, 303.

55 - Vestal, *Champion of the Sioux*, 310.

56 - Utley, *The Last Days of the Sioux Nation*, 163.

57 - Mooney, *The Ghost-Dance Religion and Wounded Knee*, 858.

58 - Utley, *The Lance and the Shield*, 308; Mooney, *The Ghost-Dance Religion and Wounded Knee*, 862; Utley, *Sioux Nation*, 169.

59 - Vestal, *Champion of the Sioux*, 317.

60 - Id., 313; Utley, *Sioux Nation*, 163.

61 - McLaughlin, *My Friend the Indian*, with Appendix by Usher L. Burdick, 432.

62 - Utley, *The Lance and the Shield*, 302.

63 - Vestal, *New Sources of Indian History*, 18–19.

64 - Id., 30.

65 - Utley, *The Lance and the Shield*, 304.

66 - Id., 305–06.

67 - Vestal, *Champion of the Sioux*, 312.

68 - Ibid.

69 - Id, 314–15; McLaughlin, *My Friend the Indian*, with Appendix by Usher L. Burdick, 426.

70 - Utley, *Sioux Nation*, 164.

71 - Vestal, *Champion of the Sioux*, 321.

72 - Utley, *Sioux Nation*, 163.

73 - McLaughlin Papers, Telegram to the Commissioner of Indian Affairs, December 15, 1890.

CHAPTER TWENTY-TWO: THE REPORT

1 - McLaughlin, *My Friend the Indian*, with Appendix by Usher L. Burdick, 464; Utley, *Last Days of the Sioux Nation*, 164.

2 - Utley, *The Lance and the Shield: The Life and Times of Sitting Bull*, 305.

3 - McLaughlin Papers, Respectfully Returned to Members of Troop F, Seventh Cavalry Assn., December 15, 1890.

4 - McLaughlin Papers, Report to T. J. Morgan, December 15, 1890. See www.primeau. org/sittingbull/mclaughlinreportondec1890.html.

5 - McLaughlin Papers, Report to T. J. Morgan, December 24, 1890.

6 - McLaughlin, *My Friend the Indian*, with Appendix added by Usher L. Burdick, 407.

CHAPTER TWENTY-THREE: BURIAL

1 - Utley, *Sioux Nation*, 165.

2 - Utley, *The Lance and the Shield*, 306.

3 - Ibid.

4 - McLaughlin, *My Friend the Indian*, 221.

5 - Vestal, *Champion of the Sioux*, 316.

6 - Id., Vestal, *Champion of the Sioux*, 317.

7 - McLaughlin, *My Friend the Indian*, with Appendix by Usher L. Burdick, 416, referencing the report of H. M. Deeble, post surgeon, to post adjutant, January 21, 1891.

8 - Utley, *The Lance and the Shield*, 305.

9 - Id., 306.

10 - McLaughlin, *My Friend the Indian*, 222.

11 - Vestal, *Sitting Bull, Champion of the Sioux, A Biography*, 317–18.

12 - Id., 321.

13 - Utley, *The Lance and the Shield*, 306

14 - Crawford and Kelley, *American Religious Indian Traditions*, 580–81.

15 - *Aberdeen Saturday Pioneer*, December 20, 1890.

16 - *New York Herald*, December 17, 1890.

17 - *New York World*, December 21, 1890; Utley, *Last Days of the Sioux Nation*, 168.

18 - Fletcher, *The Life of Sitting Bull and the Indian War of 1890–1891*, 202–03.

19 - McLaughlin, *My Friend the Indian*, with Appendix by Usher L. Burdick, 407.

20 - Vestal, *New Sources of Indian History*, 334.

21 - Ibid.

22 - LaPointe, *Sitting Bull, His Life and Legacy*, 102–03, basing his account on oral history from the children of Sitting Bull to his mother, Angelique LaPointe, daughter of Standing Holy.

23 - Green and Thornton (Editors), *The Year the Stars Fell, Lakota Winter Counts at the Smithsonian*, 286.

24 - LaPointe, *Sitting Bull, His Life and Legacy*, 97–101.

25 - Vestal, *New Sources of Indian History*, 58.

26 - Pollack, *Woman Walking Ahead*, 282; www.dickshovel.com/sittingbull.htm.

27 - McLaughlin Papers, Letter to T. J. Morgan, Commissioner of Indian Affairs, December 24, 1890.

28 - Ibid.

29 - Ibid.

30 - Vestal, *Champion of the Sioux*, 315.

AFTERWORD

1 - Vestal, *Sitting Bull, Champion of the Sioux*, 284.
2 - Anderson, *Sitting Bull*, 190.
3 - Utley, *The Last Days of the Sioux Nation*, 169; Mooney, *The Ghost-Dance Religion and Wounded Knee*, 862.
4 - Vestal, *New Sources of Indian History*, 1850–1891, 19, 21.
5 - Ostler, *The Plains Sioux and U.S. Colonialism*, 326.
6 - Id., 327.
7 - Smith, *Moon of Popping Trees*, 166–67.
8 - General Miles knew better, on December 19, 1890, he sent a report to Senator Dawes explaining the conditions of the reservation Sioux:
"[T]he government has failed to fulfill its part of the compact, and instead of an increase or even a reasonable supply for their support, they been compelled to live on half and two-thirds rations, and received nothing for the surrender of their lands, neither has the government given any positive assurance that they intend to do any differently with them in the future."
He advised that the government should place the "turbulent and dangerous tribes of Indians under control of the military . . ."
9 - Utley, *Sioux Nation*, 185.
10 - Ostler, *Plains Sioux*, 329.
11 - Id., 332; Utley, *Sioux Nation*, 186.
12 - Utley, *Sioux Nation*, 192; Mooney, *The Ghost-Dance Religion and Wounded Knee*, 866–67.
13 - Ostler, *Plains Sioux*, 332.
14 - Id., 335.
15 - Ibid.
16 - Utley, *Sioux Nation*, 196.
17 - Ibid.
18 - Id., 198.
19 - Id., 197.
20 - Utley, *Sioux Nation*, 199.
21 - Ostler, *Plains Sioux*, 336, 352.
22 - Smith, *Moon of Popping Trees*, 179.
23 - Vestal, *New Sources of Indian History*, 33.
24 - Utley, *Sioux Nation*, 210–11.
25 - Id., 212.
26 - Ibid.
27 - Mooney, *The Ghost-Dance Religion and Wounded Knee*, 871, citing figures from Commissioner Morgan's official report.
28 - Ostler, *Plains Sioux*, 351.

29 - Id., 352; Utley, *The Last Days of the Sioux Nation*, 202.
30 - Lazarus, *Black Hills White Justice*, 115–16.
31 - Photograph of body of Big Foot lying on the frozen ground at Wounded Knee, Library of Congress.
32 - Utley, *Sioux Nation*, 4; Mooney, *The Ghost-Dance Religion and Wounded Knee*, 878. Photograph of mass burial: Nebraska State Historical Society, RG 2845:13–12.
33 - Utley, *Sioux Nation*, 249.
34 - Aberdeen *Saturday Pioneer*, January 3, 1891.
35 - Utley, *Sioux Nation*, 229–30.
36 - Id., 244–45; Smith, *Moon of Popping Trees*, 202.
37 - Ostler, *Plains Sioux*, 356–57.
38 - Utley, *Sioux Nation*, 251.
39 - Id., 258.
40 - Ostler, *Plains Sioux*, 334.
41 - Utley, *Sioux Nation*, 261.
42 - Id., 271; Smith, *Moon of Popping Trees*, 201.
43 - Lazarus, *Black Hills White Justice*, 116; Utley, *Sioux Nation*, 166.
44 - Eldoes and Ortiz (Editors), *American Indian Myths and Legends*, 495.
45 - Warren, *Buffalo Bill's America*, 419.
46 - Swanson (Editor), *Chicago Days*, Essay by Reardon, "The World's Colombian Exposition," 68; Deloria, *Indians in Strange Places*, 103–04.
47 - Yenne, *Sitting Bull*, 304.
48 - Utley, *The Lance and the Shield*, 312; McLaughlin Papers, Letter to Whom it may Concern, November 1, 1891.
49 - Warren, *Buffalo Bill's America*, 218–20.
50 - Pfaller, *James McLaughlin: The Man with an Indian Heart*, 367–74.

Bibliography

This book relies on the following source material both for context and historic data.

HISTORICAL REFERENCES

Adams, Alexander B., *Sitting Bull, An Epic of the Plains* (1973)

Agnew, Jeremy, *The Life of a Soldier on the Western Frontier* (2008)

Ambrose, Stephen E., *Undaunted Courage* (1996)

Anderson, Gary Clayton, *Little Crow, Spokesman for the Sioux* (1986)

Anderson, Gary C., *Sitting Bull and the Paradox of Lakota Nationhood* (2007)

Anderson, Gary Clayton, and Woolworth, Alan R., *Through Dakota Eyes, Narrative Accounts of the Minnesota Indian War of 1862* (1988)

Anderson, Ian, *Sitting Bull's Boss* (2000)

Bray, Kingsley M., *Crazy Horse: A Lakota Life* (2006)

Brown, Dee, *I Buried My Heart at Wounded Knee* (1970)

Buckley, Jay H., *William Clark: Indian Diplomat* (2008)

Calvert, Patricia, *Standoff at Standing Rock* (2001)

Carlson, Paul H., *The Plains Indians* (1998)

Chittenden, Hiram Martin, and Richardson, Alfred Talbot (Editors), *Life, Letters and Travels of Father Pierre-Jean De Smet among the North American Indians* (1905)

Congressional Record, Vol. 18 (1886)

Connell, Evan S., *Son of the Morning Star* (1984)

Cozzens, Peter (Editor), *Eyewitness to the Indian Wars, 1865–1890*, Vol. IV (2004)

Cozzens, Peter (Editor), *Eyewitness to the Indian Wars, 1865–1890*, Vol. V (2005)

Creelman, James, *On the Great Highway: The Wanderings and Adventures of a Special Correspondent* (1901)

Crummett, Michael, *Tatanka-Iyotanka: A Biography of Sitting Bull* (2002 Western National Parks Association)

De Trobriand, Philippe, *Army Life in Dakota* (translated by George F. Will, 1941)

Diedrich, Mark, *Sitting Bull: The Collected Speeches* (1998)

Donovan, James, *A Terrible Glory* (2008)

Dorsey, James Owen, *Siouan Sociology*, published in the 15th Annual Report of the Bureau of Ethnology, Washington, D.C. (1897)

Dunn, Jacob Piatt., Jr., *Massacres of the Mountains, A History of the Indian Wars of the Far West, 1815–1875*, Vol. 2 (1886)

Eldoes, Richard, and Ortiz, Alfonso (Selectors and Editors), *American Indian Myths and Legends* (1984)

Executive Documents of the United States for the Second Session of the Fiftieth Congress, and Special Session of the Senate Convened March 4, 1889

Fear-Segal, "Nineteenth Century Indian Education: Universalism Versus Evolution," 33 Journal of American Studies 329 (1999)

Finerty, John F., *War-Path and Bivouac* (1890)

Fritz, Henry E., *The Movement for Indian Assimilation* (1963)

Garland, Hamlin, *The Book of the American Indian* (1923)

Gitlin, Martin, *The Battle of the Little Big Horn* (2008)

Green, Jerome A., and Scott, Douglas D., *Finding Sand Creek: History, Archeology and the 1864 Massacre* (2004)

Hedren, Paul L., *Sitting Bull's Surrender at Fort Buford* (1997)

Hutton, Paul, *Phil Sheridan and His Army* (1985)

Isenberg, Andrew C., *The Destruction of the Bison* (2000)

Johnson, W. Fletcher, *Life of Sitting Bull and History of the Indian Wars of 1890-1891*

Kappler, Charles (compiler and editor), *Indian Affairs: Laws & Treaties*, Vol. II (1904)

Kehoe, Alice B., *The Ghost Dance: Ethnohistory and Revitalization* (1989)

Kelman, Ari, *A Misplaced Massacre, Struggling over the Memory of Sand Creek* (2013)

Kelsey, Penelope Myrtle, *Tribal Theory in Native American Literature* (2008)

Knight, Oliver, *Following the Indian Wars* (1960)

LaPointe, Ernie, *Sitting Bull, His Life and Legacy* (2009)

Larmar, Howard R. (Editor), *New Encyclopedia of the American West* (1998)

Larson, Robert W., *Red Cloud: Warrior-Statesman of the Lakota Sioux* (1997)

Larson, Robert W., *Gall: Lakota War Chief* (2007)

Lazarus, Edward, *Black Hills White Justice* (1991)

Linklater, Andro, *Measuring America* (2002)

MacEwan, Grant, *Sitting Bull: The Years in Canada* (1973)

McGee, W. J., *The Siouan Indians*, published in the 15th Annual Report of the Bureau of Ethnology, Washington, D.C. (1897)

McLaughlin, *James, My Friend the Indian* (1910)

McLaughlin, Marie, *Myths and Legends of the Sioux* (1916)

Major James McLaughlin Papers (1855–1913)

Marshall, Joseph, *The Journey of Crazy Horse* (2004)

Marshall, Joseph, *The Day the World Ended at Little Big Horn* (2007)

Maurer, Evan M., *Visions of the People: A Pictorial History of Plains Indian Life* (1993), essay by Peter J. Powell, "Sacrifice Transformed into Victory: Standing Bear Portrays Sitting Bull's Sun Dance and the Final Summer of Lakota Freedom"

Meyer, Roy W., *History of the Santee Sioux: United States Indian Policy on Trial* (Revised Edition 1993)

Michno, Gregory F. *Lakota Noon, The Indian Narrative of Custer's Defeat* (1997)

Milton, Richard, *South Dakota, A History* (1977)

Miles, Nelson A., *Personal Recollections & Observations of General Nelson A., Miles*, Vol. 1 and 2 (1896)

Mooney, James, *The Ghost-Dance Religion and Wounded Knee* (1896)

Olson, James C., *Red Cloud and the Sioux Problem* (1964)

Ostler, Jeffrey, *The Plains Sioux and U.S. Colonialism from Lewis and Clark to Wounded Knee* (2004)

Ostler, Jeffrey, *The Lakotas and the Black Hills* (2010)

Page, Jake, *In the Hands of the Great Spirit* (2003)

Palmer, Jessica Dawn, *The Dakota Peoples, A History of the Dakota, Lakota and Nakota through 1863* (2008)

Pearson, Jeffrey V., "Nelson A. Miles, Crazy Horse, and the Battle of Wolf Mountain," 51 Montana *The Magazine of Western History* 53–67 (Winter 2001)

Pfaller, Louis L., *James McLaughlin: The Man with an Indian Heart* (1970)

Pollack, Eileen, *Woman Walking Ahead* (2002)

Powers, Thomas, *The Killing of Crazy Horse* (2010)

Rielly, Edward J., *Sitting Bull, A Biography* (2007)

Richardson, Heather Cox, *Wounded Knee: Party Politics and the Road to a Massacre* (2010)

Robinson III, Charles M. (Editor), *The Diaries of John Gregory Bourke*, Vol. 1 (2003)

Robinson, Doane, *A History of the Dakota or Sioux Indians* (1904)

Robinson, Doane, *A History of South Dakota, from Earliest Times* (1907)

Sandoz, Mari, *Crazy Horse, the Strange Man of the Oglalas* (3rd Edition, 2004)

Schell, Herbert S., *History of South Dakota* (4th Edition, 2004)

Schmidt, Martin F. (Edited and annotated), *General George Crook, His Autobiography* (1960)

Sides, Hampton, *Blood and Thunder* (2006)

Smith, Rex Alan, *Moon of Popping Trees* (1975)

Smits, David, "The Frontier Army and the Destruction of the Buffalo," 25 *Western Historical Quarterly* No. 3 (Autumn 1994)

Standing Bear, Luther, *My People the Sioux* (1928)

Strahorn, Robert E., *Ninety Years of Boyhood* (Strahorn Autobiography) (1942, Idaho Historical Society Microfilm Series)

Swanson, Stevenson (Editor), *Chicago Days* (1997), essay by Patrick T. Reardon, "The World's Colombian Exposition"

Textor, Lucy E., *Official Relations between the United States and the Sioux Indians* (1896)

Turner, C. Frank, *Across the Medicine Line* (1973)

Turner, Frederic Jackson, Essay, "The Significance of the Frontier in American History" (1893)

Utley, Robert M., *The Last Days of the Sioux Nation* (1963)

Utley, Robert M., *Frontiersmen in Blue: The United States Army and the Indian, 1848–1865* (1967)

Utley, Robert M., *Cavalier in Buckskin* (1988)

Utley, Robert M., *The Lance and the Shield: The Life and Times of Sitting Bull* (1993)
Utley, Robert M., *Little Big Horn Battlefield* (Official National Park Handbook, No. 132) (1994)
Vestal, Stanley, *Sitting Bull, Champion of the Sioux: A Biography* (1932)
Vestal, Stanley, *New Sources of Indian History, 1850–1891* (1934)
Warren, Louis S., *Buffalo Bill's America* (2005)
Washburn, Wilcomb E. (Complier and Editor), *The American Indian and the United States, A Documentary History*, Vol. IV (1973)
Welch, James, with Stekler, Paul, *Killing Custer* (1994)
West, Elliot, *The Last Indian War: The Nez Perce Story* (2009)
Wilson, James, *The Earth Shall Weep* (1998)
Yenne, Bill, *Sitting Bull* (2008)

CONTEMPORARY CULTURAL OR ATTITUDINAL SOURCES

Crawford, Suzanne J., and Kelley, Dennis F. American Religious Indian Traditions (2005)
Crow Dog, Mary, *Lakota Woman* (1990)
Deloria, Ella, Dakota Texts (originally 1932; republished 2006)
Deloria, Philip J., *Indians in Unexpected Places* (2004)
Deloria, Vine, Jr., *Custer Died for Your Sins* (1969)
DeMallie, Raymond J., and Parks, Douglas R. (Editors), *Sioux Indian Religion, Tradition and Innovation* (1987)
Petrillo, Larissa, *Being Lakota: Identity and Tradition on Pine Ridge Reservation* (2007)
Petrillo-Flora, Cornelia Butler and Flora, Jon L., *Rural Communities, Legacy, and Chance* (2013).
Smith, Paul Chaat, *Everything You Know about Indians Is Wrong* (2009)

GEOGRAPHIC SOURCES

Egan, Timothy, *The Worst Hard Time* (2006)
Norris, Kathleen, *Dakota, a Spiritual Geography* (1993)
Savage, Candance, *Prairie: A Natural History* (2004)
Zarki, Joseph W., *Badlands: The Story Behind the Scenery* (1997)

Newspapers and Magazines

Aberdeen Saturday Pioneer
Bismarck Tribune
Buffalo Echo
Chicago Tribune
Harper's Weekly
Helena Herald
New York Herald
New York Times
New York Tribune
New York World
Omaha Daily Bee
Pierre Daily Press
Rapid City Journal
St. Paul Pioneer Press
Sturgis Weekly Record
Washington Post

Other Sources

www.astonisher.com/archieves/museum/one_bull_big_horn.html.
www.dickshovel.com/sittingbull.htm
www.pbs.org/weta/thewest/resources/archieves/eight/dawes.htm
www.primeau.org/sittingbull/mclaughlinreportondec1890.html.
www.spartacus-educational.com/WWplains.htm
www.thinknd.org/resources/InduanStudies/spiritlake/historical_conflict.html
www.wyomingtalesandtrails.com/woundedk.html
Several other works and maps were also researched and considered; and extensive historical information on the Internet was reviewed, including Public Broadcast System's
   Archives of the West and the Standing Rock Reservation website.

Indian Treaties

1851 Fort Laramie Treaty
1868 Laramie Treaty
1876 Laramie Treaty

Agreement with the Sioux of Various Tribes, 1882–1883 (never ratified)
The General Allotment Act
1889 Dawes Act
1889 Sioux Act

COURT CASES

Legare v. United States (1889) 24 Ct. Claims 513
Sioux Nation of Indians v. United States (Ct. Cl. 1979) 601 F.2d 1157
United States v. Sioux Nation of Indians (1980) 448 U.S. 371

NOTES

Interpretative quotations found within the book, are provided within the context of reported events between real characters, based on actual interactions of the parties and the personality of the person to whom the quote is attributed (the source notes set forth the basis for these quotes). Second, there are oftentimes different accounts of the same event. For example, it is variously reported that Sitting Bull moved to the Grand River either in 1884 and 1887; the author chose McLaughlin's letter to the Commissioner of Indian Affairs, as explained by Robert Utley, in selecting 1884, over Stanley Vestal's date of 1887 based on oral history.

INDEX

adaptation, coerced, 22, 168
Ahern, George P., 154–55, 164–65
Allen, Alvaren, 186–87
Allison, Edwin "Fish," 127–28, 137, 150
allotment program, 164, 195–96, 201–30, 234, 256–57
American Horse, 94, 209, 211
Andrews, George, 150, 165
Arapaho Indians, 31, 33, 45
Army, U.S., 74, 75, 88–89, 96–97
assimilation, 146–47, 153–54, 168, 183, 201–4

Badlands, 26–27, 263
Bear Coat. See Miles, Nelson (Bear Coat)
Beckwith, Paul, 64–66
Belknap, William, 69
Belt, Robert, 237, 257, 269
Benteen, Frederick, 78, 80, 82
Big Foot, 238, 239, 263–64, 301, 302
    agrees to surrender, 299–300
    and Ghost Dance movement, 250–51, 298–99
Big Head, 208, 222, 226
Bismarck, 56, 139–41, 181
Blackfeet Indians, 49, 76
Black Hills, 40, 44, 53–66, 210
    considered spiritual grounds by Indians, 59
    discovery of gold in, 57–58, 68
    Sitting Bull complains government stole, 190
    U.S. government plan for, 33–34, 95
Black Kettle, 31–32, 46
Black Moon, 107, 121, 122, 255
Bourke, John Gregory, 70–71
Bozeman Trail, 33, 35, 38, 41, 44
Brooke, John, 263
Brotherton, David, 127–28, 132, 137, 138, 143
Brughiere, Johnny, 99, 105–6
buffalo, 6, 7, 12, 34, 103, 109, 118–19
    in Canada, 112, 127

importance to Plains Indians, 53–55
    last Lakota hunt, 158–60
Buffalo Bill, 184, 188–91, 266–69, 302, 303
Buisson, Marie Louise, 28–29, 63–64
Bull Head, 194–96, 250, 257, 260, 261, 270, 278
    and Sitting Bull's arrest, 273, 275–76, 279–82
    wounded and dies, 284, 285
Bureau of Catholic Indian Missions, 63, 135

Cadotte, Nick, 223–24
Canada, 104–5, 109–23
Carignan, John, 257, 267, 270, 276, 278, 295
Carlisle Indian Training School, 153–54, 187, 204
Carrington, Henry, 34–35
Catch the Bear, 185, 194–95, 277, 280, 281, 282, 283, 295
Catholicism, 63, 64, 156
Cheyenne Indians, 31, 33, 45, 46, 49, 68–69, 72, 76, 83
Cheyenne River Agency, 104
Chicago, 302, 303
Chivington, John. M., 31–32, 46
Civil War, 11, 30
Cleveland, Grover, 212, 214
Cody, William. See Buffalo Bill
Collins, Mary, 196–97, 241, 257–58
Congress, U.S., 19, 37, 42, 60–61, 228
Corps of Discovery, 8, 11
Crazy Horse, 36, 56, 74–75, 92, 107
    and Battle of Little Big Horn, 80–81, 88
    death of, 108, 166
    refuses offer to buy or lease Black Hills land, 61–62
    run-in with Miles, 106–7
Crazy Walking, 240
Cronau, Rudolf, 151, 152–53

About the Author

Norman E. Matteoni is a long-time student of the American West and the life and times of Sitting Bull. Both a legal scholar and practicing lawyer, he has written extensively in law review articles, appellate briefs and a two volume treatise on the Law of Eminent Domain in California. He also is an amateur photographer, and in 2008 he photographed areas of the northern plains, home of the Lakota.